What Reviewers Say About <u>Girltalk</u>

"It's kicky. It's fresh. It's fun. It's also serious. It's *Girltalk*. No soap boxes, no sermons, no nonsense. . . . *Girltalk* is a winner and should be owned by every young woman."
—*Columbus Dispatch*

❁

"Carol Weston, who has been writing for teens since she was a teenager, offers straightforward advice in a lively, appealing style. She provides information and guidelines, not rules."
—*Houston Chronicle*

❁

"Carol tells it all . . . and from the point of view of someone not much older than the teens she is addressing. In other words, someone they might actually listen to."
—*Good Housekeeping*

❁

"Weston's approach is informal, like an older sister answering her younger sister's questions. She doesn't beat around the bush."
—*Dallas Times Herald*

❁

"If every girl in America used *Girltalk* as her personal guidebook through adolescence, then we would have a country filled with well-informed, confident, self-respecting young women."
—*Miami Insider*

❁

"Captures all the turbulence of the teen years . . . with big-sister solicitousness and reliable sources."
—*Houston Post*

❁

"Carol Weston has written a book that can tell you about all the kinds of problems that girls run into . . . crammed with tips about what to say and do. Try your library or bookstore right away."
—"Ask Beth"/*Boston Globe*

What Readers Say About <u>Girltalk</u>

Girltalk has been all around my classroom, from girl to girl, from cover to cover, and we all loved it.

❧

I've never read a book like yours—one that seems like the author is speaking right to you and you only.

❧

On a scale of 1 to 10, I would give *Girltalk* a 25.

❧

Girltalk answered all the questions that I didn't have the nerve to ask my mom.

❧

I must have read and reread *Girltalk* three trillion times. My friends and I gather around it and use it as a guidebook to everyday life.

❧

I love it to pieces. My mom calls *Girltalk* my bible because everywhere I go I take my book.

❧

I now know how to say no, thanks to you.

❧

I used to smoke but because of your book I gave it up.

❧

You wouldn't believe how much your book helped me. In the section on colleges, you had me so inspired I wanted to start college next week.

❧

Slowly day by day I'm getting to have confidence in myself.
Thank you so much.

Other Books by Carol Weston

For Girls Only

From Here to Maternity

Girltalk About Guys

How to Honeymoon

GIRLTALK

All the Stuff Your Sister Never Told You

THIRD EDITION

Carol Weston

HarperPerennial

A Division of HarperCollins*Publishers*

Dedicated to the memory of my father,

WILLIAM WESTON

Several pages of this updated and revised third edition were originally published in *YM, Girls' Life,* and *Your Prom.* Grateful acknowledgment is made to the editors for permission to reprint adaptations of that material.

HarperCollins books may be purchased for educational, business, or sales promotional use. For information please call or write: Special Markets Department, HarperCollins Publishers, Inc., 10 East 53rd Street, New York, NY 10022.

Designed by Jessica Shatan

Library of Congress Cataloging-in-Publication Data
Weston, Carol.
    Girltalk : all the stuff your sister never told you / Carol Weston. —3rd ed.
    p. cm.
    Summary: A comprehensive guide for teenage girls on questions ranging from skin care and weight control to AIDS and college admissions, and including quizzes and answers to actual letters from teens.
    ISBN 0-06-092850-6
    1. Teenage girls—Juvenile literature. 2. Teenage girls—Conduct of life—Juvenile literature. [1. Teenage girls. 2. Conduct of life.] I. Title.
    HQ798.W43 1997
    305.235—dc21   97-13674
                                                      AC

01 02 ❖/RRD 15 14 13 12 11

Contents

2. Friendship: You Don't Like Everybody; Why Should Everybody Like You? 57

3. Love: Falling In, Falling Out 87

4. Sex: What You Should Know Before Saying Yes 124

Acknowledgments

I want to be brief, but I'm feeling awfully grateful. And since *Girltalk* has enjoyed three lives, there are many editors, experts, and others who have kept me and the book going. Here's a bouquet of thanks to:

All the girls who have sent me letters that made me laugh and sigh and think and shake my head and remember why I write what I write and how tricky it can be to make the leap from confusion to confidence.

All the editors who cared about this book: Irv Levey, Janet Goldstein, Kristen Auclair, Peternelle van Arsdale, Susan Weinberg, Dawn Raffel, and Jeanne Flagg.

All the dermatologists, pediatricians, gynecologists, psychiatrists, psychologists, plastic surgeons, dentists, and other doctors who answered questions, questions, questions. Among them: Dr. Daniel Foitl, Dr. David Binder, Dr. Armand Simone, Dr. Herbert Lazarus, Dr. Max Kahn, Dr. Nina Freund, Dr. Irving Distelheim, Dr. John FitzGibbon, Dr. Sarah Ackerman, Dr. Stephanie Bird, Dr. Adam Romoff, and especially Liz Pennisi, R.N., too.

The Centers for Disease Control for their information and patience.

Alana Kaufman of the American Anorexia/Bulimia Association, and others who work at the hot lines that give me facts and figures and give teenagers help and hope.

Beth Fredrick of the Alan Guttmacher Institute for all that sex education.

Lawrence Momo, director of college counseling at Trinity School, for looking over the college chapter.

Ragdale Foundation, a writers' and artists' colony and idyllic place to work.

Craig Herman, Michelle Pipia, and the publicists, producers, radio hosts, book reviewers, and booksellers who have been invaluable in spreading the word.

Matilde Reategui, Molly Woodroofe, Ed Abrahams, Katie Goldstein, Cathy Roos, Patty Dann, Evie Gurney, Maureen Davison, Nina Sander, and Marsha Nelson for hitting the high notes.

The *New York Times* (always informative), my book club (always fun), and my friends (who make all the difference).

Marybeth Weston, role model and Mom, for reading my first draft, red pencil in hand.

And finally, my family: Elizabeth and Emme, my enchanting daughters, and Robert Ackerman, my amazing husband. How did I get so lucky?

Hello

I'm impressed with you already. I don't always read introductions.

I'm glad you picked up *Girltalk: All the Stuff Your Sister Never Told You.* I put my heart and soul into writing and revising it and I'm thrilled that this third edition is ready to go.

My aim is to help you get through puberty . . . and into college. No matter how old you are, whether eleven or nineteen, I promise you will find this book useful. Even if you have a big sister and terrific parents, they may not be there exactly when you want to know more about breast size or résumé writing or eating disorders or financial aid. Or they may not know the very latest on depression, dyslexia, date rape, drug use, or Depo-Provera. Or maybe you'd feel funny asking about periods or crushes or popularity or sexual orientation or whatever makes you curious.

Girltalk is full of the stuff I wanted to know when I was growing up and the stuff it took me years to figure out. It includes excerpts from my preteen and teen diaries, as well as over 150 letters from girls—I've been a sort of Dear Abby since 1985 and I write the HELP! column in *Girls' Life.*

I have no sisters, but there were many times when I could have used some late night girltalk. Writing this book, I imagined I was a college student, home for spring break, and that I suddenly noticed that my kid sister was growing up fast. If I wanted to give her information and advice on how to make sensible choices and take care of herself, the time was n-o-w. Out poured the first edition—and in poured letters from around the world!

A dozen years later, I'm proud that *Girltalk* is still a friend and reference for so many girls. The first edition was a best-seller in England, and the second edition was translated into Chinese and Russian. In the past decade, I have also written for *Seventeen, YM, Teen,* and *Cosmopolitan* and have been a guest on scores of talk shows. (Yes! I've talked on the tube with Oprah, Ricki, Sally, Montel, Phil, Geraldo!) Best of all, my husband and I have two wonderful daughters, Elizabeth and Emme, so now there's always lots of girltalk in our home.

How should you read *Girltalk*? Straight through? Skipping around? It's up to you. It can be both a bedside buddy and a personal encyclopedia. The *Body* chapter talks about breasts, menstruation, weight control, working out, and staying healthy. The *Friendship* chapter tells how to make and keep friends and what to do if you get smothered by one friend or dumped by another. *Love* describes how to tell if a guy likes you, how to flirt without sounding like an idiot, how to get a romance off the ground, and how to break up without breaking down. *Sex* covers abstinence, contraception, sexually transmitted diseases, pregnancy, do-it-yourself orgasms, homosexuality, rape, and everything you need to know before saying yes. Flip to *Family* if you want to get along better with parents and siblings or stepsiblings or if you fear that you (or they) may be a ripe candidate for counseling. *Education* covers study habits, semesters abroad, learning disabilities, harassment, and how to choose and be chosen by a college. *Money* explains how to get odd jobs and real jobs, ace an interview, and shape your future. *Smoking, Drinking, and Drugs* is full of facts because what you don't know can hurt you. And finally *Quizzes* lets you know how jealous you are, how well you know your best friend, and whether you and he are a good match or whether you are *too* nice.

Way back when, my English teachers told me, "Write what you know about." That's what I've always done. One reason I remember my teen years vividly (when some adults would just as soon forget theirs) is because I adolesced all over the place. I was a teen at a suburban public school, an urban private school, on a farm in southern France, as an au pair in Madrid, Spain, and at an Ivy League college. Without even realizing it, I was examining the teen years through different camera angles and taking notes in diary after diary.

What's great about being your age is that you have it in you to become whoever you want—and you're becoming yourself.

So here it is, the best (and biggest) *Girltalk* yet. More letters, more answers, more information, more hot lines, more wisdom. And even some websites. It's not easy staying up-to-date and down-to-earth, but it's a privilege to keep trying.

Thank you for choosing my book. Get ready, get set, get comfortable, and keep reading.

1 BODY

Looking and Feeling Your Best

❀

Too fat, too flat, too tall, too small—hardly any of us is 100 percent happy with our appearance. It's especially hard for you now. Your body may be growing in all directions, blemishes may freckle your face, hair may be sprouting here and there, your period may be a mystery. What is going on inside you anyway? Are you stuck with your features and figure?

Beauty does make a difference in first impressions. But so do friendliness, a sense of humor, intelligence, thoughtfulness. And with a little effort, anybody can look attractive.

Since you and your body are together for the long haul, you need to learn to take care of it. This chapter will show you how to make the most of your attributes and how to be your most healthy and radiant.

Do Guys Worry About Their Bodies?

Before we launch into a discourse about breasts, periods, diets, and female concerns, you might be wondering if guys ever worry about their bodies. Answer: They certainly do.

Sure, a few wink in the mirror each morning and think they're God's Gift to Manhood—and Womankind. But most wrestle with puberty-related anxiety.

Guys wonder whether they're tall enough, whether their pecs and biceps bulge enough, whether their chest, facial, and pubic hair will ever grow. They wish their voices would get deeper and stop croaking. They wish they weren't hungry all the time. They're tired of having braces and pimples and being clumsy and lanky. They wish they were more handsome and that their hands wouldn't sweat when they ask you to slow dance.

Guys worry extra in gym showers, locker rooms, and bathrooms because they figure someone might be checking out their private parts. And someone probably is! Guys don't just worry about size; some even worry that their organ is crooked!

Here's another male concern: wet dreams. Guys your age sometimes wake up to find they've ejaculated during the night, and they wonder if that's normal. Yes. It's also normal for guys to get erections at odd times—in the morning, in math class, or even when taking a foul shot in basketball.

Many guys feel uneasy about their sexuality. Are they oversexed if they masturbate a lot, undersexed if they don't? If they have an orgasm quickly when they masturbate, does that mean they'll be premature ejaculators in years to come? If they haven't started dating, or if they've played sex games with other guys or admire their male coach, does that mean they're gay? If they have an X-rated fantasy involving a married woman teacher, does that mean they're perverted? No, no, no, and no. Guys grow at different sexual speeds and need not be alarmed by early imaginings or experiences.

In one important way, girls have an advantage over guys in the Worry Department. Most guys don't discuss their growing pains, whereas, luckily for us, most girls do. It's not uncommon for a girl to complain, "I wish my breasts were bigger." But find me a guy who would say out loud, "I wish my penis were bigger." It's a shame guys aren't more open and honest together. They have as many questions, troubles, and fears of inadequacy as girls, but fewer outlets. Guys tease and taunt each other, yet usually worry alone. They don't even have many magazines or books to consult. But you do. So keep reading!

Everything You Ever Wanted to Know About Breasts

Back to us girls.

If you're like me, you sometimes get fed up with your figure. Why can't your breasts be medium instead of mountains or molehills?

It's frustrating that your body's timetable answers to hormones and heredity, rather than to your own wishful thinking. If you haven't started developing yet, you may be feeling shortchanged. If you've been developing for years, you may worry you'll wind up with watermelons. Either way, you might envy the average girls who strut around the locker room parading their bra-and-panty sets.

I envied them. I was in a mad rush to grow up. I couldn't wait to get my breasts on and my braces off, to start getting periods and stop getting pimples. At fourteen, I was a restless late-blooming flatso. I dressed behind curtains and cringed at breast jokes.

Why are you a sailor's delight? Because you have a sunken chest! What do members of the Itty Bitty Titty Committee wear instead of bras? Band-Aids! What do buxom women wear? Booby traps! Pretend you're a boy for a minute. Ahh ... doesn't that take a load off your chest? Quips circulated about ironing boards, mosquito bites, and pancakes, as well as jumbo jugs, bouncing bazooms, and knockout knockers. Poor Rebecca, girls said, was so flat she could wear her bra inside out. And people teased Sophie that she'd knock down passersby if she turned without warning.

At first hardly anybody was happy. My friend Alice was as distressed about being busty as I was about being flat. She sported baggy shirts to hide her dramatic décolletage.

It was Alice who told me of the Best Breast Test. "To find out if you need a bra, place a pencil underneath one of your boobs and see if it stays up," she explained. I ducked into the bathroom ... and my pencil clattered to the floor. Alice handed me two of her outgrown training bras anyway—"booby" prizes since she'd graduated to larger sizes. I still couldn't imagine putting them on, however. A stringbean classmate had worn a bra to a party the previous weekend and a boy had jeered, "Would you wear shoes if you didn't have feet?"

Status was at stake when we discussed bra sizes. The ideal seemed to be As in school and Bs in bust. I earned no grade: just an incomplete. Later when the subject switched to boys, books, baby-sitting, I'd sometimes still be thinking bosoms, boobs, breasts. Would mine ever grow?

I wish I could have realized that I'd make it safely to womanhood. I wish I could have foreseen that although I'd always be more Kate Moss than Dolly Parton when it came to chests, I'd end up perfectly content with my own measurements, just as Alice now feels good about her body. (Nowadays, I actually prefer undershirts to Wonderbras.)

Not that curves aren't cool and coveted. *Playboy*'s pages tend toward the well endowed, and some breast-oriented fellow once paid $1,040 at a London auction for a 36-D bra worn by Marilyn Monroe. But I now know that small-breasted women have admirers, too. What's more, sagging is not a problem for us, and while it's hard to look voluptuous, it's sometimes easy to look slim. (And, yes, nursing is easy for small-breasted women.)

Most American girls' breasts start swelling when they hit double digits, turning ten or eleven. Many girls develop earlier; many, later. African-American girls tend to show signs of puberty (pubic hair and fuller breasts) a year earlier than white girls. Menstruation itself can occur a year or more after the growth of pubic hair and breasts—more on that later. Some girls develop at the same rate as their friends. But many are ahead of or behind the pack and feel self-conscious or impatient. It's nice to know you're not the only one who has anxiously compared your chest with the next girl's. It's even nicer to know that ultimately most girls make peace with their bodies.

The catch is that if you feel like a freak in the meantime, that's the image you project. Who wants to hang out with a girl who is totally preoccupied with her bust? It's not true that guys favor girls who are "built." Guys like girls who are comfortable with themselves.

Although many girls are concerned about being concave or convex, I hope you can appreciate your own shape. Bodies look their most attractive when they are firm and toned, whether they resemble hour-glasses, pears, or beanpoles. The days of girdles, bustles, corsets, falsies, and bandoes are behind us. Now big is beautiful, flat is fine, and medium is marvelous. So throw back your shoulders when you walk. Take off your T-shirt when you swim. Get out of the slumber party sleeping bag when you undress. Don't be like me who agonized too long over nothing—if you'll pardon the pun.

Have you ever wondered about breast surgery? Mammoplasty is not a neat option; it's a last resort. And no reputable surgeon would operate on a girl under eighteen. Still, you may be curious about breast reduction and enlargement. (Some women with inverted nipples choose to have them surgically altered, too.)

Let me tell you about Tammy. In high school, Tammy's body was petite, but her breasts were enormous. She got shoulder cuts from her tight bra straps and backaches from supporting her heavy, drooping bosom. She felt out of proportion and never got used to her vital statistics, or to other people's constant comments. "I felt like walking breasts," she said.

When Tammy was eighteen and seemed fully developed, she and her mother visited a few doctors. They agreed she might be better off with a little off and that she was old enough to undergo the major surgery of breast reduction. She went to the hospital, was given general anesthesia, stayed several days, paid several thousand dollars (some of it covered by insurance), put up with a lot of pain—and emerged less buxom.

Most people thought she'd lost weight, but they didn't guess where. Tammy already had a boyfriend, so her love life didn't change, but she did begin to feel better about herself. She has some scars under her breasts and around her nipples. And she may never be able to nurse. Nonetheless, she has no regrets. Yet her case is highly exceptional.

How about the other extreme? Can you make your breasts more bountiful? Ads in the back of magazines are mostly rip-offs. Some feature exercises that make your back wider, not your front. Your measurement increases, not your cup size. Others feature creams that temporarily irritate the bust, making it bigger because it is swollen.

No doctor in his right mind would say yes to a teenager who wanted breast augmentation surgery because teenage bodies (and minds) are growing and changing. But over one million women have had breast implants. Many did so after a mastectomy because of cancer. But most did so for cosmetic reasons. There is controversy over the long-term safety of silicone implants, which is why most doctors now use saline implants, though even those come in silicone bags.

I do know an adult who got silicone implants before the Food and Drug Administration began limiting their use. The plastic surgeon marked the creases where her breasts fell, gave her a local anesthetic, cut along the creases, and developed a pocket in each breast. (Ugh!) Inside each pocket, the surgeon tucked a silicone-gel-filled plastic bag, sewed careful stitches, and added a supportive dressing. The procedure took over an hour, but she wore the dressing and a supportive bra for weeks. After the operation, she said she felt as if someone was stepping on her chest, and now she sometimes worries that her implants may be time bombs. (Complications could include infection, hematoma, or loss of the implants.)

The hefty cost is not usually covered by insurance. And new breasts feel firmer than natural breasts. Some women complain that theirs are rock-hard and never jiggle. Many others worry about safety and side effects, from allergic reactions to lumping of tissue to chest pain to autoimmune disorders to implant rupture or leaking. Sometimes further surgery becomes necessary years later. For women with implants, the early detection of breast cancer may also be more difficult, which is really scary since one in nine (one in nine!) American women may someday develop breast cancer.

Breast cancer among girls and young women is very rare, and even lumps or some white or yellow discharge from the nipple may be normal. But consult your doctor if your breasts start changing after you are seventeen, or if your mother, grandmother, aunt, sister, or stepsister has had breast cancer. Be on higher alert if the family member was young when diagnosed. Everyone, regardless, should do a quick breast check after her period each month. How?

1. In the bath or shower (since wet skin is slippery), keep fingers flat and move them over your breasts, checking for lumps, knots, and thickening.

2. Lie down in bed or on the floor. Put your right hand behind your head, and with your left hand, check your right breast. Move your fingers in circles around your nipple, including the area around your armpit. Repeat with the opposite hand and breast.

3. Sit up, and with arms overhead, inspect your breasts in front of a mirror to check for changes. Squeeze each nipple gently to check for discharge. Questions? Call (800) 4-CANCER.

Since you are probably still developing, your breasts *should* be changing, so please don't go into panic mode. Two-thirds of the diagnosed cases of breast cancer are in women *over* fifty. Still, there's no harm in getting in the habit of doing this monthly self-examination, because the earlier cancer is detected, the easier it is to treat.

Let me tell you, I'd rather have my own soft minibreasts than expensive worrisome bigger ones. It's sensible to accept your body. (These days, some men get pectoral implants and some women get calf and buttock implants, but I think that's vanity gone overboard, don't you?)

The best breast advice of all is to grin and bear them—whether they're big, small, or slightly asymmetrical.

Is Your Period a Question Mark?

Can you imagine how scary it would be to start menstruating if you didn't know anything about it? Suddenly you'd be bleeding! Down there! I'd have been petrified if I hadn't known that the menarche (first period) is as much a part of puberty as developing breasts. Even if you've had your period for years, you may not understand it completely or know what to do about cramps or tampons or pads.

My first encounter with the paraphernalia of periods came when I was about six. My brother and I found white cylindrical cardboard tubes in my mother's bathroom wastebasket. We slipped them on our fingers and played puppets. Little did we know they were Tampax applicators!

Years later, in fifth grade, my friend Alice (the one who was practically born with a bra on) was sleeping over, and we compared what we knew about menstruation, which wasn't much. We made a pact to tell each other when it happened, and sure enough Alice started her period that year.

Most American girls start between ages eleven to thirteen, but starting anywhere from nine to sixteen is not uncommon, and when you start varies according to factors such as race, diet, weight, and percentage of body fat. A girl's first period usually occurs after her breasts have begun to develop and her pubic hair has begun to appear. African-American girls tend to start earlier than white girls. Why? No one quite knows. Very skinny girls tend to get their periods later than heavier girls. Why? Because once you get your period, you are capable of becoming pregnant, and Mother Nature doesn't want very skinny girls to be pregnant. Why not? Because if there were a famine, their fetuses might starve. (Mother Nature didn't realize there'd be so many grocery stores around.)

Anyway, my body was in no hurry at all. I still remember when my lab partner Colleen came by after school in seventh grade. At the doorstep she announced, "I have my friend."

"She can come in, too," I said, and then noticed she was alone.

Colleen rolled her eyes. "I mean my period," she said.

By ninth grade, almost all the girls I knew whispered about their "time of the month." I'd think: When will I start? This week? This year? In school? On a date?

When I finally got my period, I was fifteen and a half and had been going out with a guy for six months. The first time is rarely a dramatic flood for anybody; usually it's just a little red on the toilet paper you're using or a few drops of blood on your underpants, with little warning beforehand. (Wash stains out with cold, not hot, water.) When I started, I felt relieved, and my friends seemed to think it was a cause to celebrate. My mother said, "Congratulations, welcome to the sorority."

This is the gist of what menstruation is all about. Once you start menstruating, you are capable of having a baby, and every month your body gets revved for possible motherhood. A tiny egg (you're born with thousands) matures in one of your ovaries, is released and sent down a fallopian tube, and eventually reaches the uterus. Meanwhile, your uterus, or womb, has been preparing for the egg's arrival, and its lining is now thick and velvety. If the arriving egg is fertilized by a sperm, your uterus is ready to protect and nourish it. The fertilized egg, or ovum, will grow in your uterus, and in about nine months, you'll have a baby. If your egg hasn't been fertilized (you haven't had sex or you've used contraception), then you're not pregnant. Your uterus has no use for the thick, spongy lining it has been building up. Much of the lining is therefore cast off, and that, along with some blood, body fluids, and the disintegrated egg, makes up the six or so tablespoons of reddish brown menstrual flow that flushes out through your vagina for three to six days each month. Once you start menstruating and your cycle becomes regular, you'll have periods (except during pregnancy) until menopause, which usually occurs when you're between forty-five and fifty-five.

Are your periods already regular? Mine didn't become regular for over a year. Even if yours are, you may sometimes miss a month or several months. As long as you know you're not pregnant, some irregularity shouldn't worry you. Nerves, plane rides, poor nutrition, weight gain or loss, even a cold can throw off your cycle. Mysteriously, sisters' or roommates' menstrual cycles sometimes become synchronized when they live together, so their periods may be off schedule when this first happens. Many very athletic women often skip periods, although they are still fertile. If you are extremely thin and are skipping periods, try to gain weight, and they may begin again. If you're worried about your cycle—it's very irregular or painful—keep careful track of when you get your periods and talk to a doctor.

Do you know when you're about to get your period? I usually mark a small *x* on my calendar on the first day of each period so I'll know approximately when to expect it the next month. Most girls' cycles are about twenty-eight days, but they range from twenty-two to thirty-four days. Some girls may worry that their period is late, but if they have kept track, they'll realize they simply have a long cycle.

Sometimes I'll be supersensitive or weepy or strung out, and the next day, bingo—I'll get my period. I don't usually suffer from headaches, backaches, cramps, cold sores, or nosebleeds, as a few of my friends do, but I'm prone to a blemish or two, I feel heavy, and once in a while my breasts get so tender, it hurts just to walk down the stairs! That's my warning that my period is on its way. Other times I'll have no symptoms at all, or my symptoms will come a full week before my period.

It's smart to be aware of your own premenstrual symptoms so you'll carry a tampon or pad in your purse (a good idea anyway). If you think you're about to start, wear a thin pad or liner to school and wear panties at night (not your new white ones). Try not to scream at some innocent person just because you are short-tempered. (Studies show that there are more family arguments, traffic accidents, crimes, and even suicides among premenstrual women than other women. I write this not so you'll have an excuse to weep or wail, but so if you are screeching at your sister or boyfriend at that time of the month, you'll consider stepping back and saying, "You know, let's talk about this another time.")

Symptoms vary from woman to woman and from month to month. They depend on your body and your attitude. If you think, "This is the week I get depressed and bitchy," you'll probably get depressed and bitchy. But if you think it's kind of neat that your body has rhythms and you stay busy and don't make a fuss over it, your period may come and go before you know it. Don't skip gym or postpone tests just because your body is functioning normally.

If you are among the minority who hate that time of the month because you feel sluggish, edgy, bloated, and sore, you should know that your periods will probably become easier in a few years and that in the meantime, several nonprescription and prescription drugs can help relieve premenstrual syndrome (PMS) and painful periods (dysmenorrhea). If you are among the few who find PMS downright debilitating, ask a doctor about ibuprofen or even low-dose antidepressants.

But don't reach for medication every time you have a slight ache. A brisk walk, a cup of tea, or a hot bath may help you feel better. Or try a heating pad or hot water bottle. Or gentle exercises: Lie on your back with your knees up and move them in a small circle, or lean facedown on your forearms and shins and let your abdomen (and uterus) relax. Because your uterus is swollen and taking up more room than usual at the start of your period, you may want to avoid heavy meals.

Women who are on the Pill rarely suffer premenstrual discomfort and are as regular as clocks, but the Pill is not for everyone—more on that in the *Sex* chapter.

What should you do when you have your period? Everything you'd do otherwise! Skate, play tennis, dance, go out. Shower each day, eat healthfully, get lots of sleep and exercise. If you have intercourse, use contraceptives because although you're least likely to be fertile during your period, menstruation is no guarantee that you won't get pregnant. (Even if you've never had your period, you may still be fertile.)

Using too much salt is never good for you, and it's particularly smart to avoid it now, since it makes you retain fluids and look and feel puffy. You're losing iron, so eat meat, eggs, raisins, and whole-grain bread, or ask your doctor about iron supplements. Liver is also wonderful for you if you can stand it—I can't! (But I like pâté!) The calcium level in your blood is down, so drink plenty of milk or calcium-fortified juice. Your blood sugar is down, so eat small healthful snacks (not sweets) to keep it up. Now is an especially good time to take daily vitamins. Alcohol, by the way, affects you more than usual at this time, so beware.

Constipation can be a problem around your period. If it is for you, exercise and eat bran, vegetables, salads, apples, prunes, and other fruits; drink plenty of water, juice, or even coffee. (Have you tried reading on the john?) Regular bowel movements are crucial to overall health and extra important now to avoid cramping.

Which should you wear, tampons or pads? Do you realize how great it is to have a choice? Before 1921, women wore cloth diapers they washed and reused. Next came bulky napkins attached with belts. In 1936 Tampax Tampons were introduced. Hallelujah!

Most pads have an adhesive side that sticks to the inside of your panties. You can choose thin or thick pads—also called napkins, shields, liners—depending on your flow. When you change pads, throw out the old one rather than flush it, so it doesn't clog the toilet. If you're not having your period but are scared you might spot or start in the middle of a class or movie, wear a liner as a safety precaution. (Some spotting may be normal, particularly if you use the Pill or if you've gained or lost weight. Otherwise, see your doctor. Some white or yellow discharge is also normal and may be a sign that your period is on the way. But if this "sneak preview" is very clumpy or unusual for you, call your physician.)

What about tampons? I find them more convenient than pads for the first day or two because they're smaller, less messy, and more comfortable, and there's no odor. They're a must for gymnastics or swimming.

Some tampons come with tube applicators (such as Tampax), and others you push in with your finger (such as o.b.). Some have plastic applicators, which make for easy insertion for novices, but those are not biodegradable so are not ideal for the environment.

Manufacturers also make deodorant tampons, but some women are allergic to them, and most women prefer tampons that are as natural as possible. (100 percent cotton and unbleached is ideal.) There is no odor anyway until your menstrual flow meets the air, and by then you're throwing the used tampon away—in the trash, wrapped in lots of paper, or in the toilet, if you are positive the plumbing is excellent.

Most tampons come with directions for first-time users. If you haven't tried them, buy small or junior tampons and give it a go when you next have your period. Relax, read the guidelines, aim the tampon toward the small of your back, and push it in just far enough so it's comfortable. (You should hardly feel it.) You may go through several before you pop one in right, but inserting tampons is like whistling—once you get the hang of it, you'll never forget how. Don't practice when you don't have your period, though, because dryness makes insertion difficult.

Can young girls use tampons? Sure. Most girls have a thin layer of skin, called the hymen, that partially covers the opening of the vagina. But the hymen rarely seals the opening completely, so just as there's room for your flow to come out, there's room for your tampon to go in. (In case you've heard otherwise, you're a virgin if you haven't had intercourse, whether your hymen is or isn't intact.)

Use the tampon with the minimum absorbency required. For example, when your flow is light or medium, use a slender or regular tampon. When your flow is heavy, usually on day two and three, use a super tampon. (Heavier girls sometimes have heavier flows.) Still worried? You can always wear a tampon with a pad as a backup. Change your tampons every four to eight hours. When exactly? Relax and gently pull on the string. If the tampon doesn't budge, it's not yet time to change it. When it is time, the tampon will slide out easily. Changing too often can cause irritation. On the last day or two of your period, try pads and liners (such as Light days, Stayfree, Carefree, or always), instead of tampons.

In high school, my friends and I used to be afraid we'd stain our white pants or skirts. If you're careful, you need not worry. Maybe I've been lucky, but I've never yet sprung a serious leak. And even if you stain your underwear, you won't instantly stain your "outerwear."

We also worried that tampons would get lost in our bodies. That can't happen because your cervix, which is the gateway to your uterus, is too small for a tampon to slip through. If it did somehow slip up your vaginal canal, you'd just wash your fingers and tug it out. But that possibility is highly unlikely. And it can't slip down because your vaginal muscles hold it up.

You may have noticed a printed warning about toxic shock syndrome, or TSS, enclosed in your box of tampons. A lot of research has been done since an outbreak in 1980 to learn about this rare and sometimes fatal disease that is often associated with tampon use. Symptoms include a sudden fever (102 degrees or over), vomiting or diarrhea, a rash, dizziness, and faintness. If you have these signs, contact your doctor immediately, and if you are wearing a tampon, yank it out!

Before you panic, let me stress how rare this illness is. According to the Centers for Disease Control, in 1980, back when you probably weren't even a zygote, 886 cases of TSS were reported among fifty-two million menstruating women. Three years later, the number was down to 324 cases. Now doctors rarely even hear about TSS. Leprosy is more common! What changed? Rely brand high-absorbency tampons and others, which opened into a balloon shape, were taken off the market. And since more women are now aware of TSS, more are alternating tampons with pads. So be informed, but don't lose sleep.

Some women like to douche after their periods. That's unnecessary because your vagina is like a cat—it cleans itself. Some douches actually kill helpful bacteria. If you do douche, don't do so more than once a week and don't mistake it for contraception.

By the way, do you ever feel embarrassed when you buy tampons or pads? You shouldn't. Half the population buys or has bought or will buy them. Besides, you don't quake when the guy at the counter sees your toothpaste, soap, deodorant, or perfume, do you? Tampons or pads are just one more way of keeping clean and confident. So no blushing in the drugstore! (You might consider buying—or asking your mother to buy—some supplies before you start, so you'll have protection at the ready.)

On the other hand, while you should never feel ashamed of menstruation, you don't need to get out the megaphone every time your period comes. Menstruation has been a taboo subject in the past, and I'm not encouraging you to be hush-hush about it, but don't go to the other extreme, either.

(For what it's worth, I feel the same way about going to the bathroom. I prefer, "Excuse me, I'll be right back" to "I've gotta take a leak." But then I'm the type who runs the tap water when I'm in the powder room and others are within earshot.)

Once you've hit your teens, you may want to start seeing a gynecologist (male or female) instead of your pediatrician. Before your pelvic exam, the doctor will ask about your medical history, your cycle, and when you had your last period. Keep a menstrual record chart and a list of questions you may have and bring them in. (Doctors are great at answering questions, and they've heard it all: everything from "When am I going to get my period?" to "What's this little bump down here?" to questions about sex, contraception, and even bed-wetting.)

What to expect next? You'll probably slip into a paper smock and lie back, your feet in stirrups. The doctor will check your breasts, put on a rubber glove and check your vagina and rectum (it only takes a second), and take a Pap smear with a cotton swab to send on a slide to the laboratory. (If you start to feel embarrassed, try silently spelling your best friends' last names backward.) Remember, too, that your doctor is not being a pervert; he or she is trying to make sure you're healthy. Of course, if you'd be more comfortable with a different doctor, tell your parent. Annual checkups are less expensive at Planned Parenthood or a city clinic than at a private office. Examinations aren't fun, but once you're a woman, they're important. And knowing you're in good health gives you a great sense of well-being.

The Right Height

Just as you can't control how big your breasts will be or when your period will come, you can't control your height. It's a given, so the sooner you accept it, the better.

My short story is that I was the runt of the litter. My brothers are both over a foot taller than I. Even my mother is an imposing five feet seven inches, but, as she explained, "You take after Grandmother." And Grandmom was a shrimp.

In school, I was always at the end when the teacher lined us up by height. Instead of seeing eye-to-eye with people, I saw eye-to-neck.

I finally put my size in perspective and stopped fretting. I also stretched a few inches skyward and am now a towering five foot two, eyes of blue. For me, the bright side of being petite was that I went out with lots of guys, tall and small. I still receive terrific hand-me-downs (and hand-me-ups) from friends my size and larger. And I'm the last one to get wet when it rains!

Are you tall? You may feel like a giraffe now, but you'll be lucky in the long run. (Aren't you tired of waiting for the long run?) Tall women look elegant in clothes that make shorties look frumpy. On the job, they look authoritative. Another plus? Tall women can eat more than their short sisters. Be grateful, too, that you can reach the top closet shelf and see the movie, no matter who plunks down in front.

If you are afraid you'll soon be ducking under doorways, take heart. You may have reached the end of your growth spurt. A girl's growth spurt starts about the same time as her period and usually lasts one or two years. That's when you're shooting up up up, and past the guys. It takes guys a couple of years, but most catch up.

If you ever feel you're all arms and legs, fear not. That's normal, and your body will sort itself out sooner than you think.

Whatever your height and proportions, stand straight and wear clothes and shoes that suit you. Don't wear high heels constantly, though, because they aren't good for your feet or back. Shopkeepers, friends, magazines, and moms can help you figure out which styles work best for you.

Excited About Exercise

Don't think exercise. Think making friends, feeling stronger, losing weight, and living longer.

I don't love the idea of exercise. But I love to bicycle, ski, skate, swim, rollerblade, hike, and dance. My friend Judy and I used to jog almost every day in summer when we were neighbors. It was a great way to keep in shape and have one-on-one visits. It was also perfect for getting to know people better. I used to be timid about asking a guy out for Friday night or a girl over for dinner, but I was brazen about inviting Brad or Nell to go on a long, talkative jog.

More and more women are taking up cross-country in school or running in marathons. If you want to take up running, start slowly and walk when winded. Also warm up and finish by stretching. Don't run near traffic or at dusk, and when you come up behind somebody, say "Excuse me" or "On your left," so the person doesn't think he or she is about to be ax-murdered.

My friend Jen isn't a runner, but when we get together, we talk and walk—for miles. My former roommate Ellen and I figured out how to blab even while swimming! We'd meet at the pool, grab kickboards, and do laps while talking. Exercising alone can be ideal, too, whether you work out to music at home or go rollerblading solo. Signing up for a sport in school is good for your body and your social life.

A few months ago, I joined a gym. No, I don't have a personal trainer. But I do have extra energy, thinner thighs, a firmer fanny. (As they say, "If you want a smaller butt, get off it!") Can you go to a gym or Y or your parents' health club? Or can you get your family to invest in a stationary bike, treadmill, or some other high-tech machine for everyone's cardiovascular health?

If you exercise before a meal, you'll burn calories faster. Plus, if you've just worked out, it's easier to feel health-minded and forgo the sundae. My favorite times to exercise are before dinner (when I'm tempted to snack) or first thing in the morning (so I start my day awake).

You may be getting enough exercise in gym, but why not go out for a sport or enlist a friend with whom to run or play tennis regularly? A minimum of twenty minutes of aerobic exercise three times a week is crucial for health and well-being. You can find that time. (Better still, try for forty minutes five times a week.)

Walk whenever possible. Even if you have your license, why bother with car keys and parking when you're only going half a mile? The same with elevators. Don't press the button—climb the stairs!

One thing I like about exercise is that it makes me feel I've earned my daily shower. When I step in hot and sweaty, I feel extra-clean and fresh when I step out.

I even jogged on my wedding day, with Judy, my maid of honor. My mother, aghast, was afraid we'd fall and have to hobble down the aisle. Instead, jogging made us both feel less nervous. And our cheeks looked naturally rosy.

Too tired to exercise? Nonsense! A twenty-minute walk can invigorate you as much as a twenty-minute nap. Regular exercise gives you energy rather than sapping it.

Raquetball, running, ballet, gymnastics, snowboarding—they're all great, but you can also burn calories and tone muscles by walking briskly instead of shuffling your feet. Or by lifting weights or doing bent-leg sit-ups as you watch TV. Or by pressing your feet down while studying as though you alone are preventing the floor from rising.

Staying in shape now can also make it easier to stay in shape later. Just look at Martina Navratilova and Mary Decker Slaney.

Here ends my Physical Fitness Pep Talk. Don't obsess about it, but do exercise. It'll lift your spirits, improve your complexion, firm flab, relieve stress, increase your self-confidence, strengthen your heart, speed your metabolism, and leave you full of vim and vigor. Studies show that girls who get regular exercise, whether it's competitive, social, or solo, even get better grades. So don't get distraught or depressed about your chnging body. Take charge of it by staying fit and finding an activity that you can enjoy now and for the rest of your life.

Winning the Weight War

Do you eat to live or live to eat? Most people do both, and even if you would briefly consider trading in your brother for a pepperoni pizza, that doesn't necessarily mean there's cause for concern.

However, weight control *is* a problem for too many of us. No one wants to be roly-poly fat or starvation skinny. Yet it can be difficult to eat healthful, balanced meals and maintain a comfortable in-between weight. Are you so calorie-conscious that weight is controlling you, rather than the other way around? Are you dieting desperately or feeling guilty every time you eat even though friends swear you're a toothpick? Or are you chubby but unwilling to recognize it or chunky just to spite your gymnast mother or health-nut father? Schools provide guidance counseling and drug and sex information, but rarely teach nutrition. Yet that should be a required course! For the first time ever in the United States, overweight individuals outnumber normal-size ones. Fully one-third of the population is obese! Most of these portly people are in their fifties, but many are teens and preteens.

The media are partly to blame. Food commercials say eat! eat! eat! but the actress munching the brownie is skinny! skinny! skinny! Fashion magazines brim with mixed messages. On one page: the latest fad diet. On the next: new pie recipes. Even Barbie may be partly at fault. Long-haired and long-legged, she's a 36-18-33 (in human terms). Girls bond with her at an impressionable age, and forever after many have unrealistic expectations of what bodies should look like.

So what do you do? Your boyfriend gawks over svelte models in intimate apparel ads, but if you're together at a fancy restaurant, he doesn't want you to order just a salad. Your mother says you could stand to lose a few pounds, then prepares lasagna, your favorite, because she loves you. When you try on bathing suits, you wonder if the designers are comedians.

In my house, it was my father who stuffed turkeys, fried bacon, stirred gravies, rolled dumplings, flipped crêpes, whipped cream, and grated chocolate. I cleaned my plate with gusto.

Somehow I managed to get away with it and be a bit of a stick—until senior year of high school. That's when I went to France to live with a French family. France! Home of tempting breads, pastries, cheeses, and haute cuisine! Suffice it to say I overindulged. And my metabolism caught up with me.

I scarcely realized I was gaining weight because I thought of myself as the skinny-bones I'd always been. Yet when I returned to Armonk, New York, everyone seemed more interested in the dozen pounds I'd put on than in my fluency in French or impressions of the Louvre.

I cut back on my munching, bought a calorie counter, and stayed seated at dinner while my brothers hopped up for seconds and thirds. Most of the weight fell off pretty fast. Since then, however, I've had to watch myself, work out, and not gobble cookies with abandon.

The trick is to be sensible. You don't want to be fat—but you also don't want to be neurotic about every half-inch of flesh on your body. You need nutritious food for fuel and growth. According to one study, nearly two-thirds of girls aged thirteen to eighteen are trying to lose weight. But that's lunacy. Dieting should not be the norm. I mean, c'mon. Most girls look totally fine. It's only when they compare themselves to tall, thin models (a distorted image of the female shape) that they get obsessed or depressed.

Me, I'd rather be a few pounds over my ideal weight than diet endlessly, frantic about calories. Weight fixation is a major brain drain, and failed diets undermine self-esteem.

Besides, even if you do lose a pound per thigh and two off your behind, you still won't be tall and blond if you're short and brunette. Your life won't change just because you shed five pounds. It might change if you start feeling more outgoing, active, and self-assured. People respond to a gain in confidence as much as they do to a loss in weight.

Cut out the snacks and soda, and work to become fit instead of fat now because you are setting your eating patterns. Good habits now mean good health later. School-age kids are judgmental and, as the saying goes, if you don't watch your figure, no one else will. But if you already look fine, relax!

The following section on weighty worries offers fifty tips. I really hope you don't spend your life jumping on and off the diet merry-go-round.

Nor should you be on a perpetual diet because your body will simply make do on less food by slowing your metabolism. (Art Buchwald says the word *diet* comes from "to die.")

Strive to stay sane about all this. Confidence is cumulative. So accept yourself or change. It's hard to get psyched to diet, but if (and only if) you truly need to, drop some pounds by modifying your eating. You can win by losing.

Don't Window-Shop at the Bakery and Forty-Nine Other Do's and Don'ts for Healthy Eating

You have to eat. But steer clear of empty calories and 530-calorie Big Macs—a nutritionist's nightmare! Better to nutritious calories. It's better to load up on fruits and vegetables and to read the labels on foods you buy or eat. Become a savvy consumer who knows the difference between grape juice (good for you) and grape drink or soda (sugar water). Drink low-fat milk or calcium-fortified orange juice and eat cheese, yogurt, sardines, or tofu because girls need lots of calcium now to prevent osteoporosis later. Too many older women end up with shortened spines or fractured hips.

Are you thinking about becoming a vegetarian? Don't just stop eating meat. Stock up on peas, beans, nuts, legumes, and whole-wheat pasta and bread. Read about healthful balanced diets and go organic when possible.

You should exercise to improve muscle tone and keep bones strong, but playing an hour of volleyball does not entitle you to pig out on pecan pie à la mode. If you're portly, do yourself a favor and pass on the pie. Or have a taste of a friend's.

Here are fifty more ideas:

1. ***Don't*** eat if you're not hungry.
2. ***Do*** eat slowly, putting your fork down between bites and talking during the meal.
3. ***Don't*** take big portions. Take small portions. Think slivers, not slabs.
4. ***Do*** stop before you're full because it takes about twenty minutes for your belly to figure out what your mouth has been up to.
5. ***Don't*** take big bites. Take small bites.
6. ***Do*** drink lots of water all day long. Keep a pitcher of water in the fridge, a teapot on the stove, and a sports bottle on your desk.

7. ***Don't*** eat absentmindedly. Enjoy what you're consuming, or don't bother. (The first two cookies are scrumptious. Can you really taste the sixth?)

8. ***Do*** exercise regularly and remember that muscle weighs more than flab—but looks better. Swimming, blading, jogging, gymnastics, dancing, skiing, bicycling, and even jumping rope are great for fitness, fun, and all-over trimming. Think appearance and health, not just pounds.

9. ***Don't*** waste calories on soda. Drink water or calorie-free herbal teas or nutritious juices, such as tomato or grapefruit.

10. ***Do*** keep peeled carrots, celery sticks, cherry tomatoes, grapes, clementines, and other vegetables and fruits ready for snacking or for trips.

11. ***Don't*** buy fattening foods, and ask the family shopper to skip the candy aisle. It's much easier to resist when it's not around. Never go to the grocery store on an empty stomach.

12. ***Do*** think of getting through one day at a time if you're dieting, rather than bumming out over the prospect of three weeks without Häagen-Dazs.

13. ***Don't*** ever take diet pills without a doctor's go-ahead. Some are dangerous; others make you irritable; others make you lose water, not fat. If you're curious about fen/phen or Redux or some other pill, ask a professional.

14. ***Do*** eat varied well-balanced meals daily that include foods from the five major food groups: grains and cereals; fruits; vegetables; meat, poultry, and fish; and dairy products.

15. ***Don't*** weigh yourself every day because you'll get compulsive and your scale won't immediately register last night's bag of Doritos. If you're dieting, weigh yourself at the same time every few days and don't expect to lose more than one or two pounds a week.

16. ***Do*** be patient if you're dieting wisely but losing slowly or if you've reached a plateau. Some people have faster metabolisms than others.

17. ***Don't*** get discouraged if you're dieting and people don't notice your weight loss right away. You don't notice every two pounds they gain and lose.

18. ***Do*** take a walk, phone a friend, run an errand, or chew sugarless gum when you get a food craving or feel tempted to down donut after donut.

19. **Don't** skip breakfast. Your body will thank you more for breakfast than it will for an extra seven minutes' sleep. Instead of skipping meals, eat small meals.

20. **Do** learn that spumoni is more fattening than spinach—potatoes are more caloric than tomatoes, etc. Without memorizing charts, learn which foods might as well be applied directly to your thighs.

21. **Don't** talk about your diet all the time. You'll bore everybody silly.

22. **Do** keep busy, and food will become less important.

23. **Don't** blow the rest of a diet day just because you snuck a Snickers at lunch.

24. **Do** order fish, chicken, salad, or something light when eating out.

25. **Don't** have one potato chip. It's easier to have none. (Popcorn or pretzels are better for you, yet also hard to eat in moderation.)

26. **Do** remember that calories count even when it's your birthday, even when you're on a date, even when you have a test that day, even when the cookie dough is raw, even when you're standing up, even at parties, and even when you're just snitching a bite from someone else's plate.

27. **Don't** mistake your new womanly roundness for unsightly flab.

28. **Do** use a small plate if your dinner looks pitiful on a big one.

29. **Don't** feel you have to polish off every bite of your dinner at a restaurant. (Portions tend to be huge.)

30. **Do** cut down on salt because salt makes you retain excess water. Season your food with pepper and spices. (Canned veggies come salted; eat fresh or frozen ones.)

31. **Don't** eat with abandon on Sunday in preparation for a diet you might start on Monday.

32. **Do** blot your pizza with a paper napkin if it looks extra oily and you're not dining with the Queen.

33. **Don't** imagine that "low fat" means no fat or that "fat-free" means "calorie-free."

34. **Do** consider taping a picture of you-at-your-tubbiest *or* sleekest on your fridge. (I know someone who wired his fridge with a gadget that asks, when the door is opened, "Are you really hungry, Fatso?")

35. ***Don't*** leave a knife on the cake plate. It makes it too easy to slice off a taste when you really are just passing by.

36. ***Do*** brush your teeth when you want to put something in your mouth. The just-brushed feeling will cut down on your desire to munch.

37. ***Don't*** fry when you can boil, broil, steam, grill, or bake.

38. ***Do*** buy tuna packed in water instead of oil; canned fruit in its juice, not in syrup; low-fat milk, not whole milk; thin-sliced bread, not regular bread; white meat (e.g., chicken, fish), not red meat (e.g., burgers, steak).

39. ***Don't*** window-shop at the bakery.

40. ***Do*** consider writing down everything you eat during one week if you're trying to lose weight. That can help you figure out when extra calories slip into your diet. It also curbs eating when you report cheating.

41. ***Don't*** snack without asking, "Is this worth the calories?"

42. ***Do*** pick up a five-pound bag of flour after you lose your first five: That's how much weight you no longer lug around.

43. ***Don't*** become a vegetarian (or vegan) unless you research exactly what you'd need to eat each day to get enough protein and iron.

44. ***Do*** learn how to use chopsticks. They'll slow you down when you eat Chinese food.

45. ***Don't*** sit through TV food commercials—press mute or change the channel.

46. ***Do*** consider making rigid rules for yourself. It may be easier never to snack after 9 P.M. than to test your will-power every evening.

47. ***Don't*** underestimate the pleasure of holding back. When you pass up the blintzes, you'll feel strong and virtuous.

48. ***Do*** consider meeting instead of eating. You could try Weight Watchers or Overeaters Anonymous or another support group if you can't lose on your own.

49. ***Don't*** drink diet sodas or use sugar substitutes that specifically warn they contain additives that have "been determined to cause cancer in laboratory animals." (Granted we're talking rats, not people, and doses, not packets, but I'll take my tea plain, thanks.)

50. Do stop dieting when you've reached a sensible target weight.
You may want to lose a few extra pounds since you may gain a
few back. But quit when it's quitting time and then work on
maintaining. Don't congratulate yourself with Fig Newtons.
Treat yourself to a pair of pants—in your new smaller size.

Losing Too Much: Eating Disorders

If preoccupation with food interferes with your life; if you see yourself
as plump even though others swear you're underweight; or if you truly
believe that if you were thin, you'd be happy, you may be prone to an
eating disorder.

Many girls never just eat—they pick at food or gorge themselves,
starve or stuff themselves compulsively. And many do permanent damage to their bodies.

About eight million Americans, mostly female, suffer from eating disorders. About 1 out of 100 teenage girls is anorexic, and up to 5 percent
are bulimic. Among obese women, up to 40 percent have binge-eating
disorders. Famous people who have struggled with eating disorders
include Princess Diana, actress Jane Fonda, singer Paula Abdul, and
singer Karen Carpenter—who died of anorexia.

If you think you have symptoms of one or more of the following eating
disorders (there is some overlap), you are not alone. But you probably
can't cure yourself alone. Take vitamins and try to go three days without
feasting or fasting. If you can't, contact a doctor or one of the centers
listed at the end of this section. They can recommend support programs, self-help groups, clinics, or counselors in your area. They can
also talk to you about short-term individual therapy; family therapy;
and, if necessary, Prozac, hospitalization, or extended-care therapy.

Some treatment clinics like Renfrew (800-736-3936) are expensive.
Others like Center for the Study of Anorexia (212-595-3449) charge on
a sliding scale. Some accept Medicaid or Medicare; others do not. Your
inquiry will be strictly confidential.

Anorexia Nervosa

Pam is in her late teens. She is a perfectionist. She is as emaciated and
bony as a prisoner of war or a famine victim, but she insists that her
belly sticks out and she wants to lose a little more weight.

Her friendships have changed. Her family is worried. They think she
looks skeletal and urge her to eat more. But that just makes her defiant,

so she hardly touches the food on her plate. Pam thinks about food a lot, and she cooks for others. But while food fascinates her, eating repels her. So she feeds her dinner to the dog, or hides it, or throws it out when no one is looking. When someone *is* watching, she may eat, but may later take a laxative or an enema. Occasionally her willpower falters and she binges, but afterward she vomits or fasts with added determination.

Losing weight makes Pam feel in control. Her parents have always demanded a lot, and she expects a lot of herself. After Pam shed the five pounds she wanted to lose, she kept dieting and exercising rigidly. She is plugged into the idea of putting as little as possible into her body. It gives her a sense of power, even superiority, to know she can live almost without food; she can resist what others find irresistible.

From 120 pounds, she's down to below 90. She's lost some hair as well as weight. Some of her skin is scaly. She feels cold and bundles up. She has problems sleeping and suffers from constipation and sudden muscle cramps. When her periods stopped (amenorrhea), Pam wondered if her whole system was shutting down. But she hadn't felt too comfortable about menstruation or the prospect of a future pregnancy anyway. What finally scared Pam was that she went from feeling superenergetic to debilitated. And when her sister came home from college, she took one look at Pam and started to cry.

Pam has a classic, all-too-common case of anorexia nervosa. If she doesn't get help soon, she could die or suffer lifelong problems. There *is* such a thing as being too thin.

Anorexia nervosa has been described as a psychosomatic and psychosocial illness in which irrational fear of being overweight leads to compulsive dieting. It can affect anybody, but 90 to 95 percent of sufferers are women, especially young American women. Anorexia itself is culture bound. (You don't see many Asians, Hispanics, blacks, or Native Americans wilfully wasting away.) Some women diet successfully or lose weight in an illness, then continue dieting until they've lost as much as 25 percent of their original body weight. About 1 in 100 women may be anorexic, and 1 in 10 of those with serious cases die; they starve to death or die of infections or heart failure. Others wait too long before they seek help; although they recover, they've done irreparable damage to their bodies because of drastic chemical imbalances and malnutrition. Even their bones are irrevocably weakened.

What should you do if you recognize that you or a friend may be anorexic? Seek help. Talk to your family. Or school nurse. Or doctor. Or contact one of the organizations listed.

Treatment will entail putting on some weight, learning to eat a balanced diet, and therapy to overcome the phobia of weight gain and to deal with underlying troubles. Recovery is possible.

Bulimia Nervosa

Jessica's weight is pretty normal. Her friends don't even realize she has a problem. But Jessica knows she's a compulsive eater, and she feels depressed, disgusted, and guilty. At times, that guilt sends her back to the kitchen, where she eats a box of cookies, a bag of doughnuts, half a pie, or a quart of ice cream. She scarcely pauses between bites because she doesn't want to acknowledge what she's doing. After a pig-out, Jessica goes straight to the bathroom and vomits.

At first, she thought throwing up was a great way to eat her favorite foods without gaining weight. That was back when she had to use her finger to make herself vomit. Unfortunately, her unhealthy whim led to frequent self-induced vomiting, and now when she bends over, the food comes up on its own. Her mouth hurts and sometimes bleeds, and lately Jessica has been depressed by her feast-or-famine eating patterns. Her fixation with food has gotten in the way of her social life. It has also diverted her attention from her other problems.

Jessica spends a lot of time in the kitchen and bathroom. She binges about a dozen times a week. Sometimes she gorges on spaghetti, crackers, and bread instead of sweets. Sometimes she gets rid of it by using a laxative, enema, or diuretic instead of vomiting. But her weight doesn't fluctuate much—which frustrates her all the more. (Food is quickly absorbed, so bulimics throw up only about half of what they eat.)

Her mother thinks that Jessica simply has a healthy appetite. No one suspects that Jessica has a problem, because she covers her tracks. She hides her food. When she wants ice cream, she doesn't go crazy at Carvel. She has two cones there, then goes to Swensen's, Steve's, Baskin-Robbins, and Dairy Queen.

Once she stole $20 from her mother's wallet for food. That made her feel terrible, and *that* made her binge extra. She wishes she could stop, but sometimes she panics and is afraid she has forgotten how to eat normally.

Jessica suffers from bulimia. If she continues to binge and purge, she may cause permanent damage to her body.

Bulimia (literally, "ox hunger") is common among women in high school and college and is more prevalent than anorexia. Some anorexics "recover" only to become bulimic, or vice versa, which means they haven't really faced the conflicts behind their eating disorder. Also, just as some anorexics may avoid facing their sexuality by regressing to an almost prepuberty state physically, some bulimics mask their curves in fat. Many bulimics were repeatedly physically or sexually abused and began hating their bodies early on.

A bulimic's habits are harmful. By vomiting right after eating, the bulimic throws up not only calories but water and digestive fluids as well. This can cause dehydration and a serious imbalance of body chemicals. The stomach acids that come up the esophagus and pour into the mouth can cause bleeding, gum disease, and tooth decay. Fasting leads to malnutrition and kidney problems and may stunt growth. Abuse of laxatives and enemas can make the bulimic prone to constipation and bowel lesions. In severe cases, the bulimic's eyes may be bloodshot and the hands and feet may be numb. Often the bulimic feels out of control, isolated, and depressed.

If, like Jessica, you are binging and purging and are always eating because of emotional, rather than physical cues, you need help. Talk to your family or doctor or one of the groups listed. You can learn to mod- ify your eating behavior, take responsibility for your body, express ten- sions in more constructive ways, and be nicer to yourself. You will get better and, with determination, you will stay well. But the longer you are bulimic, the harder it is to recover. If you have a friend who is bulimic, share these pages with her. (And if you feel like skimming or skipping ahead, go for it. I won't mind—I won't even know! I'm just try- ing to be thorough because you never know what you—or someone you care for—will be curious about.)

Binge Eating

Meghan is overweight—and hates it. Her friends think she is too lazy to diet, and some former friends tease her. Meghan knows her weight is out of control. She doesn't just overeat at meals, after all, she goes on frequent hours-long 2,000-calorie-plus binges. Afterward, she feels dis- gusted and guilty. But unlike a bulimic, Meghan does not try to throw up or take an enema or run to the gym. She doesn't have a purge of choice. She just keeps gaining weight. At 5 feet 6 inches and 240 pounds and climbing, she worries that she'll wind up obese.

Meghan hates her body and sometimes herself, and when she eats wildly, she tries to numb the negative feelings that overwhelm her. Once in a while she'll go on a diet, but it's a yo-yo—before she knows it, she's sabotaging herself, off on another binge.

Her doctor tells her she needs to lose weight. Her mother does, too, but her mother drinks too much and has been preoccupied with her own weight ever since Meghan was little. Meghan herself knows that she isn't fat because of indifference or genetics or thyroid problems. She knows she is overweight because she's troubled. What she may not know is that willpower alone won't get her on track. She needs therapy, maybe even low-dose antidepressants. She needs to forgive herself. And she needs to work through her food issues and to get to where food is not running—and ruining—her life.

If you or someone you know is binge eating, there is still time to turn things around. It will take effort, but the sooner you get help, the sooner you'll get better.

National Association of Anorexia Nervosa and Associated Disorders
(ANAD)
P.O. Box 7
Highland Park, IL 60035
(847) 831-3438

American Anorexia/Bulimia Association (AABA)
293 Central Park West, Suite 1R
New York, NY 10024
(212) 501-8351
http://members.aol.com/AmAnBu

Anorexia Nervosa and Related Eating Disorders (ANRED)
P.O. Box 5102
Eugene, OR 97405
(541) 344-1144
http://www.anred.com

Body Sweat, Body Smells

A couple of years ago, you hardly perspired, let alone had body odor. Now some of your glands are working hard to keep you cool, and that may mean underarm wetness. Some say, "Horses sweat, men perspire, and women glow," but while *glowing* sounds pleasant, *smelling* is another story.

Fight back! Shower or bathe daily. If necessary, use deodorant, stick or roll-on. (Pressure sprays can pollute the atmosphere.) Change brands periodically, since each product can lose some effectiveness once your body gets used to it. Wear cotton or well-ventilated clothes.

While we're talking body odors, is gas ever a problem? If so, avoid notorious foods, such as beans, cabbage, radishes, and spicy foods; don't drink too much apple cider, apple juice, or soda; don't chew gum endlessly. And eat s-l-o-w-l-y.

Want to smell like lemons, flowers, or exotic essences? Don't live in a bubble bath, because that can cause vaginal or urinary irritations. Instead, consider perfume. To sample testers, spray a little on your forearm, wait a few minutes, and sniff. Your nose gets confused after three or four fragrances, so it may take a week to decide which to buy. Don't go too sweet or heavy, and remember that a little goes a long way.

Skin Care (Sun Goddesses, Beware!)

Do you have a peaches-and-cream complexion? Do you even know anybody who does? Often when you want to look your best, your skin may look its worst. (*Teen* is truly a four-letter word!) More than 95 percent of the population runs into some acne trouble at some time. Many girls find their hormones are going haywire and pimples are popping up on their faces with the dependability of dandelions on a spring lawn.

The good news? Proper care can improve your complexion, medicated makeup can hide your blemishes, girls' skin troubles are generally not as bad as guys', and your flare-ups are only temporary. Soon your angry skin will calm down—and you can start worrying about wrinkles!

My teen diary is loaded with skin worries, such as: "*My face is a pimple patch but not as bad as usual.*" After a year or two of private battles, I went to a dermatologist.

He wrote out a prescription for antibiotics; recommended a cleansing soap; and told me to drink lots of water, eat a good diet, and get enough sleep and exercise. He also said not to touch my face, rest my chin or forehead in my palms, pick blemishes, or squeeze blackheads. I followed orders, and my skin got better (as did my complexion complex).

If your skin is polka-dotted, consider seeing a dermatologist. Sure you could wait to outgrow your acne, but that could take years and leave scars. Dermatologists can also attempt to get rid of warts and pock-marks, and they should be consulted immediately if a wart, mole, or scar ever changes.

You're tired of that Dennis Rodman look? Ask your dermy to remove your tattoo. Ink can be removed with a laser, but be patient, it may take several treatments to get rid of your ex's name or that blotchy rose. (If you don't have a tattoo, I'm not going to talk you into getting one. Not every tattoo "artist" is reputable or competent, let alone artistic or legal, and some can be dangerous—cases of HIV and hepatitis have been traced to contaminated tattoo needles.)

Back to zits. New antibiotics and effective soaps are constantly being developed. A derivative of retinoic acid (vitamin A) helps reduce the plugging of pores. Many dermatologists prescribe antibiotics, such as tetracycline and erythromycin. Whenever a doctor prescribes a treatment, it is essential to follow directions precisely and to let the doctor know if you are pregnant or if you become aware of any side effects (using antibiotics can make you more prone to developing a yeast infection).

Should you quit eating chocolate, cola, pizza, or French fries? Maybe. Most experts say diet has little to do with pimples. You know your skin best, so you be the expert. If you eat a Mounds bar, does your face erupt with little mounds? Experiment (after your period, so you don't throw off the results).

Pimples do not live by food alone, and no matter what you eat, you may be a bit of a craterface for a while. Acne outside is a sign that you're maturing inside. You may break out around your "time of the month" or when you are stressed or scared or excited—or for no reason at all. Acne is not affected by sex life. And acne is not a losing battle because you win in the end.

Meanwhile, don't forget to wash (not scrub) your face. Many pimples despise soap and water and will pack up and flee if you wash regularly. Your best zit-zapping plan of attack is to wash with soap and warm water morning and night and rinse well with cool water before patting dry with a clean towel. Wash your back and chest when showering, and keep your hair clean because greasy hair means greasy skin. If you are going to apply makeup, wash your face first.

If your skin is sensitive, try Neutrogena or other mild soaps. If your skin is dry, use a gentle creamy soap and a moisturizer. If your room is overheated, you can buy a vaporizer or put a pan of water on the radiator for added moisture. Prone to chapped skin? Smear lotion on your elbows, knees, hands, and feet.

OK. Let's say you've been drinking water, eating healthfully, minimizing stress, washing well, and exercising, and you don't even *use* makeup, let alone sleep with it on. Yet you still wake up every once in a while with a pimple the size of a tepee at the end of your nose.

What should you do? Wear a Band-Aid to school? Say to friends, "Can you believe this horrendous zit? I'm so ugly! My face looks like a relief map of the Andes!" Stay home and watch talk shows? No! Your best bet is to dab on a little medicated makeup and forget about it. In high school, my handsome older brother Mark once told me he didn't mind when his date had a blemish or two because it made him less self-conscious about his own slight acne.

Hang in there. Your face will soon clear up, and I doubt there will be a single telltale scar.

A is for Aging, B is for Burning, C is for Cancer

True or false: You love the sun, you want a tan, and you don't care if you look like a prune in thirty years.

I hate to be a killjoy, but if you answered *true,* watch out. The sun is more dangerous than it used to be. Ozone depletion means more ultraviolet rays are hitting us—and too much exposure to the sun can cause skin cancer. A tan is simply evidence of sun damage—it's your body's attempt to protect itself from ultraviolet radiation. Even if you don't get a dreaded cancer, a sun worshiper's skin can become dry, leathery, and lined, and you may someday wish you could step into a time machine and throttle your former self.

Besides, you *can* enjoy the sun sensibly, without burning or inviting melanoma. Here are a dozen tips.

1. Always bring a T-shirt or long-sleeved blouse and sunglasses with you to the beach or pool. Buy a cute hat to protect your cute face.
2. Start gradually. If you lie in the sun for a full hour on day one, you won't look stunning by nightfall; you'll look like a lobster in pain. And if you're indoors up North all year and suddenly vacation for a week in the tropics, protect yourself with sunblock.
3. Douse yourself with sunscreen before and during sunning and

after swimming. If you pour on the baby oil, you'll burn to a crisp. Use a product that has a sun-protection factor (SPF) of 15 or greater and that also blocks out the UVA and UVB lights. (The A really is for Aging; the B, for Burning.)

4. Don't trust those clouds. Around 70 to 80 percent of the sun's ultraviolet rays shine through them.

5. Don't broil at midday. The sun is strongest—and most harmful—from 10 A.M. until 2 P.M.

6. Know thyself. If you have fair skin, you may burn easily. If you have dark skin, you still need to protect yourself.

7. Don't use a sun reflector. The skin under your chin and earlobes is particularly sensitive.

8. Stay away from sun lamps or tanning salons. They can be dangerous. And why wither your skin without getting the fun of the sun? If you insist on a tan, play it safe with a self-tanner or bronzer cream.

9. Take extra precautions if you live in the South, the mountains, or wherever sun rays are especially fierce.

10. Take extra care if you're skiing because snow reflects the sun's rays.

11. Know that birth control pills and certain antibiotics can make your skin more susceptible to burning or blotching.

12. Use a moisturizer after catching rays, so your skin will stay smoother longer. For the best benefits, apply after you wash or bathe while the skin is still moist.

A Nose Is a Nose Is a Nose and All About Ears

You've tackled your skin troubles. What about the rest of your face? To be thorough, I'm going to tell you about cosmetic surgery—but don't expect me to recommend it.

For starters, it's expensive, it hurts, and it won't guarantee you'll be elected class president or prom queen. Plus, by replacing your distinguished feature with an ordinary one, you're losing part of your individuality. Barbra Streisand might never have made it if she'd had an everyday nose. Who nose?

So think twice, then twice more before you decide on plastic surgery. Is your life really being ruined by your nose or ears? Or is it your attitude that needs fixing? If you change your hairstyle, don flashy earrings, make up your eyes, apply lipstick, and smile—won't that do the job? Besides, your face may still be changing and growing, and most surgeons won't operate until you're at least sixteen.

Say you are sixteen and you're sure—really sure—you want to see a different face in the mirror. Talk to your parents and family doctor. Find a competent specialist or you could end up looking worse instead of better. Elective surgery can cost thousands and is not usually covered by health insurance unless it is medically necessary.

Consider having the operation the summer before college or before a family move. And don't expect miracles.

I visited my friend Miriam after she had her nose reshaped. "I had local anesthesia, so I didn't feel much, but I'm sore now," she said, sounding as if she had a terrible cold. For several weeks after the rhinoplasty operation, she had to avoid sun and take care not to bump into anything. (No Eskimo kissing that summer!) But when she started college, instead of feeling like Pinocchio, Miriam felt pretty. Instead of wasting time worrying about her schnozz, she directed her energy elsewhere.

Are you all ears? Many big-eared women hide their ears under hair, scarves, or hats. But some opt for otoplasty. A good-looking friend of mine told me that when he was growing up, he endured several nicknames, such as Dumbo, Elephant Ears, and Mr. Spock.

"Kids are so mean!" I said. But when Ben showed me an adorable photo of a flappy-eared eight year old, I almost burst out laughing.

Fortunately, he laughed first. "They stuck straight out!" Ben admitted and told me about his operation. "It was June and I'd broken my leg playing football. My mother came up with the idea, and since I was laid up anyway, I figured why not. The doctors cut away a little cartilage and pinned my ears closer to my head. Then I wore a bandage for a week. That, with the cast, and I looked like a wounded soldier. Anyway, my leg healed and so did my ears."

Rather than protruding, Ben's ears now lie flat against his head. (Men account for about 40 percent of cosmetic ear surgery and about 30 percent of nose jobs and chin jobs.)

Ear piercing is a kind of cosmetic surgery, although it's small potatoes next to the dramatic physical and psychological transformations associated with rhinoplasty and otoplasty.

If you want to pierce your ears, first be sure you can. Do you bleed more than most people? Are you unusually prone to allergies and infections? Do you have keloid skin or skin that scars easily? If you answered no, no, no, no, then yes, you can get your ears pierced.

But get your parents' go-ahead. And if they want you to wait, *try* to be patient. Remember that lots of people (like me) have gone happily through life wearing clip-ons. (Then again, you might mention that you're thinking of piercing either your ears, eyebrow, nostrils, or navel—you just can't decide.) You suddenly do have permission to pierce your ears? Go to a doctor or qualified jeweler (not a friend).

Piercing your ears is not expensive, and it doesn't hurt much. Be sure to keep your gold posts in for as long as possible before wearing other metals or wires. And at first, always swab your ears with alcohol to minimize the risk of infection. If your ears become red or swollen, consult your school nurse or doctor.

One last thought about ears. Don't blast music too loudly through your headphones and don't live at concert halls. Millions of kids have suffered some hearing loss from loud music.

Eye Deal

Do you need glasses? One out of every two Americans and one in four teenagers does. Seeing your best is part of looking your best. Don't squint or let your grades sink or say a mere hi in the hall because you can't identify the cute guy approaching you.

In college, I went to the theater with my friend Gilbert and, feeling coy, tried on his glasses. What a shock! I could see the actors' expressions rather than just fuzzy features. I hadn't realized what I was missing. An optometrist confirmed that I needed glasses for plays, movies, and driving. So I got framed! Now I love seeing leaves on the trees, feathers on the birds, windows on the skyscrapers, faces in the crowds.

Do you get headaches after you read? Is your vision blurry? Do you have trouble making out road signs, small print, subtitles, or words on the blackboard? Get your eyes checked annually. If you need glasses or contact lenses, don't wait around.

Glasses come in all sorts of attractive shapes, colors, tints, and styles. Some people look better with them on than off. Some invest in a backup pair or in prescription sunglasses, too. Ask the store about discounts for the second set. And ask about lenses that are safe, scratch-resistant, and able to block out ultraviolet light.

Contacts often cost more than glasses, require more care, and take some adjusting to. The payoff is that contacts don't change your appearance, often offer better vision, and won't slide off your face when you're jogging. Your eye doctor can help you decide if you want soft, hard, disposable, or extended-wear contacts with tinted or clear lenses and can tell you how to clean, disinfect, remove, and replace your lenses to minimize the risk of infections or other complications.

Ignore Your Teeth and They'll Go Away

My first dentist was a horrible bald man with a tic. He used to make me kiss him on the cheek each visit and was stingy with the Novocaine. "Raise your hand if it hurts," he'd say, then ignore me as I waved wildly. His motto was probably: Drill, fill, and bill.

We changed dentists. My new one is friendly, painless, and capable. My only complaint is that sometimes he asks, "How have you been, Carol?" then pops a water-sucking gizmo under my tongue so all I can mumble is "Fffah, jjus ffahn."

Twice a year this dentist gives me sunny sermons about oral hygiene. Use a brush with soft bristles morning and night and replace it every few months. Floss religiously. Carry a toothbrush in your purse for after lunch. "At least rinse your mouth at the water fountain or in the bathroom," he pleads, "and stay away from sticky sweets and sugar-coated gum." "Coffee, tea, and cigarettes stain your teeth," he warns, "and cola rots them."

Run your tongue over your teeth right now. Do they feel coated and grimy or slick and clean?

Does the tap water in your town contain fluoride? (Chances are fifty/fifty.) Fluoride helps strengthen teeth. That's why a fluoride toothpaste is the best cavity-fighter. Do your gums bleed when you brush? Periodontal (gum) disease is common, and treatment is expensive and painful. So floss now before plaque takes over. Your family may even want to invest in a battery-powered toothbrush and gum stimulator, such as Interplak.

Do you ever have halitosis? To prevent bad breath, use a mouthwash and brush your teeth, your tongue, and the roof of your mouth gently with toothpaste. If you're going out, don't eat onions or garlic bread. Carry mints with you, or eat an apple. Your breath is still bad? You may have indigestion, an infection, or tooth decay, so see your dentist or doctor.

A college friend and I thought up a tactful way to inform each other when we had stale breath. We'd say "B²" (for bad breath) just as many people say "XYZ" for "examine your zipper" (less humiliating than "your fly is open").

What about braces? No one says they are fun. I was a Tinsel Teeth when I was fourteen. In ninth grade, I once wrapped my retainer in a napkin at lunchtime, bussed my tray, and accidentally threw my lumpy napkin away. I realized what I'd done in the middle of geometry and went racing to the lunchroom custodian. But the trash can had already been emptied into the huge garbage bin outside. Crestfallen, I returned to class. Twenty minutes later, the loudspeaker blared, "Will the girl who discarded her retainer please report to the cafeteria?" Talk about feeling stupid! The custodian and I were soon sifting through four garbage bags. I found my retainer, but had lost my cool!

Yet I am happy now that my bite is right. If you have braces, remember you're not the only one, and your teeth will soon look fabulous. Meanwhile, consider investing in a water jet for brushing with braces. And keep going to your dentist for cleanings even if you're a regular at the orthodontist. Hold off on lipstick if you don't want to accent your mouth. But don't stop smiling.

You may want to ask your dentist or orthodontist about invisible or lingual braces. If your smile could be prettier, ask about bonding, bleaching, filing. (Something to "chew on" anyway!) And it's not too late to invest in dental sealants, which are plastic coatings applied to your molars to protect them from tooth decay. Go to a pro—put your money where your mouth is!

Your wisdom teeth probably won't appear for several years. If you're lucky, they won't appear at all or they'll grow in straight. If not, welcome to the club. You may have to get them removed—which means, instead of getting money from the tooth fairy, you give it to the oral surgeon.

After your teens, you'll be less cavity prone. But the teeth you have should last a lifetime (that's over seventy-eight years for most women), so take care of them—and drink that calcium-rich milk!

Hair Care

Back from brushing your teeth? Good! I hope you're happy with your hair. I'm pretty happy with mine. I wore it long in high school and I've had it short ever since. Mine is the wash-and-wear variety, but I understand the angst of those with less manageable hair. My college roommate got up hours before class to wash, dry, and straighten her hair. My mother stayed up late at night to wash, dry, and curl hers.

Shall I tell you three dumb things I did with my hair when it was long? First and worst, I hunted in it for split ends—a waste of time and a good way to go cross-eyed. (Getting my mop chop broke that habit in a hurry.) Second, I sprayed a bleach product in it when I was ten. Months later, when the brown roots grew in, my half-and-half hair looked really special, let me tell you. Third, I didn't know about brushing tangles out *before* shampooing or about conditioners, so I often emerged from a shower with a head full of sailor's knots. End of confessions.

How about you? Are you shampooing as frequently as you need to? Meryl Streep said that to be beautiful, "You hold in your stomach a lot, and you just wash your hair a lot." I wake up with "bed-head," so I wash mine every morning. If your hair is dry or in dreadlocks or tight braids, you'll obviously shampoo less often.

Choose shampoo for dry, oily, regular, or damaged hair or for a dandruff problem. Then switch brands occasionally because your hair may get used to a product and not come as clean the twentieth time as it did the first.

Why do the directions suggest you lather and rinse, then repeat the whole process? Because that way you'll use up the shampoo in a flash and quickly shell out another $4.99. Unless you let your hair get so greasy you could fry an egg in it (heaven forbid), one sudsing should suffice. Work up a lather in your hands; then massage your scalp with fingertips, not nails. And be sure to get out all—*all*—the shampoo. Until your hair squeaks, don't hop out of the shower. (And don't hop out until you've shaken off and done most of your dripping—or you'll flood the floor.)

If you have dry, brittle, or damaged hair, use a conditioner. Combing your hair with a wide-tooth comb or brushing it with a straight brush with soft bristles and rounded tips will help, too, because that activates oil glands. Let your hair air-dry when possible.

When your hair is wet, don't brush it. Comb it with a wide-tooth comb. Some hairs will fall out whenever you comb or brush. Don't worry unless you're losing hair in chunks. To wash combs or brushes, use shampoo.

The following are foolproof ways to destroy your lovely locks: Braid strands so tightly they snap off at the hairline. Tug off curlers, barrettes, or elastics violently so hairs break. Blow-dry hair with high heat and no attachments between curls and red-hot wires. Get your hair permed or chemically straightened too often. Eat too much junk food.

Q: Do women look best in long or short hair?

A: They look best in hair that is well styled and well kept up.

But whom can you trust with a pair of scissors?

Keep trying different places until you find a stylist you like. If you admire a friend's cut or braids, ask who did it and make an appointment. Once you're in the chair, trust the pro or speak your mind. Don't let anyone whack away a foot of hair or twist your hair for hours while you save your tears for Mom. If you are happy with the job, remember the stylist's name and become a regular.

Don't hide behind your hair. Long hair needs to be trimmed every few months. Short hair, every six to eight weeks. Hair grows fastest in summer. Sounds expensive? Sometimes you can save money by shampooing at home or skipping the blow-dry. Call and ask. Or have a competent friend do the job.

What about body hair?

About two years before your first period, your pubic hair probably started growing in, straight and fine at first, then coarser and darker. About six months before your first period, your underarm hair may have begun to appear. You may even have a few tiny hairs around your nipples.

Lots of young women (in France, for instance) don't get rid of the hair on their legs and underarms. If the hair doesn't bother you, don't bother it.

If you *do* want silky legs and smooth underarms in summer or all year long, you may want to start shaving. Don't rush it, though. Once you begin, your hair won't grow back quite as fine as it was, so you may have to continue shaving.

Shaving is easy. Use a cream or soap and try not to nick yourself. If you're shaving in the tub, be sure to clean it afterward so you won't leave a ring for the next person.

You could try an electric razor. (Not with wet legs or the experience would be shocking!)

Waxing is another alternative. You can buy a do-it-yourself product or go to a salon, where it hurts less and costs more. The effect of waxing is long-lasting, and the technique is popular in Europe.

Using a depilatory on your legs seems slow and messy to me, but that's another option.

Do you have a mustache? I do. Not a handlebar, but a noticeable nuisance nonetheless. Every so often, I have to tweeze or wax or cream the fine hairs off with a depilatory. It beats five o'clock shadow!

Some women prefer bleach—but some look like they have white mustaches. If the problem is serious, consider electrolysis. It's not cheap, but it is permanent because it destroys hair roots. Your physician can recommend an electrologist. Don't expect overnight wonders. I know someone who had periodic appointments with an electrologist for several years.

Ditto all the above for any other unwanted body hair: on your chin, belly button, thighs. If your eyebrows are very bushy, or if you have an almost-eyebrow between your eyes, you may want to tweeze or cream or wax away those hairs.

Then again, if you like how you look, and it's low-maintenance, more power to you. Mexican artist Frida Kahlo painted self-portraits in which she seems to have one eyebrow—and her work is wonderful and highly prized.

Nice Nails

Modesty is fine, but it's crazy not to recognize and enjoy your good qualities—particularly if you're going to feel awful about one puny pimple or one unwanted hair.

That said, I hope you won't slam your book shut if I tell you straight out that I have nice nails. I didn't always, but I do now.

The thing is, I bit my nails to the quick in high school. The class creep once walked past me in the hall, jammed his hand upside down in his mouth, and pretended to gnaw—a cruel imitation of yours truly.

He made his point. Not only were my nails ugly, but the nibbling habit itself was ugly.

I tried to quit. I tried bad-tasting polish. I tried wearing gloves during scary movies. I tried nail hardener. I taped my mouth shut while doing homework. I wore Band-Aids on my stubs at night. I got a professional manicure. But I didn't stop for good until my husband proposed.

Rob presented me with an antique diamond ring that had belonged to his grandmother. I couldn't wear such a beautiful ring on such an unsightly hand, so I dredged up all my willpower and kicked the habit.

If you're a biter, you don't have to get engaged to break the habit. When you're truly ready to quit, you'll quit. (I say that, but even now I sometimes slip.)

Check your nails. Maybe you've never bitten them, but are they looking their best? Are they ragged or uneven or dirty? Are they so long they look like curling claws? People *do* notice.

Use an emery board to file your nails. If you want to polish them, remove all old polish and start with a clear base coat. That strengthens them and keeps them from turning yellow if you use colored polish. Let each coat dry before applying the next. Polishes last longer if kept in the refrigerator. Polish can be pretty—or provocative. But it's better to have bare nails than to go out with messy or chipped polish.

Cosmetics and Clothes

A girl in my high school, Vivian, always stood tall; wore chic, pulled-together clothes; did her makeup just right; and carried herself confidently. She assumed she was beautiful, and no one questioned her.

Looking over my senior yearbook, I see that she was cute, but no cuter than Judy or Jen. Yet because Vivian made a point of looking her best, she glowed with self-assurance. She didn't come off as vain or affected. She came off as striking.

Attitude and self-esteem really are half the battle. Remember the song from *West Side Story*? "I feel pretty, oh so pretty . . . " Maria had the right idea. If you think pretty instead of mousy, others start thinking of you as pretty instead of mousy.

Positive thinking alone can't turn an ordinary girl into a Perfect Ten. But if you like yourself and play up your best features with makeup and clothes, you can suddenly look better than ever. As Helena Rubenstein said, "There are no ugly women, only lazy ones." And as Cindy Crawford said, "Even I don't wake up looking like Cindy Crawford."

Makeup is a remarkable option. Just consider the before/after faces in magazines. Or rent *Tootsie, Victor/Victoria,* or *Mrs. Doubtfire.* I didn't wear any makeup in my early teens and I rarely do now when I'm home writing. But I love putting it on when I go out. A little brown eyeshadow, dark mascara, eyeliner, blush, lipstick—and abracadabra, I look and feel more glamorous! Face-painting is fast, creative, and one of the pleasures of being female.

Inexpensive makeup often works as well as the expensive stuff. (You're paying mostly for the packaging and advertising.) Experiment, but don't borrow a friend's eye makeup. If your eyes or skin get irritated, try hypoallergenic varieties. Also beware of free makeovers—the beautician will encourage you to spend $39.50 on supplies afterward.

With makeup, less is more, and soft and subtle look prettiest, especially on girls and especially during the day. Study magazines and friends. And don't wear so much that you feel homely without it. If you wear none at all, that's A-OK, too.

What about clothes? Do you have a passion for fashion? I can't afford to overhaul my wardrobe every season, but I like to keep an eye on mannequins, models, and peers. And I try to play up accessories—hats, belts, necklaces, earrings.

Keep your clothes clean and in good repair. Give things to charities (bonus: it may be tax deductible). Put out-of-season clothes away. Check out sales.

Figure out what colors and styles are in vogue and look best on you, then try new combinations. Some clothes make me look dumpy, while others make me look slender. Dark colors flatter me, but pastels wash me out. Accent your best figure feature with bright colors and downplay your worst with dull ones. Trade clothes with friends; give and accept hand-me-downs. Create your own style.

You project your personality, interests, and mood through clothes. Are you feeling artsy, sporty, sophisticated? Show it! If you're romantic, you may favor velvet and lace. If you're athletic, you may prefer sweats and workout clothes. You don't always have to dress one way, and even if you wear a uniform to school, you can probably find a way to add a little flair.

Looking like everybody else is fine, and safe, but why not express yourself?

Even Beautiful Girls Get the Blues

Yes, there have been times when I'd have swapped my mug for the face of a cover girl and my body for an actress's show-stopping curves. But those of us who haven't won any beauty pageants should remember that those who have don't necessarily lead happier lives.

One of my high school pals is a model, yet although black-haired, green-eyed Danielle always looks terrific, she doesn't always feel terrific. She's not deluged by dates. (Are guys scared of her? Are her expectations impossible? Do guys assume she's taken?) When they do call, Danielle wonders if they care about her or if they're after sex or just want to show her off like a trophy.

Meanwhile she's already worrying about what she'll do in five years when her face-based career could come to a thudding halt.

Danielle has few girlfriends with whom to discuss her insecurities.

"When I meet a girl, I feel I have to bend over backward being nice or she'll think I'm conceited," she said.

Her confession shamed me into realizing that when I meet a knock-out, I'm not always my most amiable. Part of me feels threatened and almost wants to believe that although she's stunning, she's also shallow, boring, or quick-tempered.

You may be more magnanimous. You may have no trouble immediately liking a girl who is gorgeous, brilliant, talented, rich, happy, and seemingly picture-perfect. If so, you deserve a *Saint* before your name. Most of us want to glimpse a filling in that dazzling smile. We want our goddesses to be human.

Another pitfall of being beautiful is that beauties are often judged by ridiculously high standards. Have you ever seen a model in a magazine and instead of thinking, "She looks exquisite," thought, "She's looked better" or "She's not *that* amazing"? It must be tough knowing the pressure is on to look breathtaking day in and day out.

I'm not saying we should feel sorry for gorgeous women or assume that *lovely* means *lonely*. But it's good to look at the flip side of beauty. Plus, like Avis, we fair-to-cuties try harder, and that can mean developing personality and intelligence—traits that never fade.

Sleep Tight (Waking Up is Hard to Do)

Too many teens are sleep deprived. Unlike most adults, teens generally need a full eight to nine hours of sleep—though they rarely get them. And unlike most adults, teens' body clocks are set so that they would naturally sleep late and stay up late—though they rarely get to.

After your parents conk out, are you still going strong? Chatting on the phone or on-line, watching TV, doing homework, or reading? (Uh-oh. Is it past midnight right now? Put me down. I'll be here when you get back, pinky promise.)

Ready or not, rested or not, school starts mercilessly early. So try to get enough sleep. One study found a correlation between lack of sleep and lower grades. Another confirmed the obvious link between sleep and mood. Sleep is restorative and keeps your resistance up. Shakespeare called sleep the "chief nourisher in life's feast." If you've been dragging around, sleep more. Or go to bed early at least one night a week.

If you're sleeping away half the day or napping constantly, however, you may be using sleep to escape. Insomnia may be a sign that something is troubling you and needs to be talked about. (Weird fact: sleep researchers report that many people who complain of sleeping poorly actually sleep perfectly well.)

For most people, nodding off is not a problem. When it is, skip the coffee, cola, tea, or chocolate at night because they contain caffeine, a stimulant. A cup of milk or chamomile tea, accompanied by a warm bath or not-for-school book, is a more soothing choice for the wide awake. Don't take sleeping pills; they're addictive. And try to think of occasional insomnia as an opportunity: to do schoolwork, write in a diary, read a short story, or surf the Net.

When you're ready for bed, take off socks and underwear and put on a comfortable gown or pajamas. Lie on your back on a firm mattress, ideally without a pillow or with a fairly flat pillow. In that position, your spine is aligned, none of your organs or limbs is squashed, and you won't wake up with a crick in your neck or your cheek all puckered with wrinkles from the sheets. Now breathe rhythmically from the bottom of your lungs through your nose. Imagine yourself floating. Tell your muscles to relax, one by one. Drift. Zzzzz . . .

Mono and Your Health

In my freshman year at college, my motto was: Work hard, play hard. For two months, I got up at 7:30, went full steam until dinner, studied until 9:30, partied until 1:30. Late to bed and early to rise proved unhealthy and unwise and was the start of my demise!

To put it more succinctly: I got mono.

It was a cold November, I was run-down, I hadn't been wearing my hat or gloves, and I'd been ignoring a sore throat. The lymph glands in my neck began to swell, and I remember watching somebody jog (my sport!) and thinking, "How can he have so much energy?" I went for a finger-puncture blood test, and my fear was confirmed.

My case of infectious mononucleosis was diagnosed early, but there are no magic-cure pills. "Get plenty of rest and sleep and eat a balanced diet," was all the doctors could recommend. "Avoid contact sports because if you rupture your spleen, you're in big trouble."

I took it very easy for a week and felt better fast. But some cases of mono knock people out for months. If you've had it once, however, you're unlikely to get it again.

Anybody can contract mono, but teenagers are the most susceptible. Although it's been called the kissing disease, you can get it without kissing, and it's not as contagious as you might suspect. It's more contagious in the incubation stage (before it's diagnosed) than afterward.

The Epstein-Barr virus causes mono, but don't confuse mono with chronic fatigue syndrome. The symptoms of mono go away in a matter of weeks, whereas chronic fatigue hangs around, and sufferers feel tired, tired, tired, on and on and on. If you feel like you have a flu that won't go away, talk to your doctor. He or she can test for and treat diseases.

If you went on vacation or to a camp in a place where deer ticks were a problem, mention this to your doctor. You may have Lyme disease. If your best friend or sister or boyfriend has a particular virus, say so. You may have the same virus. Or perhaps you are depressed (more on this later), and you need, not rest, but exercise, therapy, and possibly a low dose of antidepressants. Be honest with your doctor. The more clues you provide, the better detective he or she can be, and the faster you'll get back on your feet.

I hope you are generally healthy. I hope you eat well, sleep well, exercise enough, drink water, and wash your hands often. I hope you stay healthy even when others sneeze and sniffle. If you take vitamins or medication, always down them with plenty of water. If you're on antibiotics, follow the directions and, if indicated, finish the bottle even if you're feeling better. Consult a doctor before mixing medicines.

Do you know anyone who obsesses or complains about every itch, cough, or bruise? Hypochondriacs can be tiresome. Yet when you have bizarre pains or symptoms, do take them seriously. A school nurse or doctor may say, "It's nothing, false alarm," but then your mind will be at ease. Or maybe you have a common cold and need to be reminded to rest, drink fluids, and gargle with salt water. Or maybe your stomach or head hurts from stress, not physical factors. Fine. Psychosomatic bellyaches still ache, so it's important to know you may need not an antacid, but to start untying the knots.

In the *Sex* chapter, I'll tell you all about sexually transmitted diseases. Illnesses not commonly associated with sex or teens aren't covered in this book. If you don't have diabetes, epilepsy, anemia, asthma, or scoliosis, count your blessings. If you do, you're not alone. Call the Epilepsy Foundation, for instance, at (800) 332-1000 or Asthma Foundation (800) 822-2762 or Diabetes Foundation at (800) DIABETES to learn more. Follow your doctor's advice, take extra good care of yourself, and try not to let the condition get in the way of things too much.

Physical Disabilities

Many people take their youth and health and "normal" bodies for granted. Others have treatable learning disorders or disabilities, which I'll talk about in the Education chapter. Others have physical birth defects, cystic fibrosis, muscular dystrophy, cerebral palsy, or other diseases; are deaf or blind; or become paralyzed from accidents.

I'm not suggesting we thank our stars each day for our twenty fingers and toes and our ability to wiggle them—although that's not a bad idea. I am saying we should treat all people, disabled or otherwise, with respect, not with condescending courtesy, unwelcome pity, cruel teasing, or awkward avoidance. Too many people act as though disabilities were contagious and disabled persons were also retarded or unfeeling.

As Ted Kennedy, Jr., whose right leg was amputated, eloquently put it, "Disabled people are not unable people. . . . we are people first and disabled second." And look at Franklin D. Roosevelt, a much-beloved president who was confined to a wheelchair. Elected four times in a row, he got the country moving again even though he himself could barely walk.

Helen Keller was deaf and blind, and she wrote, "I thank God for my handicaps, for, through them, I have found myself, my work, and my God." She also wrote, "The most beautiful things in the world cannot be seen or even touched. They must be felt with the heart."

If someone is deaf and can lip-read, don't shout. Face the person, speak slowly, and enunciate well. If someone is blind and hesitating at an intersection, offer help without insisting. If you're baby-sitting for a young girl and she points and says, "Why is that boy in a wheelchair?" don't scold. It's natural for her to be curious. Tell her it's impolite to point, but give her an answer. "Maybe because of an accident or an illness or because he was born with weak legs. He uses the wheelchair to get around." If you yank the child away, you're reinforcing the mistaken notion that it's uncomfortable to be around disabled people.

Have you ever been with a friend who has parked in a space reserved for the handicapped, then gotten out limping and giggling? To someone else, the convenience of the space is not a laughing matter. I'm for finding another parking place and being glad you're able to walk the extra yards.

If you are or have recently become disabled, it may be hard at times to accept your limitations and society's prejudices. I hope you'll ultimately concentrate on what you *can* do and not get bogged down in what you can't. Counselors and rehabilitation centers can help, and you can tap into this family web site: http://www.familyvillage.wisc.edu.

Speaking of Body Language

Ever notice the ads that show before/after shots of women who have supposedly lost weight, increased bust size, or gotten rid of pimples and varicose veins? In the before pose, they're slouching and frowning. In the after photo, they're standing tall and smiling. No wonder they look better! That's body language.

Body language can speak louder than words. A wink can start a romance, and a hug can stop a quarrel.

My mother always got after me to—ready?—stand up straight, pull back my shoulders, tuck my fanny in, not wrinkle my forehead, look people squarely in the eye, and shake hands firmly without fracturing fingers. My response was usually an exasperated polysyllabic "Mah-ah-ahmmm!" but now I'm grateful. Because I learned to look confident, people started treating me as though I was confident, and I began to feel confident.

Do you have teachers who move and gesture while they lecture? You probably pay more attention to them than to the ones who sit behind the desk, arms folded, shoulders drooping. Teachers can tell if you're fascinated or bored by whether you're leaning forward attentively or slumping and drawing on your shoe. So sit up—your grades may go up, too.

Caution: You can't always read strangers correctly because body language varies from person to person and culture to culture. For example, some people look down to show respect, rather than maintain eye contact. European teens do more cheek-kissing than we do. And the Japanese prefer bowing to handshaking.

No matter where you are, you probably want your body to show that you are warm, open, and friendly. But before we go on to the *Friendship* chapter, here are some letters I've received about topics in the *Body* chapter.

Dear Carol ...

Dear Carol,
   I am 13 and I wear a 34C bra. I have been wearing a bra since second grade. Boys try things they shouldn't—I decked one kid—and I'm sick of it. All the girls at school envy me, but I envy them.

Dear Carol,

I'm sort of big and boys whistle at me. What am I supposed to do? Stare at their crotches and say, "Hey, that's a big wiener you got there!" Boys do that. They're always saying, "Hey, those are some great tits." I hate that!

Dear Carol,

I'm 17 and still wear a 34A bra. I feel very self-conscious about my flat chest. Every female on my mother's and father's side is well-endowed. They say I'm a late bloomer, but I'm afraid I'm going to stay this way forever. Help!

Dear Carol,

All of the popular girls have big breasts. They probably have their periods too. I am 12 and I'm embarrassed to death to change in front of them in gym because I am so flat-chested. I'm as flat as a first grader. Is there anything wrong?

Dear Carol,

I'm not fully developed. But when I get cold or when I'm changing, my breasts start to shrink. Is this normal?

Dear Carol,

My left breast is a tad smaller than my right, though you can't tell with a bra on. Should I worry?

No, you shouldn't, and neither should the girls whose breasts are bigger or smaller than the class average. As for breasts (especially nipples) that respond to cold . . . don't everyone's?

No one is as aware of your body as you are, and unless there's a true problem, a teen can't do much about her development. No wonder puberty is awkward! Some girls mature way before other girls, and most girls mature way before boys. Attractive women come in all sizes, of course, and the real goal is not to change cup size but to accept yourself. This takes time! Before I became comfortable with myself, some friends and I used to exercise to the horrendously sexist chant, "We must, we must, we must build up the bust, the bigger, the better, the tighter the sweater, the boys will look at us!" I shudder to remember!

And what happens when boys do look? Many of them are goons about it. And what can you do? Not much. It's hard to ignore them, but it rarely helps to say, "Grow up!" or "Yeah, and where are *your* pecs?" There is hope though: the worthwhile guys will get their acts together eventually.

Dear Carol,

I want to talk to my mom about girl things, but I'm embarrassed to. I want to shave my legs, but she says wait. I also want to wear a sports bra, but how can I ask her?

Some moms have trouble recognizing that their kids are growing up. Others just need a nudge. Tell your mom, "I feel embarrassed about this, but I want to talk to you about girl things." Or try, "When can we go shopping for a bra—tomorrow or Saturday?" Or ask politely which kind of razor she thinks works best. Sometimes the way you phrase a question makes a difference in the answer you get.

Dear Carol,

When you are wearing a tampon, can you take a shower with it in? Can you go to the bathroom with it in?

Yes. Or you can take the opportunity to remove it beforehand and insert a new one afterward. If you're not going to change tampons while on the toilet, just push the string out of the way.

Dear Carol,

I haven't started menstruating yet, but it scares me to lose that much blood. Does my body make more blood to replace the blood that is lost? Help! I'm bloody scared!

Your body makes, then sheds, that blood and tissue every month. So there's no real loss. But remember to take your vitamins and eat spinach, raisins, red meat, or other sources of iron.

Dear Carol,

I'm 14. My periods aren't always regular and I know that's normal. But it worries me that the symptoms of pregnancy and periods are similar (mood swings, backaches, tender breasts, being tired) because even though I'm a virgin, I keep thinking that maybe somehow I could have gotten pregnant. The only way I could have is this: The day before I went to tennis camp for a month, my boyfriend and I took a shower together. The only thing we did was kiss. Nothing else. Is there any way I could have gotten pregnant?

No. Sperm don't swim that well! (See the *Sex* chapter.) The new environment and active schedule at camp, however, could throw off anyone's cycle. (P.S. Don't get carried away during future showers!)

Dear Carol,

My period is off and on. My whole junior high is going on a trip, but I don't know if I want to go because I am scared I am going to get my period and I'm scared to take pads with me.

Don't miss out! Take the trip! Pack pads, just in case, and wear pantiliners if you're anxious. If all the junior high girls who sometimes get nervous about menstruation stayed home . . . every school day might look like Take Our Daughters to Work Day!

Dear Carol,

Can masturbation prevent me from getting my period?

Nope.

Dear Carol,

Do you think I've gotten my period yet? I'm 13, and two months ago, I started getting spots. Last week it did that for just one day.

Sounds like a start to me. You'll probably be getting more regular periods soon.

Dear Carol,

I wrote to you a while ago. I asked if I should tell my friends I started my period even though I hadn't. You told me not to lie so I didn't. I'm glad you told me not to lie, because guess what—I got it! And then I was able to tell my friends for real. So I wanted to write and thank you.

Thank you.

Dear Carol,

I just started getting acne on my back. It's so bad that if acne was a cash crop, I'd be a millionaire. I wash my back and have tried lots of soaps, but it won't go away. My mom wants to take me to a dermatologist, but I don't want to go.

Why not? Doctors are on your side. And you're lucky to have a smart mom. Many girls tell me they want to see therapists, gynecologists, dermatologists—even hair stylists—but their mothers object. If your parents want to consult a specialist, go for it.

Dear Carol,

I've read your book three times, but there's one part I can't get out of my system. I am 17 and I developed epilepsy a few years ago. In the Disabilities section, you say to "count your blessings" if you don't have any diseases. I have a disease and I still count my blessings. A lot of the diseases you mention are controlled by medication. I have been seizure-free for nine months now. Kids used to make fun of me when I was having seizures, and the memories are painful. I'm not mad at you, but people should be more sensitive.

You're absolutely, positively right. Thank you for writing.

Dear Carol,

I have diabetes and am scared to tell my friends. Once, I fainted in school and didn't know what to say to them. When they ask if I want candy, and I say no, they think I'm weird. Should I tell them my secret?

Here's what I look for in a friend: warmth, intelligence, sense of humor, and a good attitude. It doesn't matter if the person has diabetes or freckles. How about you? If you found out your best friend had asthma, would you drop her? No. But you'd probably be curious and ask a million questions. Before you go public, talk to your doctors and parents and become as knowledgeable as you can. If you think diabetes is weird, scary, or embarrassing, your friends may, too. But if you accept yourself, others will accept you. When you're ready, and friends ask why you're saying no to candy, tell them how you take care of yourself. Call your local hospital for information or the American Diabetes Association at (800) DIABETES to find out about support groups and same-age pen pals.

Dear Carol,

I'm 11 and I have a little sister who just turned 2. My mom started toilet training her and wants me and my other sister to let her watch us go to the bathroom. Mom thinks it will help her learn to use the toilet. My other sister doesn't mind, but I hate it. There are certain things I can't even do when someone's in the bathroom with me. My mom thinks I'm being silly and yells at me when I go in without my little sister. Is it so wrong to want privacy when I'm using the toilet?

No. Going to the bathroom is not a spectator sport. Some people aren't modest, but many are—especially girls whose bodies are changing. Tell your mom that you'd be happy to play with or read to your little sister but that, sorry, you don't want company in the bathroom and you think that is reasonable. You're entitled to pee in peace.

Dear Carol,

I'm ashamed even to write this, but I sometimes wet my bed. When I get invited to a sleepover or a slumber party or something, I always make an excuse. I can't believe I still have accidents.

Your problem is far from rare. It has a name—enuresis—and it's genetic, which means that a parent of a bedwetter may have had the same difficulty. Talk to a doctor. Treatments include an alarm device or even a prescription nasal spray, Desmopressin, that can help you get through a sleepover, slumber party, or sleep-away camp. You'll probably grow out of this, but meantime, I hope you can get over the shame because the condition is not your fault.

Dear Carol,

One of the inner folds of skin outside my vagina is slightly larger than the other. Is that a problem or is that normal?

It's normal.

Dear Carol,

I'm 14. I used to be sort of fat, but I lost 20 pounds over the summer. Some people in my school remember me as a fat sixth grader and tell stories about me. How can I get them to forget the old me and see the new, thinner me?

If you forget the chunky girl you left behind, they will, too. All teens are self-conscious, and it can take a while for your self-image (and confidence) to catch up to your new body, whether you've lost weight, gained weight, grown four inches, or had a nose job. Remember Hans Christian Andersen's ugly duckling? He has no idea he has become a beautiful swan until he is surprised by his own reflection.

Dear Carol,

I eat and eat and don't gain a pound. I'm glad I'm not fat, but I'm not thin either—I'm skinny. In a bathing suit, my bones stick out. I'm 5'7" and weigh only 100 pounds. How can I gain weight?

Make milkshakes by tossing ice cream, banana, peanut butter, milk, and ice into a blender or food processor. Snack on nuts, raisins, cheeses. Eat between-meal yogurt. Avoid junk food but enjoy seconds. Go on the seafood diet: You see food, you eat it! I was a bean pole, too, but I grew out of it, as will you. For better and worse, metabolisms can change in a hurry.

Dear Carol,

I have a BIG problem. I am 13 years old and weigh 210 pounds. You're probably thinking, "Gosh, she's a blimp. Why doesn't she go on a diet?" Well, I have tried over and over, but I live with my four-year-old brother who has a really big sweet tooth and I just lose control.

Dear Carol,

I'm short, but I weigh 130 pounds. My mother says it's baby fat, and my doctor makes jokes. I can't swim because there's no pool. I can't jog because my mother doesn't like me to go out alone. I can't bike ride because I don't have a bike. How can I shed pounds fast?

Dear Carol,

My parents aren't very happy with me, and neither am I. I feel like the fat lady in the circus. I'm ugly, I have no friends or personality or excitement. I know I need to lose weight but I don't have enough self-confidence to do it. Someday, though, I want to go to the pool without a T-shirt over my bathing suit and to the store to try on a size 7 or 9. I would sell my soul to the devil to be thin. Thanks for taking time out of your busy schedule to read my insignificant letter.

No letter is insignificant, and no one should sell her soul to the devil. If you're not feeling strong enough to go on a diet, try to picture how strong you'll feel once the diet starts paying off. Don't wait until your brother grows up or the town builds a pool. Swear off ice cream now and exercise with a partner or in front of a workout video. Try to feel smug and virtuous (not deprived) when others eat brownies. Where there's a will, there's a way, so summon your willpower and take some weight off—then take your mind off dieting, so you can better enjoy these years. It's not easy, but you can lose a pound *this week* if you want to. And then you can start giving yourself credit for trying to lose weight instead of beating yourself up for having weight to lose.

The following are excerpts from letters I've gotten over a five-year period from a girl who is now in college.

Dear Carol,

Guess what??? I've lost 5 pounds!!! Can you believe it? I'm so happy! I practically starved myself, but it was worth it! I went about two weeks on water and sugarless gum. I'm really hungry, but I'm scared that if I eat anything, I'll eat compulsively. On Friday I started feeling dizzy and I fainted in the hall at school. Somebody took me to the clinic, and the school nurse gave me some Tylenol and made me eat an apple. I told her I'd eaten a huge lunch because I didn't want her to ruin my diet, but she made me eat the dumb apple anyway . . .

You said I may be developing an eating disorder. I eat! I ate a few bites of salad a few days ago! I eat around my mom, too, but I take a laxative afterward. For once, I'm actually losing weight. That's what's important! I've been taking vitamins daily, but I'm having a hard time sleeping, so now I'm taking Valium at night . . .

When I read your letter, I ate a salad and I didn't take a laxative. I did it for you. You said to stop taking Valium and I have. Today I had two cherry tomatoes, two radishes, eight green grapes, one quarter of a peach, and a celery stick. I hope that doesn't make me gain weight. I got a little carried away. I still feel tired and weak, and I fainted again. I will ask about getting a counselor . . .

Carol, I think I'm becoming bulimic. I reread that section in your book, and I've been eating, then vomiting. First I thought I would do it for a while, then stop. But it hasn't helped me lose weight, and I can't stop! I hate to tell my new counselor because she'll be so disappointed in me. My mouth has gotten real sore and I have no energy . . .

I tried to commit suicide. I took some sleeping pills and cut my wrists. My mother took me to the hospital and my counselor went, too. She stayed with me. I ate some of my dinner and then went to the bathroom and threw up. My counselor figured it out, and the next day she took me to an eating disorder clinic. I've got to go twice a week until I'm better . . .

I got in trouble with bulimia again. I've been in the hospital for a week and have had an IV in my arm continuously. It's really sore. It seems I have a severe "electrolyte imbalance." I was dehydrated, too, and I have a swollen esophagus. I can't believe how stupid I was to let this happen all over again. But no one understands how alone and empty you feel when you're totally obsessed with losing weight. I wish I could find someone who has gotten through this . . .

Eventually, she did find some counselors who were recovered anorexics and bulimics themselves. And she did get through it.

If *you* are becoming obsessed with losing weight, or if you have other body or health concerns, get help today.

Your body needs to last a lifetime.

And now let's talk about friendship, OK?

2 FRIENDSHIP

You Don't Like Everybody;
Why Should Everybody Like You?

❀

The phrase "just friends" makes little sense to me: Friendship should never be trivialized.

It takes time and effort to make new friends and keep old ones. It's not easy to overcome shyness, listen to someone else's troubles, phone or write when you're busy, and get together with the girls when you'd rather spend time with a guy. But it's worth it. I don't collect coins, stamps, or cat figurines, but I guess I collect people. Friends are one of the staples of my life.

Friends congratulate and console, heighten pleasure and ease pain. Judy sent a bouquet of flowers when an editor offered me the chance to write this book. And I was matron of honor at her joyful wedding. Jen drove for miles to be with me after my father died. And we talked for days after she broke up with a man she loved.

You can get by without being popular; you can live without a boyfriend; you can survive without one particular best friend. But if you have no friends, you're missing out. After all, a friend who likes you teaches you to like yourself. Friends exchange the gift of self-confidence. This chapter is about making lasting friendships with girls and guys and, most vital, making friends with yourself.

Girlfriends Last Longer Than Boyfriends

I'm not knocking romance or saying that sweethearts never go platonic or high school honeys never marry. But chances are, in ten years, you'll still be in touch with some of the girls who are close to you now, whereas the guys in your life now will be in someone else's life.

In high school, I spent thousands of hours with a terrific green-eyed curly-haired boyfriend. Today we exchange Christmas cards. I also spent endless afternoons with Judy and Jen. Today, though we live in different cities, we keep in touch by phone and by letter and visit each other when we can.

Same thing happened in college. I dated Chris, Walter, Steve, Alger— lots of guys, lots of fun. But most of the Yale males I keep up with are the ones I never kissed. Meanwhile, the girls I knew in classes, dormitories, and dining rooms are still my buddies. When Helen, Ellen, Sally, Amy, Sonia, and I got together at a class reunion recently, we had a blast.

Among my mother's closest friends are her grade school chums. They called themselves the CHAMP club, named for Carolyn, Helen, Anne, Marybeth, and Polly. They've been friends for decades!

Don't turn down dates. But do be aware that your summer loves may not last until fall, whereas the friendships you make with girls now may last a lifetime.

Ten Ways to Make Friends

You'd like to make friends and widen your social circle? Don't just stand there—smile, laugh, talk, listen, ask, whisper, admire! As Ralph Waldo Emerson said, "The only way to have a friend is to be one."

1. Figure out whom you want to be friends with and why. If you want to be friends with Jenna because she's popular or Tanya because she's pretty, it will probably be more difficult and less rewarding than if you want to be friends with Sue because you both love to write or Katherine because you're both into hiking. Your future friends are the people with whom you share interests. Choose them because of their qualities, not their status.

You can also learn by observing the people you want to know better. Why do you wish Lexi was your friend? If it's because she is always "up" or funny or considerate, then cultivate those traits in yourself.

2. Get involved with after-school activities. Don't just hang out at home or at the food court at the mall. Sign up for extracurrics. Join soccer or field hockey or track or gymnastics. Be good at sports and be a good sport, too. Or join chorus or band or computer club or the student council. Stars in your eyes? Try out for the school play. If you don't make it, don't stay home. Help with sets or lights or props or programs.

When I joined the Byram Hills French Club, I met fellow francophiles. When I volunteered to work with handicapped kids in nearby Mount Kisco, I made friends with some popular older students who had never before lowered themselves to say hi to me in the halls. When I became manager of the Boys' Lacrosse Team, I got to know some great guys.

By being active and on the go, you keep meeting people, and you stay busy and interesting. Besides, someone who is enthusiastic about lots of projects usually makes better company than someone whose main extracurric is sitting around. So don't spread yourself too thin, but don't sit there like a blob of mayo.

3. Introduce yourself and remember names. Don't wait for someone to make formal introductions or for a person to decide he or she would like to meet you. March right up and say hello. When I say, "Hi, I'm Carol," to someone I've never met, she doesn't look at me funny. She says hi back.

I wasn't born with a skill for remembering names. But I've learned to be good at it. It's easy. When someone introduces herself, listen to her name and repeat it: "Glad to meet you, Margo." A few sentences later, use her name again: "Margo, where are you from?" Make a point of catching the name the first time, and you won't forget it so quickly.

Some people try to remember names by associating them with the person. Blair is blond; Paul is tall. Whether you remember names by paying attention to the first go-around or by using an elaborate mnemonic device, it's a knack you should acquire a.s.a.p.

What if you say "Hi, Tim" in the lunchroom, and Tim doesn't remember your name? He may feel embarrassed as he mumbles an unadorned hi. But he may also ask his friends who that friendly girl is. Be extra nice to the new kids at school and to those who seem to be trying to expand their social circle. They will be grateful, and you may discover some terrific new people.

4. Master the art of conversation. Don't you hate when you're in the middle of telling a story and someone interrupts? You're describing your movie date with Raleigh. "No sooner did the lady behind the counter hand me my popcorn," you say, "than I slipped and spilled it! Raleigh turned around and—" Then some loudmouth butts in, "You know, my dad said they don't use real butter on popcorn at the movies. They use this oily yellow stuff that . . . "

You'll make friends faster if you let people finish their sentences and thoughts. Let them talk, and listen to what they're saying. If someone says she just got back from vacation, don't immediately chime in, "So did I." Ask, "How was it? Where'd you go?" If she says she went white-water canoeing down the Colorado River, don't say "Huh." Encourage her to tell you more by nodding, looking her in the eye, asking questions requiring more than a yes/no answer, saying "Really?" and peppering her paragraph with "That's amazing" and "How incredible." What if that same popcorn fan interrupts her story? Wait it out, then invite her to pick up where she left off by saying, "So what *did* you do when the boat toppled?"

People like to talk about themselves, and a good listener is rare and always appreciated. (As humorist Fran Lebowitz quipped, "The opposite of talking isn't listening. The opposite of talking is waiting.") Besides, you can learn more by listening than by talking.

That doesn't mean you should give your tongue to the cat. But just as run-on sentences don't thrill your English teacher, nonstop chitchat won't win you instant pals. If you're sparing no details ("Last Friday, or maybe it was Thursday, I'm not sure, anyway, Robin and I went to that lake, you know, the one with the pier that's really long, anyway, so he goes, 'I like this place,' so I go, 'It is pretty,' and he goes, 'Yeah,' and we looked at the clouds—there was this one that looked exactly like a scoop of vanilla ice cream . . . "), you're boring somebody. Beware, too, of talking too much about yourself. Don't become an egotist who is me-deep in conversation.

Ideally, conversation should run about half listening, half talking. If you tend to be too quiet, force yourself to speak up more in class and at meals. You don't have to expound on Central American politics, but say something. Make a deal with yourself that every day you will hold a brief conversation with at least one girl, guy, teacher, librarian, or someone you hardly know. A little shyness can be endearing, but if you're *too* timid, some will misinterpret your shyness as snobbery. Worse, you aren't meeting people. Yet you have nothing to hide. You have as much to offer as the brazen kids—who sometimes feel anxious, too.

Tip: If you're at a loss about what to say, get in the habit of skimming newspapers or magazines, the teen variety or ones like *Newsweek, Time,* or *People.* The more informed you are—about the latest movies or scientific discovery—the more comfortable you'll feel in different conversations.

5. Develop charm. Is charm something you're born with? Not necessarily. If your father is a Boston-bred ambassador and your mother is a Southern belle actress, and they've spent years readying you for your debutante ball, the odds *are* in your favor. But anyone can learn to be irresistibly charming, to guys and girls.

Charm is empathy with style. It's making sure no one feels left out. It's telling your friend's parents that you've never tasted such fabulous zucchini bread (if it is truly delicious). It's offering a hand when needed. It's being supportive instead of sarcastic. It's answering the question "Are these pants too tight?" with "I think your other pair is more flattering" (rather than "God, you've gained weight!"). It's helping someone get his foot out of his mouth instead of laughing at his faux pas. It's apologizing when it was your fault. And when it wasn't, it's saying, "I must not have explained this very well," instead of, "I can't believe you screwed up!" It's giving a guy the benefit of the doubt. It's making a girl feel good by tuning in, drawing her out, and showing with and without words that you are enjoying her company. It's listening to the end of a story when you realize no one else is. It's appreciating the best in people and things and not being too self-centered. (How many snobs does it take to screw in a lightbulb? One. She holds it to the socket and waits for the world to revolve around her.)

As you first practice charm, you may feel phony or manipulative or as though you're trying too hard. But soon it should feel more natural and become more genuine.

People like people who like them. So if you find someone you like, and project that fondness or respect, you have a head start on turning a stranger into a friend.

6. Give and get compliments graciously. Flattery may not get you everywhere, but it won't hurt in your quest for friends. When you admire something, say so. As Catherine the Great said, "I praise loudly;

I blame softly." Everybody loves a sincere compliment, so praise gener-
ously. "What a great necklace!" "Your handwriting is so pretty." "Our
basketball team would be nothing without you." "You drive really well."
"You have the sunniest smile." Hardly anyone would greet a warm compliment with a cold shoulder.

If you want yours to have extra impact, pay tribute to something that
usually goes unnoticed. If you ran into Tiger Woods buying a ham on
rye at a deli, you wouldn't make an impression with "You play golf
really well." Same principle with classmates. Yet you'd be surprised at
how delighted the school quarterback would be if you told him he has a
beautiful voice or an amazing smile. (Don't be insincere. False flattery
will endear you to nobody.)

You're not a compliment butcher, are you? Some people mean well,
but their compliments come out backhanded, so instead of sowing the
seeds of friendship, they're paving the path of animosity. I once made
the mistake of telling a girl, "You've lost a ton of weight!" instead of
simply, "You look wonderful." My slim acquaintance looked more grim
than grateful.

Other gems to avoid: "Your complexion looks clear today." "Your hair
looks so shiny—you must have washed it." "This is really tasty; you
didn't cook it yourself, did you?"

And when the tables turn? Do you accept compliments gracefully? If
a guy says, "I like your shirt," do you immediately say, "I like yours,
too"? Do you gasp, "You're kidding, I've had it for *eons*"? Do you
explain, "I picked it up for $3.99 at a garage sale in Kansas City"? The
best way to accept a compliment is to smile and say, "Thank you." If
you like, you can add, "That's nice of you to say."

Beware of fishing for compliments—you might come up with a boot!

7. *Don't rush it.* Friendship at first sight? Could be shaky. You'll hit
it off with some people instantly, and you'll click with others fairly fast,
but friendships, like plants, take time to grow. Some friendships that are
quickly made quickly fade.

If you try to hurry a friendship, you may come off as pushy or too
intense. If you ask dozens of questions, you may seem nosy instead of
amiable. Don't be too modest, but if you toot your horn loudly or launch
into your life story, you'll sound like you're in a job interview instead of
a social situation.

In college, I was having lunch with a friend named John. The subject was mountains, and he was telling our table about how he'd climbed Mount Kilimanjaro. I was so impressed I nearly fell off my chair. Not only had John scaled such heights, but he had never mentioned it before. If John had described the same feat when we'd first met, I would have been impressed, yes, but I might also have thought, "What a showoff" or "I bet he couldn't wait to get that in."

So take your time making friends.

8. Be willing to risk rejection. Just as you don't like everybody, everybody won't like you. Some people just aren't going to be as amicable as others. Their loss.

In the meantime, be known for your niceness. If you hide in a shell, you won't meet anybody, let alone cultivate friendships. Open up, be visible, take a chance. State your views, not what you think will make you accepted. Then if Gillian acts snooty, you wouldn't want to be her buddy anyway. (Who wants snooty buddies?) If she's kind, it was worth the risk.

Is everybody gossiping about you behind your back? Probably not. When you get right down to it, it's egotistical to think your personality is such a hot topic of debate. And what if the lunch table *does* discuss you the second you get up to bus your tray? Relax. If you're a warm, caring person, you have no reason to worry. What they're saying might be all good. As Oscar Wilde put it, "There is only one thing worse in the world than being talked about and that is not being talked about."

9. Arm yourself with zest and zeal. When I ask an acquaintance, "How are you?" and she grunts about backaches, allergies, and fights with her sister, it doesn't make me want to join her for a bike ride. Snarls and complaints won't help you make friends.

If you are sad, share it with those who are already near and dear, but don't dump on people you scarcely know. "Sorrow is like a precious treasure shown only to friends," says an African proverb.

I remember one guy in high school who never smiled. I'd say, "How's it going?" and he'd shrug and murmur, "Ehhh." I'm not proud to admit it, but I never did make the effort to find out what was bugging him.

You don't want to come off as Suzy Sunshine. But if you act happy and confident for two days and say an audible, positive hello to lots of new faces, you may be amazed to find they'll cheerfully greet you back. The next thing you know, you'll be *feeling* happier, and the smiles will come on their own.

10. Give parties. One way I made friends after moving to a new town was to give parties. When word is out that you're throwing a party, near-strangers sometimes start falling all over themselves to become your pre-party bosom buddies. Sure you see through them. But at least you are all taking the time to get to know each other.

What kind of party should you give, invitations only or open house? Find out what your parents will allow. How about a slumber party with six to eight girls? It's fun to have séances, levitations, ghost stories, refrigerator raids, and time to talk. If everyone brings her own sleeping bag, it shouldn't be too much trouble. Or invite the guys. A pot-luck dinner or brunch is not much fuss. Tell one guest to bring the bread, another to bring dessert, another to bring hors d'oeuvres, and so on. You can provide the main course (spaghetti?), and everyone can pitch in on the cleanup. Or have a blind taste test of four different brands of frozen pizza.

Other ideas include barbecues, picnics, and get-togethers that wind up at a movie, pool, or skating rink. How about playing charades or your newest board game? It may be easiest and least scary to invite people over without trying a theme, but theme parties are fun. That's when you're supposed to wear only black or white or come in costume (or pajamas!), or when you give high tea and the guys appear in jackets and ties and the girls arrive in last year's prom dress or the bridesmaid gown they wore only once. If you have friends who like to bake, you could give a cookie party. Everyone brings a different kind of cookie, samples some of each, then takes home a small assortment.

Don't wait for someone else to give a party and then hope that Sarah, Robbie, and Jack show up. Draw up the invitation list yourself.

The Pursuit of Popularity

The word *popularity* hardly exists in college. There are many groups of friends, and no one thinks about which is "cool" or in or right or best. Yet you're not in college, and being popular may matter to you now.

It mattered to me. For a long time, all I wanted was to be popular. No such luck. The twins and their chic circle did me the favor of talking to me, but I was never important to them. Wanting in and not getting in was lousy for my ego, but thank heavens Judy talked some sense into my head.

"What's so great about the twins?" she wanted to know.

"They're popular," seemed like a pretty feeble answer, but I ran it by her anyway.

"The masses look up to them. Big deal! They may be perfectly wonderful, but they've never been wonderful to you. With all the nice people out there, I can't believe you're hung up on them. Will it damage your reputation if you are seen with less popular people? Will it injure your image? I swear, Carol, sometimes your values make me ill."

At this point, I'd usually want to tell her to can it. But Judy was a genuine friend who knew me thoroughly and liked me anyway. And she had a point. Since the popular crowd wasn't spending time worrying about me, it was pretty crazy for me to spend time worrying about them.

If you are popular, congratulations. If not, relish your close friends and try not to care about the others. It may help to realize that popularity has a flip side. Sure it must be fun to be a trend-setting center of attention. But some popular girls feel cramped by their clique.

Melissa, a college friend, told me about the disadvantages of her high school popularity. She said she felt terrible when she won the class election because she knew her opponent cared more about school issues. "And I hated when my clique got into shoplifting. I didn't want to steal, but I felt I had to—I'd lose popularity points if I didn't. There were sides of me the girls never knew. Since they liked me because I was funny, I felt I always had to be 'on.' If I was depressed, I couldn't cry. Sometimes it was as if I didn't have any friends." Melissa sighed. "I'd be lying if I said I didn't enjoy feeling liked and important. But it made the transition to college hard. No one here knew they were supposed to bow down to me. I was one more lowly freshman. Except I was full of myself."

A clique can be a crutch. Members feel secure, but they're taking their identity from the group and letting group values mold their characters, rather than becoming unique, self-reliant individuals.

Although you may not be as popular as other girls, your friendships may include a closeness that some popular girls have not found.

Your Friends Don't All Have to Like Each Other

One advantage of not belonging to a clique or *the* clique is that you can have many diverse friends to suit your multifaceted personality. It used to bother me that Judy and Jen didn't like one another as much as I liked each of them. But they had friends whom I didn't take to, either. And why not?

It also struck me as odd that during vacation, I'd write such varied letters. Gossip about cute boys to Lauren. Pontifications about the meaning of life to Norma. Was I being phony? Was I being the person each wanted me to be, rather than the person I was? No; I had chosen several friends for my several selves. Different people bring out different sides of us. Twosomes can be easier than threesomes, anyway, and talking one-on-one on the phone can be easier than trying to have a serious conversation in the school cafeteria.

If your friends Seth and Mallory are incompatible, see them separately. If Arin doesn't understand what you see in Nancy, that's OK. If she puts you down for making plans with Nancy, examine her motives. Critical people are often insecure. Is she jealous or worried you'll stop being as close to her? Reassure her that you value her friendship as much as ever. Maybe Arin's concern is that Nancy may be a bad influence—she smokes and hangs out with guys who drink or do drugs. Decide for yourself whether she's right and whether to heed her warning.

When you have friends meet, up their odds of taking to each other by making introductions that lead into conversation. Say, "Anna, I'd like you to meet Nicole—she can play "Für Elise" on the piano, too." P.S.: Don't be so worried about whether everyone else is having a good time that *you're* not having a good time.

Can a Guy Be a Friend?

Sure. It is often hard to be friends with an ex-boyfriend, yet it's easy to have other guys as friends. Your friendships with your lab partner Ed, your neighbor Norm, or your pal's brother Matthew are probably fun in their own right, and they also help you feel comfortable with guys in general and give you insights into the male psyche.

My friend Gilbert and I went to movies, plays, meals, and parties together. We didn't flirt; we talked. We didn't worry about the impression we were making or if our hair was sticking up; we were at ease. I could discuss some subjects more easily with him than with girls, and I felt safer going to some places with him than with girls. While we never "went out" in the romantic sense, we went out together all the time—and years later attended each other's weddings.

Some of the best romances start as platonic friendships, but if you suddenly find you're smitten with a friend, proceed with caution. Don't immediately back him into a corner by declaring your passion. Why? Because if the feelings aren't mutual, it can be uncomfortable for yours to be out in the open. And if they are, but the fling doesn't work out, it's hard to go back to the fraternal bond. (R.J. and I got along great until I had to go and kiss him. After that, we felt awkward and the friend-ship—maybe not as solid as I had imagined?—went down the tubes.) If a male buddy has a one-way crush on you, consider dropping gentle hints about your other romantic interests and don't lead him on or make a big deal of his changing feelings. His crush may pass. His friendship can endure.

You may sometimes feel jealous of your guy friend's girlfriends, and he may envy your dates. Be sensitive and make time for each other. Your mutual friendship may outlast your separate romances.

Fights and Friends

Even the best of friends argue. That's fine. It's better to express resent-ment openly than to let hostility build. But it's also better to lose an argument than to lose a friend. And no matter how solid a relationship is, it's still fragile if it's not handled with care.

If you get a D+ on a test you really studied for, you may be angry. Don't take it out on your chums, thinking they'll love you no matter what. Don't say, "You really tick me off the way you flirt with every hot-tie in sight" if what you mean is, "I'm so mad Mr. Pryor gave me a D+ on that stupid test." Instead, share your frustration. Too many people vent displaced anger. They blow up at friends and family when their rage stems from a different source.

What if you are genuinely peeved at a friend? What if Jill made plans with you and canceled at the last minute, and it's not the first time?

You could proclaim, "You take me for granted." But Jill might say, "I do not." You could insist, "You always stand me up or come two hours late." But Jill might counter, "I've never once been two hours late." She'll be right, you'll be wrong; she'll have learned nothing, and you'll be madder than ever.

A smarter approach would be to address the issue as specifically, tactfully, and rationally as possible. Don't diffuse your case with a gen-erality, and don't lose your case with an overstatement. Say, "Jill, next time we do something, I'd appreciate it if you showed up—on time. It hurts me that I seem to take our plans more seriously than you do."

Keep your voice down, talk slowly, say "I . . . " instead of "You . . . " (that sounds less accusatory) and mix positive with negative. Instead of lighting into her, say, "Your friendship means a lot to me; that's why I feel let down when you seem not to care. It's also why I was glad two weeks ago when you came to my piano recital on time."

At the end of an argument, try giving each other a hug. If you can't—you're still fuming—keep hashing things out.

Whenever you're unleashing anger, less is more. A boyfriend and I once agreed to meet outside the door of a concert hall, but I ran into a pal and went ahead inside as he parked. It turned out by the time he'd found a space and looked for me, the concert had begun and he couldn't get in. When I met him later, I sheepishly asked, "You mad?" He could have blasted me nonstop for twenty minutes. Instead he simply said, "No. Disappointed." I felt like a first-class inchworm.

Are you and your friend disagreeing about which movie to see? Compromise. See her choice this week, yours next week. Are you becoming competitive? Talk it out; take pride in her talents; strive to outdo yourselves, not each other (you're friends, not rivals). Are you on opposite sides of the abortion issue? Don't shout, "I can't believe you think that!" Say, "I feel differently." You don't have to agree on everything (you're friends, not clones).

Do you give in too easily? Some girls back down and beg forgiveness when they have done nothing wrong. Don't be belligerent, but don't apologize for breathing or sob at the first sign of a confrontation.

Before *you* start a fight, have your facts straight. Before you explode, "Why didn't you invite me to your bas mitzvah?" be sure your invitation isn't in the mail.

Eleanor Roosevelt said, "Nobody can make you feel inferior without your consent." When someone insults or teases you, don't fight or cry or raise your voice—that's his intent. Ignore the comment or ask, "Why do you need to put others down to build yourself up?" It's usually best to fight fire with water. Later you can decide whether his "Your breath could kill a herd of hippos" was pure maliciousness or whether you should rinse with mouthwash.

What about when you're the one who's out of line? Did you spread a secret when you should have kept your trap shut? It's too late to clean up that mess, but don't make matters worse by ignoring your friend. She has a right to be upset. Listen and accept the blame. You could protest, "I didn't know it was such a deep dark secret." But should you have known? Rather than be self-righteous, admit your mistake and apologize sincerely. (By the way, while you'll win an audience if you gossip, you'll win respect if you don't. And secret-keepers get a bonus: You wouldn't believe all the juicy gossip I hear since friends know I'm close-lipped.)

In college, some friends and I once talked and played music until 4 A.M. The next day the girl on the other side of the thin walls told me she'd slept terribly. She was about to launch into a tirade about how rude and selfish we'd been, but I disarmed her (saving her lungs, my ears, and our rapport) by pleading guilty. "It was rude and selfish of us. I apologize, and it won't happen again." I made sure it didn't.

Staying Friends

Can you remain close when your friend moves or goes to college? Absolutely. Samuel Butler said, "Friendship is like money, easier made than kept." Yet with a little effort, friendship *can* be forever. My family moved when I was in the middle of sixth grade, so I could no longer sleep over at Debbie's once a week, but I managed to keep up with her, and we still see each other. When I left new high school friends to study in France, I made *amis* abroad but stayed in touch with buddies at home.

Obviously I've let go of lots of peripheral pals over the years. And lots have let go of me. (Some people want to leave their past behind, and some can't be bothered to call or correspond.) But it's not hard to stay friends for keeps if you both want to.

How do you stay close? You show that you continue to care. Some long-lost friends simply pick up where they leave off. But many want to keep up the communication while they're apart—and not just on birthdays.

Write letters. It's not a chore; it's fun. Scribble a note during study hall or after a date when you're too wired to go to sleep. Send photos and news of mutual pals. Keeping up a correspondence often strengthens friendships. Some people can express on paper what they repress in person. For instance, it can be easier to write "Alexa, I miss you" than to say it. Plus, petty aggravations don't get in the way of long-distance friendships. So write every so often. It takes less time, money, and energy than you'd ordinarily be spending on each other. Writing may also help you sort out your own feelings. Don't be super-rigid about who owes whom. It won't hurt you to send an extra missive, but it could hurt your friendship if you both keep silent just because you've lost track of whose turn it is.

I have a few postcard pals. Writing a postcard takes three minutes and costs next to nothing. You don't have to fuss with an envelope, and you can pack in piles of news. Why not make a pact with a faraway friend to exchange frequent postcards? Liven up the deal by agreeing to send the artsiest, wackiest, or tackiest ones you can find.

If you're both on-line, send E-mail. Or send a personalized tape or videocassette. That takes longer and works only if you both have a tape recorder or camcorder and VCR. But hearing or seeing your friend is the payoff.

Maybe you can visit each other during summer or vacation. Expect some changes, initial awkwardness, and late-night catching up.

And how about the telephone? You could call each other at set times, say every other Saturday morning or the first of every month. The danger is the bill. Call at night, on weekends, or during other not-too-expensive times, and keep it brief.

Telephone Tactics

How true is the stereotype? Do teenage girls and telephones really stick together like P.B. and J.? When I remember how Judy and I tied up the line for hours (we lived right next door to each other) and how Jen used to call me when I was baby-sitting and sometimes the Matusows wouldn't have left yet and Dr. Matusow would answer and Jen, the chicken, would hang up—well, I still blush to think of it.

You may be spending over a thousand hours on the telephone during the next few years alone. So follow these telephone tips. And use the phone book. Calling 411 gets expensive, and if you know Daphne's last name, you don't have to call Emily to get her number.

1. After you dial, let the phone ring at least six times. The person may be outdoors, in the bathroom, on call-waiting, or just sliding a cake into the oven. (Don't you hate when you skin your shin on the coffee table while lunging for the phone—only to catch the dial tone?)

2. Say, "Hello, may I please speak to Grace?" or "Hello, Mr. Green. This is Carol Weston. May I speak with Grace, please?" It's more polite than "Is Grace there?" If Grace answers and says, "This is she," don't laugh—that's what she's supposed to say.

3. Don't play guessing games. Introduce yourself immediately. Unless your name is unusual, give your last name, too. I know lots of Johns, and it is embarrassing when I'm not sure which one I'm talking to from the start. Even when I phone my aunt, I'll say my full name because she won't be expecting to hear from me and may know other Carols. If I'm talking to an editor, I may even identify myself beyond my name. "Hello. This is Carol Weston. I sent you the quiz on First Ladies. . . ?"

4. If the person you called sounds rushed, ask, "Did I catch you in the middle of something?" or "Do you have a minute?" or "Is this a bad time?"

5. In your lowest, least shrill voice, gab. Pretty voices are more pleasant than dull or squeaky ones. You know how people say, "I never forget a face?" Well, many of us never forget a voice. You're concerned with the way you look and smell; give equal time to the way you sound. Really. (Oh, and chewing gum on the phone sounds terrible.)

6. If you're talking on the phone, talk on the phone. Don't also watch TV or slurp stew. I hate it when someone phones me, then bangs around in the kitchen. I want to believe the person called to converse, not to make a chore go faster. If you're on with a motormouth, and you want to do more than say, "Uh huh, uh huh," then at least be discreet about it. Sort your books or CDs quietly or file your nails.

7. After you've talked, don't say, "I gotta go now." Say, "Well, it's been good talking to you; I'll see you Monday" or "I better let you go but thanks for the science assignment." (If the caller won't get off, say, "Well, Amanda, thanks for calling" or "My mom needs the phone," or "I'm glad you phoned, and I'll see you at Stephanie's.")

8. When you first answer a call, make your *hello* sound warm even if you're feeling grisly. If it's not for you, take the caller's number and message, and *write it down.* That way your family won't mind taking messages for you. (You *do* have a pen and pad by the phone, don't you?) If you have to leave a message for someone, ask, "Do you have a pen?" It's a polite way of making sure your message gets written down.

9. Does your friend's family have an answering machine? Don't crack up or hang up. Just say, "This is Francesca Smith at 444-4444. I'd like Max to return my call when he has a chance." Say your phone number slowly and clearly—and then repeat it. (It's annoying to have to rewind a tape nine times to decode someone's number.)

10. Does your family have call-waiting? It may be worth the few dollars a month because then your brother can't pace around screaming, "Get off, I'm expecting a call." When you hear the click-click, say, "I better get that call, but I'll talk to you tomorrow, OK?" If you've barely got on with caller number one, say, "Would you hang on half-a-sec?" then get on and off quickly with caller number two. Say, "Mrs. Warren, I'm on the other line. I'll have my mother call you when she gets in." And write it down! If it's important or a long-distance call, ask the person to hold on and get off with caller number one. (My apologies if this seems obvious, but more than once I've spent my long-distance money on static while the person I called is jabbering away with someone else. Or I've chatted on and on, then felt like a fool when the person finally mentioned, "Listen, I'm on call-waiting . . . ")

11. Don't let an unknown caller know when you're alone. Say, "My father can't come to the phone right now; may I take a message?"

12. When to call? When it's evening in California, it's past midnight in New York. If you always call at dinnertime or after 10 P.M., you may be losing points with friends' parents. Try not to call someone more than once in an evening.

13. Don't be caught in a lie. In the era of technology, if Gretchen says, "I called all weekend" to a person with an answering machine, or "Your line was busy all night" to a person with call-waiting, it could be discovered that Gretchen, however well intentioned, is full-of-it.

14. When an operator says, "This is Dorothy, may I help you?" say, "Yes, Dorothy." By using her name, you'll brighten her day.

15. If you ever get obscene or phony phone calls, after the caller has spoken, calmly say, "Yes, Operator, this is the call I'd like you to trace." If the calls are repeated, ask the phone company to look into it. If you have Caller I.D. or the * 69 option, the mystery is solved.

16. If you want to play an off-key "Happy Birthday" to someone on a push-button phone, here's how: 886809, 8868#9, 88*7532, ##9568. (Don't just take my word for it. Go check!)

Being a Good Guest

I remember when my friend Debbie's mother invited me for dinner. "We're having liver," she said. I told you how I feel about liver in Chapter 1, and there was no way I was going to subject myself to such a meal. But did I have the guts or know-how to decline graciously? I did not.

Within earshot of Debbie's family, I called home and said, "Dad, the Kirks invited me to dinner, can I stay?"

"Sure," said my father.

"Oh c'mon, just for dinner."

"I said you could," my father replied.

"Pleeeease, Dad? . . . Well OK, then could you pick me right up?"

Fortunately, my father figured out my ploy and, within minutes, was in front of Debbie's house, tooting his horn. But there are easier ways to wriggle out of a dinner invitation.

A simple "I can't tonight, Mrs. Kirk, but thank you, I appreciate your asking—and I'd love a rain check" would have done nicely. Parents eat up that kind of courtesy.

Whether you are accepting or declining an invitation, always say thank you. And if you have spent the weekend or vacation week at a friend's house, write a quick note afterward to her parents. The longer you put off writing the thank-you note, the better it has to be.

Other good-guest thoughts:

- If you'll be spending a few days with a family, bring a gift: home-made bread, a jar of fine jelly, pretty soaps, a plant, or book. If you're good with a camera, take pictures and send them copies.
- Don't be too shy with your friend's parents. Try to start a conversation by complimenting the dinner or surroundings or saying, "Hannah tells me you're a professor; that must be interesting."
- Offer to help wash and dry dishes; pitch in.
- Make your bed and be as neat as possible in the bathroom, and don't leave damp towels around.
- Mind your manners: Napkin in your lap, don't start eating until the hostess does, use the outside fork first, break your bread and butter it piece by piece, don't slurp your soup or tea . . .
- If you sense your friend or her family might want a moment alone, go read a book or magazine. Don't expect to be entertained every second.

- If your friend's family is taking you out to dinner, don't order until they do. You'd be embarrassed if you asked for shrimp cocktail if they were planning to go for just main courses.
- Leave when you planned to or you'll wear out your welcome. As Ben Franklin put it in *Poor Richard's Almanack*, "Fish and visitors stink in three days." And as Jane Austen wrote in *Emma*, "It was a delightful visit . . . perfect in being much too short."

When Friendships Change

What if you don't fit into your clique anymore? Maybe you got in with them when you felt insecure, but now you realize they aren't your type. Maybe all they care about is Saturday-night keg parties and you think drinking is stupid. Whatever the reason, you want out. What do you do?

If it's your group's stealing, smoking, drinking, exclusivity, or wildness that makes you uncomfortable, you could consider saying so. Without being judgmental, say that you feel rotten after you shoplift or you don't see the joy in getting high all the time. (You may discover that some of them aren't as hyped about it as they had led you to believe.)

The best way to start moving away from a clique is to be extrafriendly to girls outside it. That's what a friend of mine did. "I used to smoke pot with my friends all the time," she told me. "Then one weekend I went with my family to visit a college out East with my older brother. The campus was beautiful, and I realized I'd want to go away to school, too, and that I was blowing it. My grades were terrible—my whole group was totally unmotivated. Right then I understood that if I could just do better in school, more doors would be open to me. So when I got back home, instead of calling my buddies, I called this other girl, who was straight and a good student. I made plans with her and gradually got in with her friends. About two weeks later, one of my old buddies was stoned in the girls' room and sneered, 'God, you used to be so much fun.' It was rough. But I'm at a good college now and I love it here."

When friendships shift, it can ache as much as or more than breaking up with a guy. It'll hurt if your tomboy friend turns into a young lady overnight or if your neighbor gets a boyfriend and discards you like scrap paper. You used to be able to think aloud together. Now you each worry that the other is taking everything wrong. Try to be patient, accepting, and open about the adjustments you're making. True friendship can survive.

I remember a heart-to-heart Jen and I once had. We'd both been quietly feeling smothered. Somehow the responsibility of being best friends in junior high had gotten to us. We each needed time for other people. After several uncomfortable weeks, we talked about our concerns. Imagine our relief when we discovered we'd both been upset about the same thing! Jen and I decided to be "bestest" friends instead of "best" friends. That left us feeling less possessive and obligated to each other, yet just as caring. Once we stopped feeling as though we *had* to spend every waking moment together, we had more fun when we *chose* to see each other.

I also remember a run-in with Judy. As I confessed to my diary, "*I feel like I don't have a best friend. Judy's changed. I'm sick of her telling me my faults. Her frankness is beginning to nauseate me.*" Suffice it to say I'm awfully glad we made up, and Judy's candor is still one of the traits I like most in her. So don't let ordinary squabbles and moodiness damage extraordinary friendships.

Of course, just as you'll continually add friends to your life, you'll also "weed" your garden of friends. It's natural to outgrow some pals or find you are growing in different directions. (She likes horses; you like boys.) You'll want to stick by a friend who is going through a hard time (parents' divorce, problems at school), but what if there is no legitimate explanation for a friend's change or selfishness? What if a fickle friend is ditching you in favor of someone more popular? Or what if you and a friend just don't click anymore? You could try clearing the air. You might say (on the phone or in a note) that you've noticed things have cooled off between you but you'd like to work at staying close. Or you could decide to drift away with as few hard feelings as possible. If your pals have been friend-hopping, it may be time for *you* to go friend-shopping. (Always try to have more than one bosom buddy—you can't get it all from one friend.)

Grudges and hate are a waste of energy. I resented a friend-turned-bitch for almost six months until I realized that while I was practically developing an ulcer, this hot-and-cold girl was dating, partying, and not giving me a second thought.

Don't bother hating people because they don't accept you or because they threaten you or because you see in them some characteristic you don't like in yourself. (Oscar Wilde again: "None of us can stand other people having the same faults as ourselves.") Channel your feelings elsewhere; focus on your friends, not your enemies.

Ten Ways to Lose Friends

Friendships can be forever, but too often, they fall apart along the way. If you want to keep your friendships in good repair, don't sabotage them. Heed this what *not*-to-do list.

1. Agree wholeheartedly when your friend says, "I acted like such a jerk" or "My party was a total failure."
2. Neglect your friend whenever a guy comes into the room. Drop her whenever a guy comes into your life.
3. Stay on and on, leaving only when you're pushed out the door. Then, as soon as you get home, phone to talk.
4. Use your friend for her homework, car, hand-me-down clothes, or social status. Develop a crush on her crush and flirt shamelessly.
5. Become a bore: Constantly whine and complain, blab endlessly about your diet or boyfriend, or turn anything anyone says into a springboard for you to talk about yourself.
6. Become dependent and get jealous every time your friend talks to anyone else. Act like you own her.
7. Be so envious of your friend's grades, clothes, looks, athletic abilities, relationships with guys, or whatever that you no longer enjoy her company or what *you* have.
8. Demand that your friend tell you everything. Promise not to tell. Spill the secrets.
9. Criticize and say "you should" a lot; try to change your friends and run their lives.
10. Notice when you need your friends but not when they need you. Call when you're upset but be impatient with their tears.

Be Your Own Friend

If you like yourself, others will like you, too. Even if the popular girls *don't* know you're alive, and James *doesn't* ask you to dance, you are still a good, worthwhile person with lots to offer. Believe in yourself!

Focus on your bright side. If you're speaking up in biology class and a little voice inside you whispers that you sound like a nincompoop, tell it to shove it. Listen instead to the voice that's whispering, "Hey, you know your stuff." This is hard to pull off when you don't know a mollusk from a molecule. So try to be the smartest, warmest person you can, then give yourself the approval you deserve.

Recent studies have shown that from age fourteen, girls are twice as prone to depression as boys. Equally alarming is that at the age of nine, most girls feel confident, but by the time they hit high school, fewer than a third report feeling confident, assertive, and positive about themselves. White girls seem to lose their self-assurance even faster than black and Hispanic girls. Social scientists are still trying to make sense of these findings, but some speculate that many girls' sense of self-worth is too tied in with body image. We're too fixated on the physical— concerned more about looking OK than feeling OK.

Some insecurity is normal. There were times, I'll confess, when I'd catch a glimpse of myself in the mirror and think, "Carol, you are the fattest thing that ever waddled." But other times, I'd think I was so cute, I'd want to pinch my cheeks. So why not give yourself a break? Why not make peace with your body? And why not concentrate on pluses instead of minuses? Why not listen to the Yes? I could sink into total despair if I thought about all the guys who didn't ask me out, all the essays I wrote that didn't sell, or all the skills (like singing or sewing) I haven't learned. Or I can bask for a moment recalling good times I have had, books I have had published, skills I have acquired. I'm for basking; how about you?

When you consider your personality, give yourself credit for being energetic instead of clobbering yourself for being short-tempered. (Then work on lengthening your fuse.) When you look at your past, emphasize sunny-side-up periods; don't brood on scrambled ones. If you insist on recalling what a geek you were last year, think about how you've grown since then. And how tough times help you appreciate happy ones.

Do you bad-mouth yourself? Stop. Don't discredit yourself by saying, "I'm a bitch; I can't help it" or "I'm a jinx; it's my fault we got a flat." When an unlucky thing happens, think "What a drag!" not "I'm unlucky." Be less hard on yourself. Measure yourself by reasonable— not impossible—standards.

In short, give yourself a pat on the back instead of a kick in the butt!

When you're in the absolute pits (and we all fall in occasionally), talk it over with someone, but don't moan endlessly to your friends. Do something active you can be proud of and start pulling yourself out. Do a five-star job on an assignment. Or astound your parents by cleaning the kitchen. Or go on a longer-than-usual bike ride. Or listen to upbeat music, watch an absorbing movie or video, read a fun magazine, take a hot bath. Write in a journal. Start a scrapbook or look one over. Volunteer to help someone who needs you—that will lift your spirits, too. Tackling a project that isn't fun per se (organizing your closet, doing homework, working for a humanitarian or environmental cause) can also make you feel better. Do something you know you do well or try something you've never tried. The course to take after you've struck out is to get back up at bat and hit one.

Believe me, I get the blues and the blahs, too, and I can go off the deep end with the best of them. I'm not saying you should ignore anger or sorrow or let them build up inside you. But after you express negative energy, sit down, close your eyes, breathe deeply, and think "calm." The world isn't all black and white. There are still people who love you and things you can feel good about and things you can do to get back in gear.

You could stay bummed for ages, but what's the point? Why not strive to keep things in perspective? Why shoo happiness away? Whatever is upsetting you will probably pass. Things could probably be worse, but aren't.

One technique that has helped me is to keep a list for a few days of what I've done—not what I *have* to do. Tuesday might say nothing more than "exercised, showered, dressed, read paper, read three articles on drunk driving, had a sandwich, wrote two pages, sent a postcard to Aunt Lisa, bought typing paper, ate dinner with my family, called John and Linda, read a García Márquez story." For me, that's a fairly typical fine day. Yet when I'm down, that can feel like an I-didn't-get-anything-done day. Keeping a list helps me see straight.

Even if you do get a C– on a test, don't let it hold you down. Don't think, "I'm such an idiot; I'm going to flunk out for sure." Think, "I didn't study hard enough; next time I'll do better."

Don't let yourself wallow too long. If you do call a friend, don't just unload your woes. Listen to her insights and advice. If you can't shake a long-term depression alone or with the help of friends and family, see a counselor or therapist. I've done that, and the sessions were just what I needed to get through a difficult period. (I'll tell you about it in the *Family* chapter.)

Before you seek professional help or sign up for antidepressants, though, think about this: In some ways, *wholeness* is as important as happiness. Feeling down helps you grow up and become sensitive, wise, and empathic. Feeling low is part of being human. And you can't always expect smooth sailing—especially if you're making waves. (Ups and downs are to be expected. It's staying consistently down that may be a cue that you could use outside intervention.)

If you're comfortable with yourself, you'll feel lonely less often. Everyone is alone from time to time (even on Saturday nights), but try to think of those hours as precious solitude, not painful loneliness. Learn to entertain yourself, whether by reading, cooking, exercising, gardening, surfing the Net, putting on music and conquering your cluttered desk or drawers, whatever!

As Abraham Lincoln put it, "Most folks are about as happy as they make up their minds to be." I won't quibble with honest Abe. Happiness doesn't just happen. You have to invite it over and welcome it in. Be true to yourself and do things that please you and things that please others. Even happiness can be a habit. Even depression can be habit-forming. You may have to work at being happy and you can't be happy all the time, but self-contentedness (which is how Aristotle defined happiness) is within your grasp. So seize the day! Squeeze the moment! (Bonus: Happy people tend to be healthy people.)

Since I'm ranting and raving about how you should like yourself, I'd better add: Don't go overboard. If you become conceited or smug or self-satisfied, you'll drive near and dear ones away. A little modesty, please. There's room for improvement in everybody—in you, in me, even in the girls you envy and the guys you adore.

Speaking of guys (always one of my favorite pastimes), after the letters section, we'll talk about that elusive stuff called love.

Dear Carol...

Dear Carol,
Everybody always says "Just be yourself," but I don't know who I am yet. Is that weird or what?

No! That's what adolescence is about—the chance to start figuring it all out.

Dear Carol,
Help! My best friend in the whole world, Molly, is sick of me because I have started to follow her around, talk like her, dance like her, act like

her, and dress like her. It's just that I love everything about her. She's popular and I want to be like her.

Don't be her shadow, be her friend! You can admire and emulate Molly, but give the girl some breathing room. And while you're figuring out which of her qualities you want to copy, think about the ways in which you'd like to be different, too.

Dear Carol,

I just started a new school and I am a likable person. But a girl from my old town has been sticking to me like Superglue. And I mean 24-7! I want to make my own friends and get in with a good crowd. She is holding me back. Help!

No one can single-handedly hold you back—unless you let her. You can make new friends by joining the photography club, debate team, Save the Earth committee (maybe without telling your friend?), by sitting with other people at lunch and in class, and by inviting other girls over after school. With luck, you won't have to spell things out to Superglue . . . and you may even find that as you see her less, you'll like her more. (If you have to give an explanation, put a spin on it. Say, "I'm glad we're still friends with each other and that we're making new friends, too.")

Dear Carol,

My friend is always comparing my grades to hers. If she gets a better grade, she'll congratulate me. If I get a better grade, she'll ignore me and act stuck up. In the summertime Caroline is the best friend a person could ask for. But now that school has started, I've been hanging around another girl. The thing is, I'm feeling really guilty about it.

Put the guilt aside. It's smart to have more than one close friend, and you have every right to make new friends (while still being nice to current ones). You could even tell Caroline what you told me—that she's the best friend a person could ask for, but that you wish she wouldn't worry so much about grades—at least, not yours.

Dear Carol,

Mary used to be my friend, but now she's gotten in good with Brandi who is really popular. Now Mary ignores me, says stuff about me, puts me down, laughs at what I wear, etc. If Brandi had worn the exact same thing, Mary would have liked it. How can I get close to Brandi like Mary is? And what's wrong with Mary—or is there something wrong with me?

All too many friendships take nosedives during these years. It hurts. It stinks. It happens. Mary is insecure and is trying to build herself up by putting you down. Not very nice in my book—and this *is* my book! It may seem like the whole school consists of popular kids and their followers, but look around; there are many other girls (and guys) out there. Instead of getting totally hung up on Mary and Brandi, you'd do well to keep your dignity and reach out to kids outside their limited orbit— kids who will appreciate you.

Dear Carol,

I have two friends, and when they get in a fight, they say, "Which side are you on?" And I don't know what to do because if I go on one side, I'll lose a friend, and if I don't go on either side, I'll lose two friends.

Say, "This is your fight, not mine," and refuse to get sucked into it. You shouldn't have to choose or lose.

Dear Carol,

Last year I was known as a "bad girl." Truth is, I've never taken a drug in my life and I'm a virgin. This summer I put together an innocent look and I like it. I stopped wearing "slutty" clothes and so much makeup. But how am I going to convince the rich preps that I never really was loose or wild? How can I get rid of my old reputation? (Forgive me for spilling my guts on paper. Oops! Splat! *** There goes another one!)

Dear Carol,

Last year, a girl moved here, became really popular (I think people were scared of her), and told everyone she was going to beat me up. She didn't, but she humiliated me in public, so everyone thought I was a wimp. Now she's moved away and school is about to start. What can I do to reverse the bad effects this girl has had? I think she has ruined my life.

Reputations change, lives aren't ruined that easily, and it's never too late to clean the slate. Anyone can start a new year with a new look and a new attitude. Gather up what's left of your self-esteem, march into school without posturing or cowering, and make an effort to be friendly to new people (not just to your old crowd or the school's hailed heroes). Join a team or club or choir. *Everyone* changes over the summer, so have an open mind when September rolls around—and others may, too.

Dear Carol,

My friends make fun of me whenever I use what they consider a big word. The other day I said something was "frivolous," and they nearly died laughing.

Smart people laugh last. My brother Mark was called a Brain in high school (when he would rather have been labeled a Jock), but recently on the game show "Jeopardy!" he won thousands of dollars and a trip for two to Hawaii! Don't use polysyllabic words just to impress someone, but never play dumb.

Dear Carol,

Usually I am cheery, but right now I hate the entire world. Elsa is a friend of mine who gets invited to all the parties and who made cheerleading, which I didn't. This wouldn't seem so bad because I have friends, too. At least I thought I did. But lately if I mention I talked to So-and-So, Elsa says, "Oh really?" (in astonishment), "I just talked to her and she said she can't stand you. We were even making jokes about you." Elsa seems to enjoy conveying these messages. I can't even talk to her on the phone without discovering at least two new people who hate me. Is it supposed to make me feel better to know the truth? It makes me feel worse. I used to feel self-confident. Now I feel rotten about myself.

With friends like her, who needs enemies? Elsa sounds awful! She's trying to flatten you, so don't buy into it. Other people may act like they like her because they're afraid to get on her bad side. But the best thing to do with friends like Elsa is to make them ex-friends—quickly and quietly.

Dear Carol,

Right before I moved, my best friend, Amelia, started acting as if she could care less about me. It really hurt because we were always inseparable.

Maybe Amelia left emotionally, so she wouldn't feel like the one left behind. (Get it?) She may have also decided to get started in her scramble for new friends. Write or call Amelia, and tell her you miss her. You can both enjoy a long-distance friendship (punctuated with fun visits) for the rest of your lives. In the meantime, turn off the *Home Improvement* reruns and get busy with the here-and-now of your new school.

Dear Carol,

I'm 16 and have a big problem. It may not seem like much, but it's been eating at me for months. I want to know if it's normal to be jealous of your best friend. My best friend Lily is one of the sweetest most terrific people in the world. Things were great for almost five years until we went on a vacation to Disneyland together. I couldn't help noticing that every guy we met (vendors, operators, tourists) flirted with her. None of them so much as looked at me. Now I'm always noticing how guys can't take their eyes off her. I feel like such a traitor for not being happier for her. Please tell me how to get over this—I don't want to ruin our friendship.

Jealousy is natural, and friendship rivalries are as common as sibling rivalries. You are clearly sensitive and caring and need not feel ashamed. You could mention your feelings to your friend. But work on developing your best traits and skills, so you become less vulnerable to jealousy. Who knows? Your friend may also envy you. (By the way, you'll find that having a terrific and attractive friend has plenty of pluses. Her suitors have friends, too, after all.)

Dear Carol,

For a while all I wanted was to be popular. My eyes lit up when a girl named Heather asked to sit with me at lunch because Heather was popular. But then I told her about my friend Jennifer, and she said, "You can't be friends with her. She's a nerd." So I stopped being friends with Jennifer. What a fool I was! I was accepted by the popular clique, but I never really fit in. And now Jennifer doesn't like me anymore. Which I can certainly understand. How can I tell her that I've reformed?

Call and say you miss her and invite her to do something really fun with you. She may come around when she sees that you're sincere.

Dear Carol,

There's this girl in my class who thinks she's so cool. She acts like she's Miss America. I get so annoyed!

She probably annoys other kids, too. But don't let her problem be your problem. Since she's not losing sleep over you, don't lose sleep over her. Do more things to make you proud of yourself, and you'll stop minding when she acts proud of herself.

Dear Carol,

I wrote my old friend a letter saying very nicely that I didn't want to be friends anymore. She wrote me back saying that I was stupid and ugly. I know it's not the right thing, but I want to get back at her. What should I do?

Nothing. You hurt her feelings so she hurt yours. Now let it go. Who knows? Someday you two may even make up and be friends again. Next time, instead of breaking up with a girl so officially, just stop calling or making plans. Just pull your oar out of the water.

Dear Carol,

Three of my friends are starting to shoplift. It started with candy, but now they take bigger stuff. No one has been caught, but I'm worried.

When Ben Franklin said, "God helps those who help themselves," he was not referring to shoplifting. It's OK if you choose to do nothing, but why not tell the closest friend that you think stealing is risky and wrong and you're afraid she might get caught? She may be ambivalent about it herself—and glad to know that you'd respect her even more if she cut out the crime. There *is* such a thing as positive peer pressure.

Dear Carol,

I have a friend who is really nice to me, and we have a great time when it is just us. Once we get around other people, she is rude and makes fun of me. I know she is just joking, but it hurts my feelings.

When she teases, you have two choices. You can laugh along and say, "You're right! My sense of direction is a joke! I could go the wrong way on a one-way street!" Or you can tell her (when you're alone), "We're good friends and I feel hurt when you make fun of me, so I wish you'd stop."

Dear Carol,

I told a friend a secret, and the next day it was all over school. What do I do?

Put it behind you. The school has. Most people are so preoccupied with themselves (and the hole in *their* tights and the zit on *their* nose and the rumor about *their* crush) that they aren't as focused on you as you fear. Nonetheless, do not confide in that girl again. Many people can't resist turning someone else's big drama into their small talk. Next time, confide in a cousin or friend from another school—or your own journal.

Dear Carol,

There are these five cool girls in my class. I want to be in their group, and a lot of people think they're the best. I'd do anything to be popular and I always try to impress them. Every day I give them gum or candy. The other day they read my secret diary and saw who I like. Then they started laughing at me. I feel like they are using me.

Better to base a relationship on affection and trust than on gum and candy. Stop shortchanging yourself by trying to buy attention. Drop out of the Fab Five fan club and find less visible girls who can become more valuable friends.

Dear Carol,

I did something really terrible and I don't know what I can do to fix it. I thought my best friend stole my boyfriend (which she didn't do—she would never do that) and when we got into an argument about it, I blurted out, "At least I still don't wet the bed." Now the whole school knows her secret, and she is devastated. I'd do anything to take back what I said—I even tried telling people it was all just a lie, but nobody believed me. She knows lots of embarrassing stuff about me, too, but she would never tell anybody. But she says we can never be friends again after what I did. I know I deserve it, but I hate not being friends with her anymore. Is there anything I can do to make it up to her?

I can tell that you are genuinely sorry, but since you hit her where it hurt—and in public—she's too mortified to be in the mood to help you feel better. This friendship may be over for good, with both of you learning the hard way to be more discreet. If you want to try to salvage things, write her a heartfelt note saying you'd do anything to turn back the clock and you hope someday she'll forgive you. She probably misses your friendship, too, so there's an outside chance of reconciliation. (By the way, the bedwetting is not her fault. See page 53 of the *Body* chapter.)

Dear Carol,

I'm 13 years old. My friend Amanda was talking about killing herself, but I figured she hadn't succeeded before, she won't this time, so I kept my mouth shut. Two days later, she was missing, and then they found her in a lake. She was dead. I went into a state of depression because it was my fault she died. They entered me in a mental hospital. When she died, I put a note in her coffin that said, "Dear Amanda, I'm sure this isn't what you've been planning to hear, but I don't feel sorry for you. I'm angry. You were always the strong one, and you're not strong, you're weak." I wish God would give her a second chance. She just needed someone to hear her. I would give my life for hers. Mine's already destroyed. I can't walk and I don't talk to anyone. You're the first and the last.

What a tragedy for Amanda and for everybody who loved her. You certainly have grieved for her and your anger is understandable. But don't turn that anger on yourself. Though her life ended terribly, yours is still ahead. You didn't kill Amanda; she killed herself. And you now need to start walking, talking, and living again. Maybe you can express your pain in a poem or painting that you can dedicate to her. Let the mental health experts in the hospital help you through the trauma and sorrow of her death. Or talk to your parents about trying another treatment program.

I, too, lost a friend to suicide. The sadness afterward was long and leaden. I wish my friend had been able to get the right counseling from a psychotherapist and the right medication from a psychiatrist. I wish she'd been able to hang on until she found the way back into her life instead of the way out. She obviously felt desperate at the end, but depression lifts, and I believe she could have gotten through the tunnel and emerged to enjoy the years—decades!—ahead. We should have been friends forever, she and I. But after suicide, there is no turning back, no second chance.

If *you* have a friend who is talking about suicide, confide in an adult you trust. In this case, it is much more important to get help than to keep a secret. (*See* Teen Suicide on page 195)

If *you* have thoughts about suicide, get counseling now. The high anxieties of junior high and high school (popularity, pecking orders, and fade-in, fade-out friendships) usually end with graduation. Yet suicide is final and unforgiving. It is a permanent solution to a temporary problem.

3 LOVE

Falling In, Falling Out

✿

Love is wonderful. And love is a mess.

Love is dopey smiles, giddy phone calls, deep talks on long walks, singing in a snowstorm, squooshing into the same section of a revolving door, identifying with every lyric on the radio—and feeling excruciatingly alive. Love is also dashed expectations, quarreling because you care, missing him the moment he says good-bye, aching when he flirts with someone else, longing for another letter, losing sleep over nighttime daydreams—and feeling blissfully deranged.

Love? I'm still trying to figure it out myself. It's the most complex emotion going. Heady, heartbreaking, poignant, breathtaking. And *I love you* means different things to different people at different times.

So while I can offer facts about menstruation and eating disorders, and while I can provide rights and wrongs about applying for a job or to college, I can't claim to have a hold on love. Love knows no facts, few rights, few wrongs. Love is full of contradictions.

Nonetheless, here's a chapter full of tips. How to let guys know you're interested; how to keep dates fun; how to let love last; and, sigh, how to survive a breakup.

Just keep in mind that love is something you have to learn the hard way—which, lucky you, also happens to be the fun way.

Getting Started

The first love letter I ever received was in third grade, in Mrs. Gemunder's class. A blond named Billy passed a scribbled scrap of paper from the third row on the left, where he sat, to the second row on the right, where I sat. It read, "Do you like me? ____Yes ____No."

This was exciting. I immediately checked Yes. But I wasn't going to make myself vulnerable for nothing. No fool I, in my brand-new cursive handwriting, I added, "Do you like me?" I handed the note to my neighbor and watched as it passed from person to person to person to Billy. Billy read it. He looked up. He met my gaze. He smiled.

Ah, things were so simple then.

By junior high, they were complicated.

Why? Partly because I was love-hungry, desperate to be going with somebody. It scarcely mattered whom: I was in love with love. Here are some typical lines from my diary:

Tuesday: I don't think Jake likes me. But Nat (yuk!) told a kid he'd ask me to dance every dance at school. I'll say no!

Thursday: In dance class, Jake danced with me. He likes me!! I decided to change my future slumber party to a boy-girl party.

Wednesday: Jake doesn't like me. I bet he likes Danielle.

Thursday: Jake doesn't like me because I like him.

Friday: I'm not going to say hi or anything.

Thursday: I've given up on Jake. He doesn't like me. I like Evan a little.

Saturday: The dance was OK. Jake didn't dance with me and Nat did only once.

Wednesday: I got thrown in the lake by ninth-grade boys. Fun!

Friday: My party was a success, but no boy likes me.

Monday: In Music, I wrote a note to Jen about boys and Mr. Parsons took it and said he'd read it aloud if I didn't behave. I behaved.

Friday: I don't know what boy to like.

Saturday: Dave is so cute and strong. So is Hugh. So is Walter.

Friday: The last dance of eighth grade wasn't that good because no good boys like me.

Sunday: I am so in love with everybody.

Thursday: I went in a rowboat with Walter.

Tuesday: *Hugh Dalton may have seen a CW+HD on my French book. God!*
Wednesday: *I love three-ring pretzels.*

Fortunately, I didn't permanently give up boys for pretzels. By age fourteen, I had a new curly-haired crush. According to my diary:

> *Jen and Judy prodded me and I mustered up all my courage and asked him, "Are you going to the concert tonight?"*
> *"Why?"*
> *"Oh, I don't know."*
> *"Are you?"*
> *"I was planning to . . . "*
> *"I'll be there."*
> *Then at 6:45, It happened. He called. He looked up my number and used his finger seven times for Me!. . .*

Guess what? After that fateful concert, he and I ended up going out for three shining years.

So don't despair. There will be dry spells in your love life, times when you think, "It's not fair, even garbage gets taken out!" Fill those boyfriendless days with friends, family, work, sports, books, and yourself. And remember that it's A-OK not to have a boyfriend. It certainly beats settling for someone scummy.

Be patient. Girls are usually ready for romance long before boys are. But there's enough love to go around. If you send out signals, love is bound to come your way.

What signals? Keep reading!

Sending Out Signals

You can't force someone to like you. But you can stack the odds in your favor. How do you let the would-be Love of Your Life know you're interested without seeming too forward?

Easy. Sort of. Remember the *Body* and *Friendship* chapters? Wash your hair, watch your weight, dress your head-to-toe best. Be on the go, be a good listener, project confidence even when your stomach is doing flip-flops.

Well, all that advice applies whether you're looking for girlfriends or a boyfriend. Try not to be self-conscious. You have yak attacks with girls, so don't clam up with guys. Don't avert your eyes in the hall or stare at your shoelaces at the track meet. Even if he turns your knees to mush, try to be your attractive, easygoing, approachable self. (*Approachable:* That means not always being locked inside a group of eight girls.) You can even flirt a little.

Flirt? Yes. Flirting without being a flirt is an art. If you flirt with every guy in sight, or with someone else's boyfriend, girls will resent you and guys won't take you seriously. But if you never flirt, the guy you're wild about may consider you one of the crowd forever.

You don't like the word? Call it something else. Flirting is simply an informal way to let him know you enjoy his company without going out on a limb. It doesn't mean batting your lashes, winking, giggling, looking him up and down, or cooing, "Your cologne smells diivvviiiiine." You don't have to come on to him. Just try a smiling, straightforward "Hello." Or pay him a sincere compliment. Ask questions and show interest in his thoughts and plans. Glance his way—but don't stare.

Flirting should give you both a boost. When it's too one-way or in-your-face, that doesn't make the other person feel flattered or intrigued. It makes him/her feel uncomfortable. And if it's a person in power (say, a teacher or boss) making unwelcome advances, that's not flirting either. It may even be harassment—more on that later.

I used to worry that my mind would go blank during fourth period in the library when I was about to run into my curly-haired crush. So I actually kept a hidden list of things to tell him. (He wasn't always able to play Mr. Cool as we talked, either. Once two of his friends flew a paper airplane at him that read, "How's your love life?")

Some girls like to enlist mutual friends to test the promise of romance. Third-party inquiries can work or can backfire, so use discretion. Unless you're pretty sure he likes you back, I wouldn't confront him directly or make your crush public. That will only make him feel he has to give you an immediate green light or red light when he may want to keep getting to know you without any extra pressure.

Do send out nonverbal signals. Look at the guy, look away, smile ever so slightly. Pull your chair closer to his. Mirror his gestures. Touch his arm gently as you make a point. Whatever. It should feel relaxed and in the spirit of fun. It should communicate: "I'm friendly; I like you"—not "I'm lonely; I need you."

Tune in to what his eyes and body are saying. Don't jump to happy conclusions just because he's maintaining eye contact. But if he is making small talk and paying attention to you, encourage him. Guys get acute anxiety attacks, too, and many are reluctant to make the first move because some fear being teased by friends and some fear the Big R (Rejection!). If he says something tentative like, "I'll see you at the game," say something positive like, "I hope so." If you both adore the same band and he says, "We should catch one of their concerts," say, "I'd love to." (But don't pant, "Yes! Yes! Anytime! I'm always free.")

What if his eyes are lighting up, yet he's not issuing any invites or almost-invites? Are you bold enough to ask him out, or almost ask him out? If so, try something like, "Isn't it great that a pizza place opened on Main Street?" He'll put it together that if he invites you for pizza, you won't turn him down. Of course, if he's a victim of the "once burned, twice shy" syndrome, you'll have to be extra patient. Maybe you could suggest studying together or ask him to join you and a group of friends at a park or bowling alley. Again, remember that while boys are notoriously fast once things get cooking, they're slow, slow, slow to pick up the phone in the first place. (So don't bring your life to a standstill while awaiting his call!)

I know a woman who flirted with a guy who flirted back, but made no plans. Finally she got up her nerve and oh-so-casually mentioned, "I'm having a party tomorrow night if you'd like to drop by." He said he would. And she? She ran home and frantically organized a get-together with all her friends. Know what? The couple is now happily married!

Warning: Keep your flirting low-key and ambiguous. If you're coming on like a steamroller, he may run for cover.

A date once told me, "Hey, I don't want to get married," to which I retorted, "I didn't propose." But perhaps I had been sending out I-sure-would-like-to-go-out-with-you-all-the-time signals instead of I'm-having-fun signals.

It's happened to me the other way around, too. Gordon wasn't eager, he was overeager, and that sent me packing. According to my diary: *"I really like Gordon, but at sentences like, 'You're good for me' and 'Do you realize you single-handedly got me out of a depression?' I withdraw. I'm also uncomfortable when he stares into my eyes, which he does a lot."*

So show him you're interested, but don't go overboard. Once in a while, especially if he's so-gorgeous-you-could-just-die, you may have to tell yourself, "Down, girl, down!"

On Your Mark, Get Set—Relax!

Will the real you please stand up? If your crush doesn't respond to the real you, he'd make you a lousy boyfriend and there's no point in longing for him. But if you are yourself—your best self—and he's smitten, what could be better? You can relax, say what's on your mind, and know that he cares.

It may turn out *you're* the one who is not as interested as you once were. It's easier to fall for a stranger on whom you can project storybook qualities than for a human being with good and bad traits. If you find your crush doesn't have the fantasy personality you'd conjured for him and that you're on different wavelengths—well, that's an important discovery.

If he's talking football and you hate football, you could pretend to be enthralled as he explains a strategy. But at best, you'd be dooming yourself to boring afternoons watching games on the tube or on the field. Molding yourself into the girl you think he wants will leave you stifled. Plus, if Mr. Football finds out he's been feeling amorous about a nonexistent sports fan, he won't be too pleased, either.

Developing some of your sweetie's interests is a compliment. Pretending you already share them is not.

Icebreakers: Twenty-three Ways to Launch a Conversation

Flirt? Relax? Maybe you think you can't even strike up a conversation with a guy, let alone pull your chair closer and be your nice normal self. Fine. Let's backtrack.

You might be forgetting that lots of guys are as intimidated and tongue-tied as you. Most would welcome it if you took the first step. The shy guy in your choir, the soccer star, the genius in your computer club—they may all have noticed you but not known what to say. So for Pete's sake (and Dan's and Adam's and your own), speak up!

Here are twenty-three conversation starters. Don't memorize them because they're not slick pickup lines. They're just natural ways to get a discussion rolling. Ready?

1. How did you figure out question number 12? (He's behind you in math, looking over his homework.)
2. What good movies have you seen lately? (You're side by side in a ticket line.)
3. Did you see who scored that goal? (He's in front of you at the lacrosse game.)

4. Why can't they ever serve lobster tails? (You're waiting for the mystery meat the cafeteria has the gall to call lunch.)

5. What was your old neighborhood like? (He's new in town.)

6. What an adorable dog! (Or terrific boots or handsome sweater or great car.)

7. Do you have change for a dollar? (While he's checking, keep talking.)

8. Do you know where there's a bookstore near here? (Maybe you can walk toward it together.)

9. Hi. (He's bound to say hi back.)

10. Have you been here before? (You're at a tourist site, a baseball stadium, a doctor's office.)

11. So where are you from? (A tried-and-true standby to be used on trains and chairlifts, in lines, at parties, beaches, concerts, fairs—you name it.)

12. How far do you usually run? (You've caught up to him and now maybe you'll do a mile or two together.)

13. What time is it? (When he answers, compliment him on his watch or say, "Phew! I thought it was later," and say why you're relieved.)

14. May I share your history book? (Don't forget yours on purpose, but if you left it in your locker, don't miss an opportunity!)

15. I know you from somewhere—did you ever go to Camp Sloane? (This age-old question lets you find out about each other's background and interests.)

16. Been here long? (You're in a long line or at a subway or bus stop.)

17. Have you ever had Señor Véguez for Spanish? (You've both just received your course schedule for the next term.)

18. I can't believe it's raining again! (Cliché, but discussing the sky gets conversations off the ground.)

19. Where did you learn to type so fast? (Or draw so well, take photographs, read palms, fix cars, dance, shoot hoops, or play guitar.)

20. Doesn't this remind you of a scene from _____? (Fill in the blank with any favorite television show, film, or book.)

21. You're Amy's brother, aren't you? (As if you had the slightest doubt—but that's his cue to ask who you are.)

22. Did you read about the senior lounge plans? (Or about any other school, local, or national news item.)

23. Weren't you absent yesterday? (Why not let him know that class just wasn't the same without him?)

Think up your own questions, too, because breaking the ice is step one to melting his heart.

Is Cupid Stupid, or Does He Just Have Poor Aim?

You aren't breaking the ice and sending ask-me-out-ask-me-out-ask-me-out signals to the wrong guy, are you? Try not to fall for your sister's boyfriend, your art teacher, the married letter carrier, your handsome gay neighbor, your minister, or the loner who has been chatting with you provocatively on-line. Do you have tunnel vision for a famous basketball star or musician? No problem, as long as you don't care if he cares back. Is your heart sold on the popular guy every other girl is head-over-heels over? Great—you may be the winning wooer. But brace yourself for the likelihood (alas) that he won't single you out. What if you've been flirting for months with the same guy and are convinced you could rock happily together as grandparents, yet he still scarcely knows you exist? You're inviting the blues.

Some girls subconsciously pick out-of-reach guys. Deep down, they don't feel ready for the possibility of intimacy, commitment, or connecting with someone who might argue with them or fall short of their impossible standards. It's safer to love from afar, and if unrequited passion doesn't daunt them, no harm done.

However, if *you* are ready for the real thing, why not shift your energies? Give up gracefully on the movie idol. Focus on the sensitive and available, though less widely acclaimed, guys. Look again at the boy next door; stop writing off the foreign exchange student.

Maybe you think you can't help it. You want an honest-to-goodness relationship, but you've flipped for the Class Babe who happens also to be your best friend's boyfriend. He's forbidden, but he's the only one who fuels your fantasies.

All I can say is, you'd be wise to take a deep breath, yank out Cupid's arrow, and find a more suitable object of your affections. Don't pine away, lovesick. Sometimes Cupid misses his mark.

My pragmatic advice may seem unromantic, but it'll probably make you happier in the long run. It's hard to avoid crazy crushes. It's hard to control desires. But you can do it. A crush is like a small flame. You can fan it into a forest fire or, if it's hopeless or off-limits, you can snuff it out.

If your love life, real or imagined, tends to be painful, look for a pattern. Are the guys you go for all the kind your mom hopes you'll marry? Good—if you like them as much as Mom does. Are they nice even though Mom wouldn't take to them? OK. But if you're always aiming too high or too low, or if the guys are all sexy but shallow and oblivious of you, or if one after another is abusive, mean, taken, gay, faraway, unattainable, or your basic Mr. Wrong, try to be kinder to yourself. Try to end the destructive pattern. Don't keep thinking you'll be the one to reform a guy.

You're also not doing yourself any favors if the instant you get a guy, you tire of him and try to make another conquest. Or if you and your boyfriend are going strong, yet you flirt suggestively with every other attractive guy around.

The point isn't to have a boyfriend, after all. The point is to have a healthy, warm, wonderful relationship with a boyfriend.

Should You Date Older and Younger Guys?

My high school honey was a year older than I, and my husband is two years younger. Younger boys aren't all immature and older men aren't all lecherous. However (I bet you knew a *however* was coming), if your sweetheart is years younger or is already well out of his teens, that does give me pause.

Let's say he's *years* younger. That may make you feel safer than you would if you were going out with a peer. Fine. But be sure you also feel secure with guys your own age who may challenge you more.

Is your boyfriend not a boy but a man? Going out with an older man may give you status and prestige. The price? Growing up fast, ready or not. You'll be a woman for the rest of your life, but you're a teen for only a few precious years. A man may not be content to snuggle and kiss for hours (one of the finest features of teen romance) and may up the sexual pressure. He may also be bored by your tales of bombing a test or blowing up at your brother, yet you're entitled to share such stories.

One high school friend told me later that in the long run, she felt that going out with Rick, who was in his late twenties, was not a smart move. She couldn't take him to the prom or out with her friends. And she got so used to adult company that even at college, she found the students childish and felt alienated. Plus, as she got older, she stopped idealizing Rick, and that didn't always thrill him.

Although you may be proud to have won the attentions of an older guy, ask yourself why he isn't dating women his own age. Sure, it's because you're so terrific, but even *you* may be still more terrific when you have more years of maturity and experience behind you.

Some men love the intensity and enthusiasm of young girls—girls who supposedly aren't jaded and haven't "seen it all." But you want to be loved for yourself, not your sweet-young-thing innocence. Is your older man intimidated by marriageable career women? Does he revel in the hero worship you may be giving him? Are *you* using *him* because he has money, a car, an apartment, sophistication? Or because he's a father figure? Your caring may be genuine, but it can't hurt to question his motives and your own.

I'll talk about sex in the next chapter, but if you are becoming intimate with an older man, please note that if you're under sixteen or eighteen (depending on the state), it's not called sex, but statutory rape. And sometimes it is rape. Six in 10 girls who had sex before age fifteen report having been coerced into it—often by older men. Many fathers of babies born to teenage mothers are *not* teenagers themselves. Older men are also more likely to have a sexually transmitted disease than younger men.

Pretty soon, age gaps will hardly matter. Twenty-one? Twenty-five? Twenty-nine? Three adults. But the same gaps among eleven-, fifteen-, and nineteen-year-olds can mean batting in different ballparks.

Should You Date Someone from a Different Ethnic, Racial, or Religious Background?

I went out with a philosophical Spaniard for nearly four years. The idea of a Madrid marriage did occur to Juan and me. But I wondered if Spain's happy-go-lucky mañana mañana style would drive me up a wall. Would I get homesick for America? Would I be able to write well in English in Spain? (It worked for Hemingway, but he was Hemingway!) Bottom line: Would our love truly be enough to make up for my leaving family and friends an ocean away?

Maybe. Maybe not. Juan and I broke up for other reasons—but that's another story. The point here is that keeping a relationship in top form isn't a breeze under any circumstances (witness the divorce rate), and marrying someone of a different nationality, race, religion, or background can make harmony even harder.

Yet who's talking marriage? As for dating (and friendship), go out with whomever you want. Broaden your horizons. Gain insights from other people's perspectives. Expose yourself to other values and customs. I'm grateful for the years with my "Don Juan."

If your romance turns serious (or if your parents make life miserable), *then* ask yourself serious questions. Multiracial couples usually do encounter extra friction and conflicts. Do you have substantial doubts about the rocky road ahead? (Everybody has some doubts.) Do you love your guy for his personal qualities? (Or do you want to prove to yourself and the world that you are open-minded, color-blind, tolerant, and big-hearted?) Love can't always conquer all.

My parents got married when crossover marriages were much more taboo. Mom was born in Texas and Dad was born in Russia, and it worked for them.

Intermarriages are becoming increasingly common. Today more and more Asians and Hispanics are marrying outside their ethnic groups, and 1 out of 100 married couples in America is a black-white couple. About two million children now live in homes where the parents are of different races.

Ask your heart and your head what is right for you.

Saying No Nicely

All right, so there you are, relaxing, laughing, asking questions, and hoping you're charming Rob. But no. You're charming Elmer. And Elmer asks you out. (Goons tend to have impeccable taste.)

What do you do?

If he says, "You wouldn't like to go with me to the school car wash, would you?" and, indeed, you wouldn't, say no. Say it nicely, but say it fast. "I'm sorry, thanks for asking," is sufficient. If you say, "I'm studying that day," then Elmer may ask you out another day, and it would be cruel to show up at the car wash with someone else. So don't tell a lie you'll be caught in. If Elmer is an out-of-towner who doesn't know your friends, you could say, "Thanks, but my boyfriend wouldn't like that!" That's a white lie, but it spares his ego. If he gives you the creeps, don't give him a mixed message; don't say, "Oh, I would have loved to—maybe another time?"

What if Elmer is persistent? What if he asks you out five Saturdays in a row, and every time you say you're busy, he asks about the following week? What if he invites you to the prom and it's only September?

Most guys can take a hint, but some need you to spell out the deflating truth or they won't get it. If you must break the news to Elmer that he's not your type, be gentle. Say something like, "Elm, you're a good guy and I'm flattered by your calling, but I want us to be friends, OK?" You could even tell him that you admire his fun-loving spirit but he's just not right for you. Use tact, but make sure he gets the picture because you don't want to give him false hopes.

What if—miracle of miracles—your Ideal Boyfriend calls and asks you out for Friday, but you've made plans you can't break? Don't give him the "I'm sorry, thanks for calling" line, or he may interpret it as a polite brush-off. Be effusive. Say, "I'd adore seeing that movie with you but I can't miss my grandmother's eightieth birthday dinner. Could we go Saturday or another day?"

Perceptive guys learn to tell the difference between a don't-call-back no and a please-call-back no.

But why should they be the only ones to put their egos on the line? Even if you're too scared to ask him to a school play, you can still phone and ask about algebra homework. If he wonders whether you're more interested in him than in the assignment—so much the better. (Note: This doesn't mean you have carte blanche to call him three times a night. And if you're bold but he's cold, you have to accept this even though it's not the reaction you had hoped for.)

Twenty-Eight Things to Do Besides Meet at the Mall

The good news is that sometimes, just sometimes, the guy you like likes you, you start seeing each other, and presto—you become an item.

By now, you've gotten strikes and gutterballs, shared popcorn at the movies, watched videos, munched pizza, wandered the mall, and even played computer games and miniature golf. Running out of rendezvous? No! The fun has just begun.

When your guy says, "What do you want to do?" don't shrug your shoulders and say, "I dunno." That's not being pleasantly agreeable— that's boring! Whether you live downtown or in the country, have spending money or are broke, there are plenty of plans to make. (P.S. Many of these would be fun to do with girls, too.)

1. Study the portraits at an art museum and imagine what the people might have been like. Or check out other museums to find dinosaurs, antique autos, jukeboxes, wax figures, gems, cartoon art, costumes, and arrowheads.

2. Explore a college campus; attend a concert, film, or lecture.

3. Go to a farm and pick strawberries, apples, or pumpkins.

4. Bake chocolate chip cookies. Follow the recipe on the yellow Nestlé Toll House bag—but leave out the brown sugar, baking soda, and salt. (Trust me.) Deliciousness guaranteed. Give him some to take home.

5. Listen in on an interesting case at the courthouse; discuss how you would vote if you were jury members.

6. Pack croissants and jam in a basket and head east to a hilltop to witness the sunrise. Or meet just before sunset with a picnic, Frisbee, poetry book, or sketch pad.

7. Go to the races and watch cars, horses, sailboats, or runners speed to the finish line.

8. Sign up for a free introductory dance class at a studio. Or go skating together—holding hands required.

9. Browse at an antique store or rummage sale. Pick out one-of-a-kind gifts for each other.

10. Take karate or cooking lessons.

11. Visit a pet shop and fall for the kittens, puppies, bunnies, and lizards.

12. Check newspapers and bulletin boards to find out about concerts, country fairs, auctions, outdoor art shows, church bazaars, car shows, boat shows.

13. Plant an outdoor garden or a windowsill or potted herbs.

14. Have tea and crumpets at a fancy hotel.

15. Play tourist in the metropolis nearest you. Go to a skyscraper's observation deck and locate the landmarks below. If possible, take an architectural tour, a horse-and-buggy ride, or a boat tour. Or walk, walk, walk.

16. It's windy? Go fly a kite!

17. Raining? Stroll under one big umbrella, then head inside to play Monopoly, Scrabble, or cards.

18. Go to a zoo and pause at the aviary, snake pit, and monkey house. Or go to an aquarium, watch the sharks get fed, then figure out how the lionfish, ghostfish, and unicorn fish got their names.

19. Rent a bicycle built for two and head to the waterfall only you know how to find.

20. Splurge on a play—matinee or evening.

21. Many health clubs offer free classes to prospective members. Work up a sweat together!

22. Attend a professional football, baseball, soccer, hockey, basketball, tennis, or other sports game.

23. Is there a river or stream near you? Rent a canoe or rowboat, take along poles and bait, and go fishing.

24. Take advantage of a local business that offers free tours: from a newspaper plant or television station to a pretzel factory, paper mill, or stock exchange.

25. Feed the ducks and geese at a pond. Feed the sparrows and pigeons at a park.

26. Meet for breakfast at a diner or upscale restaurant. Order different items and split them half and half.

27. Take a walk at a botanical garden, conservatory, or arboretum and see how many trees and plants you can identify.

28. You live near a planetarium? Study the exhibit on constellations, and that night, grab a blanket and star-gaze. No planetarium? Find Orion anyway. And the Dippers. And maybe Mars.

The Way to a Guy's Heart Just Might Be My Cheesecake

I can't promise that. The fifties are behind us. But I *can* promise you that this recipe makes a mean cheesecake for him or your friends or family. So if all else fails . . .

Take 1½ pounds of cream cheese (that's 3 8-ounce packages) out of the fridge and let it soften.

Make a big graham cracker pie-shell crust. Recipes are on boxes of graham cracker crumbs, but here's what I do: Take 2 cups of crumbs plus ¼ pound (1 stick) of melted butter plus ⅓ cup of sugar and 1 large tablespoon of cinnamon. Mix together. Pour into a 9-inch pie pan, pat down the mixture hard and evenly to form a crust, and chill in a freezer for about 10 minutes. (Ready-made crusts are not as tasty or as big.)

Preheat oven to 375 degrees.

Make the filling: With a beater, blend the 1½ pounds of softened cream cheese with 1 cup of sugar. Mix in 3 eggs, one at a time. Add 1 teaspoon of vanilla and 1 tablespoon of lemon juice. Blend until smooth. Pour into the prepared crust.

Bake in a preheated oven for 35 minutes.

While you're waiting, mix 1 pint (a little less is OK) of sour cream with 2 tablespoons of sugar and 1 teaspoon of vanilla. When your kitchen timer (you have one, don't you?) rings, take out the cheesecake, turn the oven up to 475 degrees, and spread the sour cream mixture right on top of the hot cheesecake.

Return it to the 475-degree oven for 5 minutes.

Take it out, let it cool at least 15 minutes, then pop it into your fridge to chill for three or more hours before serving.

The cheesecake can be eaten as is or garnished with chocolate shavings, fresh strawberries, raspberries, or blueberries. *Bon appétit!*

(Now what can *he* cook to dazzle you?)

Nine Awkward Situations and How to Handle Them

Even the best evenings go awry.

Of course, some girls turn purple over nothing. If they need to go to the bathroom during intermission, they ignore nature's call, twist their legs, wriggle in the lobby, suffer through Act 2, and finally bolt from their date's car without so much as a good-night kiss. That's boneheaded. Instead, they could have simply said, "Excuse me, I'm going to the bathroom. I'll be right back." A guy won't be put off—he'll probably say "Good idea," and visit the men's room.

Then there are the girls who are too flustered to eat in front of guys. They fear the guy will think they're piglets or will laugh if they spill gravy on their sleeves. Question: Are you appalled that boys eat to stay alive? Question: Would you crack up uncontrollably if a boy got ketchup on his cuff?

When you're dealing with guys, it sometimes helps to ask yourself what you'd do if you were with your best friend. If you had to go to the bathroom or were sloppy with the soy sauce, you'd pull through. You'd take it in stride. So listen, if your package of Goobers flips upside down at the movie theater and they all go clattering down the aisle, laugh, don't cry.

Here are nine sticky situations.

1. You came to the game with a guy who likes you but whom you consider a friend. During half-time, you go alone to buy popcorn, and the guy you've adored for months appears, strikes up a conversation, and says, "Come watch the rest of the game with me." What do you do?

•Smile, talk, offer him some popcorn, and tell him you'd love to watch the game with him, but that you can't today because you came with your pal Matt. If you sparkle, he won't be discouraged. Who knows? His interest may even double: You're not only attractive and popular, but you're considerate, too. Feeling brave? Suggest that you sit together next week.

2. Watching fireworks at the amusement park was fun, but now you feel as if you're battling an octopus. You don't want to put him off entirely, but you don't want to go any further yet, either. And struggling to hold down his roaming hands has taken the fun out of kissing. What do you do?

•You could fiddle with the radio, apply fresh lipstick, ask about his childhood, announce that you're starving—but why not speak your mind? Tell him straight out that you like him, but you don't like feeling so pushed. If he's a decent person who cares about you, he'll adjust his pace to yours. If he continues the passion play, tell him you'd like to go home and don't go out with him again. His loss.

3. You've had a crush on him for weeks and this is your very first date, a double with a pair of his friends. After the movie, you all pile into your guy's car, which is parked on a side road. Suddenly the couple in the backseat grows quiet, the windows start steaming up, and you know it's not global warming. Your guy drapes his arm over your shoulders. You're torn: You feel attracted to him, but also self-conscious and rushed. What do you do?

•Realize that he, too, may be ill at ease. Perhaps he's feeling pressured by his backseat buddies. Suggest taking a walk or going for a bite to eat nearby. That way you can get to know each other better before taking the next step.

4. All week you've been psyched for your blind date. Your aunt gave you such a buildup about her colleague's son, you were expecting a cross between Adonis and your favorite rock star. But when the doorbell rings, you find yourself shaking the sweaty hand of a 200-pound boy with bifocals and braces. "Want to go dancing?" he lisps, and you think, "As if!" What do you do?

•Make the best of it. Suggest a movie and stay open-minded. Sometimes the king of the nerds can be a prince of a guy—or, at least, introduce you to a guy more your type. If you're friendly without leading him on, you'll feel good about yourself. Later, shake his clammy hand before he has a chance to try to kiss you. If he's already puckered up and lunging forward, turn your head so his lips land on your cheek. (P.S. Tomorrow you can rant at your aunt.)

5. He obviously likes you because he's asked you out every weekend for a month. But each evening ends the same way: You talk until midnight, then he leaves without a kiss. The anticipation is driving you crazy! You'd make the first move, but you're shy, too, and you've decided you don't want to initiate. Still, you can't go on meeting like this! What do you do?

•If you think he likes you only as a friend, try to appreciate the friendship for what it is. But if you're pretty sure he's just too timid to take action, subtly let him know you'd welcome his advances. Sit close to him, or if you're walking, brush against him gently. Leave your hand near his, or say, "Let me fix your collar." Linger before getting out of the car or at the doorway. Look into his eyes. Let your gaze wander briefly to his lips. Or give him a peck on the cheek. He'll take it as a go-ahead.

6. He's being so quiet you could scream. It's a twenty-minute drive back to your home, and you can't single-handedly keep the conversation going that long. Usually he's talkative, but tonight it's Monosyllable City. What do you do?

•Is he silent because he's angry or upset? Ask what's on his mind. Say, "You seem a little quiet. What's going on?" He might want to open up.

If you think he's just feeling shy, realize that he probably appreciates your breezy efforts to keep the conversation rolling. Ask friendly questions: "What's the best vacation you've ever taken?" "Do you remember when you first met your little brother?" "Who's the worst teacher you ever had?" What *would* you really like to know about him? Remember, too, that you don't have to be "on" all the time or fill up all the airwaves. Is silence golden? Well, silver at least, and it is natural.

7. Your parents don't like the guy you're going out with, and he senses it. The one time you invited him to dinner, the tension was chowder thick. Now, at a concert, he suddenly asks, "Your folks don't like me, do they?" What do you do?

•Let him know your parents criticize *all* your friends because they feel protective. (Then ask yourself if your polite explanation is true, or if there are legitimate reasons behind their coolness.) It is possible that your folks wish you'd spend more time with them or worry that you've been slipping in school, and they are unfairly using your guy as a scapegoat for other concerns.

To help everyone get along, remind your parents of your friend's strengths and accomplishments. And tell him about their interests. If he can get your dad talking about mystery novels and your mom talking about music, they may establish a rapport after all.

Before you meet *his* parents, make sure he smooths the way for you. It's better to ask his mother, "What do you enjoy most about being a realtor?" than to have to start from square one with the awkward, "Do you work?" First parental meetings usually go best when they are brief and informal.

8. You're having dinner together at an Italian restaurant. You've just taken a bite of linguini when your old boyfriend—and his entire family—stroll in and plunk down at the next table. Suddenly you can hardly keep track of what your guy is saying. What do you do?

• You could shovel down your noodles and make a run for it. Instead, just explain the situation, excuse yourself, and say a quick and gracious hello to your old beau and his family. Get it over with. Your date shouldn't object. Greeting your ex shows you're mature enough to remain on speaking terms with someone who meant a lot to you.

And if you're *not* on speaking terms? Explain your uneasiness, and discreetly shift your chair so you won't be facing that table: You want to concentrate on the him-and-now. After dinner, you could suggest having ice cream cones elsewhere for dessert—your treat.

9. A guy you like takes you to a boring party twenty miles from your home. After a few hours, you want to leave. He doesn't. You feel stuck because you came in his car, you don't know anyone else who could drive you home, and you don't want him to think you're a jerk for wanting to go already. What do you do?

• Since you like him, it might be worthwhile to stick it out a little longer. Summon your second wind and introduce yourself to two strangers, or start a new discussion with your guy about sports, family, movies, pets, school, news events. Yet your feelings count, too, so whether you have an official curfew or not, remind him that it's getting late. (You might even whisper that you'd hoped you two would have a moment alone before saying good-bye.)

If he wants to stay another hour and you want to leave now, agree to exit in thirty minutes. If thirty minutes comes and goes and he still refuses to budge—or if he's not willing to compromise in the first place—tell him you're going to find a safe way to leave. Call home. Call a friend. Call a cab. You're going out to enjoy yourselves, and you don't have to put up with a bad situation any more than he would.

Eleven Surefire Ways to Ruin a Romance

(No, silly, I don't recommend them.)

1. Be a policewoman: Now that he's your possession, don't let any female thieves near him.

•Wrong! Just because you want him doesn't mean everyone else does. Your heartthrob might be another girl's Elmer, and vice versa. Besides, if you play the smothering policewoman, your guy may bristle and play criminal—running in the opposite direction. Stop worrying. Relationships that are trusting and sturdy can withstand a few external distractions.

2. Play hard-to-get and other games.

•If you've been doing all the giving, calling, and caring, you may want to lean back to see if he'll lean forward. I won't argue. But if you get in the habit of trying to arouse jealousy, play mind games, or second-guess each other, conflicting messages will shoot back and forth, and your romance may become a jumble instead of a joy.

3. Talk about commitment on the first date.

•Bad idea. Don't worry so much about tomorrow that you hardly enjoy today. Neither of you should swear eternal loyalty to each other, anyway. Love is not a trap. If you start making him feel bad for not spending every second with you, you may end up with lots and lots of time on your hands. Remember: Pushy people push people away. As folk wisdom dictates: If you love someone, let him go. If he comes back, he's yours. If he doesn't, he never was.

4. Worry about his ex.

•She's his *ex*, remember? You're his now. Everybody is entitled to a past. Work on making this current romance as mutually satisfying as possible.

5. Be dependent: Now that you've paired off, you don't need anyone or anything else.

•Boring! A guy and girl can't be everything to each other. Don't let your love life become your whole life. Don't let it eclipse your other friends and activities. Besides, if you spend time apart, you'll have more to talk about when you're together.

You'll also be less broken up if you two ever break up. Going out with someone should add to your self-esteem, yet a girl who always depends on a guy may wind up feeling like a half-person.

6. Take him for granted.

•Some girls forget that relationships, like potted flowers, need to be taken care of. Other girls take their guys for granted because they figure, "If he likes me, he mustn't be as great as I'd thought." No matter how long you've been seeing a guy, if you still care, let him know.

7. Open old wounds.

•Suppose he did go out once with the class tease while you were away. You've rehashed the episode nineteen times since then, he's begged your forgiveness, and you've granted it. Now what?

Let it go. Get on with the present. Going over and over past bruises just prolongs the hurt.

8. Love him only when he's feeling cheerful and strong.

•Not nice. You may be most drawn to him when he's up and confident, but he needs you most when he's down and out. If he's a good and solid guy, don't be a fair-weather girlfriend. (If, however, you've come to realize that he's a moody, selfish, downbeat dog—you're not stuck for life.)

9. Get hung up on three little words.

•If one of you whispers "I love you" and the other isn't ready to echo the phrase, it doesn't have to be a problem. Some people are afraid of the words but not the feeling. Others drink two beers, get horny, and say "I love you" when they mean "I want you."

It's good to try to recognize the differences between "in love," "in like," and "in lust." However, as my poetic mother put it, it's not always necessary to "label it love or libel it lust." When my high school boyfriend and I were first going out, I wasn't ready to verbalize my emotions. I told my diary: *"We concluded that we have very strong affectionate feelings for each other. He calls it love. I call it nothing."* (By the way, I finally came around!)

If you profess love prematurely, your guy may panic or question the depth of your emotion. And if you two break up a month later, you may both feel more confused and distraught than if you hadn't given a name to your feelings.

10. Analyze the relationship to death.
•If you spend most of your togetherness time monitoring the progress of your relationship, rather than enjoying it, you'll sour it. Sometimes one evening of fun can do more to recharge a romance than three of heavy discussion.

11. Harbor unrealistic expectations.
•You're infatuated. Just as the music, movies, and magazines promised, it's heaven—for about two weeks. Then he criticizes your dear friend. And you blurt out that he's a snob. He acts sullen. You get bitchy. Should you scrap the relationship, figuring it has run its course?
No! Once you get past all the grand, magical stuff, you find the nitty-gritty of two imperfect individuals trying to connect with each other.

So don't set yourself up for disappointment. Don't put your guy on a pedestal, then frown when he falls off. Don't count on transforming him. No one is too good to be true. If you want your "main squeeze" to be thoughtful, funny, smart, athletic, and so cute that everyone does a double take, you're asking too much. (Do *you* meet those standards?)

I'm not saying you should settle for whatever guy comes along. You should expect to go out with a good guy who treats you well. But your love won't stay superintense every day. And it's OK for Prince Charming to muddy his white horse once in a while.

I could go on, but the point is this: Once you get a romance flying high, don't force it into a crash landing!

Breaking Up Without Breaking Down

Breaking up? Maybe you and your boyfriend can turn things around. Love is moody. Have several heart-to-hearts before you accept heartbreak and heartache.

Yet maybe, sigh, your waxing love has waned for good, and no one is to blame. Or you both realize that as much as you care, you just aren't each other's soulmate or future spouse. Not everybody you go out with is someone you'd want to go out with forever. Which means you'll probably survive more than one breakup in your life.

Bummer. Breakups are hell. In college, I remember looking out my third-story window onto the courtyard below and seeing the guy who'd just suggested we "cool things" flirting merrily with another girl. In grad school, breaking up with Juan hurt terribly because I simultaneously lost my boyfriend and best friend. Plus we both still harbored leftover love.

My high school honey and I? We broke up more than once. You've heard of false starts at track meets, right? Well, we had a few false ends. From my diary when I was sixteen:

> *I guess I was having my doubts. Apparently he was, too. He said he wanted to talk. He said the world is too big not to see other people. He was afraid of getting so serious.*
>
> *"Face it, our lives and friends are completely different."*
>
> *"But it hasn't mattered."*
>
> *"But it has."*
>
> *He asked if I wanted to give breaking up a try.*
>
> *"No, but I don't want you to feel obligated." By now, I was crying.*
>
> *"You really do care, don't you?" We kissed. "I love you; maybe I love you too much."*
>
> *We said good-bye.*
>
> *He stood in front of his car for a while, looking down and at me.*
>
> *Then he left. I sat on the grass in front of our house. Ten minutes later, I heard his rumbling Saab coming back!*
>
> *He said, "I was driving away and I said to myself, 'You stupid ass—what did you do that for?'"*
>
> *I smiled. "We gave it a try."*

Should we have broken up then and there? Perhaps. False ends are usually indicative of problems, and we eventually did part ways. Of course, reconciliation can be fun. (*"I'm falling in love all over again. Like when we first met. . . ."*) But dragging out pain is a drag.

Can *your* relationship be saved? Is it worth saving? Deep inside, you and your guy probably know when it's *sayonara* time. When the relationship is more exhausting than exciting. When costs outweigh pleasures.

If you ever break up with a guy because he is abusive or alcoholic, don't feel guilty. In many ways, you're doing him a favor because he may then have to confront his problems. Don't ever give a guy an ultimatum ("I'll break up with you if you don't . . . ") unless you are prepared to follow through.

How do you go about breaking up? Gingerly. The process can be likened to removing a Band-Aid. You can do it gradually, pulling each fine hair as you go. (Ooooooouuuuuch!) Or you can yank it off. (OUCH!!!) It hurts either way. Falling out of love is harder than falling in. As Pablo Neruda wrote, "*Es tan corto el amor, y es tan largo el olvido.*" ("Love is so brief, and forgetting is so long.")

As painful as breaking up is, however, remember that the end of one thing is the beginning of something else. And breaking up beats clinging to a threadbare, one-sided, or mismatched relationship.

Sometimes these insights come fast, sometimes not. Do tell yourself: If your love was meant to last, it would have. And that freedom has its frills: You've been missing out on the fun of flirting, playing the field, and spending time with your friends and yourself.

Among the other fish out there are sharks and minnows, but also lots of good catches. What initially charmed your ex will charm your next. Or who knows? What *irked* your ex may charm your next.

If you've been given the shaft, remember the bad times. After a breakup, we have a tendency to recall long talks and long kisses and to forget fights and not-so-hot feelings. His smoking irritated you? He was a tightwad? Great. Write down all the reasons behind your breakup and remember them as you grieve.

But do grieve. Tears help you heal, and you can't expect to be over him instantly. In fact, the hurt you feel now is a tribute to your love and your ability to love.

Breakups don't always come complete with explanations, and that can add to the confusion. If you and your guy can be gentle and honest with each other about why the curtain is closing, it may help your mutual growth and recovery. But too often, it doesn't work that way, and you're both left to puzzle it out on your own. You may even feel as if you were watching a movie and somehow missed the last scene.

Stay busy! You could feel sorry for yourself for weeks, but you have better things to do. Dress up and see your friends. (Remember—the ones you didn't neglect just because love entered your life?) Don't bicycle past places where you used to park. Don't listen to Your Song. Put away his photograph. Work out. Get your hair cut. Buy a shirt. Take up a new extracurric. Read a novel. Go to a movie. Write your grandmom. Cuddle your cat. Spend an evening with old friends—and I don't mean Ben & Jerry. It's okay to stay in bed for one whole day if you want—but then get up and at 'em.

At first, you'll see flashbacks and mull over your last conversations, but fill your time so you don't sink into too much self-pity, guilt, rage, or remorse. (A little is natural.) Try not to suffer from withdrawal for too long.

If you meet someone else right away, he'll lift your spirits. Yet it's best not to race into romance on the rebound (or to get involved with a guy who's doing that). Give yourself time alone first. Patch your broken heart before you give it away again. It's only fair to both of you. Sometimes relationships overlap, but that makes healing harder.

Can you two remain friends? Some former couples pull off that stunt. If you can swing it, more power to you!

I do recommend trying to end things in a peaceful, dignified way. Don't threaten, beg, bitch, or scream at him. Don't bad-mouth last week's Mr. Wonderful to your pals. Don't hope he'll see the light and come crawling back. (Or if *you* instigated the breakup, don't try to get back together if you know you'll just be ending things farther down the road.) You'll retain more self-respect if you can thank your guy for the good times, wish him the best, and move on.

(Then again, if he was a two-timing, double-crossing, total jerk about the whole thing and you want to blast him, I won't stop you. A loud breakup may help you deal with your anger. Or wait until you're alone; then punch pillows or tell all to your journal or best bud—a trustworthy local one or a faraway friend.)

Above all, don't conclude that love isn't worth it. Your broken relationship was not a waste of time. You enjoyed it and learned from it.

After you begin to feel stronger, get back into the ring. Not that there's anything wrong with going a long time without a boyfriend. But do check out the smorgasbord: Mario, Jeff, Bryson, Drew, Darryl, Pierre, Paul. . . . Variety is spicy. And trial and error isn't such a bad way to go.

Lasting Love

Some romances take nosedives, others wind down and die natural deaths, and a few last a lifetime.

Tonight over dinner, a woman told me about her high school reunion. She described a bunch of adults milling around a gym wearing name tags attached to photos of their former selves. "I saw three old boyfriends," she said. "Dull! Dull! Dull! Neither Jay nor Karl nor Danny appealed to me. Boy, I'm lucky I made it to Jeremy."

I tell you this because back in high school, she never imagined that being dumped by Jay, Karl, and Danny would be something she'd be thankful for one day. Yet love isn't always supposed to be forever.

Summer romances are especially notorious for being intense, wonderful, and short-lived. Why do so many sunny romances chill in the fall? Because you and your guy have less free time, you're back under the student-body microscope, you may live miles apart, and the starry infatuation stage may be about up by September anyway. If you want to try to keep the romance going, by all means do. A fling *can* last a lifetime. But most just become happy memories.

People change and drift in different directions. And great boyfriends don't always make great husbands or fathers, anyway. Be aware, too, that, to a certain degree, you may now be bewitched by love in general and not by Gregory in particular. Do you mostly adore Gregory, or do you mostly adore adoring and being adored?

There's no way to control how long a relationship lasts. For now, if you want your current love to continue, try to be friends first and foremost. Give each other room to grow—none of this yearbook signing "stay just the way you are" nonsense! Keep your cards on the table. Keep your humor about you. If the magnetism lasts and you remain compatible as you mature—if you grow up without growing apart—your love just may endure.

Getting married while you're a teen, however, is usually shortsighted. Teenage girls often envision the rosy side of marriage (a permanent date, a kitchen, your very own bed-for-two) and forget about the added responsibilities of running a home (laundry, vacuuming, checkbook balancing). If you have superhigh expectations of what a marriage is, look around at the married couples you know—your parents, relatives, neighbors, friends' parents. That's marriage: for better and for worse. Marriage can be marvelous, but it doesn't make other troubles go away. And marrying to escape problems often just causes more problems.

One joke says that marriage isn't a word—it's a sentence. A Jewish proverb puts it this way: "Love is a sweet dream; marriage, an alarm clock." Of course, marriage should be and can be wonderful—but not if you latch on to the wrong guy or make a decision prematurely.

The younger a couple marries, the higher the chance of divorce. The overwhelming majority of teens who marry when one or both are under eighteen end up divorced. In America, 97 percent of women and 99 percent of men between the ages of fifteen and nineteen are unmarried. Most states require parental consent before a minor can get married.

The average marrying age for women is 27—five years older than it was in 1971. How can you know now whom you'll want to eat breakfast with when you're fifty-nine? Take your time before choosing a life partner! Why jump from life-with-parents to life-with-husband anyway, without first going to college, getting a job, and enjoying the world alone or with roommates your age? If you marry well, you'll probably spend most of your life married—which is great—but it's also an argument for dating different people now.

I have a friend who called off her wedding at the last minute. I admired her guts. As she put it, "Better to be mortified this month than miserable for years."

Before you marry anybody, soon or someday, make sure you thoroughly (thoroughly!) discuss your attitudes about money, children, sex, health, housework, education, religion, where to live, personal goals, and everything else under the moon. You're not both going to live with one of your parents, are you? (Their roof, their rules.)

Should you live together someday? It's up to you. If you do, may I suggest a one-year limit to the arrangement? When the time's up, marry . . . or set each other free. I know too many women who spent their twenties living with a man who suddenly realized that, gosh, while he liked playing house, he wasn't interested in actual *commitment*. By then, the woman was hearing the tick tick tick of her Baby Clock, and the man was off playing Peter Pan with someone else. Fair? No. Nature never was.

Obviously, you don't have to think about marriage yet. But women in their twenties should begin to step back, look at the Big Picture, and be realistic about career, marriage, motherhood—and the enormous challenge of finding a balance.

Love Notes

LOVE AT FIRST SIGHT OR WHEN THE CHEMISTRY IS RIGHT:
When Rob and I met, a zing definitely flashed between us. Yet I still say love at first sight only holds up if it survives a second glance, a third stare, and a fourth cross-examination. Intrigue at first sight? *That* I'll buy. Falling in love is lovely, but so is stepping in, and it's OK if you and your guy didn't feel immediate thunder.

HE SAID HE'D CALL BUT HE DIDN'T:
Guys do that. They say, "I'll call you" at the end of a date even when they won't. It's not to string you along. It's their way of being polite. Like

when we say, "Thanks, I had a good time" even though the evening turned out so awful that it would have been better to have stayed home and changed the kitty litter. Of course, your guy might be shy. Or he might call in a few weeks. If you can't stand the waiting game, call *him*. At least you'll find out where you stand.

THERE'S NO SUCH THING AS A FREE DINNER:
If he wants to pay, I won't quibble. Just don't order the most or least expensive entrée on the menu. But why not offer to share expenses or invite him out once in a while? Say, "My treat." (That's more graceful than "Let me pay.") Don't let a guy spend big bucks on you if afterward one of you is going to feel you owe him $24.99 of hot-and-heavy making out. If you invite *him* to the theater or a prom, let him know ahead of time that you plan to treat (or that you hope it's OK to split expenses).

EVEN IF YOU FIND MR. RIGHT, THINGS WILL GO WRONG:
Not such bad news, really. It keeps you on your toes.

CHIVALRY IS ALIVE AND KICKING:
Feminism is great, but I also like when a man holds a door open for me, and I make a point of holding doors open for men—and women. If a guy helps you on with your coat, don't lecture him on women's rights. If he opens the car door for you, don't give him a speech; get in, lean over, and unlock his door for him.

LOVE AND LOOKS:
If you run into your crush when you're wearing sweats, don't cringe. Smile. He looks cute in *his* sweats, doesn't he? On the other hand, do always try to look presentable. And if you know you'll be seeing him, make an extra effort to look decent. Love makes people blossom, but then many take it for granted and go to seed. Beware: Love is blind, but not for long!

GUYS GET NERVOUS, TOO:
Once my brother Eric had an 8 P.M. date with our neighbor Amy. He came into my room at 7:45 to ask, "Do you think I should be a few minutes early, right on time, or a few minutes late?" I said I didn't think it mattered. But that exchange mattered to me—it taught me to relax because guys quake, too.

THERE IS SUCH A THING AS BEING TOO HONEST:
Yes, you should keep the lines of communication open, speak your mind, and not lie. But no, you don't have to name names and tell your boyfriend precisely how far you went with each of your former honeys. Don't unburden yourself by lumping the burden on him. You also don't need to share every little thought that pops into your head or tell him how you hate your fat thighs and fantasize about liposuction. (Blecch!) *You* decide where to draw the honesty line. Love is sometimes saying what you think the other person wants to hear instead of the truth, and sometimes saying the truth instead of what you think the other person wants to hear.

WHOEVER SAID A GIRL CAN'T GIVE A GUY A FLOWER?
Not me.

LIFE CAN BE EXHILARATING EVEN WHEN YOU'RE NOT IN LOVE:
Absolutely! After all, *you* count too. In *Reviving Ophelia,* Mary Pipher, Ph.D., wrote this about a girl: "Suddenly she cared more about being liked by athletes than about being an athlete." I hope you strive to define yourself by who you are not whom you're with.

LONG-DISTANCE LOVE:
I've been there. It can work. But exchanging eloquent love letters that skim above daily strife makes it easy for you both to romanticize the relationship. When you're actually about to see each other again, allow for an awkward period of getting reacquainted.

GOING OUT WITH MORE THAN ONE GUY AT ONE TIME:
I've been there, too, and it's not as much fun as you'd imagine. It takes a lot of psychic energy really to care about two guys—and I, for one, never have been a fan of roller-coaster rides. If you think you and your guys can handle a triangle, OK. But if you sneak around, you may get caught, and you'll probably feel guilty. What about just casually dating more than one guy? Sure, why not?

LOVE BETWEEN WOMEN:
You are not alone if you suspect or somehow have always known that you're more attracted to girls than to guys. It is not clear what deter-

mines sexual orientation, but having crushes or falling in and out of love happens whether you are straight, lesbian, gay, or bi. This chapter was written about girls and guys, but if you are lesbian, I hope some of it had relevance for you. As Rita Mae Brown wrote, "The only queer people are those who don't love anybody." In the next chapter, I write about homosexuality and coming out, and I provide hot lines for getting more information.

Kissing, Etc.

I'll keep this brief because some of you may not be kissing for a few years, and others of you may already have your kissing style down pat. When the time is right, just take off your glasses and be soft, sensual, and creative. Kissing expresses caring. Don't feel compelled to break any kissing-without-breathing records or to jam your tongue into the guy's mouth if you don't want to. Beware of beard burn. And (uh oh, here comes a dumb joke) don't ever say to a vampire, "Wanna neck?"

My high school boyfriend and I sometimes argued about PDA. He took offense because I didn't want to play kissy-face in public. Once he even asked, "What are you going to do on your wedding day in front of all those people?"

Decide how you feel about the *whos, hows, wheres,* and *whens* of kissing. Kissing and cuddling go a long way. Sex doesn't have to enter the picture for a long, long time.

Television and movies make it look as though some adults rush from making out to making love. Some do. Yet instant sex is often sound and fury signifying nothing. And many adults miss all the kissing, hugging, back-rubbing, freckle-hunting, and hand-holding. Many also can't get beyond short-lived passion. And many are not careful and wind up with an unwanted pregnancy or disease.

How did *you* first find out about intercourse? Did Olivia tell your whole table one day at lunch? Did you stumble on a racy book when baby-sitting or learn at a slumber party? Did your mother sit you down to discuss The Facts of Life? Did it suddenly all make sense when you were watching a nature show on PBS or when you were outside and saw two chipmunks mating? We'll talk about sex next, but first, time for some love letters . . .

Dear Carol ...

Dear Carol,

I'm 16 and I'm too shy to talk to guys. I can't bring myself to say any-thing, even to boys I like, even when they say hi first.

Judging from my mail, zillions of girls are shy. (I was, too.) Yet if a boy says hi and you don't, he may not know you're shy—he may think you're stuck-up or that you don't like him. Even the poised and popular get bashful, but they somehow manage to untie their tongues. You can, too. Saying hi back is easy. Even if your heart is racing and your knees are knocking, you can eke out a pitiful two-letter hi. Getting beyond hi is a little harder, but think ahead about what to say. Anything from "I like your shirt" to "I saw a great movie" to "You have a good accent in Spanish" to "Did you hear about the earthquake / Supreme Court decision / upcoming concert?" Start practicing on people who make you less nervous. Say "Nice earrings" to a friend, teacher, neighbor, librarian, or saleswoman, and just watch how easy it is to get a conversation rolling. Next thing you know, you'll compliment your crush, he'll smile and say thanks, and you'll *want* to come out of your shell.

Dear Carol,

I want somebody (anybody) to go out with me at my school. But I'm too shy. Help!

'Scuse me? Being shy is one thing. Being indiscriminate is another. Figure out which guys you like most and why. Then get in there with the smiles and hellos.

Dear Carol,

To meet guys, everybody always says, "Join the newspaper or yearbook or choir." Well, I go to a private all-girls school. How about some advice to us for a change?

If your choir is predominately soprano, check out the guys beyond your school walls. Join the mixed choir at church or go on the outings your synagogue sponsors. Go to dances or plays at "brother" or coed schools. Study in the town library, work at a local ice cream shop, or volunteer at a food pantry or hot line. Hit the mall or the Y or plan a party. Organize a Walkathon fund-raiser for the homeless and do it with boys' schools. Write an article for your paper about what girls and boys think of single-sex education—and interview boys to find out! Summer? Sign up with a coed camp or travel-abroad program or try to get a job in a busy place.

Dear Carol,

Whenever I see this guy Matt, my heart starts pounding. We look at each other in class, and I think he likes me, but why doesn't he ask me to go out with him? One day at lunch, he sat beside me. I almost had a heart attack. He took my orange and put it in my chili. I picked up his orange and put it in his chili. We both laughed and laughed. Later in class, he was poking this girl Amanda in the side and she was laughing like it was the greatest thing that ever happened to her. I felt so jealous. But when he did it, he was looking at me. Sign me . . . wonderfully dazed and confused.

What lobster and champagne can do for an older couple, chili and oranges can do for a younger couple. Sounds like Matt likes you. The trick, however, is to enjoy a budding romance as it develops instead of trying to push it from stage to stage. Most twelve-, thirteen-, and fourteen-year-old boys aren't ready to declare love or go public with feelings. Slow down, and relish the ride.

Dear Carol,

This boy in my class and I are starting to like each other more than as just friends. He even said so. All my friends told me to write him a letter and ask him if he would go with me. I was sure he would say yes. But when he gave back the letter, it said, "Not now, maybe later." I felt like a moron. Do you think he will stop liking me?

Probably not, but I still recommend enjoying a relationship instead of rushing to label it. Most boys would rather flirt outside the school spotlight. And though many girls like the added status of a guy's affection being official—that kind of pressure often scares guys away. Next time, instead of cornering (and embarrassing) a boy, just put up with the suspense a little longer.

Dear Carol,

About one month ago at Skateworld, I bumped (literally) into this incredibly cute guy. I apologized, but he just smiled the most wonderful smile and skated away. Soon after that I had to go home (I was with my friend's family), and now I can't stop thinking about him. I'm always daydreaming. I can't even concentrate on school. At night I think about him, too. I just know he was perfect, and I'm in love!

Are you in love or are you obsessed? Was he a perfect mate or a perfect stranger? (No one is perfect—not him, not me, not you.) That moment at the rink may have romantically awakened you, but having a crush is no reason to let grades slip. Instead of projecting stellar qualities on the mystery skater, you'd be better off getting to know the guys in your school or neighborhood (popular ones *and* as-yet-to-be-discovered ones). Stuck on the smiler? Maybe you can find him again at Skateworld, and this time talk to him—maybe even invite him to have hot chocolate. He might say yes (hurray!) or he might say, "My girlfriend wouldn't like that." Either way, you'll find out fast whether he's worth all the daydreams.

Dear Carol,

I went to a dance and met this guy. I got his phone number, and my friend started pressuring me to phone him. Eventually she phoned him pretending to be me. He wanted to go out, but I wished he had said it to me, not her. I told my friend I didn't like it that she called him, but she said, "I got you a date, didn't I?"

Your friend had no business impersonating you on the phone. If she meant well, you can tell her why you don't want her manipulating your love life. If you think she was up to no good, however, beware. Some pals are poison. In the meantime, call the guy again or meet him in a public place (since you don't really know him or his background) and find out more about each other—and your own feelings.

Dear Carol,

All my friends are going out with guys, and I feel like a total loser.

Being attached does not make you a winner, and being unattached does not make you a loser. Next time you feel melancholy, list all the girls in your class and try to write a boyfriend's name next to each girl's name. Voilà: proof positive that everyone else has not paired off. Even girls with boyfriends sometimes feel bored or mad or sad or full of doubt. And some worry that they are missing out on the freedom and fun of hanging with girlfriends and flirting with whomever they choose.

Dear Carol,

There's this boy I like as a friend, but he told his friends he had a crush on me. He's not real popular and the next day, word was all over school that we were going out. Everybody keeps asking me, "Do you really have a crush on Brendan?" And I say no. But they tease me and I feel as if I should hit Brendan on the head and say, "I AM NOT YOUR GIRLFRIEND!"

Don't do it. The poor guy has good taste, and his public rejection is penance enough. Relax. Rumors never last.

Dear Carol,

My boyfriend and I are fighting because I chat with boys on-line. It's just harmless stuff, but I don't know how to tell him to stop worrying.

How would you feel if he chatted with girls on-line? Would you be amused? Interested? Threatened? His mixed feelings are natural and show he cares. So don't belittle him—one real boyfriend (if he's terrific) is worth several cyberbuddies. On the other hand, if your boyfriend is full-throttle jealous, that can be a problem. (You are entitled to talk to other boys, electronically or face-to-face.) For now, reassure him of your affection for him, spare him the details of your chat sessions, and help boost his self-esteem by telling him what you like most about him. (And remember: Never give out your real name or number during those "harmless" chats.)

Dear Carol,

I've liked this boy since the second day of school, but I don't know how to tell him that I like him.

Don't tell him. Show him. Instead of putting him on the spot, just smile, sit by him, pay attention to him, compliment him, ask questions, and start noticing whether he's talking and smiling back. He is? Hip hip hurray! He isn't? Accept this and cut your losses. (Who needs an unenthusiastic boyfriend?) Be patient and before long, someone you like will like you back.

Dear Carol,

I went to a friend's boy-girl party where only couples were invited. We played truth-or-dare. Every couple got dared to kiss each other on the lips or cheek. Everyone kissed on the lips (for the first time) except two couples. We were one of them. I didn't think that my boyfriend or I were ready. My friends say kissing isn't a big deal, but I'm not sure. Is kissing a big deal?

Yes. And if you take your time and wait until you do feel ready for that first kiss, it will be more meaningful than if you had simply succumbed to peer pressure and gone along with the crowd. Keep trusting yourself.

Dear Carol,

I'm 13 and very, very shy. There's this one boy I've really really liked for four years. But he barely knows I exist. I only get up the courage to call him once in a great while, and when I do, I run out of things to say. He never really joins in or asks me anything. On the last day of school, I gave him a letter. It told him how much I like him. I also wrote my phone number and told him to call if he had the chance. Well, the summer is almost over and not one call. My mom and all my friends are sick of hearing about him. They say I should give up on him, but I just can't. He seems like my whole life.

Don't let a guy become your whole life—especially when he's showing so little interest. When the writing is on the wall, it's best to read it. Shy? You told your crush you were interested. For many guys, knowing a girl cares is all the welcome mat they need. But this guy is not responding. That's a shame. Yet it'd be more of a shame to spend four more years worrying about someone who is not worrying about you. When it comes to love, persistence doesn't always pay off. There are over ten million *other* teenage boys in the United States alone, and it's time to stop being fixated on the one who is not returning your calls. I say: Give up on him without giving up on love. Someone more deserving will notice you soon.

Dear Carol,

I am 13 and I have just one question. How do you French-kiss? My boyfriend and I have kissed, but we haven't Frenched yet. I have the feeling he knows how, but the problem is, I don't. So if you would write down the details of how French-kissing starts and ends and how to hold him in the process, it would be helpful. But I need the information very soon so please HURRY!!! Thanks.

Girls nationwide are panicking about puckering. But guess what? There are no rights and wrongs to kissing. So relax. If he explores your mouth with his tongue, you can gently do the same . . . if you want to. How to hold him? Do what comes naturally. Put your hands on his back, neck, shoulders—whatever seems comfortable. Remember, too, that most guys don't want girls who have been fine-tuning their kissing on the entire hockey team. A boy won't hold it against you if you're a little nervous—he probably is, too.

Dear Carol,

I am only eleven and I am totally crazy about a forty-three-year-old man. I met him because my dad is his supervisor at work. I am afraid that if my dad found out I liked him, he wouldn't let me go on walks with him anymore. See, I meet him at his house and then he takes me to Taco Bell. Should I keep doing this?

Whenever you think, "I hope my parents don't find out," that should tip you off that something is . . . off. Meeting this middle-aged man at his home sounds inappropriate and potentially dangerous. It's one thing to have a crush on an older guy. It's another to have secret private meetings with him. Read the next chapter and please be careful. If he touches you intimately, he'd be breaking the law—and compromising your physical and emotional health.

Dear Carol,

I have a semiproblem. I've been going out with this guy for almost three months. Now I don't know. I'm not trying to be mean, but I'm kinda getting tired of him. I haven't felt like talking to him in a few days. Most of the time I've been busy (really!) but I may be busy all summer. Help! I'm afraid if I tell him, he'll hate me forever. Maybe I'm too young to go with anyone—that's what my mom would say!

Not every romance is supposed to last forever. Some girls are so hell-bent on landing a boyfriend, they hate to admit (even to themselves) that the guy wasn't worth all the fuss, that the romance has run its course, that the twosome got tiresome. There's no crime in wanting out of a relationship, and if it's time to write a Dear John letter, do so. Or be tactful and direct. Say you feel too young to be going out exclusively with anyone. Say you hope you can stay friends. While it's not sporting to deep-six a relationship right before finals or The Big Game or right after the guy's parents announce a separation, there's no point in spending weeks spinning your wheels in a relationship that's going nowhere.

Dear Carol,

I just read the love chapter of your book and I cried all the way through it. About three months ago, I broke up with my first real boyfriend, and I haven't had another since. Last night I went to a dance and he was there. It hurt so much to see him dancing with other girls. Even though I danced with other guys, I had the most miserable feeling inside me. We used to have something really special, but we just grew further and further apart. I miss him so much. We never really said good-bye. One night when we went skating, I knew it was almost over. But we never officially broke up. He said he'd call me but he didn't. It's been three months now, and I'm not over him at all. Will it ever get any better? My mom says, "There will be other people," but who is she kidding? It took me almost seventeen years to get him.

Will it get any better? Yes. It took almost seventeen years to launch your love life; it may take just a matter of months to keep it going. It is difficult to get over a first love. But your first love needn't be your last. Stay busy and try to remember the bad times as well as the good ones. After a breakup, you can spend months biking by your ex's house, poring over old photos, dialing his number and hanging up, and feeling as mixed up as a Picasso portrait. Or you can do some pining, nestle up with all your old Beanie Babies, and then dry your eyes and decide, "Enough is enough." I'm for moving on instead of letting your life come to a standstill. Besides, as Tennyson put it, "'Tis better to have loved and lost than never to have loved at all." If you think you need some official "closure," consider calling or writing him to say that you're hurt but you're healing, or, if possible or necessary, talk to a counselor. You are able to love and you will love again.

Dear Carol,

Last summer I went to Europe for two weeks with some friends. I met a man who was 26. I was 16. We shared one day together. It was the most wonderful time I had ever had in my life. I knew I was falling in love and that it wasn't just a one-night stand. We both cared for each other a lot. He meant everything he said and wasn't playing with my feelings. I ended up having sex with him—I knew I was ready. The next morning he dropped me off at the hotel, and we kissed and hugged and cried and didn't want to let go. At least I didn't. He promised to write and at first he did. But then I started getting letters only once a month. And then none at all. Last week and the week before I telephoned and a lady answered and I hung up. It's now been nine months since we've seen each other and I still feel very strongly about him. I even cry myself to sleep wishing I could be with him again. I would have died for him, I loved him so much.

The Wizard of Oz told the Tinman, "Hearts will never be practical until they are made unbreakable." Too true! I don't know where we would all be without waterproof mascara! But the thing is, while I feel sad for you, I also hate to see you spending more time crying over a guy than you did going out with him. You would have died for him you loved him so much? C'mon. You shared one day and a handful of letters. A lot can happen fast, but you're too young to spend all your energy looking backward instead of forward. Maybe you're crying not just for him but for lost innocence and a bruised ego. OK. Recognize that. And since he's far away, it's easy to idolize him. Accept that, too. But now, do yourself a favor and change the channel! He's moved on and you should, too. Breakups are extra hard when couples have been intimate. At sixteen, you may not have been as emotionally ready for intimacy as you thought. Sex, after all, comes with its own complications.

4 SEX

What You Should Know Before Saying Yes

❀

If you're not yet having sex—three cheers. If you are, I hope that you don't have sex for the wrong reasons: Your friend is involved in an X-rated romance or your sister has already done it or your boyfriend is putting on the pressure or you think you gain points if you score.

Sex should someday become a pleasurable, meaningful, guilt-free part of your life. But sex before you're ready or sex with the wrong guy is no fun—and can be dangerous. So proceed with caution. There are good reasons why you should wait.

This chapter is for those who are already sexually active and for those who intend to be virgins until their wedding night. It gives the lowdown on contraception, pregnancy, abortion, self-stimulation, sexually transmitted disease, homosexuality, rape, incest, and other topics you may wonder about.

To Do It or Not to Do It: That Is the Question

Once upon a time, unless you were married, you didn't want anybody to think you'd gone all the way. Now lots of teens don't want anyone to think they haven't. Years ago, girls couldn't say yes. Now many can't say no. Back then, some dreaded the thought of being sweet-sixteen-

and-never-been-kissed. Now some fear they'll be sweet-sixteen-and-never-been-____.

Let's just say too many girls are forgetting that virginity is not something to get rid of or feel ashamed of. Too many are feeling rushed.

If you are a virgin, you may be asking yourself if you are ready for sex. Yes? No? Maybe so? It's a tricky question because it brings up many other questions.

- Do you feel free to say no?
- Are you responsible enough to use birth control every time and mature enough to have a baby or an abortion if it fails?
- Is he responsible enough to wear a condom to protect you both from sexually transmitted diseases?
- If having sex goes against your parents' values, can you handle doing something they (or you) consider wrong?
- Do you love the guy, and does he love you?
- Are you two friends and not just partners in passion?
- Will you feel good about the decision the next day?
- Have you weighed the pros and cons?
- Will it mean as much to him as it will to you?
- Do you truly desire him physically? (Most girls don't feel intense sexual desire in their early teens.)
- Could you still reach your goals if you got pregnant?

I'd want to answer all yeses on that miniquiz before saying yes to any guy. Sex at any age before you're ready is a bad idea. It's better to let sex be something to look forward to. The suspense and wanting and anticipation make the eventual act more special.

If you can wait, wait. If you have doubts or are ambivalent or think you would have regrets, wait. If you think having sex is the way to get or keep a boyfriend, wait. If you think your decision is based on wanting to rebel or wanting to conform, wait. If you would freak out if the condom broke, wait. If you haven't become an expert in birth control and sexually transmitted diseases, wait.

What if your boyfriend is pressuring you? You're both in love and have been petting for months, and he says he's frustrated out of his mind? What if *he's* ready but you're not?

First of all, saying no to a boy can mean saying yes to yourself. And heartless though this may sound, nobody ever died of "blue balls." It doesn't maim a guy to have an erection and then not come (have an orgasm). That happens to him when he sees a sexy movie or thinks about bikinis during class. (I was sixteen when I wrote in my diary, *"Judy and I were discussing erections. Can boys calm down or do they have to let it out? Eric [my brother] enlightened me that they can calm down."*) Second, lots of guys would prefer the frustration of not making love to the frustration of not kissing, so it's unfair for them to make you feel so guilty. (His relief is not your responsibility.) Third, if you have sex for his sake, you're shortchanging yourself; you should be making love *with* him—not *to* him or *for* him. Sex goes both ways. It's not one person letting the other do things or one owing the other something. Fourth, many guys feel it's their duty to play offense while you play defense. Your boyfriend may be no more experienced than you and may even be expecting you to set limits.

Lines? Some guys use a variation of the ancient "You would if you loved me." You can reply, "You wouldn't insist if you loved me." A guy who doesn't care enough to be patient and respect your point of view doesn't care enough. Or he might argue, "Everybody else is." Fine. Why isn't he with everyone else? Or he might try the old, "We might die tomorrow." True. But we probably won't. And the only way to stay sane is to have confidence about the future: your own and the world's.

Beware: Drinking or getting high together may make you less certain of where you stand. Don't dilute your principles. Don't blur your boundaries. If you mean no, say it—seriously, not coyly. Let him know that your refusal is not a rejection of him. Sure, you are attracted to him. Sure, you have the urge to merge. But sorry, sex goes against your values and is risky and you just aren't ready.

Having intercourse means literally and figuratively opening yourself up to someone else. That's a Big Deal. Even if you're not a virgin, it's still a Big Deal—it's always a Big Deal. If you went all the way once with someone, you don't have to do it again with him or anyone else unless you want to.

Are you concerned about what you think your friends think? Believe it or not, virgins in your school are probably the silent majority. Seventy percent of fifteen year olds are virgins, and at age sixteen, over half the girls are virgins. By seventeen, it's about fifty-fifty, but the scale doesn't tip until age eighteen. Most of your peers wait until their mid-to-late teens. And 1 in 5 never have intercourse during their teen years. In other words: Everyone is *not* doing it.

Once you've said yes to someone, it is harder to say no the next time. It also becomes harder to sort out how you feel about the guy. And if you and he do break up, (as most teen couples do) the split may be more painful and confusing. Also consider this: Some couples aren't as sexually compatible as others. What if sex isn't so great with you and Ned? Will your relationship go down the tubes?

Girls who do have sex should be discreet. To kiss and tell is all very well, but it's wiser to kiss and shut up. I'm amazed at how much I knew in high school about people I shouldn't have known anything about. My diary is peppered with tidbits (names changed), such as this: *"Lance Harmon and Polly Shoor screwed when she was super-drunk"* and *"Mike is very upset with Diane for telling that they went to second. He found it 'intimate and personal.' Diane did, too, but she told Jen who told Carol who told Judy who told Steve who is best friends with Mike and mentioned it to him."*

So if you aren't going to keep your legs crossed, at least keep your mouth shut! Then if gossips gossip, tune them out. "Tease"? "Slut"? "Prude"? Labels are idiotic. Try not to use them or listen to them. Some nice girls do and some nice girls don't.

Talking to Parents About S-e-x

Don't assume your parents are up on the latest about contraception or STDs (sexually transmitted diseases). But don't assume they're hopelessly naive either. You didn't get here by immaculate conception, you know. Many kids and parents don't talk about sex and don't want to. But since most teenage pregnancies are unplanned and 1 in 4 teens gets an STD each year, it would be better if everyone were franker and more informed.

Are your parents into playing ostrich? Or are they waiting for you to bring up the subject? For parents, figuring out when to tell you about the Facts of Life is like figuring out when to tell you about Santa Claus. Parents want to preserve their children's innocence, but they don't want them to be the last innocents on the block.

If you want to broach the subject, here are some ways. While perusing the newspaper, say, "AIDS is really scary, isn't it?" In the car, mention, "A girl in my class went on the Pill so her periods would be less painful." While watching TV or a movie, say, "Sex, sex, sex. What about birth control?" Over dishes, say, "I was reading this chapter about sex, and I can't believe one million teen girls get pregnant each year."

Your mom or dad may be surprisingly candid or helpful. Or they may be uncomfortable and disapproving. Are there other adults—relatives, teachers, godparents, or friends' parents—you can talk to?

It's hard to be both a perfect daughter and a perfect girlfriend, and asking your parents to bestow their blessings on your sex life may be asking too much. Yes, some moms do help their daughters get birth control devices. But most don't. Most feel awkward about the whole subject and don't want to feel cornered into approving of what you may be doing. Even if they *can* handle it without flipping out, they may think that it's not OK for them to say it's OK.

If you are a virgin and intend to stay that way until marriage, tell that to your parents—put their minds at ease. If you think they already suspect that you are not, casually mention that Responsibility is your middle name. (I hope it is!)

Ideally, you and your parents won't have The Talk. You'll have many talks over many years. But not every family is ideal.

What if you no sooner say, "I was reading this chapter about sex—" than your dad says, "What? Gimme that!" and wings this book out the window? Then I'm sorry for the stupid suggestion and I'm glad you were able to join me through page 128.

Do-It-Yourself Orgasms

I have nothing against masturbation, but I hate the word. It sounds so clinical. About as sexy as the word *genitalia*. Plus *masturbation* conjures up some of the leftover hogwash that people used to preach: Touch yourself and you'll go blind! crazy! both!

The fact is, if you're clueless about your clitoris, masturbation is a perfectly healthy and acceptable way to learn about your body.

More teen boys than teen girls masturbate regularly, but the girl who has discovered that stimulating her clitoris or clitoral area can bring pleasure and relieve tension is far from rare. I write this not so you'll jump into bed with yourself once you get to the last paragraph. I write it so you'll know there is nothing shameful or even unusual about exploring and arousing your own body. You're not guilty; you're normal.

Some "sexperts" even argue in favor of self-stimulation. Alone, a girl can learn how to climax and then feel confident about her ability to have an orgasm. Later with a partner someday, she may be more apt to come or better able to show him how to help her come. That beats feeling frustrated or worrying that you're frigid or thinking you're the only one who has never felt the rhythmic throbbing and doesn't know what the fuss is about. Masturbation also makes more sense than having sex when you're in lust but not love.

Some girls worry that they are "spoiling themselves"—they fear they'll never come "the regular way" with a guy once they are used to manual stimulation. Yet only a minority of young women regularly reach orgasm during intercourse without additional stimulation of the clitoris. Some macho lovers may feel that if the friction going on between his penis and your vagina isn't enough to make you come, it's your fault. More mature and understanding men may be eager to help you climax by touching your sensitive clitoris and clitoral area before, during, or after intercourse.

Some girls find their own private orgasms may be more intense than orgasms with a lover. No crime in that. Sex with a caring partner is still more gratifying than sex by yourself.

I don't mean to be making a sales pitch for masturbation. But girls are lucky. They can do it without making a mess. And solo sex can't make you pregnant or give you a disease. So if you've already discovered that you can give yourself an orgasm alone—you don't have to apologize. Because it's not so terrible to love thyself. (In Woody Allen's movie *Love and Death,* a countess praises his sexual prowess, and he says, "I practice a lot when I'm alone.")

Sex? Who Me?

I remember the June night when my boyfriend first suggested we make love. I was stunned. I'd thought about it in the abstract, and we'd done our share of kissing, but somehow it had never occurred to me that sex—real-life stark-naked, get-down-to-it sex—had anything to do with me, with us. It's all in my diary:

> *We were lying down in the grass and he said, "How long have I known you?"*
>
> *"Six months, ten days."*
>
> *"Loved every minute of it."*
>
> *I kissed him and said, "You're so nice. Everything you say and do is nice."*
>
> *"Do you think making love to me would be nice?"*
>
> *"Yes. Wait. What? No. What?"*
>
> *"You didn't catch that, did you?"*

"I guess not."
"Why not?"
"I don't know."
"You must have a reason."
"I'm only fifteen. I'm not ready."
"When will you be ready?"
"I don't know."
"Best answer I've heard from you yet."
I pushed him away and laughed.
He said, "You're not serious, but I am."

It left the evening with a question mark. I am lucky. He is nice—but too fast. I'm not that bitterly opposed to losing my virginity—but not at fifteen. And what about pregnancy and disease? And what if he's not a virgin?

Much, much later, I found out that he was a virgin. But in some ways, I lost my innocence that night. Not earlier when I first learned the Facts of Life. Not later when we finally made love. But that June tenth at Wendy's when I realized with a jolt that sex and I would not be strangers forever.

True Confessions: My First Time

Your first time is important. You remember it forever. Not that times two and three are run-of-the-mill or that sex should ever be less than memorable. But there's only one first time, and the moment stays with you, for better and for worse. Are you expecting instant ecstasy? Don't. Many guys and girls find the first go-around is clumsy, no matter how meaningful and poignant. Even some virgin brides and grooms find the first time awkward.

I hope your first time is with a steady, caring partner. That's how it is for most women. Others give away their virginity to someone who is so busy "getting laid" that he doesn't even appreciate the momentousness of the moment. That's the old everyone-else-is-doing-it-so-I-might-as-well-get-it-over-with-approach. A bummer if you ask me.

My first time was also my boyfriend's first time. We were in love and we'd waited and postponed and planned and were responsible enough not to insist on spontaneity. Nor did we want to be high or drunk; we wanted to be *there*. So we discussed the logistics, got birth control, and finally tried to do it. And tried and tried. I was tense and scared and, as I confessed afterward to my diary, *"It took an hour of true struggling."*

Then the condom broke and so did the mood as I rushed to the phone to call Planned Parenthood. (The phone call was eventually followed by a test, but I was lucky and wasn't pregnant.)

To be honest, making love that first time was neither painful nor particularly enjoyable. I didn't bleed (many women do) and I didn't come (most women don't).

In my diary, I reported the lack of blood and commented, *"Maybe my hymen isn't even broken,"* and *"Maybe I'm still a technical virgin."* Yeah, right, and maybe Elvis is still out carousing. Perhaps my wonderings were part ignorance, part wistful thinking. It isn't easy to say good-bye to girlhood.

It's Easy to Get Pregnant; It's Easy Not To

You can skip every other section in this book if you want, but read these next few pages. Maybe not this year, maybe not next year, but before you get involved in a sexual relationship. I'd never made love without contraception until my husband and I decided we wanted to have children. Our daughter Elizabeth was born exactly nine months later. Contraception works. Use it. There's no reason to be unexpectedly expecting.

More and more teens are saying no to sex. And more and more teens are using condoms the first time they have sex. But too many other teens still don't realize how important it is to protect themselves.

If you are sexually active, I won't stand in front of you waving a chastity belt. But if I could, I might show up waving a condom. Sex without contraception is like skydiving without a parachute. And there's no such thing as casual sex because there's no such thing as a casual baby or casual abortion or casual miscarriage or casual sexually transmitted disease.

These are the hard facts:

- Each year, over one million American teenagers get pregnant. (That's about 3,000 a day.)
- About half have babies (500,000 babies).
- Half of all surprise teen pregnancies occur within the first six months of ever having sex.
- One in 3 American babies is born to an unwed mother. (Forty years ago, it was 1 in 20.)
- Of all teenage pregnancies, 85 percent are unplanned. (55 percent of adult pregnancies are unplanned.) Babies shouldn't be accidents!

- Teen condom use has doubled recently, yet one-third of teenage girls used no protection the first time, and one-fifth never do.
- Each year, 10,000 girls aged fourteen or under have babies. (One in 25 that age gets pregnant—and gets cheated right out of childhood.)
- By age eighteen, 1 in 4 teenagers will have become pregnant at least once. (One in 4!)
- Nearly 1 in 5 unmarried teenage girls who gets pregnant becomes pregnant again within a year. Within two years, nearly 1 in 3 has a repeat pregnancy and 1 in 4 has a baby. (One teen mom, several kids: not an ideal scenario.)
- One in 4 black women and 1 in 7 white women are moms by age nineteen. (The pregnancy rate among Hispanics is also on the rise—*¡cuidado!*)
- Compared to other teens, if your family is poor, you are more likely to have sex at a younger age, more likely to get pregnant, more likely to have a baby, and more likely to stay poor.
- Despite some recent progress, the United States still has the highest teen pregnancy rate in the developed world. (We're hypocrites. We sell beer and cars by touting sex, but then blush and sputter rather than educate teens.)

If teens were better informed, these statistics could become less lame, less disturbing. It's not JUST SAY NO. It's JUST SAY KNOW.

Worldwide, things are improving. The global population is growing at an alarming 100 million people a year. But contraception has caught on. Women in poorer countries used to average six children each; now it's down below four.

In America, change has been less dramatic. Parents and daughters still get flustered over the topic of sex. Racy songs, TV shows, movies, and music videos get everybody all fired up, but offer few clues about contraception. In school, sex ed may mean a lecture about fallopian tubes, rather than a crash course on condoms. And when someone suggests making condoms available, politicians and the PTA tend to go ballistic.

Women need to be able to protect themselves from disease and unwanted pregnancy. How? By not having sex (abstinence) or by being prepared. Should men be encouraged to accept a bigger role in birth control? Absolutely. But don't count on their taking care of things. We're the ones with wombs; we're the ones with more to lose.

Some girls (and this kills me) hesitate to get contraceptives because that's consciously admitting that they're having sex and they're not ready to face that fact. They figure "Since I'm not using birth control, I'm not *really* having sex." Listen, if you're not ready to be responsible about intercourse, you're not ready for it. Which is fine. And smart. What's not fine is to deny what you're doing and wind up another statistic. Don't ignore the cause-and-effect nature of sex and pregnancy. If you're adult enough to have sex, be adult enough to protect yourself.

Other girls feel contraceptives take the romance and spontaneity out of lovemaking. Hellloooo! Pregnancy, disease, and babies don't do much for romance and spontaneity, either. The idea of reckless sex may seem all very nice during those minutes of heavy breathing. But it's not worth the worry as you pray for your period and pray you didn't contract a disease.

Still other girls don't use contraceptives because they are afraid their parents will find out. First of all, pregnancy is scarier than upset parents and a lot harder to hide than pills or condoms. Second, no state has a law that requires a minor to get parental consent for contraceptive services. You can buy condoms in any pharmacy and convenience store, and, in most cases, if you go to Planned Parenthood or any other family planning clinic for prescription contraceptives, by law the clinic will *not* notify your parents. (Gynecologists are there for you.) Finally, if your mother did find your pills or condoms, there's a chance she might be more relieved than outraged.

Some girls have sex without contraception because they think they want a baby. They imagine sweet smiles and booties and aren't aware that babies get screaming hungry at 4 A.M. and throw up a lot and aren't toilet-trained for almost three years. Babies require work, attention, and money. Toddlers require work, attention, and money. Children require work, attention, and money. And what if you want to go to a movie some time during the next ten years? Who's going to baby-sit? As Roseanne Barr put it, "There's a lot more to being a woman than being a mother, but there's a hell of a lot more to being a mother than most people suspect."

If you think a baby would bind you happily ever after to a guy, you haven't met any of the thousands of unwed mothers whose former boyfriends are long gone. (Many boyfriends deny paternity and refuse to pay child support.) I meet lots of single teenage moms when I'm on talk shows. Most are tearful and overwhelmed and say things like, "I didn't think it could happen to me" and, "He said he'd love me forever."

Guess what? It's easier to father a child than to be a father.

Look, no one is saying you can't be a mom. But why not wait until you've jumpstarted your own life? Why not wait until you've reached a few personal goals and saved some money and found a co-parent you love?

I know lots of intelligent girls and women who were unhappily surprised by pregnancy. One had a baby daughter, gave her up for adoption, and still thinks and wonders about her. Several had abortions and felt sad for months afterward. Two got married, and if you ask me (I know you didn't, but I'll tell you anyway), I don't think either marriage will last. In couple number one, the husband feels trapped and resentful. And couple number two's baby boy was born severely handicapped, and so far neither groom nor bride seems willing or able to cope.

Sure, some unexpected pregnancies lead to happy endings. But lots don't. Planning parenthood really is the way to go. And you need a better reason to have a child than that you didn't know how to prevent one.

Birth Control Methods

"No woman can call herself free until she can choose consciously
whether she will or will not be a mother."
—Margaret Sanger, founder of Planned Parenthood

The decision to have sex and the decision to have a baby are very different decisions. If a sexually active teen does not use birth control, she has a 90 percent chance of getting pregnant within the year. Contraception is crucial for couples of all ages. American women are having sex earlier, marrying and having children later, and having fewer children than they used to. That means they need to think about birth control during much of their lives.

Abstinence is obviously the best method of birth control. Saying no makes sense and more girls are saying no.

Sterilization is popular among married parents—the man gets a vasectomy or the woman gets her tubes tied—but sterilization is not for teens.

If you are having sex, what method is best for you? Some contraceptives require responsibility from your partner; some don't. Some protect against STDs; some don't. Some have been around for ages, some are new, and some (like the sponge) came and went.

Condoms and the Pill are by far the most widely used methods of birth control among teens. I'm going to tell you about all the methods, starting with condoms, since they are the cheapest and easiest to get, and moving on to the prescription methods that you can get from a doctor or clinic. All methods have some side effects or drawbacks. If you experience dizziness, blurry vision, shooting pains, or any worrisome unexpected physical change, immediately call your doctor or clinic. You know your body best!

Need more information? Contact Planned Parenthood Federation of America at (800) 230-PLAN or, on the Internet at http://www.ppfa. org/ppfa. Or tap into http://www.agi/usa.org for the latest research from the Alan Guttmacher Institute. And don't buy into any myths. You're kidding yourself if you think that by douching, having sex standing up, or not having an orgasm, you can prevent conception.

When it comes to sex, if you say yes, say it to him, not to his baby.

Condoms and Spermicide

If your partner uses a condom and you use a contraceptive gel or foam, you have nearly a 99 percent chance of not getting pregnant. More and more couples use condoms because they are cheap, accessible, safe, and small enough to carry around and because they protect against pregnancy and most STDs. Condoms can literally save your life.

Condoms and spermicide are available without a prescription at any pharmacy and many stores. (Embarrassed? If you buy Trojans and Conceptrol, the individual behind the counter will guess what you've been up to. If you're pregnant, *everybody* will.) A handful of schools give out condoms, and some have condom machines.

Guys sometimes complain that condoms cut down on pleasure, but worrying about pregnancy and disease cuts down on pleasure, too. And just as a driver doesn't get offended when you put on a seatbelt, your partner shouldn't get offended when you ask him to use a weenie beanie. (If he complains, "It's like taking a bath with your boots on," you can always smile and say, "No balloon, no party," or "No glove, no love.") Attitudes have been changing, and according to a recent survey, most guys between the ages of fifteen and nineteen wore a condom the last time they had sex. Girls buy condoms now, too, so if you don't know how to approach the subject, you can always say, "Let's use this." (C'mon, if you're planning to sleep with him, you should be able to talk to him.) He's still resisting? Why share your body with someone who doesn't want to protect you or himself?

Condoms have no side effects (though a few women are allergic to certain lubricants), and the condom-spermicide method means you're sharing the responsibility of birth control.

If he wears a latex, lubricated condom from start to finish and you use a gel, foam, or cream containing nonoxynol-9 (inserted before sex like a tampon), you're both protected from unwanted pregnancy and disease.

Condoms are more likely to break if they are old, have been stretched, have been stored in a wallet or hot glove compartment, or are unlubricated. Never use oil-based lubricants (such as vaseline, cold cream, and mineral oil) with a condom. And yes, condoms come in different sizes. Some guys figure out which work best when they are alone—if you catch my drift.

How do you use the condom-spermicide method? Before penetration, he unrolls the condom onto his erect penis (leaving a one-half-inch space for the sperm-filled semen if the condom doesn't already have a reservoir tip) and you insert the foam or gel into your vagina. These products vary; follow directions. You can also put some inside the top of the condom before he puts it on or on the outside of the condom once he's wearing it. After ejaculation, as he withdraws, he should hold on to the rim of the condom so it doesn't slip off. Use a new condom every time you have sex.

The condom-spermicide combination works because sperm are trapped in the thin rubber sheath, and if the condom breaks, the sperm-killing foam acts as a backup. Effective, easy, and a particularly good choice for first-timers (since there's no need to see a doctor) and for couples who don't have an exclusive relationship (since condoms protect against disease). Me, I wouldn't sleep with someone who sleeps with others—especially in the age of AIDS.

In the United States, 6 in 10 sexually active women between the ages of fifteen and nineteen have had two or more sex partners, and guys get around, too, so don't be naive. Use condoms that come with a disease-prevention claim on the package label. Avoid lambskin and novelty (e.g., glow-in-the dark) condoms, since they do not protect against AIDS, chlamydia, or other STDs.

Don't rely on condoms alone, however, because 10 out of 100 girls who do wind up pregnant. If you rely on foams, gels, or vaginal inserts alone, you have a 22 percent chance of pregnancy. Use both—this is no time to save money or bother!

The Pill

The Pill does not protect against disease, but as an oral contraceptive, it has some real advantages if taken without fail at about the same time each day. The doctor may prescribe a twenty-eight-pill packet (a pill a day keeps the stork away) or a twenty-one-pill packet (take one a day for three weeks, then skip the week of your period before starting again). Once the first fourteen pills are taken, a woman can have sex with complete spontaneity and without fear of pregnancy.

Birth control pills come in two forms: the regular pill (which contains synthetic hormones similar to progesterone and estrogen) and minipills (which contain only progestin). Both pills work by suppressing ovulation. With no ripe-and-ready egg present, a woman can't become pregnant. Used properly, it's almost 100 percent effective. No muss, no fuss. It even makes periods regular, shorter, and less painful. Your doctor can recommend which type of pill to take and speak with you about how long you can stay on it.

The Pill was approved by the FDA (Food and Drug Administration) way back in 1960. Most experts agree that the low-dosage pills now on the market pose no serious health hazards for young women. Most say that the benefits outweigh the risks. Not only is the Pill safer than childbirth, but it actually protects *against* ovarian and uterine cysts or cancer. The Pill has been linked, however, to increased risk of blood clots or circulatory problems.

Girls who smoke and women over age thirty-five should probably not go on the Pill. Who else should think twice? Girls who are quite underweight or who do not yet have well-established periods, girls who have certain medical problems (such as high blood pressure), and girls who are forgetful and might miss a day. For most sexually active girls, the Pill may be an ideal method of birth control. (But unless you are engaging in regular, frequent sex, I don't think it's worth it to fool with your body chemistry. On the other hand, don't have sex simply because you are already on the Pill!)

Does the Pill make you gain weight? When I was briefly on the Pill, I didn't get puffy. Nor did it cause me nausea, spotting, depression, or headaches. But some girls do suffer these or other side effects. (Call your doctor if you have concerns.) If you stop using the Pill and keep having sex, use other birth control methods. There is no "grace period," no free couple of months.

Does the Pill protect you against STDs? Nope. That's why a woman on the Pill also needs to make sure that her partner wears a condom. One quarter of Pill users always use condoms as well—the others are taking too big a chance.

Diaphragm and Spermicide

Have you ever seen a diaphragm? Picture a flexible beige mini-Frisbee with a rubber ring around the edge. A doctor measures you to determine what size you need before prescribing the diaphragm. He or she should check you again yearly to make sure the size is right, and more often if you gain or lose more than ten pounds or are a newcomer to sex or have a baby or an abortion. The diaphragm is not effective if it doesn't fit properly or if it has a hole or tear in it. So replace it at least every two years and make a habit of holding it up to bright light to check for a rip or filling it with water to check for a leak. (Heard the one about the lady who kept her diaphragm near the bed—tacked to the bedpost?)

A diaphragm is not much more complicated to put in or take out than a tampon, and a doctor or nurse will show you how. Once it's inside, you shouldn't be able to feel it.

Anywhere from six hours to six seconds before intercourse, you should prepare the diaphragm by squeezing at least a teaspoonful of spermicidal jelly or cream into the bowl of the dome and around the rim. Before you insert the diaphragm, pee and wash your hands. After intercourse, leave it in for at least six hours but never over twenty-four. If you make love again during this time, insert more jelly or cream with a plastic applicator without removing the diaphragm. Later, after removing the diaphragm, wash it gently with warm water, dry it, and store it away from heat in its container.

The diaphragm prevents pregnancy because the rubber barrier in front of your cervix physically blocks the speeding sperm, and the jelly or cream chemically kills them. Used properly, it works 97 percent of the time, but because some girls and women put it in incorrectly, forget to use it, run out of jelly, or lose or gain weight but don't get remeasured, its effectiveness is about 83 percent.

The diaphragm is convenient if you want to have sex during your period because it catches the menstrual flow. I'd especially recommend it if you are responsible, comfortable with your body, and if you have sex only once in a while and don't want full-time birth control for part-time sex. Used properly, it offers some protection against STDs, but if you're prone to urinary tract infections, it can make matters worse.

Depo-Provera

Depo-Provera is for the sexually active but forgetful. It is an injection (yes, a shot) that a nurse or doctor gives in the buttocks or arm every three months. Taken four times a year as scheduled, it is 99 percent effective as contraception, though it provides no protection against STDs.

Depo-Provera, like the Pill, uses a synthetic hormone to prevent pregnancy. The ovaries go into a sort of resting state and stop releasing eggs. The monthly uterine lining also stops forming, and menstrual bleeding itself ceases or becomes irregular. In other words, your period may disappear—or become unpredictable. Other side effects? Weight gain. And possible headaches, nausea, bloating, or joint pain, as well as an increased risk of breast cancer. (Nothing is as simple as it seems!)

If you opt for this method, the first injection is given during the first five days of your period because it's essential to make sure that you are not pregnant. Women who have abnormal vaginal bleeding or who have a family history of breast cancer, stroke, blood clots, diabetes, depression, or liver disease should not choose this method. For more information, talk to your health care provider.

Norplant

Effective, reversible, long term, and convenient, Norplant was approved by the FDA in 1990. What is Norplant? Six little matchstick-sized rods that are implanted in a fan under the skin of the upper arm in a procedure that requires local anesthesia. Norplant starts working within twenty-four hours, protects against pregnancy for up to five years, and has a failure rate of less than 1 percent. (How? The rods or capsules release levonorgestrel which tells the pituitary gland to stop the ovaries from developing eggs.) Norplant can be removed at any time, and fertility is restored. The device and its implantation require a high one-time cost (many hundreds of dollars), but this is ultimately cheaper than buying five years of protection in pills or condoms. (Medicaid may even cover the costs.) Insertion and removal should take about 15 to 20 minutes and must be done by a trained doctor, but not all doctors know how to do it, and if scar tissue forms, removal can be more complicated.

Drawbacks? Many women have irregular spotting or bleeding and many complain that the device is visible and can be felt beneath the skin. Others have headaches, weight gain, and upper-arm scarring. Some women should not use this method (e.g., women with diabetes, liver disease, breast cancer, or blood clots). And it works slightly less well in women over 155 pounds. Norplant, like the Pill, also offers zero STD protection.

Norplant has been used by over a million women in dozens of countries for many years, but its long-term effects are still being studied.

Withdrawal

Don't count on it. It takes a whole lot of willpower for a guy to pull out the very second his pleasure is most intense. Even if he means to withdraw before ejaculating, he might slip up, and that means millions of sperm racing in search of your egg. I know I couldn't relax if I was depending on someone else's self-control to keep me from getting pregnant.

Even if your partner does withdraw in time, it may still be too late. A few drops of clear, lubricating, sperm-filled liquid may be secreted even before he ejaculates, and all it takes is one sperm (and one egg) to make a baby. Men may produce as many as eighty million sperm daily, and they keep making more—they don't run out.

Q. Why does contraception involve millions of sperm and just one egg?

A. Because men hate to ask for directions.

Look, withdrawal is better than nothing, but why take chances? In actual use, withdrawal is only 70 to 75 percent effective. As far as protection against STDs, its effectiveness is zero.

Rhythm

Q: What do you call people who use the rhythm method?

A: Parents.

I bet the guy who sings, "I got rhythm, I got music, I got my girl, who could ask for anything more?" ends up with more: a houseful of babies! While it's wise to know how the rhythm method works so you know when you are most and least fertile, it's risky to rely on rhythm as a means of birth control because your cycle changes. In theory, rhythm is only 87 percent effective, and in practice, it's only 79 percent effective. That means each year, out of every 100 women who rely on rhythm, 21 get pregnant. We're talking about a lot of upset ladies.

When are you most fertile? At about the midpoint of your menstrual cycle (about two weeks after your period starts). When are you least likely to get pregnant? During menstruation (not everyone's favorite time to do it anyway). Quick review: Assuming you have a regular twenty-eight-day cycle (and for most women, that's a false assumption), if your period begins on January 1, you will ovulate and be most fertile sometime before and around January 14. One of your ovaries will release a single egg into one of your fallopian tubes, and that egg will travel toward your uterus. Your egg can be fertilized anytime during the next two days, and sperm can live inside you for up to four days. So if sperm meets and fertilizes egg anytime that week—presto, you're pregnant. The rhythm system therefore says: No sex before, during, or after ovulation. So you would abstain (or use other contraception) at least from January 11 through January 17 in that hypothetical cycle.

Many conscientious women do more than mark their calendars. They check for variations in their cervical mucus and body temperature and note conditions (stress, travel, sickness) that could cause an irregularity in their cycle. Such precautions make rhythm—which is also called the calendar method or natural family planning—a little more effective.

The problem with rhythm for girls who don't have regular cycles is that they can't predict when they are ovulating. If you have a period the first week in January and not again until the second week in March, it's hard to know when you were most fertile. Other girls may be absent-minded and have trouble remembering which days are the safest.

Still others might feel passionate on a "dangerous" day and not be responsible enough to say no.

Rhythm is safe and is sanctioned by the Roman Catholic Church. I do *not* advise it as your sole method of birth control. But I do recommend that you learn when you are most fertile. Why? So that now you never ever take a chance during those times, and later, when you may want to start a family, you'll know when you'll be most likely to conceive. Remember that rhythm or no rhythm, you can get pregnant anytime—even during your period.

Cervical Cap

The cervical cap, approved by the FDA in 1988, works like a diaphragm but fits extra-snugly on the cervix and can be worn longer (though it sometimes develops an odor). It is, however, somewhat trickier to insert than the diaphragm, and very few teens have chosen this method.

Intrauterine Device (IUD)

IUDs work well, but they are controversial and are not recommended for young women and women who have never been pregnant. They're better for women who have already had kids and cannot use other methods of birth control. Why? Side effects. Some users get heavy periods and cramping. All users risk perforation of the uterus, tubal pregnancy, spontaneous abortion, and increased chance of pelvic inflammatory infection, which, in severe cases, could lead to sterility. They also offer no protection from STDs.

Condoms for Women

A female condom, or "vaginal pouch," is a polyurethane sheath that lines the vagina and is about seven inches long. It protects against STDs, but most women find it bulky and difficult to insert.

Emergency Contraception

Morning-after pills? Yes! There is a way to stop pregnancy in its tracks—to block a fertilized egg from implanting itself into the uterus. The method has been used for years in New Zealand and Europe and on American college campuses and rape crisis centers. Studies show that the abortion rate goes down when emergency contraception is available.

How does it work? Ask your doctor or health practitioner, but basically a first dose of two or four ordinary birth control pills (depending on the brand—not all brands are effective) must be taken within seventy-two hours of intercourse. A second dose of the exact same size must follow twelve hours later. (If the pill is Ovral, for instance, each dose is two white tablets.) Used properly, this method prevents pregnancy 75 percent of the time. It is safe, though you may feel queasy and you may bleed after you take the dose. (Some women take Dramamine to cut down the chance of vomiting—and having to repeat the treatment.)

If sex was forced or the condom broke or you forgot to use birth control and you're panicking about the possibility of pregnancy or abortion, call the Emergency Contraception Hot Line at (800) 584-9911 or, on the Internet, explore http://www.opr.princeton.edu./ec/ to find out who in your area can prescribe the pills to you. Do not try these pills without professional supervision, since there will be cramping and bleeding and the method may not work. And do not use this method as regular birth control. This is for urgent cases and is much harder on your body than regular contraception.

What If You Are Pregnant?

I hope you're dipping into this section out of idle curiosity. I hope you're a virgin or are now abstaining or use birth control whenever you make love.

But you may be reading this because you're pregnant.

Pregnant. It may not seem fair. Perhaps you've only had intercourse one measly time in your whole life. Or maybe you and your boyfriend were always careful about contraception—except once. Or maybe you believed a crazy myth like you can't get pregnant the first time or you can't get pregnant if you don't come. Or maybe you thought that getting pregnant now somehow made more sense than postponing motherhood until you have a job or degree or husband.

So you missed a period, were feeling tired and occasionally nauseated, had to urinate often, and noticed your breasts and belly beginning to swell. Did you wait around to see if your next period would come? No. You took a home-pregnancy urine test or went to a clinic (in your town or nearby) for a blood test. You flunked. You're pregnant.

Now what? For a short time, you may be a basket case. Or you may deny it. Talk to the counselors at Planned Parenthood or some other clinic, your boyfriend, or even your parents. They may be disappointed, but they may come through for you. Telling a friend may be a comfort, but if your friend tells a friend, your news could become public.

Start considering your options, each with pros and cons. Calculate how many weeks pregnant you are, learn as much as possible, and decide what's right for you. Your boyfriend may beg you to keep the baby. Your girlfriend may advise you to have the baby, then give it up for adoption. Your parents may urge you to get an abortion. Easy for all of them to say. What do *you* want to do?

It's your decision, and neither your parents nor the baby's father can legally keep you from having an abortion—or force you to have one. Think about yourself first—before baby or boyfriend, friends or family. I'm going to tell you about your choices. You're the one who has to make the decision and live with it.

Keeping the Baby

Before you decide you want a baby, think about what you're getting into. Having a baby is not like having a doll or Tamagotchi, or baby-sitting for two hours, then leaving with money jingling in your pocket. A baby is a huge responsibility. And as Elizabeth Stone said, "Making the deci-

sion to have a child . . . is to decide forever to have your heart go walking around outside your body." I didn't feel ready to have a family until
I was thirty—are you sure you are ready now?

Over a half-million teens each year decide to have and keep their
babies. Some start out hopeful but end up feeling trapped, resentful,
and cheated of their childhood. Child abuse and neglect of babies born
to teens is more common than among older mothers. Would you find it
frustrating to wear maternity clothes while slim friends wear sexy
dresses? To be stuck inside changing diapers, or comforting a sick child
while buddies are out partying? To drop out of school or have to go on
welfare while friends are graduating from high school and getting jobs?
To swear off all alcohol, tobacco, and drugs while pregnant and breast-
feeding? Maybe you want to finish being a kid before you have a kid.
You probably will be able to offer a baby more in the future. Being a
mother with no money, no husband, and no degree is hard. Having a
baby too soon can stunt your growth. Grim but true: Suicide is more
common among girls who are mothers than among girls who are not.

Be realistic. Can you afford a baby? Are you mature enough to handle having a baby now? Healthy enough for pregnancy, labor, and motherhood? Willing to give the baby all the attention it demands? Will you
get married or raise the child alone? Picture your situation a year from
now; five years from now. Will the baby's father be able to help you during all this? Most teenage mothers are unmarried, but if the father signs
papers acknowledging paternity now, you'll be legally able to collect
child support later.

Some teens decide to have and keep their baby, and it is a wise,
happy choice. The baby's father is proud and supportive and can earn a
living for the couple and the child. Or the teen girl's parents care for the
mother and baby and the teen is able to continue her education and
career plans. Obviously, if you are an older teen and you and your
boyfriend are already engaged, your chances of feeling good about
keeping the baby are better than if you are fifteen and the baby's father
doesn't want a thing to do with you. But many couples who marry
because Baby's on the way end up miserable. And daughters of teenage
mothers are more likely to become teenage mothers themselves. Teen
poverty and teen motherhood go hand in hand.

In some countries, single mothers are outcasts. In Japan, for instance,
teens postpone sex, pregnant teens have abortions, and only 1 of 100
births is to an unwed mother. In America, 30 out of 100 births are to sin-

gle mothers. It's good that we're not hung up on stigmas. But is it good that so very many children don't start off with a two-parent family?

If you decide to have the baby, see a doctor now and start getting prenatal care and taking prenatal classes. If you think you might have a sexually transmissible disease, go to a doctor for tests and possible treatment or your baby could be born blind, deaf, retarded, or with health problems. To make sure your baby is born as healthy as possible, take prenatal vitamins, drink milk, and eat nutritiously. The birth defect spina bifida, for instance, can be easily prevented if the pregnant woman consumes folic acid, a B vitamin. Cut out junk food—you and your baby are both growing and competing for nutrients. Don't drink, smoke, or take drugs while pregnant. Drinking is linked to birth defects and smoking, to small, weak babies and premature births. The incidence of premature and underweight infants and infant mortality is higher among teen mothers than mothers in their twenties. And 1 out of 3 teen girls who have babies have inadequate prenatal care. (When you do see a doctor or even dentist, say that you are pregnant, since X-rays could hurt the fetus.)

If you decide to have your baby—if your baby is a wanted baby—do all you can to start its life right.

Ending the Pregnancy

Miscarriage is not uncommon. Your pregnancy may end itself. But don't count on it. And don't try to make it happen.

Emergency contraception (see page 142 or call (800) 584-9911)—is an option during the first three days after intercourse. During the first seven weeks, there may soon be another option, RU-486, or mifepristone. Despite swirling controversy, the FDA approved the drug in 1996, and in France, women have been using RU-486 since 1989.

Mifepristone is for women who know early on that they do not want to carry the baby to term. It will be especially welcome to rural women who cannot find a local doctor who performs abortions and to women who fear the protests that sometimes besiege abortion clinics.

While medical abortions promise to be more private and readily available than surgical abortions, RU-486 is not a magic unpregnancy pill, and even in France, it's not as easy as *un, deux, trois*. It's not as if you take it and then get your period, period.

The pregnant woman must first go to a clinic to register for mifepristone tablets. She takes the drug, and it prevents a fetus from attaching to the uterine wall. In two days, she returns to the clinic to take miso-prostol, which makes the uterus contract. Within four or more hours, she bleeds and the embryo is expelled. Finally she returns for a follow-up visit.

In some women, the drugs don't completely work and a D&C (dila-tion and curettage) or vacuum aspiration is needed. In other women, the drugs cause excessive cramping or bleeding or nausea. Nonetheless, many health experts are glad that the wait for this safe alternative to surgical abortion is, at long last, ending.

Another drug, methotrexate, can also be used to end pregnancy dur-ing those first seven weeks. Methotrexate stops embryonic growth by blocking cell division. At a clinic, the woman receives an injection which she follows five to seven days later with misoprostol.

Visit http://www.popcouncil.org on the Net for more information.

Many pregnant teens—nearly 40 percent—end up having a surgical abortion. It's not an easy decision, and afterward, some feel guilty, sad, and wistful. But many also feel a deep sense of relief, especially if the pregnancy was the result of rape or incest or loveless sex. Or if the girl knew in advance (perhaps through a sonogram or amniocentesis) that the baby would be severely abnormal or unhealthy. Or if the girl's own health was at stake.

Girls who choose abortion often say they realized that they were not emotionally or financially ready for a baby. (Yes, it's better to realize this before starting a life.) Others decide that they want their child's father to be part of the family—not some guy who got lucky while she got unlucky.

A first-trimester abortion is performed during the first twelve weeks of pregnancy and is safer, cheaper, and simpler than a second-trimester abortion. (So make up your mind. Don't let time make the what-to-do-if-you're-pregnant decision for you.) Having one abortion by a competent gynecologist won't damage your reproductive organs, but having several abortions, particularly later abortions, may make it harder for you to carry a future pregnancy to term. The longer you wait, the more compli-cated and expensive the abortion.

In 1973, the Supreme Court legalized abortion in all fifty states in a decision called *Roe v. Wade.* Many people still question a woman's right to choose. Some groups put the well-being of the embryo above the well-being of the mother. And some clinics do not offer information about this option. Decades ago, some girls who could not turn to doctors tried their own abortions. They shoved coat hangers up themselves or drank horrid solutions or threw themselves down stairways. Many died. If you jump out a second-story window in the hope of ending your pregnancy, you could end your life. Or you could end up pregnant and crippled.

Each year about 1,400,000 women have abortions in America. Most of the women are young, and poor women are three times more likely than other women to have abortions. About 3 out of 5 teens who have an abortion do so with the knowledge—and support—of at least one parent. Abortion rates are now declining, and the availability of next-day pills and RU-486 may further bring down the number of surgical abortions.

Early abortions can be performed quickly in many clinics. Ninety percent of abortions take place in the first trimester. Doctors administer anesthesia (usually local), dilate the cervix, and insert a tube attached to a suctioning device that removes the developing egg and placental tissues. (Picture a very gentle minivacuum.) The procedure takes ten or so minutes and is followed by a few hours of recovery in the clinic. Do not leave until a doctor confirms that the abortion is complete. Then take it easy for a few days—and no sex or tampons.

Second-trimester abortions are usually performed in hospitals and involve general anesthesia. Afterward, the woman may have cramps and bleeding, and should refrain for two weeks from having sex, using tampons, swimming, or taking baths.

"I'm pro-choice," one friend told me, "but it's not like I wanted to have an abortion. No one wants to have an abortion. Still, the decision wasn't hard; it was more . . . sad. I was sixteen—I wasn't ready to be a mother. So my boyfriend and I went together and after that, we were a lot more careful."

If you want to learn more about abortion, ask. Some states require parental consent or the approval of a judge or counseling or waiting periods. Ask. For the nearest Planned Parenthood to you, call (800) 230-PLAN. Or call the National Abortion Federation at (800) 772-9100. Abortion is legal and you can find a sympathetic listener.

Giving Up Your Baby

Maybe abortion is against your principles. Or maybe you're too far along in your pregnancy to have a safe abortion. So you're going through with your pregnancy. You're seeing a doctor and taking good care of yourself because you want to deliver a healthy baby.

But you've decided not to keep it. Thousands of teens each year choose the adoption option. They realize they are too young or too alone to be the kind of mothers they'd like to be.

If you are considering adoption, some may ask, "How can you give away your baby?" but you have to ask yourself, "How can I keep it?" Others may think you're coldhearted. I think it is bighearted to offer your baby to a couple who desperately wants a child, has been waiting for one, and is ready and able to give yours the future he or she deserves. There are more couples who want to adopt than available babies to be adopted. (The number of children placed for adoption has declined dramatically in the past few decades.)

Some couples place ads in school papers, but you will probably want to contact a licensed adoption agency that belongs to the Child Welfare League. Look up Adoption Agency in the phone book or ask your doctor or prenatal care counselors for referrals or call the National Council for Adoption in Washington, D.C. (202) 328-1200 or the National Adoption Center (800) 862-3678 or National Adoption Hotline, (202) 328-8072. Find out as much as you can before you sign any papers. The baby's father's parental rights have to be waived (given up), too, before the baby can be put up for adoption.

In many cases, when the child is eighteen or twenty-one, he or she can try to contact you (or you can initiate contact) through the agency. Some such reunions are heartwarming; others are disillusioning. If you never want to get in touch with your baby, you don't have to. In many cases, the mother may hold her newborn and say a final good-bye. Some mothers write a letter to their baby and give it to the agency to give to the child years later.

Some mothers opt for open adoption. The birth mother makes an arrangement with the adoptive family to be involved in the child's life. Still others leave the baby temporarily in a foster home and visit regularly while making the decision. Downside? If the birth mother chooses to give up the child after all, the waiting period can make separation harder. And it is best for the child to have one stable home as soon as possible. A mother never forgets that she gave birth to a baby, but if she knows that she placed the baby in a loving home, that can help soothe the ache and begin the healing.

All these choices are hard. Once you have made your decision, commit yourself to it and work to feel good about it. I wish you luck now and I beg you to use contraception in the future. (Many teen pregnancies are repeat pregnancies.) Or swear off sex for a while. As they say: You can go further if you don't go all the way.

Think I'm coming down hard on you? Older and married women also get pregnant without intending to. When it comes to birth control, almost everyone should be more careful.

Quick Quiz on Prom Pressures

On a lighter note, sharpen your pencil and your wits and pretend it's prom time.

1. Your crush invites you to the prom (you're psyched) and says he plans to book a room at a hotel (you're ambivalent). You

   a. pump yourself up for the biggest night of your life.

   b. smile and mumble, "OK," but plan to back out later.

   c. say, "Save your hotel money—my parents will never let me stay out that late."

2. You love your boyfriend but want to remain a virgin. He keeps hinting that he hopes that will change on prom night. You

   a. figure you'll see how you feel that night.

   b. tell him ahead that you adore him but know for certain that you are not ready for the big step.

   c. hope things don't get awkward or testy after dancing.

3. At the prom, you're already tipsy and your date keeps refilling your glass with contraband alcohol. You

   a. decline and say, "No more for me. I want to remember tonight."

   b. keep drinking and wind up blotto.

   c. say nothing but stop imbibing.

4. Your best friend is doing a semester abroad and her boyfriend and you are going as buddies to the prom. She knows this and trusts you both. What she doesn't know is that you're now in the backseat of his car and he's loosening his cummerbund. You

   a. swear each other to secrecy and let your passions go.

   b. press Pause and tell him you don't feel right about this.

   c. kiss for hours but then draw the line.

5. You and your boyfriend started having sex months ago. On prom night he remembers the corsage but forgets the condoms. What to do?

    a. No problem—you pull a condom out of your purse.

    b. Go for broke anyway—making love without birth control will make the night extra special.

    c. Fool around without actually having intercourse—you don't want the sperm and the egg to have the last dance!

Answers

1. c. Voice your reservations before he makes his reservations. (Blame it on your parents if that makes things easier.) Don't talk yourself (or get talked) into having sex. And don't lead him on only to disappoint him later.

2. b. Hope? Figure? No, no, no. *Tell* him to keep his expectations in check. Say that your decision is based on how you feel about sex, not how you feel about him.

3. a. or c. When you drink, your judgment slides downhill and you may make a sperm-of-the-moment decision that you'll regret later. Prom night is worth remembering, so quit while you're ahead instead of drinking yourself stupid—or sick.

4. b. Whoops. It would have been better if you hadn't gotten into this tangle. Now it's your call. On the one hand, all's fair in love and war and there are no rings on any fingers. On the other hand, she's your *best friend,* and how would you feel if the tables were turned? (Answer: Like hell.) What's the potential between you and this guy anyway? Are you really destined? (If so, why rush the romance?) To kill a friendship for a quickie is crazy. So keep your shirt on. Smile at her boyfriend, acknowledge your mutual attraction, feel good about it even, and call it a night. If the guy's decent, he'll actually feel better (at least emotionally!) about drawing the line. Whether to tell your friend later about this abbreviated kiss is your decision, complete with pros and cons. (Next time don't complicate your life so much, OK?)

5. a. or c. No contraception, no intercourse. That's the rule for birthdays, prom nights, Valentine's Day, and everything in between, whether you're a virgin or haven't been one for years. Either come prepared or stop short of penetration.

Straight, Lesbian, Gay, Bi: Sexual Orientation

Most women are sexually attracted to men, and most men are sexually attracted to women. That's heterosexuality. Many women are sexually attracted to women, and many men are sexually attracted to men. That's homosexuality. And still others are sexually attracted to both women and men. That's bisexuality.

What determines a person's sexual orientation? No one really knows. It's probably nature and nurture, which means it's probably a given, not a choice, with outside factors having an impact, too. Approximately 3 to 5 percent of women and up to 10 percent of men are homosexual.

Many lesbian adults say that they always knew they were gay. As teens, some were comfortable and open about it. Some were secretive and played it straight, leading double lives. And some felt ashamed, isolated, and desperate. Gay teens are three times more likely to try to kill themselves than straight teens, and 1 out of 3 teens who actually commits suicide was gay or lesbian.

Other lesbian women say that it wasn't until college or afterward that they discovered they were drawn more to women than to men. As teens, they may or may not have had boyfriends and they may have been as in the dark about their sexuality as they were about their future careers.

Way back when, there was little understanding of same-sex relationships. It wasn't until 1973 that the American Psychiatric Association stopped listing homosexuality as an illness. Nowadays, homosexuality is more accepted. But things still aren't easy. Gay men need to be especially careful about HIV and AIDS, and gay men and lesbians have to be wary of discrimination. There are still many intolerant, insensitive, insecure people who get into name-calling and gay-bashing. (I hope you never tell or laugh at jokes based on ignorance or cruelty.) And there are still many families that have enormous difficulty accepting their child's orientation. (Dad: "If you're out of the closet, you're out of the will!" Mom: "But you can't be. I've already picked the caterer for your wedding. . . .")

If you are a young teen and are not sure of your orientation, don't conclude that you are gay just because you are a tomboy or feminist or have a crush on your female teacher or had an erotic dream about your best friend. We are all surrounded by magazines and movies brimming with supersexy women; it'd be nearly impossible not to notice their appeal. Even same-sex games of "doctor" when you were a child mean little about your sexual self. Give yourself lots of time to figure out your identity, sexual and otherwise. Some women go out with other women in college but end up marrying men and considering their college liaisons an experimental phase.

If you are an older teen and you know—you just know—that you prefer women romantically and desire them sexually, you may be wondering about coming out. "When you finally come out, there's a pain that stops, and you know it will never hurt like that again," wrote Paul Monette. Even so, take your time about going public. Yes, it would be ideal to be frank with family and friends. But what if your family goes into temporary shock or mourning? What if your friends or co-workers act weird or E-mail the news to people whose business it isn't? Coming out is a big step, and not one that is easily reversible. If your community is homophobic or hostile to lesbianism, it may be smart—not cowardly—to stall before you emerge and try to educate them. Most lesbians who are open in college did *not* come out in high school.

Then again, who knows? Perhaps when you come around to coming out, lots of people will be there for you. Perhaps, given time, your family will accept you and appreciate your honesty. Perhaps your friends will say, "Cool," and ask all about it. (Some might worry that you're attracted to them; others might be offended that you aren't.)

Let's say you're a high school senior and you believe that closets are for clothes and you're 100 percent sure you're gay and 100 percent ready to tell your closest friend. Question: Is she ready to listen? Find out by making an offhanded remark like, "I was watching Montel Williams, and someone came out right on TV." If she says, "Eww! Gross! A faggot or a dyke?" or asks, "Came out of what?" take note: She is not your perfect first confidante. If she says, "Huh. I wonder why the person didn't tell her folks privately," then you may proceed. You could also talk about the music of k. d. lang or about how Melissa Etheridge and her partner became parents or the controversy over TV's Ellen DeGeneres coming out and confiding to a therapist played by Oprah. Drop hints. You might eventually say, "Do you know anybody gay?" When she shakes her head, you can smile and say, "Yes, you do."

If you are still having trouble accepting yourself, you can't expect others to be all-accepting right off the bat. Before approaching loved ones, you might want to talk anonymously and confidentially to informed and caring strangers. You can call the Gay and Lesbian Anti-Violence Project's twenty-four-hour hot line at (212) 807-0197. Or the Gay and Lesbian Youth Hotline at (800) 347-TEEN, evenings, Thursday to Sunday. Or the Bridges Project at (215) 241-7000. In New York, the Hetrick-Martin Institute for Lesbian and Gay Youth (212) 674-2400 offers free counseling for teens aged twelve to twenty-one. To reach the National Gay and Lesbian Task Force, call (202) 332-6483, or tap in on-line at http://www.ngltf@aol.com. On the Internet, you'll be able to find gay chat rooms, but be wary even in cyberspace of victimization or of someone older trying to hit on you. (Don't give out your real address.) Parents, Families and Friends of Lesbians and Gays, at (202) 638-4200, offers a brochure called *Coming Out To Parents.* And I recommend renting *The Celluloid Closet,* a documentary that shows how far Hollywood has come in depicting homosexuality.

If you feel discouraged because your home or hometown is light-years behind the times, keep in mind that you'll soon be liberated. Many colleges have gay organizations that welcome new members, and many cities have gay neighborhoods. In the meantime, there are people nearby who are going through similar struggles—and might become future friends or potential partners. Note: Just because you and someone else are both gay doesn't mean you have to like each other.

Shakespeare wrote, "Were kisses all the joys of bed, one woman would another wed." Today some lesbians do have wedding celebrations (and not just on *Friends* or *Roseanne* reruns). And some same-sex teens escort each other to the prom.

Wouldn't Shakespeare be surprised?

The next section is on sexually transmitted diseases. While lesbians don't have to worry about unwanted pregnancy (phew!), no one can afford to be ignorant about STDs.

STDs (Sexually Transmitted Diseases)

I don't want to give you the impression that sex is dangerous and scary and will leave you either pregnant or diseased. Sex can be wonderful. But it's most wonderful when it's worry-free. And it's most worry-free when you're informed, careful, and protected. (Abstain or use condoms!)

We'll try to zip through this section. I'm not up to thinking about pus, warts, sores, or bodily fluids any more than you are. But when it comes to STDs, what you don't know *can* hurt you.

STDs are also sometimes called VD, for *venereal disease.* They are incredibly common, and they are all avoidable, though they are not all curable. Over twelve million Americans contract an STD each year. Two-thirds of the cases occur in people under twenty-five, one quarter to teenagers. Each year 1 out of 4 sexually active women between fifteen and nineteen seek treatment for an STD. Women are more susceptible to infection than men.

You know about AIDS, but do you know that there are dozens of other STDs? One in 5 Americans has already caught an STD! One in 20 will get one this year. (Remember when all you worried about getting from boys was cooties?) Millions of women have one or more STDs and don't even know it because symptoms can be subtle. Yet if people carry a disease without knowing it, they can be spreading it willy-nilly even as it is spreading inside them.

I do not tell you untrue horror stories. Masturbation will not make you go blind, crazy, or sterile. But STDs can. Some can give you cancer; some can kill you. And 100,000 women each year become infertile from STDs. STDs do not go away by themselves. If you suspect you have an STD, call a doctor, a family planning or Health Department clinic, or the National STD Hotline at (800) 227-8922 or (800) 653-HEALTH. Pronto! You can hear taped information or speak to a counselor. The call is free and will not show up on your phone bill. Or check out the American Social Health Association at http://sunsite.unc.edu/ASHA/. You may be able to be tested free and confidentially. Call and ask. STD tests are no big deal, but they are not a routine part of checkups.

Some STDs, such as AIDS, herpes, and genital warts, are viruses with no known cures, though there are medications that can relieve some discomfort. Other STDs can be cured readily (praise be to Sir Alexander Fleming, discover of penicillin!), but you have to know you have them before you and your partner can be treated. (This is one case where you *should* kiss and tell. If you don't want to call your partner, a public health adviser can notify him without revealing your name.) Take *all* the medicine prescribed to you even if your symptoms disappear after just a few days. Then return for a follow-up examination, and don't have sex until you and your partner are fully cured—or you'll just ping-pong the disease back and forth.

STDs can be particularly serious in pregnant women because some can be passed on to the baby. Syphilis can harm the fetus, and babies can get chlamydia, gonorrhea, and herpes during birth, so treatment during pregnancy can make all the difference.

If you have several sex partners (who have several sex partners who have . . .) or if you have a classic telltale symptom (a sore, swelling, an unusual discharge or bleeding, pain, or a persistent itch in the genital area), get tested. Don't postpone it because early symptoms can go away while the disease itself continues coursing through your body.

You don't get STDs from toilet seats, hot tubs, swimming pools, or mosquitos. You get them from unprotected sex. So don't have sex. Or make love only with someone who is uninfected and who isn't having sex with anyone else (are you sure?). And use lubricated latex condoms every time you have sex and use a spermicidal jelly, cream, or foam containing nonoxynol-9 (which can kill germs, too).

Because AIDS is fatal, people are naturally more worried about the HIV virus than about other STDs. But the others are common, and you need to beware of them, too. If you are a sexually active teen and figure that no guy you fool around with would ever have an STD, listen to this. Each year, 4 million Americans contract chlamydial infections, 1.4 million get gonorrhea, 750,000 get genital warts, 500,000 get genital herpes (30 million already have it!), and some 130,000 get syphilis. Contrary to popular belief, teens aren't immune or immortal, and people with STDs that cause open blisters and sores are also more at risk for HIV infection, since breaks in the skin make it easier for the virus that causes AIDS to enter the body.

A few pages from now, I'll tell you all about AIDS. But first, a word about other STDs and a few nuisances, too. How do you and your boyfriend broach the subject of STDs? Say "I just read this chapter about STDs and I was surprised by some of the statistics." Or simply begin with, "AIDS sure is in the news, isn't it?" Or, "Let's talk about STDs, for both of our sakes."

Chlamydia

Chlamydia is the most common STD. Almost 75 percent of infected women have no symptoms (like burning, discharge, pus, or nausea) until there are complications (like infertility, ectopic pregnancy, and chronic pelvic pain). Girls fifteen to nineteen appear to have the highest infection rate of any age group. Antibiotics can cure chlamydia, so if you think you might have been exposed, ask to be tested. It would be too sad to find out a decade from now that last summer's hot romance blew you and your husband's future chances of getting pregnant.

Gonorrhea

If a woman has unprotected sex with a man who has gonorrhea, she has a 50 percent chance of getting it. Though easy to get, the "clap" is hard to detect. Symptoms include yellowish discharge, pain during sex, and urinary burning—or nothing at all. Gonorrhea is quite curable, but left untreated, it can lead to arthritis, heart trouble, or pelvic inflammatory disease (PID), which, in turn, can scar the fallopian tubes, making it hard or impossible to have a baby. If at risk, get tested regularly. Penicillin is usually the drug of choice, but different strains require different antibiotics.

HPV or Genital Warts

Highly contagious, yet sometimes practically invisible, genital warts can be removed through medication, freezing, burning, laser therapy, or surgery. Sometimes the warts are flat and sometimes they look like tiny cauliflowers. Because they may be at the base of the penis, a condom doesn't completely protect against them. The human papillomavirus (HPV) is not always curable, and sometimes the warts come back and fighting them becomes an ongoing battle. Some kinds are benign. Others are linked to cervical cancer. Every woman should have an annual Pap smear because the test helps doctors detect cancer early enough to treat it.

Trichomoniasis

Unusual discharge? Itchiness? Pain? "Trich" is hard to detect, but simple to treat, and there are three million new cases a year. It has no long-term consequences, but it is irritating (literally) and anything that irritates the vagina puts one at a greater risk of getting other STDs.

Genital Herpes

Q: What's the difference between love and herpes?
A: Herpes lasts forever.

Active herpes can appear as cold sores or blisters in the mouth or genital or rectal area or thighs. The virus—still incurable—spreads by direct contact. Condoms don't always protect against herpes because sores can be in places condoms don't cover. (That's another reason why people talk of safer sex—not safe sex.) If you have active genital herpes and have sex, you can give your partner herpes. If you have a herpes cold sore and have oral sex, you can give that special someone genital herpes. (Don't believe me? Call the STD hot line.) If he's unaware that he has herpes, he can infect you. Sufferers may experience itching or burning, pain, fever, and an outbreak of blisters that dry up and go away but then reappear at unpredictable intervals. Flare-ups usually become milder and less frequent but during active phases, the area should be kept clean and dry. (Some doctors suggest using a blow dryer.) Never touch open lesions and if you do, wash your hands with soap and water afterward.

FDA-approved medications for herpes include acyclovir, zovirax, valtrex, famvir, and famciclovir. While acyclovir, for instance, can be taken in pill form or applied to sores in cream form, the National Herpes Hotline (919 361-8488) does not recommend the cream form because that can seal in moisture and it's better if sores dry out. Loose-fitting clothing also helps.

Is there a link between herpes and HIV and other STDs? Two-thirds of people who are infected with HIV also have genital herpes, perhaps because open sores are entrance points that are all-too-welcoming to viruses. During outbreaks, abstaining or practicing safer sex can be a matter of life and death. For more information, call the hotline above or the Herpes Resource Center at (800) 230-6039 or visit this American Social Health Association Web site: http://sunsite.unc.edu/ASHA. If you think you may have herpes, see a doctor while your sores are still present and ask for a culture for HSV.

Hepatitis B
About 1.5 million Americans carry this viral infection—in blood, semen, saliva, and urine. Spread through sexual contact or contaminated needles, it attacks the liver, but is treatable.

Hepatitis C
This is another treatable viral infection—also hard to detect and damaging to the liver. It is spread through unclean needles (used for drugs, tattooing, or body piercing) and from intercourse with a carrier.

Syphilis
Symptoms may include a painless oral or genital sore (or chancre) followed weeks later by a rash, sore throat, and/or hair and weight loss.

Then symptoms go away, but the disease, if not treated, can do devastating damage to the brain, blood vessels, and heart—damage that may not become apparent until years later. A 1990 syphilis surge was mostly among blacks and Hispanics in inner and southern cities, but guess who else suffered from it? Henry VIII, Napoleon, and Beethoven. Right now, syphilis cases are on the wane.

No-Fun Nuisances (That Aren't STDs)

And now a few words on yeast and bladder infections and scabies and crabs—all of which can be spread by sex but can also bedevil virgins and girls who are abstaining.

Vaginitis and Yeast Infections

Some vaginal infections are not STDs. Vaginitis is not very serious but may require treatment with pills, suppositories, and/or creams, such as Monistat. Symptoms? Severe vaginal itching or burning and an increase and change in vaginal discharge. You may be more prone to vaginitis if you douche or use deodorant sprays or bubble baths (these can irritate your vulva and kill friendly bacteria). Or if you hang out in a wet bathing suit or wear tight pants or panties or pantyhose with a nylon, rather than a cotton crotch (nylon keeps in heat and moisture, allowing organisms to grow). Or if you're taking oral antibiotics and/or birth control pills, are eating lots of sugary junk food, or are drinking lots of alcohol (these may create vaginal conditions favorable to a yeast or other infection). Or if you have sex with someone who is infected or have sex without enough lubrication. How to guard against yeast infections? Eat yogurt. Cut back on sweets. Be sure to wash your vulva with mild soap daily. And always wipe from front to back after a bowel movement. If you are sexually active, see a doctor the first time you have a vaginal infection because it's not always easy to distinguish vaginitis from an STD without testing, and a misdiagnosis is bad news.

Cystitis and Urinary-Tract Infections

Almost all women get cystitis (a bladder infection) or urinary-tract infection at least once. These infections are not STDs, but young women who have lots of sex (and use lots of spermicide) are particularly prone. If you feel as if you have to pee constantly, yet it burns like Hades when you try and nothing comes out, or your urine is bloody, see your doctor. Cystitis has been dubbed "the honeymoon disease" because one cause may be a suddenly active, vigorous sex life. A doctor can prescribe antibiotics, but in the meantime, abstain from sex, drink plenty (gallons!) of water and other liquids, especially cranberry juice with its helpful acidity, and, if possible, soak in a warm tub. Steer clear of alcohol, coffee, or tea, which may irritate your bladder even more. (If you seem prone to sex-related cystitis, try to urinate before and after intercourse and use a lubricant like K-Y if necessary.) Improper wiping can also be the culprit. Untreated, cystitis and urinary-tract infections can lead to kidney problems.

Scabies

A scientist named Bonomo discovered the itch mite in 1687, and scabies continue to plague children, teens, and adults. You can get scabies from having sex, holding hands, or simply sharing a towel with an infected person. Tiny mites mate on the skin, and then the female mite burrows into the skin and lays eggs. They may appear on hands, armpits, breasts, genital or rectal areas, or elsewhere. Scabies can be treated quickly with medicated lotions. Ask a pharmacist.

Crabs

Crabs are little six-legged lice that nestle in pubic hair and itch, itch, itch. They look like moving freckles. Fortunately, over-the-counter shampoos, such as Rid or A-200 Pyrinate, or prescription shampoos like Kwell kill 'em off. Make sure you wash and dry all your clothes and linens (on the hot setting) before declaring victory over the little beasties. Dumb joke I learned in junior high: What's worse than a lobster on your piano? A crab on your organ!

HIV and AIDS

Are you wondering why I told you about yeast infections and crabs before addressing HIV (human immunodefiency virus) and AIDS (acquired immune deficiency syndrome)? It's because you probably hear a lot about HIV and AIDS at home and in school, yet next to nothing about the diseases and nuisances that you or your friends are more likely to get.

That doesn't mean you shouldn't take AIDS seriously. God knows you should. But don't be too casual about the lesser evils, OK?

OK. Back to the HIV infection and the disease it causes, AIDS.

As of this writing, AIDS still has no cure, though many people are living longer with HIV. AIDS weakens the body's immune system and makes it unable to ward off certain infections, pneumonias, and cancers. In 1981 AIDS was first diagnosed. Today it's a plague—a worldwide epidemic.

In America, AIDS is the leading killer of people ages 25 to 44. Nearly 1 million Americans are infected with HIV; over 250,000 have died of AIDS. Globally the disease is a nightmare. Over 23 million adults and children are infected with HIV. Half live in sub-Saharan Africa.

Some Americans who tested positive for HIV or have gotten AIDS are public figures, Olympic heroes, or entertainers. Basketball star Magic Johnson, diver Greg Louganis, tennis ace Arthur Ashe, actor Rock Hudson, and pianist Liberace all got infected by unsafe sex or unlucky early blood transfusions.

Most Americans with AIDS are gay men and intravenous drug users; new cases include mostly addicts, gay men, African Americans, and Hispanics. Numbers are also rising among teens, male and female. Women account for 1 out of 5 AIDS cases, and women tend to be diagnosed later and die faster than men with AIDS.

A woman's risk of being infected during heterosexual intercourse is twenty times greater than a man's. Why? Because the vagina is moist and warm and any tiny cut (caused by rough sex or a sore from a different STD) can become a point of entry into the bloodstream. Another reason is that semen, which may be infected, remains inside the woman long after intercourse.

You may be thinking that you don't know anyone with AIDS. You may be right. But many healthy-looking teens test positive test for HIV. The virus shows up in blood several weeks or months after infection. It can take up to ten years before someone who has the HIV virus comes down with symptoms of AIDS, such as weight loss, fatigue, fevers, or lesions. Yet more than a fifth of Americans with AIDS are in their twenties, which means that lots of them became infected in their teens—and probably didn't know it. Many homeless teens also test positive for HIV, some because they traded sex for drugs or money and did so with someone who was infected.

You may be thinking that despite these high numbers, no one in your high school could possibly have AIDS. Believe me, I hope you're right. But this is how a boy *could* get AIDS. He could have been peer pressured at a stag party into having sex with a prostitute (who may have had the virus). He could have had sex with a girl who had sex with the wrong guy before him. He could have had a homosexual encounter while experimenting or trying to sort out his own sexual identity. He could have been raped. Or he could have done drugs and shared a lethal needle. Could he have gotten AIDS from a blood transfusion? Probably not after 1985, when the nation's blood supply started getting screened. Could he have been born with AIDS? Almost half the babies of infected mothers are born HIV-positive or get infected through breast-feeding, but sadly, none has survived long enough to become a teen.

And you? Be wary, not panic-stricken. You don't need to be paranoid about AIDS if you don't shoot drugs and if you abstain from sex; have sex with only one faithful, uninfected partner; or always, always, always use lubricated, latex condoms with spermicide from start to finish. (I know it doesn't sound sexy, but you're supposed to use a condom even during fellatio—oral sex—too.) The HIV virus is spread through blood and body fluids, and since anal sex can cause bleeding, it can be especially risky (and probably was not on your to-do list today anyway). Personally, I'd also avoid sex with bisexuals or intravenous drug users, since having sex with someone who has engaged in risky behavior is risky behavior.

You cannot get infected from hugging or kissing or sharing forks or towels. You can get it from contaminated needles. New needles are used when you donate blood. What about if you get a tattoo or get your ears pierced? Needles must be new and equipment must be sterile—take your health seriously!

You also cannot get AIDS from being helpful and friendly to someone who does have AIDS. People with AIDS need support, company, and compassion, not ostracism. When my cousin Jim got sick with AIDS, we tried to spend more time with him, not less. If you know someone with the disease, don't shy away—unless you yourself are sick. (Run-of-the-mill germs to you can be life threatening to a person with AIDS.) And don't assume the worst. Some people continue to live vigorously even with full-blown AIDS.

If you truly think you may have been exposed to HIV, you can get tested. All HIV testing is voluntary and confidential. Blood tests are conducted in many hospitals and clinics, and home kits can be bought at the registers of many pharmacies.

If results are negative and you haven't engaged in any high-risk behavior in the past six months, start breathing easy—and stop putting yourself at risk.

If you test positive, get counseling and medical care. There is no way to get rid of HIV. But there are combinations of drugs (some are expensive) that can prolong health and life. Many doctors are cautiously hoping that combination therapy can help transform AIDS from a fatal disease to a manageable chronic illness—from a death sentence to survival.

Why get tested? For peace of mind. And, in worst-case scenarios, so you can get medical care and protect others. Thousands of HIV-positive people live for years with dignity, vitality, and hope.

More questions? Call the National AIDS Hotline at (800) 342-AIDS. Or call the AIDS hotline that is just for teens at (800) 234-8336. In Spanish: (800) 344-SIDA. *¡Decir no a la SIDA es decir sí a la VIDA!* On the Internet, contact the Centers for Disease Control at http://www.cdc.nac.org.

One question: Now that you've waded through these sections on birth control and STDs, are you sure you want to say sure to sex?

Rape

I am lucky. I have not been raped. But I will share an experience with you that frightened me. Here's what I wrote on February 9 in the diary I kept when I was fourteen:

> *. . . Now for the unbelievable thing of the day. I was working on my math assignment after school in an empty classroom when that stupid janitor walked in. As usual he made remarks about his girl-chasing youth, and he asked whether I played around with the boys, adding, "Sure you do, sure you do" and "You're not afraid of me, are you?" (I hate him so much.) Anyway, once or twice he's touched me around the bra area. That could be unintentional but I doubt it, especially after today. Today I was sitting at the desk wearing a dress. He said, "You must get cold going around in bare legs," then rubbed my leg high above my knee and added, "Oh yes, you're wearing stockings. Are your pantyhose tight?" (What a queer!) I mumbled, "I guess so." Then he took his hand away. I yanked down my dress lower and he asked, "Why are you pulling your dress down?" Thinking it was none of his business, I just shrugged. Next he put his hand above my knee again and started working his way up. Suddenly he remarked, surprised, "Oh you have panties on underneath." Not realizing his fingers were up so high, I desperately held*

*down my dress. He said, "What are you worried about?" At this
point I was giving him really dirty looks and holding down my dress
with all my might!! He said, "What are you afraid of? C'mon, let
me have another peek." (Who does he think he is?) Finally he must
have given up and he went back to vacuuming. Now get this. He then
said, "I know what you're hiding—your little brown mustache.
That's it, isn't it? Do you comb it every night? Sure you do. Well yes
or no?" I said no. He added, "Well you put your hand on it." I shot a
really mean look at him and went back to my math. He said, "You
know I'm doing you a favor letting you in here." I retorted, "OK. So
I won't come here." He said, "You can come. You're not afraid of
me." I ignored him and finished my geometry. God!!*

I didn't tell a soul back then. Now I wish I had. For all I know, that
old man may have harassed—or molested or abused—some younger
girl. How could I have been so naive and trusting as to think there
could have been anything unintentional about his pawing my flat chest?
And why did I just sit there? Why didn't I at least shout "Stop touching
me!"? Because he was a grown-up? Because I thought adults were
always right? Was I so intimidated by and respectful of my elders that I
didn't know I could talk back and take off?

That disturbed individual scared me without scarring me. But others
have been less fortunate. It is estimated that 1 in 4 American women is
sexually abused (not necessarily raped) before age eighteen.

Never let a stranger lure you into danger by asking you to help him
look for a lost dog or by promising you a gift or by pretending to have a
message from your family or by asking you to be in a movie. Never get
into his car. It's much better to yell your lungs out or cause a big-time
scene. Say "Help me!" or "Call 911!"

Women are vulnerable. Men don't usually have to think about the
possible danger of working alone in an empty classroom or walking
unaccompanied at night. Women do. We don't need to be paranoid, but
we need to be cautious. And informed.

Did you believe any of the following myths?

Myth 1: Only girls get raped.
Truth: While the majority of rape victims are girls under age eighteen,
anyone can be raped. Rape is a crime of violence, not passion. Rapists

look for easy targets, not sexy figures. Teenage girls, old women, even boys get raped.

Myth 2: Most rapists are strangers.
Truth: Most reported rapists are "friends," acquaintances, or relatives, and many "date rapes" go unreported. If a guy you're dating forces you to have sex against your will, that's rape. If your neighbor or friend's brother or coach or telephone repairman or the father of the kids you baby-sit for forces you to have sex when you did not give consent, that's rape. If you're underage, that's rape, too. Most rapists are between fifteen and twenty-two. Some are psychopaths with criminal records. Some are good ol' boys yukking it up at the frat house. Some are family members. (*See* Incest.)

Myth 3: The victim was asking for it.
Truth: Nobody asks for rape. Rape is sometimes random, but if the victim happens to be wearing a short skirt, she is no more to blame than if she is wearing an overcoat. The rapist is to blame. A child who is molested or raped by an adult is never to blame. A woman who drinks too much or has terrible judgment about men may foolishly be putting herself at risk. But she is nonetheless not asking for rape.

Myth 4: Most rapes happen in dark alleys.
Truth: About half of all rapes and assaults happen at home—in the victim's home or at the place where she is baby-sitting or visiting. "Date rapes" or "acquaintance rapes" often occur on the rapist's turf, often on weekend nights. If you say no and he hears yes, if you resist and he threatens or holds you down in order to have sex with you, that's rape (even if he seemed like such a nice guy). If, however, you mumbled no once, but then, perhaps tipsy, became a partner in passion, you may wake up with regrets but you can't really press charges. Don't be a little girl in bed. Be clear about what you want and what you don't.

Myth 5: Most rapes are interracial.
Truth: Most rapes occur between men and women of the same race.

Myth 6: Men's sexual urges are impossible to control.
Truth: Nonsense. A man who penetrates an unwilling woman has raped her. Even if he doesn't see it that way, the law does.

How can you reduce your risk of being attacked or raped? Use common sense and take a self-defense course or learn judo or karate at school or at the YWCA. I know a 110-pound high school girl who decked a 180-pound mugger. She sure took him by surprise. Stay alert and for safety's sake:

- If you are in a home or car, make sure the doors and windows are locked.
- At night, don't walk alone, especially in rough or too-quiet neighborhoods.
- By day, walk with a friend.
- If you are out alone, walk briskly and with confidence. Don't project fear.
- If you are lost, don't ask a strange man for directions and don't give your home address.
- Make sure your parents always know where you are.
- If you feel suspicious of a man behind you, don't slow down or go toward bushes, alleyways, or dimly lit areas. Enter a store or restaurant or Safe Haven or cross the street.
- If you've got the willies and see a respectable-looking woman, walk next to her. (A man once saw me enter a movie theater alone, then went in and sat behind me. I spotted another lone woman a few rows back, sidled up, asked if I could join her— and she and I have been friends ever since.)
- If the phone rings, and you're alone, don't let a stranger know. (Why not lift the receiver, shout "I'll get it" to the walls around you, and then say hello?)
- If the doorbell rings, don't open the door without being sure who is knocking. (An unscheduled plumber? I don't think so.)
- If you're flirting on the Internet, he may say he's nineteen when he's really forty-one. Never give out your number or arrange a first date in a place that is not public.
- If you're alone on a bus, subway, or train, sit near the driver or conductor and don't prepare to get off until the last moment. No one needs to know ahead of time which stop is yours.
- If you are carrying more money than usual, carry two billfolds— one with a few bucks in case you are approached, the other for you, safe in an inside pocket.

- Don't hitchhike.
- If you are nearing your home or car, have your key ready.
- If a guy is alone in an elevator, and your instinct tells you not to trust him, don't get in. If you're alone in an elevator and as soon as someone enters, you think, "Uh-oh," coolly get off at the next floor.
- If you don't know your date well, be extra cautious about drinking or accompanying him to his room. Nine out of ten college-campus rapes involve alcohol!
- Be aware of the messages you're sending. If you hop in bed with him naked, he may assume you plan to have intercourse. If you want to kiss but don't want to have sex, state your boundaries clearly ahead of time.
- If you and a guy are going to park and kiss, avoid secluded back roads or lovers' lane setups where he or a less trustworthy man could take advantage of you. (My parents encouraged us to park in the driveway. Safe and sensible, though my brother Eric sometimes teased me when he heard the car pull in at 11:30 but didn't hear me walk in until 12:00.)
- Don't get drunk or high with a guy you don't know well.
- When you mean no, say it firmly and clearly.
- If a friend's brother or a coach or any man surprises you with unwelcome advances, say, "No! Let me go," and try to break away.
- If a phone is nearby and you need help, dial 0 or 911 to summon the police. If you want information, call the National Center for Missing and Exploited Children at (800) 843-5678 or (800) 4-A-CHILD.

Since we're imagining the worst (I trust you're not reading this alone at night in a creaky house), let's imagine the worst of the worst. You're jumped by a rapist. What do you do?

Unfortunately, there's no simple answer. It depends on you and the situation. Some advise to be passive, especially if the rapist has a gun or knife. Others say to try to repel him: vomit, drool, pee, tell him you have your period or herpes or AIDS. Many say to be assertive: Say "No!" scream, yell "Rape!" or "Fire!" or "Help!" or "Police!" (not just "Leave me alone!" because then someone might think you're arguing with your boyfriend or father). Struggle, carry a whistle, and blow it like mad. Others say to fight back if you know what you're doing: bite, scratch, knee his shin or groin, gouge his eyes, punch his stomach, bend back his pinky, beat his face with your keys or the heel of your shoe, yank at his testicles when he least expects it. (When you think about it, he may be in a pretty vulnerable position himself.) Some say to go limp: Turn into heavy, immobile weight. Others say to use psychology: Ask him sympathetically about his life or tell him your father was just killed in a car crash. Shock him, catch him off guard, outsmart him.

What would *you* do if you were approached? Think about it now.

I don't think I'd have the guts or know-how to poke a rapist's eyes out, but if I had my wits about me and there were people nearby, and I thought I stood half a chance—a big *if,* to be sure—I'd scream bloody murder and run like hell.

You knew this was coming. We're about to imagine the worst of the worst of the worst. You've been raped. Now what?

Call a friend, parent, or doctor, or go straight to the nearest hospital emergency room, rape crisis center, or police station. Call even before you bathe, clean up, or change because authorities usually need physical evidence if you prosecute, and the police may be more sympathetic if you aren't looking fresh as a rose. The majority of rapes go unreported, but if you press charges and land the creep in jail (not easy), you'll feel good about that measure of justice and knowing you probably protected someone else. (Most rapists rape again.) Many rape crisis centers provide a counselor or support team who will accompany you to the hospital or police station and help you begin to deal with your numbness, rage, humiliation, guilt, and disgust. They can also give you emergency contraception—though, odd but true, many rapists wear condoms.

Studies estimate that 13 percent of women have been victims of rape over their lifetime, with the overwhelming majority occurring during their childhood, girlhood, or teen years.

A married friend of mine was raped. She didn't get pregnant, beaten, or STDs, but she was so turned off by men and sex afterward that for a long time she was unable to enjoy making love with her husband. Finally she joined a therapy group that helped her sort out her feelings and retrieve her self-esteem and sense of control. She is now slowly learning to trust again and to blame that one man—not all men and not herself—for her misfortune. She is learning to stop demeaning herself for not having resisted and to start congratulating herself for having survived.

Incest

Sexual contact between relatives or family members is taboo and illegal but not as rare as we would like to believe. Since so many cases go unreported, it's tough to guess how common incest is and how many women have been sexually molested by their fathers, stepfathers, grandfathers, brothers, stepsiblings, halfsiblings, uncles, cousins, or other relatives—or, for that matter, any trusted adult who is considered part of the family.

Incest is alarmingly widespread among American families of every color, class, and locale. Offenders may be violent alcoholics or conservative churchgoers. Often the victims are children who are raised not to question their elders, don't realize how exploitative their situation is, and may mistakenly believe that Father knows best.

"If you don't do as I say," a father or stepfather may threaten, "I'll beat you." "If you don't let me do this now, I'll do something worse next time." "If you tell anybody, I'll kill you." "I'm your father—I should be your first man." "I love you, Baby." "Do this for me—c'mon."

The girl may be afraid to say no. She may be afraid that if she tells her mother, her mother won't believe her. Or will blame her. Or will break up the family, then hate her for it. The girl may also worry that if she does *not* tell, the experience will happen again—to her or her little sister. In cases of ongoing abuse, the girl may even develop a confusing dependence on the unhealthy physical closeness.

If you are a victim of incest, you are not alone and you are not at fault. You are the same good person you were before the offender made use of your body. The offender is messed up, not you.

If you were molested by an acquaintance once, the isolated incident may have had little impact. But if a trusted relative abused you repeatedly, therapy is in order. Seek help before your pain, anger, and humiliation can turn to scars that make it hard for you to respect and love other men. Tell a trustworthy adult who will believe you: a family member, teacher, doctor, group leader, school counselor, minister, or rabbi.

There are clinics across the country that specialize in incest-related problems. Or call the National Child Abuse Hot Line at (800) 422-4453 or (800) 4-A-CHILD. Or look in the Yellow Pages under Mental Health or Social Services or Family Counseling or Community Referral. Your father won't be immediately hauled off to jail, nor will you be thrown into a foster home. In most cases, you and your family can begin to get the therapy you need. And you can learn how not to let the difficulties of your past ruin your future.

Those who quip "incest is best" haven't been there. One of the saddest letters I ever received was from a girl named Susan. She was five-and-a-half months pregnant by the time she contacted me. *"The baby is from my stepfather,"* she wrote. *"My mother knows that I am pregnant from him. She drinks—that's her problem. He had been doing it to me when I was smaller, too. . . . My stepfather goes to bed with me every night, and one night this week he went to bed with me and made me bleed. . . . And when this happened, I was thinking my baby came out of me."* Susan and I ended up talking on the phone, and I urged her to call the child abuse hot line. She did, and social workers helped move her and her younger siblings into her grandmother's home. Next Susan went to Planned Parenthood. It was too late to consider abortion, but the doctors talked to her about prenatal care. Months later, Susan had the baby and arranged to give it up for adoption. And now? She is back in school and holds an afternoon job. With the continued help of social workers, she is trying to keep her life on track.

Here are some letters from other girls.

Dear Carol...

Dear Carol,

My friend's boyfriend asked her if she wanted to go all the way and she doesn't really want to. But if she doesn't, he might drop her. She's considering it for his sake. They are 13.

Sex is not something you do for someone else's sake. At 13, does she imagine this is her last chance at romance? If he drops her over sex (or lack thereof), good riddance.

Dear Carol,

My friend is 13 and she met a guy who is really into sex—not making love. They had sex because he is the type who, if you didn't do what he wanted, would knock you around, so she had no choice.

You always have a choice. When you don't, it's not sex, it's rape. Don't lead guys on, but know that you are in the driver's seat—even if you two are in the backseat. Why rush sex anyway? It's better to have love without sex than sex without love. And why is your friend putting up with a boy who is physically abusive?

Dear Carol,

I have a major, major problem. I've had a boyfriend named Dale for a little over a month now and he has been pressuring me into having sex. He is 17 and I am 14, but he thinks I'm 15. Lately he's been getting mad at me when I've been saying no, and that has made me mad and confused. When I've said no in the past, he's asked why. I told him I didn't want to get pregnant, and he said, "You won't. I have condoms." Yesterday I bought some Conceptrol and today I said yes. I used the Conceptrol, Dale didn't use a condom, it wasn't that great, and now I think I'm pregnant. I am scared out of my mind. I plan to call Planned Parenthood for a pregnancy test. If I am pregnant, I'm really going to freak, but I will have an abortion. Before Dale left this afternoon, he said that he didn't think we should see each other anymore and that I was too young for him. When he said that, I almost passed out, but then he said he was just kidding. Now I'm scared that he wasn't kidding and he was just afraid of being thought of as a jerk. After we did it, there was a lot of blood, and I'm still bleeding now. I'm wondering if I'm having my period (it's not regular yet). Please help.

If I were in your home, I'd give you a hug and we'd talk about emergency contraception and how to say no to lowlifes like Dale. For now, let's hope you're not pregnant. If you don't get your period, go to a clinic or buy a home pregnancy test. Though the blood could be your period, I think it's from the tearing of your hymen, the thin skin that covers the opening of the vagina.

Saying yes can be the start of a new phase of a solid relationship, but it often marks the end of a shaky one. If Dale makes a quick exit, try not to grieve over him. Get busier with girlfriends and activities. Once you start respecting yourself more, you'll find a guy who will love and respect you too. And next time (years from now?), instead of giving pregnancy as the excuse for not having sex, say you're just not ready. Setting a firm limit early on will also prevent every make-out session from turning into a tug-of-war.

Dear Carol,

I recently wrote my best friend who moved away that I had had sex with my boyfriend six times, but really I'm still a virgin. I'm 15. There's this guy who is visiting my neighbors from out of town who said (direct quote) I'm "hot" and that he wanted to have sex with me. I really do care for him even though I may never see him again. I know that I'll feel guilty and sad afterward, but isn't it better to expect these feelings than not to expect them? If I write back in tears, you can say "I told you so."

I don't want to say I told you so. And I don't want you to get hurt or sad or pregnant or itchy. It's better to wait for the right guy and the right relationship. This guy thinks you're attractive? Great. Take it as a compliment, not a reason to have sex. And start being honest with your friends. Boasting just fuels peer pressure, and that's hard on everybody.

Dear Carol,

I'm 17 years old and have been going with a guy for two years. During the past month, he and I have been talking about intercourse. We are very much in love and we are sure we want to do it. We have weighed the pros and cons and discussed birth control. The only thing holding us back are my mother and father. I've always been the "perfect child" and I'm afraid that they would lose confidence in me.

It's not easy being one man's darling daughter and another's sexy lover. Teens might wish for their parents' approval, but most teens end up being mum to Mom and having sex "under wraps." If you and your parents are close, you can broach the subject obliquely, but don't count on their inviting your boyfriend for a sleepover.

Dear Carol,

It's about the Pill. How long before and after sex do you take it? What if you have sex twice in a row?

You take the Pill at the same time every day. If you go on it, read the instructions on the packet!

Dear Carol,

My boyfriend found some of his dad's old condoms. How do we know if they're still OK to use?

Check for an expiration date. Condoms kept in a wallet or glove compartment age faster than condoms in a drawer. But use "condom sense" and splurge on new ones in the right size. It's better to be protected than pregnant. It's also possible to enjoy a lot of intimacy without going all the way. Your boyfriend can even ejaculate but not inside you. (Wanna bet this will be the page that flops open when your grandmother is trying to decide whether *Girltalk* would make a nice present for her little angel?)

Dear Carol,

I'm only in the eighth grade. The boys in my class say they use the same condoms over and over and let their friends use them.

That would be disgusting and dangerous. The boys are all talk. Don't believe them.

Dear Carol,

I came close to having sex. We were in a camper. He tried to get it in, but it wouldn't go in. Is that normal, and am I still a virgin?

A girl is a virgin until she has penis-inside-vagina intercourse. It is normal for penetration to be difficult in the beginning. Some girls have trouble because their hymen is still intact. Others have trouble because the couple is in a hurry and the girl's body does not have time to respond sexually. Lubricated condoms can help. Better still, put on the brakes until you are really ready, physically and emotionally.

Dear Carol,

I am 14 years old and I like to have my way—like dating and smoking. Neither my mom nor my grandma likes that. They're afraid I might get pregnant. I don't use birth control and I do like this boy who is 17. He wants a baby and so do I. My parents are too protective of me, and I'm scared to sit down and talk to them.

If I were your mom, I'd be protective, too. Are you and "this boy" really ready to *raise* a baby? Even your mentioning smoking and pregnancy in the same letter gives me shivers. (Smoking is unhealthy for the unborn and newborn.) Will having a baby make you feel more adult? Or will it make you more dependent on adults than ever? Yes, you can have a baby at fourteen. But you can also have one at twenty-four. Or thirty-four. Or forty. Why not finish school, travel, start a career, find a husband, and then raise a family?

Dear Carol,
  Can a gynecologist tell if one has masturbated?

Nope.

Dear Carol,
  I have a problem. This may sound gross but my boyfriend wants to have sex and I'm only 13. What should I do? I'm so confused. We've done everything else there is to do and now we're bored and want something else to do. My mind keeps saying no but my body is saying yes. My boyfriend is the hottest and most popular guy in school and I'm afraid that if I don't do this, he'll dump me.

How do you feel when you're alone with your boyfriend? Happy and wonderful? Or bored and pressured? Is this relationship helping you grow and feel good about yourself? Or is it stifling you and making you unsure of yourself? You don't need me to tell you what you already know: You don't want to have sex yet. So don't.

Dear Carol,
  I told my boyfriend I wanted to stay a virgin, and he bought mint-flavored condoms for oral sex. But I don't want to do that either.

So don't. Just because he's ready-to-go doesn't mean it's your duty to satisfy him. If you aren't burning with love and desire, why even consider being so intimate?

Dear Carol,
  I'm 12. I've never had sex with anyone, but I have a sort of pimple between my vagina and my rectum. It was sore and swollen for two days

but now it's just a small bump. Please write me. It will really take a load off my mind.

Relax. Just as no-big-deal blemishes can appear on your face, they can appear elsewhere. Other STD questions? Call the hot line at (800) 227-8922. It's free, anonymous, and won't show up on your phone bill.

Dear Carol,

I am 16. My boyfriend and I had been going out for a year and a half when we finally made love. And that's exactly what it was. It was both of our first times, which made it more meaningful. Instead of breaking up afterward (which I hear often happens), he and I were closer than ever before. Perhaps because we shared with each other something that we'll never be able to share with anyone else ever again: our first time. We always protected ourselves. A few months ago, we broke up for different reasons, but we are still close friends.

Dear Carol,

I really liked the chapter on sex in Girltalk. *I'm a virgin and have been wondering lately if it was time to change that status. The sections on birth control and STDs helped me realize the responsibilities involved. I've decided I'm not ready for sex yet and I feel really good about that decision. Thank you.*

Thank you both for the honest letters.

Dear Carol,

You are the first person I have consulted about my problem. I was riding home in the bus from kindergarten one day, and a boy asked if I would undress for him. I wasn't so sure at first, then after he told me it would be OK, I did. I think it was the biggest mistake of my life. Anyway, something happened that I don't wish to say. Now when I'm around boys, I'm very squeamish. I don't know what to do. I know this problem sounds like just another love problem, but it took a lot of guts to write this letter.

What happened wasn't your "mistake." You were just a scared kid who got unfairly taken advantage of. You may not have been raped, but you were definitely violated. Since the long-ago incident is still coloring your feelings toward guys, I suggest you spill the whole story to a counselor (or maybe your mother) instead of storing it inside and feeling ashamed. Get referrals and shop around for a good therapist. After just a few sessions, you may feel wiser, lighter, and more ready to move on.

Dear Carol,

I wish I had Girltalk *when I was younger. I am 18 years old. When I was about 10, I got raped by my best friend's older brother. No, I didn't report it because I didn't know what was happening. I got over it, but not completely. Sometimes I wake up crying and it scares me.*

Since you still feel upset about that rude sexual awakening, you, too, might want to get a little counseling (often free in college). Many rape victims benefit from therapy because it helps remind them that while the rapist was abusive, not all men are, and while the rapist was to blame, the victim was not. Will this incident always be part of your baggage? Yes. But we all have baggage, and what we can't unpack, we just carry along. It makes us, us, and that's OK.

Dear Carol,

I have a cousin who is 15. I am 12. Last summer, my cousin and I were in my room talking and taking turns giving each other backrubs. I was under my covers on my bed and he was on top of them. I had a nightgown on with no underwear, but I lifted it over my head because I wanted to get the full effect of the backrub. Did I get an effect all right! After a while, my cousin started massaging my bottom and I kind of pretended I was asleep. He also was trying to feel at my breasts. I let him do that knowing I should stop him, but it felt so good. Then he tried to get around my bottom and into the front, but by squeezing my legs together, I didn't let him—thank God. Finally, I pulled myself together enough so that he got the point, and after a while he said, "Do you know why I did that?" and I pretended I was half-asleep and said, "Mmmmwhaat?" I then felt some sticky stuff coming out of my vagina. Is that what happens when you're going to have sex so that the vagina is lubricated? I just want to forget that night with my cousin because I love him a lot and he's my friend. Is there any way to forget without facing him? HELP! I feel like such a slut for not stopping him.

You *did* stop him. Granted you could have stopped him sooner, but hitting yourself over the head for a year is penance enough. It's time to forgive yourself. You might even say to your cousin, "I'm glad we're still friends because I felt pretty stupid about that night last year." Chances are he does too—even if he pretends not to remember what you're referring to. About the sticky stuff: Yes.

Dear Carol,

I reread Girltalk *a lot and practically have parts of it memorized. Last year I was at a sleepover at my cousin's house and when we went to bed, my uncle came in the room and asked me to watch TV. I said I was tired, but he pulled me by the arm and walked me to the living room. He kept pulling here and there and finally pushed me on the carpet. He held my feet tight with one of his legs and held my hands with one arm and I started to scream but then he put his other arm over my mouth. I fought him all I could and prayed that he wouldn't, but he did—he raped me. After this I didn't say anything about it, but on the night of my birthday I tried to commit suicide by taking a bunch of pills. I woke up late and dizzy the next day, and then I talked to a counselor, who ended up calling my mother. My mom was angry and she called my grandmother and they made me promise not to tell anyone and not to report my uncle. I still get depressed though.*

Who wouldn't? You've described a nightmarish incident and a mother and grandmother who are protecting the wrong relative. I feel for you and I'm sorry your uncle acted so abominably. What a horrible experience! The good news: Your life can improve as you move further from your troubled family and as you continue therapy to understand better where they end and you begin. Speaking of families . . .

5 FAMILY

Making the Best of Your Nest

❁

So much for sex. If your mom and dad hadn't had it, you wouldn't be here. But they had more than sex. They had a family.

Some say the ideal family provides roots and wings. The catch? Most families aren't ideal.

You may have problems with parents or parents with problems. Or you may get along fine with your parent or parents but wish you could say the same about your siblings or stepparents.

If yours is an open, affectionate, supportive family, you are lucky. I bet you like yourself and I hope you are appreciative. If your family always bickers, yells, ignores, or hurts each other, these pages can give you clues about how to end destructive patterns. It's worth working toward more communication and caring, possibly even through counseling. You can't just break up with your family as you can with a boyfriend, so strive to improve things on the home front. Love takes work.

This chapter is for every daughter who is growing up, up, and away, and every family who is having growing pains.

Problems with Parents

Why aren't you all getting along as well as you used to? That's a hard one. If it's not the case in your family, terrific. If it is, fluff up a pillow, sit back, and let's try to figure out what went wrong.

Surprise. Nothing went wrong. It's absolutely normal for parents and teenagers to go through some rough times. Why? Because when you were a child, you often obeyed your parents without question, and now you question everything. You may have thought they were infallible, and now you know they make mistakes.

Consider your parents' point of view. Not so long ago, you idolized them and depended on their approval ("Mom, Dad, watch this, watch this, watch this!"). Now you eat and sleep at home but would just as soon be with your friends. You reached for your mother's hand when crossing the street, and now, when she occasionally reaches for yours— right in public—you could just die. You probably give Tuffy and Tiger more affection than Mom and Dad. Yet your parents, like you, need to feel needed and loved. They want to get along with you as much as you want to get along with them. And they have to put up with you as much as you have to put up with them.

You think it's easy for your mother? She's noticing a wrinkle here, a gray hair there—and you wake up more attractive every day. She may feel her life is becoming routine, whereas yours is (or is about to be) brimming with kisses and compliments, new people and places. Of course, she's proud and happy for you, but she may also feel a tinge of envy—and hate herself for it. It may be tough for her to see you as a person who won't need much mothering anymore. (Or maybe *she* doesn't feel old enough to have a teenage daughter, so she hasn't caught on yet that you're no longer a little girl.)

And your father? You think it's easy for him to see his darling daughter's eyes light up with every mention of Tom, Rick, or Larry? He remembers his wild teenage times and may hate to think of his princess getting tangled up with guys. Plus, he probably thinks you're as pretty as the woman he proposed to, and that may be hard for him to handle. If he's going through his own midlife crisis ("Have I accomplished what I set out to do? Is there more to life than this?"), he may be too preoccupied to sympathize or help with your adolescent identity crisis ("Who am I? What do I want to become?").

So everybody's got a different perspective, and you're all butting horns. You may quarrel because your parents are too protective, permissive, indifferent, nosy, demanding, critical of your friends, or embarrassing. Or maybe they're mired in problems of their own.

Sons complain about parents too. Mark Twain wrote, "When I was a boy of fourteen, my father was so ignorant I could hardly stand to have the old man around. But when I got to be twenty-one, I was astonished at how much the old man had learned in seven years."

Many teens—about 1 in 4—live with a single parent, usually the mother. Although I refer to *parents* in the plural, the following suggestions apply to single parents, too.

If Your Parents Are Overprotective . . .

They probably want to know where you're going and with whom and when you'll be back because they love you and worry about you. They may trust you, but not everyone else in this dangerous world. Even so, it's hard if you have the strictest parents around. How do you get them to stop treating you like a baby? Not, I repeat, not, by throwing a conniption fit; stomp, stomp, stomping to your room; slamming the door; and blasting your music. If you want them to start treating you like an adult, act like an adult. If you want more privileges, show that you can manage on your own—whether by getting up in the morning or getting a job or doing your chores—without needing to be nagged.

Margaret Mead wrote, "One of the oldest human needs is having someone to wonder where you are when you don't come home at night." True. But, are we talking 10 PM, or 11:00 PM, or midnight?

What if you'd like a later curfew? Don't whine, "Everybody else gets to stay out until midnight!" Instead, wait for a relaxed moment and ask your parents if you could have a trial compromise-curfew this weekend. Try to sound rational, not emotional, as you ask if they'll let you stay out until 11:15. Say you want to learn to become gradually more independent so you'll be able to handle college and living away. Then make an effort to be more responsible. You might volunteer to do another chore around the house—vacuuming the living room? mopping the kitchen floor?—in exchange for more freedom.

(If you're thinking, "Another chore! Whose side are you on anyway?" let me point out that a carefree childhood can be misleading. The "lucky" girls who don't have to pitch in at home often freak out when they're on their own or married because they hadn't realized how many tasks need doing. I agree, however, that it is unfair if your parents distribute chores in a sexist way. You *can* mow the lawn, and your brother *can* wash dishes.)

If your parents don't agree to the later curfew, tell them they're almost asking you to be disobedient or resentful. Or simply ask again next week, perhaps upping the check-in time by only fifteen minutes.

If they agree to give the 11:15 curfew a try, *get home on time.* If you walk in at 11:25, you've blown it. If you won't make it in until 11:20, phone ahead. If you arrive at 11:05, you may have won their trust and earned a new, improved curfew.

As far as parents' wanting to know where you're going, that's not unreasonable. No, they shouldn't give you the third degree and, no, you don't have to fill them in on every detail. But parents tell each other where they're off to and until when. It shows they care and it's important in an emergency. From my diary when I was thirteen: *"Mom, Dad, and Mark got home after 1:00 A.M. and didn't call—worrying me and Eric to death."* See? If they're going to be late, they should phone, too.

How come you don't want to tell them where you're going, anyway? Because they'd disapprove? If you are doing drugs at your boyfriend's while his parents are away, maybe you can see why your parents worry.

One more thought: If your parents and you are fighting because they won't let you baby-sit or won't let you go out on dates, *and no one has asked you to anyway,* call a cease-fire. Choose your quarrels well and don't fight when it's not necessary.

If Your Parents Are Too Permissive . . .

Maybe you feel your parents would let you do anything, and that they don't, as Rhett told Scarlett, give a damn. Frankly, they probably do.

Your parents may believe that since you'll have to learn to be self-sufficient eventually, better now, under their roof, than later by yourself. And, as with overprotective parents, they may be trying to raise you the best way they know how.

My parents were fairly permissive. They made me absolutely promise I'd never ride a motorcycle, but otherwise I had a lot of leeway. Mom and Dad's easygoing attitude made me feel trusted, not neglected.

How about *you?* If your parents' lack of rules makes you uncomfortable, and you'd like more reassurance that they care, tell them. They may have been afraid to lay down the law for fear that you'd resent them. Or maybe they're so exhausted and overworked that they haven't been as on top of your daily life as they could be. Let them know that you want more guidance or guidelines. Shock them with, "Can you look over this book report?" Or "I'll be back by 11:00. That's my curfew, right?"

Many teens wish their parents would provide more rules, so they know what's off-limits and so they have a handy excuse to go home when it's late and they're tired. If your parents never provide rules, give yourself rules. You will make your bed every day. You will start your homework before dinner. You will be tucked in by 11 P.M. Eventually you live by your own rules, so it doesn't hurt to discipline yourself.

If Your Parents Seem Indifferent . . .

What if your parents not only haven't set rules but never ask about your life, friends, schoolwork? They're so busy with their jobs and friends, they don't seem to have time for you. What if communication is zilch?

That hurts. Of course, they may be patting themselves on the back for not being nosy, nagging, interfering parents. If so, you need to let them know you'd like to spend more time together. They may be flattered, but unsure as to how to bridge the gap. A man who has spent his whole adult life getting ahead in business may not know how to be a sensitive father. You may not be able to convert him and may have to accept him as is, flaws and all. Or reject him. Or in a few years, closeness may be easier.

It *is* worth trying to get through to a stony parent. Are you trying? If your dad asks, "Where have you been?" and you say, "No place," that's not setting the groundwork for friendship. Rather than being upset that your parents aren't attentive the minute you come home from school or they walk in from work, plan a time for a visit or family meeting. Say, "How about if we make popcorn or play cards tonight after we all get our work done?" Or, "Let's take a walk after dinner." Or, "Let's go out for ice cream cones—my treat." Or, "Keep me company while I make cookies and I'll give you a plateful to take to the office tomorrow." Sound too idealistic? Try informality. If one parent is running an errand, go along. If both are relaxing in front of the television, join them. Or leave a note on their pillow or in their briefcase. "I don't say it often, but I love you."

If you need to have a heart to heart, it may be easiest in the car or on bikes or some time when you are not face to face.

Try to draw your parents out, too. Try: "How was work today?" When your parent grunts, "Fine," say, "No, tell me about it. I hardly even know what you do." If your folks are in a good mood at dinner, ask about how they met, about their first date, first kiss, honeymoon.

Don't forget the little ways to show you care. Compliment the person who made dinner. Praise your dad for trying to quit smoking or your mom for trying to lose weight. Empty the dishwasher if you know your mom hates to. Ask your dad if his cold is going away. My father used to stock the refrigerator with mushrooms (I adore mushrooms) when he knew I was coming home for vacation. It was a small detail, but it made me feel loved. By the way, if *you* do something loving, then afterward wait for applause, toasts, and thank-you notes, it doesn't count as much.

No getting around it, some parents really don't or won't or can't care. You can bend over backward to please or displease them, and it hardly makes a dent. Maybe you can forgive them someday for being emotional rocks. In the meantime, work to please yourself and reach out to other peers, adults, and family members for role models and the love you deserve.

If Your Parents Give You No Privacy . . .

According to a recent survey, about one-third of American teenagers feel their parents invade their privacy. If your parents ransack your drawers, rummage through your purse, enter your room without knocking (or without waiting for you to say "come in"), read your mail and diaries, listen in on your phone calls, throw out your old clothes or magazines, or borrow your belongings without consulting you first, you can legitimately be mad.

Have you given them reason to be suspicious? If parents find out that their daughter smokes or drinks or has sex, they may—again, for Daughter's own good—try to keep track of what she's up to.

Try to get your parents to trust you more by being more open. If a friend comes over, don't race to your room. Spend two minutes introducing her to your mom. Satisfy your parents' curiosity by telling them a little about your classmates, activities, whereabouts, and schoolwork. Instead of "I'll be out until six," say, "Ali and I are going to Stephanie's after school to work on our project about endangered species."

They are wrong if they think they have a right to know everything you do, but you are wrong if you think your life is none of their business.

In person or in a note, gently ask them to try to respect your privacy and your wish to keep some things to yourself. Don't shout, "Leave me alone!" Explain that you aren't doing anything bad and that you love them but that you need some time and space of your own. And always knock before barging into their room and ask before borrowing their scarf or reading their letter from Aunt Susan. (No double standards!)

If they won't stop snooping, you could consider hiding or locking up your personal things or leaving them in a school locker. What a shame. But take heart. Pretty soon you *will* be on your own.

If Your Parents Expect Too Much . . .

Some parents' expectations are so high that nothing you do is enough.

When I was sixteen, I wrote in my diary about a time when I fell short of my father's expectations. My verbal PSAT score was fine, but not as fine as he had hoped. *"Dad said, 'Read the paper, Carol, and you'll do better next year. Eric's score went way up; Mark's did, too. Don't be disappointed.' Dammit—I wasn't disappointed!"*

Because I was a good student, my parents got used to good report cards. At first, I wanted Mom and Dad to go nuts with pride every quarter, yet they seemed to take my grades for granted. Finally, I told them how I felt. They said they were proud even when they didn't show it. More important, I began working to please myself, not them.

If your parents expect the world, they may mean well. They may even want you to accomplish what they meant to but didn't. If they encourage you (as my parents usually did), they are being helpful. But if their plans for you are too lofty, they may be setting everybody up for disappointment.

You may have to sit them down and explain that you *are* trying hard in school. Or that mastering the flute is their dream, not yours—you'd rather concentrate on photography. Or that it's not reasonable for them to expect you to do all the cooking and cleaning and still have a life.

Some parents may never be satisfied. Try to accept this as their shortcoming and recognize your strengths even if they don't. This isn't easy, but you can do it.

Other parents may have difficulty giving praise because they're feeling jealous or inferior. If this is the case, you could subtly remind your parents how grateful you are for their help along the way.

Still others are convinced their kid is God no matter how much the kid screws up. That way they get to award themselves the Best Parent Prize every year. Positive reinforcement is the key to good parenting, but not when Mom and Dad go overboard. If you start believing you're picture-perfect, you'll be in for it later when you have to face up to your failings.

Finally, some parents—the kind I hope you have—have high hopes for you and encourage you, without undue pressure, to reach for the sky, yet want for you what you want for yourself and will love you unconditionally.

(P.S. That's a lot to ask. And sweetie, you can't expect your parents to be Super-Mom and Super-Dad any more than they can rightfully expect you to be Super-Daughter.)

If Your Parents Don't Like Your Friends or Boyfriend . . .

In fifth grade, one of my friends said, "I hate you!" to her mother, and her mother told her to stop playing with me. Me! Mild-mannered, level-headed, polite little me! She had decided I was a bad influence on her innocent child. I'm biased, of course, but I think she was mistaken. Sometimes parents' judgments are wrong.

But sometimes they are right. Come to think of it, I was an unpredictable ten year old. That very week I'd pilfered five colored thumbtacks from the police department headquarters during a Girl Scout trip!

Anyway, just as you don't like all your parents' friends, they won't like all yours. Do introduce everybody so they can give each other a chance. And don't pick friends just to please or spite your parents.

If they like some of your friends but dislike one in particular or don't like your boyfriend, obviously you aren't going to dump that person heartlessly. But ask yourself—and them—why they disapprove. Maybe your father would have trouble watching Daddy's little girl waltz off with *any* young man. Maybe your mother is jealous of your closeness with girls your age. If so, their opinions of your friends may not be 100 percent valid. Why not meet your buddies outside, at school, and at their homes more often than at yours?

Perhaps your parents have reason to believe that Greg is dishonest, is taking advantage of you, or drives too fast or that Paula hangs out with older guys and is into smoking, drinking, or drugs. Have you been swearing more than usual or acting surly or listless or sullen? Have your grades dropped? It's possible your parents put down your friend (I know you're tired of hearing this, but picture yourself in their position) for your own good.

My parents never warmed up to my brothers' friend Zeke. One evening we three kids gave a big summer party, and Mom and Dad were nice enough to stay upstairs and out of the way. Dad did, however, peer out their bedroom window from time to time to check on things. That's when he saw Zeke, slightly wasted, tossing lighted matches into the forsythia. Dad came down yelling, and I couldn't blame him.

Your parents may be particularly touchy about your boyfriend because they may be afraid you're going to get pregnant or run off and marry him. Tell them you're responsible and having fun, not making life commitments. If they haven't met your boyfriend, have them meet informally. They may decide he's not such a bad guy.

Some parents are going to like your friends so much that they may not know when to leave. If your parents always try to be too buddy-buddy with your buddies, handle the situation with care because they may be feeling a little middle-aged or lonely. Meet your friends elsewhere. Or have a short visit with your parents at your home, then explain that you are all going to your room to talk. You're entitled.

If Your Parents Embarrass You . . .

I have a friend who is embarrassed by her parents because her parents are poor. They also happen to be one of the warmest, most giving, most down-to-earth couples I know.

Other friends get embarrassed because their parents are rich. You compliment the grand piano in the hall or the painting on the wall, and the friend starts apologizing.

Try to appreciate whatever it is your parents offer and stop cringing just because your foreign-born mother makes occasional grammar mistakes or your individualist father shops in shorts and knee-highs while puffing on a fat cigar.

If you are embarrassed because your parents have drinking problems or are known to be busybodies or curmudgeons, the problem is stickier, but remember that you are your own separate person. If someone mocks you, you can say, "My mother's behavior bothers me, too, but it also bothers me when people judge me because of her." Or you can tell a teacher, "I feel terrible that my father called to complain about my grade. I'm really sorry."

Can you speak directly to your parents? Maybe. You can't say, "Mom, get rid of your accent." But you can say, "Mom, I know you meant well telling Tish to stand up straighter, but I don't think it's your place to comment on her posture." You can say, "Dad, please don't compliment me in front of friends. It was sweet of you, but I felt ridiculous when you wolf-whistled in front of Lloyd." Or tell your parents, "Please stop asking me to play the horn for company. I feel like a complete idiot when I have to perform." If your parents love to tease, you can't change them, but you can warn your friends they may be in for some ribbing.

Decide for yourself if a showdown is worth it. My father sometimes had me speak a few lines of French when we had dinner guests. I usually obliged because although I got a little embarrassed by it, he got a big kick out of it.

I also had to develop a sense of humor about Dad's quips on my budding figure. From my diary, age fifteen: *"I was going to the dance and Mom said to Dad, 'Doesn't Carol look nice?' Dad put in his usual, 'Yes, but what are those bumps on her chest?'"* Thank heavens he kept such cracks in the family!

If Your Parents Both Work . . .

If your parents both work, that doesn't have to be a problem. Coming home to quiet may be a jolt if Mom or Dad had always been a house spouse and you'd gotten used to milk, snacks, and conversations after school. You may miss that time of closeness, but there are advantages of having two working parents, besides the obvious economic ones. Since both my parents worked, I learned independence early and didn't struggle with any career-versus-marriage questions because I knew that women, like men, can have kids *and* careers. Some sacrifices have to be made, but both parents can be breadwinners and bread bakers.

If your working parents like their jobs, that can be a plus, too. If they lead stimulating (albeit stressful) lives of their own, they might be somewhat less likely to invade your privacy or be overprotective.

And if you crave more attention? Say so. Don't pout, "You're always working." Say, "I miss you when I don't get to see you."

If Your Parent Is Gay . . .

Sometimes a gay couple adopts and brings up a child. Sometimes a child is raised by two lesbians, and the biological father may or may not be part of the picture. Sometimes after a divorce, a parent comes "out of the closet" and moves in with someone of the same sex. No matter what the scenario, you're not alone if one (or both) of your parents is gay. There are some 14 million children of gay and lesbian parents in America.

Are you comfortable having two mothers or two fathers? Even if you are, it can be difficult if school friends question or criticize your home life. The more accepting you are of your home life, the easier it will be for you to talk about it. If someone does needle you, she is ignorant, and you can ignore her—or educate her.

Some gay parents choose to keep a low profile, and their kids do, too. Other parents are politically active and hope their children will want to march in Gay Rights parades. You can decide if you want your circumstances to be private or public.

Many towns and cities have organizations for gay parents and some have counseling groups for teen children of gay parents. If you're feeling confused or conflicted, set your mind at ease and speak to a counselor or join a group and compare notes with peers in similar situations.

Studies show that children of gay and lesbian parents are no more likely to become homosexual than other children. In fact, the discussions in your home may not center on sexuality at all, but on chores, curfews, and whether you can have a dog or get your ears pierced.

No matter what your parents are like and no matter what your complaints are, some days will be tougher than others. In general, the soundest advice is to be open, caring, and honest and to try to start talking as adult to adult, not child to parent. Tackle problems as they arise. You and your parents are separate individuals. Agreement isn't always possible. But harmony is worth working toward.

Parents with Problems

When you're a kid, you don't think of your parents as having any problems. Now you know better. Family strife may come from parental problems that have almost nothing to do with you. If your parents fight or get divorced, it is probably because of problems between them: changing values, loss of trust or respect, money troubles, infidelity. Or your family may be in turmoil because of alcoholism, illness, or unemployment. You may get caught in the middle and you may ache because of their problems, but their problems are not your fault. And just as your parents aren't failures if you're not happy, you aren't a failure if they aren't happy.

If Your Parents Fight a Lot . . .

My parents had a good marriage, complete with occasional arguments. When I was fourteen, I wrote in my diary: *"It hurts and upsets me when Dad uses a harsh manner with Mom because I know twenty years ago they were newlyweds."* Yet now I realize it's impossible to feel and show intense love every minute after years with someone. And sometimes arguing shows caring.

When you go out with a guy, you're trying to have fun for a limited time. When you're married, you're trying to have fun and take care of each other and make a living and pay taxes and keep a tidy home and get food on the table and maybe raise a family—for an unlimited time. It's a bigger challenge. Your parents may be very much in love yet sometimes feel the need to let off steam. A little airing of tension is healthy and productive. It may not be pleasant or even fair, but it is tolerable and normal.

And if they quarrel constantly? It's hard on you, but it's not because of you (or your siblings). Childless couples squabble, too. Even if your parents do blame you or use you as a scapegoat (I hope they don't), how well they get along is up to them, not you. Their happiness is their responsibility, just as yours is yours. If you worry that they'll split up as soon as you leave the nest, you need to realize that you can't live at home forever to serve as a buffer zone or keeper of the peace.

What can you do if they're always blowing up at each other? Not much. As my teen friend Emily says, "Try to be Switzerland and remain neutral." Try not to take sides or become the confidante of either one. Go on living your life because you can't make their problems dissolve.

You *can* attempt to make things easier on them. Try to be less demanding during their rocky times. Clean up after yourself around the house, be extra kind, offer to fix dinner for your younger siblings so your parents can go out alone. If things are getting out of control, you could (easier said than done) suggest they talk to a marriage counselor, adding, "I love you both and I hope you can work out your differences." This may help. Or may not.

Keep things in perspective. You and your siblings probably fight even though you love each other. Some well-matched parents fight a lot. Some fight for a few months, then go back to being their quiet, resilient selves. And—I hate to say it—some hold hands all the time, then end up in divorce court. Just because your parents raise their voices is no reason for you to jump to conclusions. Even if your parents are separated, they may get back together, though it's best not to count on it.

If Your Parents Get Divorced . . .

Ouch. This is official. Every year there are over two million marriages and about one million divorces in the United States. Divorce is com-

mon, and you're not alone. But divorce is painful. And it may force you
to grow up before you're ready. Your parents may start leaning on you.
You may be alone more than you like. Money may become scarcer,
responsibilities more plentiful. You may move. Or have to deal with
stepparents. Or be separated from a sibling. You may wish things were
back to normal.

They aren't—alas. And even if you'd been a total angel-pie every
second your parents were together, it's almost guaranteed they'd still be
apart now. So if you're feeling guilty, stop it. If you're hoping they'll get
back together, try to stop that, too. Get yourself to remember, if only for
a few minutes, some of their worst fights.

Accepting hard times is part of maturing. It rains on everybody's life
once in a while, and then the sun comes out again. In the meantime,
your umbrella is to try to get on with your world—friends, school, work,
sports. You need a lot right now. Don't cry alone. Talk about how you
feel to your parents. Or talk to a teacher, relative, school counselor,
therapist, friend, or classmate whose parents are divorced. Some
schools have peer support groups. Don't deny or bottle up your very
natural feelings of rage or confusion or they could come back to haunt
you. Depression, psychologists say, is anguish turned inward.

If one parent starts trashing the other or telling you things you don't
want to hear, understand that your parent is hurting, but gently say,
"Mom, I don't want to hear about how stingy Dad is or how rotten your
sex life was," or "Dad, please don't tell me about Mom's affair; I can't
do anything about it and it just upsets me—I'm sorry." It's not fair for
you to have to play parent to your parent or get caught in the crossfire.
(On the other hand, if your parents act falsely brave, tell them it's OK to
share their sadness with you. A simple "You seem down" might help
cheer them up.)

It's tricky if one parent tries to use you to find out what the other is
up to. You might say you are having a hard enough time adjusting and
you don't want to be a go-between. Say, "Ask *him* if he's dating, not
me." It's also awkward if your parents try to win you over with gifts.
Don't let your loyalties be bought. And don't let one parent make you
bad-mouth or stop seeing the other.

It might be a good idea to try to be part of any discussions about cus-
tody and visitation rights. Keep at least a spare toothbrush and some
underwear at the house where you may spend weekends or vacations.
Better yet, make one bedroom drawer officially yours.

Some kids are relieved when their parents divorce. The war is over, and the parents may end up more content, alone or remarried. Some kids have more independence than ever, and some enjoy a new closeness to both parents. One friend told me she thinks of her family not as a broken home but as two happy homes.

Other kids are devastated. They'd accepted their parents' marriage as a given, and now their family is one more statistic. Is your parents' marriage over? Coming to terms with that sad truth gets easier with time and distraction. But you can't deal with it until you believe it. Be patient with yourself. Allow yourself time to feel angry and down.

It takes a long while to get from one part of your life to another. Remember that the end of one chapter marks the start of the next. Take your time grieving for the way your family was; then turn the page. Things won't be the same, but they may come out better than you expected. And by simply surviving this terrible time, you'll probably emerge a stronger, deeper, more compassionate person. (If, instead, you let yourself become glum, cynical, or an object of pity, you aren't doing yourself any favors.)

Although your parents don't love each other the same way anymore, they probably each love you as much as—or more than—ever. If one of your parents does suddenly drop out of the picture, it's going to hurt like hell. Parents are irreplaceable. But new people always come into your life, too, and 2 out of 3 divorced or widowed people remarry. You'll be loved because you are lovable.

If Your Parents Drink Too Much . . .

The *Smoking, Drinking, and Drugs* chapter talks about alcohol. But if your parents (not you) have the problem, they (not you) are going to have to recognize it and deal with it. If your parents have one or two drinks after work every day, that doesn't point to alcohol dependence. But if that drink or two changes their character, or if they can't control the drinking or become mean, moody, sloppy drunk, or borderline comatose, then your parents may be alcoholics and you are indeed in a difficult situation. You may feel disgusted, ashamed, angry, resentful, disappointed. Keep in mind that alcoholism is a disease; it may be partly acquired, partly inherited. And you can't get your parents to change until they admit that they have a problem and are ready to work on it. I know one boy who poured out his mother's entire liquor supply, but the mother replenished it that week.

What can you do? Stay out of the way when your parents are drunk and don't provoke them. Call Alateen (800 356-9996) and meet other teens whose parents are alcoholics. Millions of problem drinkers in America are parents with children who, like you, are caught in a love/hate bind. Al-Anon is for entire families of alcoholics. You could also talk to an adult you trust, a counselor, a member of the clergy. And you could suggest (results not guaranteed) that your parents attend an Alcoholics Anonymous meeting. Be encouraging, not critical. If your parents have come to grips with the problem, they may be ready to get help. But if you keep making excuses for them or keep covering up their abuse, they are getting away with too much and may not feel motivated to change. (You may want to escape the whole scene at times, but don't do it by drinking.) For information on the Internet tap into http://www.al-anon.alateen.org.

If Your Parent Is Ill . . .

Losing a parent is the number-one teen fear, according to a Norman-Harris survey. But for the moment, let's not assume ill means dying, OK? Many of my friends' parents have survived heart attacks and cancer and complicated operations. In each case, the scare brought the family closer.

If your parent is ill, it's hard on everybody. How you did in the track meet doesn't seem to matter to anyone anymore—maybe not even to you. Your whole family is frightened, near tears, and tiptoeing around. Hospital bills may be using up the family money. You may have to take on more responsibilities than you can handle.

Talk about your worries with each other and show your love to the ailing parent with words, hugs, cards. You all need each other a lot right now. Be thoughtful and helpful. If the strains are too much, talk to a relative, a friend, or an adult outside the family.

If Your Parent Loses His or Her Job . . .

Be supportive. Your parent's self-esteem may be suffering, and your understanding, love, and respect will be appreciated. The parent may be cranky or withdrawn or may sleep or drink more than usual. Cut back your own spending and try to make extra cash baby-sitting or at other work. Maybe you could even treat for some groceries. Even if your admiration is more genuine when your parent is on top of things, your parent needs your love now. Take advantage of the parent's extra time by doing things together: walking, cooking, going to the zoo, playing games. That will be good for both of you. Every family crisis provides an opportunity for new family closeness.

If Your Parents Are Abusive . . .

If you frequently get hit or threatened, it probably doesn't help to know that millions of other teens are also beaten, neglected, or abused by their parents or that parents who punish their children like this are sick and in the wrong. If you are a victim of abuse, you need help. Your parent needs help. Your siblings need protection. You should report your parent.

It's one thing if your parent lost control once and slapped you harder than he or she meant to. That's not praiseworthy, but it may, if followed by apologies and explanations, be forgivable. But if your parent uses you as a punching bag, *you* could grow up with physical and emotional scars even though your *parent* is the one at fault.

If you've been brutally smacked around more than once, consider speaking anonymously to a counselor at the National Child Abuse Hot Line, toll free at (800) 422-4453. Or call the National Domestic Violence hot line at (800) 799-SAFE. Or call the police or talk to a doctor, relative, teacher, minister, rabbi, or school counselor. Or press 0 and ask the operator to give you the number of someone who can help. You deserve to be treated better.

Emotional abuse may not leave you visibly black and blue, but it's horrible to be picked on all the time. If the nicest thing your parents ever say to you is "Get lost" or "Our lives were easier before you came along," it becomes difficult for you to believe in yourself. Your family needs counseling, and if they won't go with you, you should go alone. Making the initial call is hard. Talking to the therapist or social worker is not so hard—it's a relief and a release.

If you cannot stay in your home, there are places to go besides your friends' or neighbors' homes. Don't rush into marriage, or you may find yourself in another trap. And don't run away without knowing where you're running to. Too many runaways end up desperate and poor and deceived; many become prostitutes or pushers or porno "movie stars." That doesn't have to happen! There are halfway houses and shelters and federal service agencies for battered teens and wives. If you are under eighteen, you have a legal right to shelter, protection, education, and support. The Legal Aid Society, Civil Liberties Union, and Child Welfare Bureau can help you.

The National Runaway Switchboard for runaways and youths in crisis is (800) 621-4000. Switchboards can serve as go-betweens for parents and teens and can tell you about running away and about getting help. Or call the Covenant House 9-line, (800) 999-9999. To reach Christian counselors, call (800) HIT-HOME or, on the Internet, visit http://www.ydi.org. Over one million teenagers run away from home each year—that's too many!

In most cases, if you have terrible problems with parents or parents with terrible problems or a bit of both, you'd be wise to get some family counseling before things worsen. There's no stigma to getting outside help. And it's better than staying in a no-win situation.

You're Crazy If You Need Counseling and Don't Seek It

Therapy is not only for the weak or the wacko. It's for the person who is smart enough to realize that she could be happier and that a trained professional could help her find that happiness.

You don't trot off to the doctor each time your tummy hurts, and I'm not saying you should run to get your head shrunk (or expanded) each time you're upset.

From my diary when I was sixteen:

> *Life is like a rerun. There's no one to talk to, and I don't want to be alone. I'm sick of pressure, even peer pressure. I'm sick of being told to pick up Eric here and there. I'm sick of Fran and I haven't even seen her yet. I'm sick of my driving teacher flirting with Danielle. I'm sick of my bosses at the pharmacy thinking I'm high-strung. I'm sick of my messy room—I never clean it. I'm sick of getting no sleep—it's 1:11 A.M. now. I'm sick of not improving at piano—I hardly practice . . .*

That's not jolly, but it's OK. It's the kind of mood that feels awful, yet mostly disappears by morning. Part of being a teen—and a person—is getting into life's ups and downs, smiles and frowns. (Now you know why I'm not a poet.)

But some problems, ruts, and moods are too big to handle alone. If you're anorexic or alcoholic or suicidal, you probably can't recover without outside support. If you've been abused, talking to a therapist can speed the healing. If your parents divorced or your sister died, an objective listener can help you cope with your sorrow. If the idea of kissing petrifies you, a counselor can help you be more comfortable with your sexuality. If you've been shoplifting or binge buying, a counselor can help you control your urges. If you've been generally down, a therapist can help you buoy yourself back up. Sometimes you feel trapped when you aren't. A psychiatrist can also find out if your depression is due to a chemical imbalance and, if so, can prescribe the necessary medication, possibly Prozac, Zoloft, or Paxil. Finding the right dose of the right drug can be challenging—and lifesaving.

Maybe your whole family could benefit from therapy. For instance, if your home life is not warm, but always freezing or boiling. Or if your father is the heavy, and your mother never even disciplines the dog. Or if it's next to impossible to adjust to your stepparent or half-brothers. Or if your home is full of misdirected anger: You all yell at each other when you're actually mad at friends, teachers, and bosses. You could put up with family friction and hope that you'll all get along in a few years. But why deny yourselves the possibility of getting along now?

Not that counseling guarantees instant family or personal happiness. You have to work toward that. But counseling is a step in the right direction. And if you're carrying around a lot of excess emotional baggage, sooner or later, you'll want to unpack.

How do you find a good therapist?

Your school guidance counselor may be able to help you or refer you to competent counselors or counseling agencies. The referral can be confidential, and your sessions can be your secret. If you belong to a church or synagogue, counseling may be available free. Ask. If a friend is in therapy, find out with whom. Your family doctor may be able to recommend a psychologist, a psychiatrist, or a licensed social worker. Private sessions are expensive but may be covered by insurance.

In your telephone directory under Youth or Mental Health or Social Services or Family Services, you may find therapists and agencies that offer free counseling or that charge a sliding-scale pay-according-to-what-you-have fee. The United Way can also help you find someone who can guide you to understanding and liking yourself better.

Short-term therapy may be all you need. Going for counseling doesn't have to mean years on the couch.

You may decide you don't respect or feel comfortable with a particular counselor. Fine. Get several other references and call them on the phone before setting up a new appointment. Or try group therapy. Or perhaps a confidential call to a hot line or an anonymous visit to a Web site or a look at self-help books can provide comfort, insights, and reassurance.

Maybe what you need is to talk to yourself. Really. Maybe your parents keep putting you down and saying you can't do anything right and now you're picking up where they leave off. Maybe instead of ever saying, "Good job!" to yourself, you always say, "I'm such a loser." If so, instead of making the L hand signal, give yourself thumbs up. Be your own cheerleader. If you just spent twenty minutes on a stationary bike, don't moan, "What a pathetic workout," try, "Yay me—I exercised for twenty minutes."

The point is, you can feel better. You may benefit from therapy or medication. Or you may be able to modify your thinking and behavior on your own. If you've lost your appetite or can't sleep or work because of troubles, don't come apart at the seams. If some people envy your popularity or money or brains, but you can't see past the 8,600 logical reasons you have for feeling miserable, seek help. It's no disgrace. What is unfair to yourself and your loved ones is to be chronically depressed for months (or years) on end, with or without good reason, yet to do nothing about it except cry and complain. And since moods can be as contagious as colds, your loved ones, upon repeatedly hearing your tales of woe, may either burn out themselves—or start keeping their distance.

An estimated 1 in 4 women will suffer from clinical depression at some point. The National Mental Health Association (800) 421-4211 can provide more information.

Teen Suicide

Suicide rates among American fifteen- to nineteen-year-olds have quadrupled since 1950. Many more girls than boys try to kill themselves, but boys go about it more decisively and succeed four times more often. In the fifteen- to twenty-four-year-old age group, suicide is the number-three cause of death, trailing homicides and accidents— many of which may be suicides. Several hundred kids aged ten to fourteen commit suicide each year, and several thousand teens aged fifteen to nineteen do so. (The actual numbers may be much higher, since so many suicides are reported as accidental deaths, even when the person pulled the trigger or drove into a wall on purpose.) Sometimes suicides follow a ripple effect. One person commits suicide and then a classmate or relative does the same, as though the first person somehow made it legitimate or OK. The domino effect is frightening—suicide is never OK.

While the number of suicides is high, the number of attempts is higher still. Some people try to hurt themselves as a cry for help, hoping to be found and rescued. Many are rescued; many are not.

There is nothing sadder than a young person taking his or her life. Depression is common and crippling, but it can go away and it can be treated. Many despairing teenagers pull through and become happy adults. The challenge is to survive the difficult periods, to be like those trick birthday candles that stay lit no matter what. Everybody trips and falls at times, but it is possible to get back on course.

Do you have a friend or sibling who is talking about suicide? Who is more than a little accident-prone? Who isn't eating or sleeping? Who is suddenly giving away valued possessions or withdrawing from everything? Don't brush it off. You owe it to him or her and to your own peace of mind to alert a responsible adult. Take your friend seriously. Now, not later.

How about you? There are reasons to feel despondent just as there are reasons to feel happy. Have you ever had a moment in which you briefly considered suicide? According to one study, 1 in 4 high school students has. You may have thought, "That'll show 'em," then realized suicide would show you, too. If you have ever attempted or seriously contemplated suicide, please, please, please see a counselor or make a confidential call to a suicide hot line—perhaps from the privacy of a phone booth. Hundreds of suicide prevention centers exist across the country. Look up Suicide in the phone book. Or call the National Runaway Switchboard (it's not just for runaways) at (800) 621-4000 or the twenty-four-hour nonreligious Samaritan's Suicide Hotline at (212) 673-3000 or the 9-line at (800) 999-9999. They can get you through a dark moment and point the way to help and hope.

Someone who is dangerously suicidal may end up spending several weeks or months in a psychiatric ward of a hospital before doctors hit on the right medication and right insights to turn the person around. But what's a few weeks? A blip in a long life. You can't rush recovery. Suggestions that work for teens who are just down (join extracurrics! get some sunshine! excel in one course!) are glib and irrelevant here. Yet antidepressants and proper therapy *can* make a difference. If you are ever in a situation where you think prescribed drugs or your therapist aren't helping, say so. You can try a different medication. You can talk to someone else. Your mental health is just as important as your physical health. Severe depression isn't a weakness; it's a disease.

Many teens kill themselves each year, leaving heartbreak, guilt, and indelible pain in their wake. But many others manage to reconnect with people and to get hold of the reins of their lives. If you hang it up, it's game over. No college. No movies. No dinners out. No naps in a hammock. No walks on the beach. No music. No Paris. No finding that fulfilling job or wonderful spouse. No kids. No grandkids. No great-grandkids.

If you are feeling overwhelmed and debilitated, I'm not telling you to buck up. I'm not saying, "Get with the program." I'm saying, "Get help." I'm also not saying, "It's your party and you can die if you want to." Because I don't think you want to *end* your life. I think you want to *change* your life. And there's a big difference.

A friend of mine tried to commit suicide as a teen. She failed—thank God. Today she is married, has a child, has a fun career, and is very grateful that she got another chance, that her rage one day as an adolescent didn't cancel out her entire future as an adult. I had another friend, as I told you in the *Friendship* letters, who was less lucky. I will always miss her, and she will miss seeing her sons grow up.

If only, if only, if only . . .

Brothers and Sisters

My neighbor Stacy's big brother swore that if she cupped her hands around a bumblebee and held them together, the bee would become tame. She spent months hunting bumblebees, finally caught one, clamped her hands, and—well, you can guess what happened. (Hint: She wasn't pleased.)

Brothers and sisters. When I was growing up, I had no sisters, but brother, did I have brothers! Just two older ones, actually. Mark and Eric. Yet it felt like a houseful.

We three sometimes got along, sometimes squabbled, and sometimes played tricks on each other. It's all in my diary.

> *I was about to go to bed when I found out Eric had set my alarm for 2:00 A.M.! . . . Mark and I tried hard to convince Eric he was balding. . . . Eric told me my faults for about half an hour including that he'd rather have been an only child. . . . Eric was mad at*

me so he slammed the car door shut. But its window shattered and that made him even madder because he'll have to pay. . . . I drove to Jen's, but Eric bicycled over and quietly drove the car away. When I was ready to drive home, I thought the car was stolen and I got hysterical. . . . Judy, Eric, and I visited Mark at Brown University. The visit was fun except that besides giving Mark and his roommate Charlie a dozen cupcakes, we were a pain. For example, Mark had a huge test, and we gave him no time to study. We twisted Charlie's pipe cleaners into little animals. We insulted their sloppy room. We made them find extra beds. We put a peeled banana in Mark's bed, and he thought it was something else. I parked illegally and the car got towed and Mark had to pay to retrieve it, etc. etc.

Somehow we've all forgiven each other, and we're very compatible now (well, not aalllwaaays, but most of the time).

Becoming lifelong friends with your siblings isn't easy. But a sibling is a sibling forever. Your bond may be all the deeper for the mischief you shared. "Blood is thicker than water" is a sort of gross way to put it, yet it's true that you can count on family even when friends let you down. Besides, who else knows you and your parents inside out and remembers the day your kitten got stuck in the filing cabinet and how Grandmom always brought hermit cookies when she visited?

I know, I know. I'm making it sound ever so rosy, but some of you are stuck between a snobby bossy know-it-all big sister and a bratty kid brother who gets away with murder. Or you've got a 100 percent perfect, can-do-no-wrong sis, and only you know that behind the charming facade, she's a number-one jerk. Siblings are for keeps? That may be the last thing you want to be reminded of.

Hold it right there. Are you even half as nice to your siblings as you are to friends and strangers? If not, that's one reason they aren't always nice back. It's wonderful that family members feel comfortable together and can take their shoes and makeup off. But if you're so familiar that you don't bother being kind, civil, or interested in each other's doings, no wonder communication breaks down.

Example: If your brother says, "Nice haircut," and you got your hair cut *last* week, you could sneer, "You're real observant," or you could say, "Thanks."

It's hard to get along with someone who hogs not only the bathroom, computer, telephone, and TV, but parents' attention as well. Some fighting is inevitable. Henry David Thoreau wrote, "Those whom we can love, we can hate; to others, we are indifferent." Jerry Seinfeld wrote, "There is no such thing as fun for the whole family." Bill Cosby wrote, "Parents are not quite interested in justice—they are interested in quiet." Bottom line: No one ever said it was easy. But getting along is a worthy goal. Here are some tips.

• *If you and your sister constantly bicker,* realize that you'd both be happier if you called a truce. Say, "Let's stop fighting. We have to find a way to get along." Try to see her point of view. Praise her instead of cutting her down. Her favorite candy is Twizzlers? Put some on her desk.

• *If you're jealous of your brother,* tell him. He may envy or admire qualities in you, and deep down he, too, may sometimes feel insecure.

• *If you think your parents favor your sister,* don't hope they'll detect your gloom, speak up. Use "I" not "You" statements. If you say, "You always ignore me!" they'll say, "Nonsense!" If you say, "I feel invisible," they may reply with compassion. Ask yourself why they are lavishing time on your sibling. She's sick? Her wedding is next month? Be patient. They don't love her more; she just needs them extra right now. (Direct from my diary: *"I feel like crying. Dinner was awful and the conversation was Eric's college choices again. What originality!"*)

• *If they label you two the Smart One and the Pretty One,* tell them Smart is beginning to feel ugly and Pretty is starting to feel dumb.

• *If your parents favor you,* you could bask in the glory, but be generous. Say things like, "Isn't Lynn a great actress?" or "Can you believe how good Lisa is in science?" When your parents play favorites (their mistake), you and your siblings may become competitive and jealous (your loss). Compliment your sibling directly, too.

• *If your brother acts like he knows everything,* tell him you're glad he's there when you need help, but you wish he wouldn't volunteer advice when you don't ask for it. Tell him you want to make up your own mind, not conform to or rebel against his ideas. He may be in a let-me-prove-how-mature-I-am phase. Things get easier once you're both more secure and independent.

•*If you always idolized your sister and then find out she's a regular human being,* that's called growing up. It's OK—but it doesn't mean you should stop treating her decently.

•*If your sister is Ms. Amazing,* stop competing and focus on what's amazing about you. Think of your family as a team: The "better" each member, the "better" the team.

•*If you and your sibling are rivals in school or athletics,* figure out what area *you* like best and work on excelling in different subjects or sports (unless you both absolutely love the same fields). Learning to cooperate and compromise with siblings helps you learn to deal with strangers.

•*If your kid brother always wants to tag along,* spend a little time with him, but explain that you want to go out alone with your friends. If you occasionally offer him your undivided attention and let him say hello to your friends, he may be more willing to respect your time out. Or tell him you'll play with him when you get back.

•*If your sister steals your boyfriends,* tell her she's hurting you. And that you're glad she approves of your taste, but even if she "wins" Kirk, she's losing more than she's gaining. She may be sacrificing sisterly love for a fleeting romance.

•*If you want to get to know a brother better,* start a conversation and listen. Instead of doing chores separately, do them together and talk. Go for a bike ride and ask his advice or tell him what you like best about him. Knock on his door and confide in him: You have a crush on Bob, or Mom has been on your case and it's driving you nuts. Ask what worries him most. Stop making fun of each other.

•*If you like your brother's friend and think feelings might be mutual,* maybe, just maybe, he can arrange a casual double date to the bowling alley. (Eric did it for me!)

•*If you and your sister share a room,* try to set a few rules about neatness and privacy and try not to let petty things get to you. Tell each other (calmly) what you like and dislike about the arrangement. And consider a curtain or room divider or separate shelves.

•*If your little sister is allowed to do things that your parents didn't let you do at her age,* get over it. She's probably mad that there are more baby photos of you than her. You'll always have reasons to say, "Not fair!" but try to find reasons to get along instead.

•*If your sister goes to camp or college,* call, write, send E-mail or cookies. It may strengthen your bond.

•*If your sister is a nerd,* don't tease her about what a nerd she is or she'll become nerdier and hate you, too. Praise her for what she does well and boost her confidence.

•*If your brother is getting married and you're worried you won't be as close to him,* expect to feel a little jealous and left out at first (I did when Eric married Cynthia), but give your brother credit for knowing a great person when he finds one. You may gain a sister, not lose a brother.

•*If your brother discourages you from taking on challenges,* prove him wrong by excelling.

•*If your sister's recent eating or drinking habits worry you,* say, "I care about you and I'm concerned that you're getting so thin (or drunk). Is something bothering you?" Don't expect her to thank you and reform immediately, but continue to show love, and she will appreciate it. If you're very worried, you could tip your parents off. (I don't mean tattling about your older sister's sneaking one beer. I mean getting help if you think she's losing control of her life.)

That's enough *ifs* for now, don't you think? It's hard to generalize because each family, sibling, and situation is different. It depends on many things, like how old you are and your relationship and family size and age gap and birth order.

Birth order. Have you heard the popular birth-order theories? Some experts believe that where you fit in your family may determine where you fit in the world. They contend:

• The firstborn, since he or she deals with adults right off and teaches younger siblings, is often bright and verbal and achievement oriented, but may be stubborn or a worrier.

- The middle child, since he or she is a practiced diplomat and referee (who, alas, may occasionally feel overlooked by Mom and Dad) is likable and socially adept.
- The youngest child, since she may get heaps of attention, may grow up confident, secure, sociable—and a little spoiled.

Of course, individuality is far more important than family position. Besides, if you're the only daughter in a family of five (like my friend Judy, a middle child), you're going to get more attention than an average middle child. And if you're a "caboose baby," born long after your siblings (like my sister-in-law Sally), you may sometimes feel like an only child.

What does it feel like to be an only child? Depends. My sister-in-law Cynthia says, "When I went to other people's houses, I thought, 'Nice place to visit, but I wouldn't want to live here'—too chaotic!" The pros of being an only child are that you may get undivided attention and feel very loved, you never have to share a room or get shoved by a bully of a brother, and you learn early to be independent and, perhaps, imaginative and a good reader. The cons are that you may get more parental attention and solitude than you'd like, you won't get the inside scoop on what makes boys tick, and you may feel less comfortable in a group of kids. If you are an only child, work on making tight friendships. And if your parents will let you, get a pet. A pet can be a family member. (I had the same sweet Siamese for eighteen years!)

My husband's mother is a twin. She experienced the advantages of always having a playmate and best friend and the disadvantages of rarely getting Mom and Dad all to herself. Famous twins Dear Abby and Ann Landers were compatible and competitive, and I bet the Olsen twins of TV and movie fame were, too. If you're a twin, you two might consider attending different schools or colleges. The connection you share will probably never fade, and it's crucial to develop separate identities. Out of every 100 babies, 2 are twins. (Twin births are up 42 percent since 1980, largely because of fertility drugs.)

If you are adopted, you may not know your natural parents or have any natural siblings, but you probably know that families who share their home and love are as close as families who share genes. I hope you feel special knowing how much your parents wanted you. I know many couples who waited patiently—and impatiently—for month after month until finally the phone rang with the happy news: "Your baby is here."

Stepparents and Stepsiblings: Step by Step

Just about everything I said about parents and siblings goes for stepparents and stepsiblings, too, but getting used to new family members is a whole 'nother sack of potatoes.

While about half of American children live with both original parents, 1 in 4 lives with a single parent, usually Mom. Among black families, over half are headed by single mothers.

Some single moms never marry or remarry. But many do. Over one thousand new stepfamilies form every day, and one-third of all Americans are in some stepfamily situation.

If you are suddenly a stepchild, you can probably make friends with someone who has gone through the adjustments you're now facing. Some teens accept a parent's death or divorce and welcome new family members. Others feel angry, upset, or threatened by any new changes. *You* may wish your stepparent would make a grand exit or that a fairy godmother would appear and whisk you away. (It worked for Cinderella.)

If you were happier before the stepmother, stepfather, or live-in lover came along, keep these thoughts in mind:

• You may chafe because you feel left out. A lot of parental attention that went to you now goes to someone else. Ask your parent to go for a walk or shopping or to lunch or somewhere alone with you. Make a date of it. A weekly date of it. It could even be a book club with three friends and their parents or a Mom's Monday Movie night. Then make it positive, not just a gripe session about The Invader or Boy Toy or Gal Pal.

• You may bristle at your stepparent because you miss your natural parent. You may even feel like a traitor for chumming up to the replacement. But play fair. Treating the newcomer like a substitute teacher or blaming only the stepparent for family upheaval makes life harder for everybody. Befriending the stepparent doesn't diminish your love for your absent parent, though it may mean that you finally have to let go of the fantasy that your parents will someday get back together.

• Try to be happy for your happy parent. Just as you need friends your own age, your parent—though he or she probably adores you—may have felt lonely at times and wished for adult company. If you are happy for your parent and sad for yourself, why not say so?

•Be relieved: With someone else to care for Mom or Dad, you won't feel depended on. You will feel freer to go out with pals or go away to college.

•Who is your wisest relative? Who is the most candid? Your cousin? Your great-aunt? Vent with them and seek their advice.

•Form a stepfamily support group at school. It can be a safe place to bitch—and to trade survival tips.

•Try to think of the stepparent as a plus, not a minus. Arrange time alone together. Let rapport or friendship develop. Who knows? If your stepparent has natural kids elsewhere, he or she may feel the same odd sense of betrayal and disloyalty you do about investing in a new relationship while missing a former one. Ask yourself if you'd still think she was a shrew or he was a thug if she or he had been introduced as a friend's parent.

•Try not to let your feelings toward your stepparent depend on whether he or she is generous or permissive. If you're expected to follow a whole new set of rules, have a family talk about compromises and trade-offs.

•Allow time for transition. Instant harmony won't happen. It may take a year or two to settle in as a family, more if you see each other only on weekends or vacations.

•Don't forget that your stepparent is making adjustments, too. Consider this: Your stepparent fell for your parent yet married a package deal. Fine. No reason for guilt. But it's not all stars-and-stripes from that end, either. If you want to get closer, one way to begin is, "I've been sort of stubborn, but I'm ready for us to try to get along." Stilted? Maybe. Effective? Probably. Or try, "It must be weird having an instant family." (If the stepparent grunts and grumbles, "It ain't what I bargained for," then my sympathy is with you.)

•If you've really tried and just can't get along—sigh—learning to deal with the stepparent will teach you tolerance and social skills. Watching the stepparent's interactions with your family will give you insights on how other families operate. If the situation is beastly, you might be able to move in with your other natural parent or with a relative or friend.

•Stepsiblings add more confusions, rivalries, dimensions, love, and good times to the pot. You're not obliged to adore your stepsiblings, but it's worth working toward (1) truce, (2) friendship, and (3) family feeling. Some stepsiblings get along better than natural siblings. If you're the newcomer and you think the daughter feels threatened, say, "We both know you're your mother's one and only, but I appreciate her trying to make me feel at home." If you're the one who will receive new siblings, call or write before the marriage and say "Welcome to the family." Realize that your parent, too, may be going out of the way to show the newcomer goodwill.

•More questions? Call the Stepfamily Association of America at (402) 477 STEP.

Relatives in the Parlor and Skeletons in the Closet

It's easy to take relatives for granted. It's easy to think of your parents' folks as old fogies, not as the ones who cradled your mom or dad, baked birthday cakes, gave driving lessons, walked down the aisle on their wedding day, and watched with excitement as your mother, pregnant with you, got bigger and bigger.

Your relatives shared memories before you were born, and they've been through crises and quarrels like the ones you're going through now. Sure it's important to dress up, be polite, and show them respect, but why not really get to know them? You probably won't like all of them, and not all of them will make time for you, but you may find you adore many of your relatives, and vice versa.

If you have a complete set of doting grandparents, you are very lucky. Let them know you love them. If one of your parents' parents died before your birth, ask about him or her. Your parent may welcome the chance to share memories.

Get to know older relatives while you have the chance. Correspond with them via mail or E-mail. Hear their stories firsthand. What was their childhood like? What were their hardest and happiest times? What were *their* parents like? What are they most proud of? How did they meet? What was your dad like in grade school? What was your mother like in high school?

You may treasure the advice older relatives give you. When I was sixteen, I wrote in my diary, *"Granddad told me to 'spar with the boys' but not to fall in love, but Grandmom said I'd be in and out of love many times before marriage."* (Grandmom was right.) If you have a video camera or tape recorder, you may want to record relatives' stories.

Or have them write stories down. The best present I ever gave my father was a journal of blank pages in which I asked lots of questions. Some of the questions were light, such as "What are your favorite forms of exercise?" (Dad wrote, "Jogging to refrigerator, fetching the mail, signing checks.") Others were more serious, such as "What was it like meeting Mom?" (Dad wrote, "From about the third date, we were bonded for good.") Now that I don't have my father, I can't tell you how glad I am to have some of his thoughts written in his own hand.

Years ago, when families didn't scatter so much, grandparents often lived with the family. In some places, they still do. When I stayed on a French farm, grandparents Mémé and Pépé lived with us, as did great-uncle TonTon. It caused some tensions, sure, but mostly it was nice for the teens to learn from the elders' wisdom and skills and for the elders to enjoy the teens' energy and enthusiasm.

Don't be embarrassed by your relatives. You are you, and they are they, and besides, nearly everybody's family has at least one eccentric but sweet uncle who saves paper bags and wears wide, garish ties and socks that slip down because the elastic has worn out.

Do you have any problem relatives? If you look deep inside almost any family—including relatives and in-laws—and open the closet door, skeletons come toppling out. Never mind the adulterous half-brother or the bisexual aunt. I'm talking about real lulus. In my extended family, a cousin shot her husband and then herself, only she died and he lived and . . . well, I'm not trying to one-up you on family sagas, but to let you know that if your stepgrandfather drinks and your cousin is in jail, *you* need not feel ashamed. (Even American presidents have wacky relatives.)

If you feel you got gypped in the Relative Department—you hardly have any or the ones you have you could do without—take heart. Certain teachers, parents of friends, and friends of parents can become like loving relatives to you.

When Loved Ones Die

When someone you love dies, it feels like the worst thing in the world. I wish I could tell you that you'll get over the loss in a hurry, but you don't. I will say that after you have mourned, you may end up stronger (if you've survived this, you can survive anything), you may have a better perspective on your setbacks (you won't say, "This was the worst day of my life" after merely flunking a test), you may become more sensitive (since you've "been there," you can empathize with other people's sorrows), and the rest of your family may grow closer than ever.

Of course, you'd probably prefer to be less strong, less wise, less sensitive, and less close to your family than to have to deal with death. Yet Death doesn't ask. And if you're lucky enough to be long-lived, you probably will have to deal with the death of loved ones somewhere down the line.

About 5 percent of Americans under age eighteen have lost a parent, in most cases, a father. Thinking about death may help us appreciate our finite lives and may remind us to show our love to those who make our lives richer.

If a relative is dying, now's the time to say how much you love and will remember him or her. After a death, you may want to write down memories or even lines that could be read at the funeral. If it's a close relative, you may even want to ask for a photo or scarf or small keepsake.

My father died in his sleep when he was sixty-eight. I still cry about it once in a while and I still sometimes say "my parents" when I mean "my mother." But I have finally gotten to the point where I can smile when I remember Scrabble games and driving lessons and cooking side by side. Or when I remember that among his things was a leather eyeglass case I'd made for him in Shop when I was in sixth grade. Or when I recall that whenever he left after visiting me at college, I waited the hour and a quarter it took for him to drive home, then phoned, and he always picked up the receiver and said without hesitation, "Yes, Snippo, I got back safely."

It took a long time, but I can finally feel thankful that I had such a caring father, rather than feel heartsick that I had him for only twenty-five years. I can feel thankful that the bond we shared is sealed and safe. And that you lose your father only once.

But it still hurts. Remember that journal I told you I gave him? One of my questions was a fill-in-the-blank. I wrote, "I'd think it was pretty neat if Carol ____." Dad answered, "published a book." Well, here's the book, but I can't give Dad an autographed copy.

Mourning is the pits. Dad was my biggest fan, and when he died, I felt stranded. My mother and brothers and I comforted each other, but we were all in pretty bad shape. Suddenly a huge hole was in our lives, and we kept falling in because we didn't know how to step around it. I also felt guilty about sobbing to Mom; she had just lost her husband, yet I was asking her for solace.

Seven weeks after Dad's death, I was still a mess: unable to work, unable to play. Dad's life was over and mine was at a standstill. A friend suggested I "talk to someone," meaning that I see a therapist. The words stung because I'd always "had my head screwed on right"—as Dad had often put it. But I knew my friend was right.

What I didn't know was whom to call. (I didn't have one of these handy-dandy books around.) Baffled, I started leafing through the phone book under P for psychology, T for therapy, and at last, M for mental health.

I was shaking as I dialed the first number. The receptionist said someone could return my call after the weekend. The weekend? I couldn't wait that long. I dialed another number, got no reply. I dialed a third number.

"My father died and . . . " my voice cracked, ". . . I'm having a hard time dealing with it." The woman on the other end said, "Do you want to come in and talk about it?" Did I ever!

I got on my bicycle, rode to the Evanston Hospital Crisis Intervention Center, met Mickey Jordan, and blubbered to her for a solid hour. I showed her Dad's picture, described the funeral, told her about the other people in my world. During the next few months, we met seven more times. The sessions with Mickey cost only $20 each and were invaluable. She helped me accept what I couldn't change and untie some knots that were in the way of my getting on with my life. She helped me figure out how to step around the abyss of my father's death. She helped me regain my lost confidence and realize that although my father is dead, he will always be alive inside me.

If someone you love dies, you may not need or want to seek professional counseling. You may find enough strength in your family, your friends, your religion, your memories, yourself. You may be able to stick to your routines and get through one day at a time. Try to pamper yourself. And don't go by any *shoulds:* "You should have been nicer"; "you should feel better by now"; "you should cry more"; "you shouldn't be enjoying a dumb television show." It may take months or several years for you to absorb the shock and believe that the loved one is gone forever. There may not be a turning point in your recovery, but there will be a turning time. Almost everybody who has grieved is left with some sense of guilt, some feeling of being robbed, and some unanswered questions. But eventually, you will accept that your life goes on and you will risk loving other people.

What can you do or say if your friend has lost someone close? Do not avoid the friend because you don't know how to act. Your friend needs you now. Say you are sorry. And be there to listen. You don't have to bring up the subject, but don't change it if your friend brings it up. If your friend's mother dies, she can't talk *to* her mother, so she may want to talk *about* her. Listen.

If her mother had been sick for years, it's not your place to say, "Her death was a blessing in disguise" or "Cheer up" or "Be brave" or "You never really got along with her anyway" or "Don't question God's wisdom" or "Maybe your father will remarry someone nice." I also never liked it when people said, "I know how you feel" because I always felt "You do not." But those people meant well, and the grieving need to be tolerant, too.

Just listen to your friend and agree that it must hurt an awful lot. Listen even if she wants to share a detail that seems horrible (how skinny her mother looked in the hospital or what it was like throwing away her pantyhose). Even if your friend acts crabby or neurotic, she probably appreciates your being attentive. Grant her a short-term "fool's license" because she may be spacy for a while. If your friend loses a family member, she may be sadder months after the fact, when the loss really hits her. And she may never be her very same old self again.

When I was in junior high, my mother learned of the death of a friend and cried and carried on for hours. I tiptoed about and stayed out of her way. Later Mom said she wished I'd gone into her room and given her a hug. Now I wouldn't need to be told.

Do you want to write a note to someone far away who has been through a loss? (I appreciated every single letter I received.) Your card doesn't have to be long. In fact, instead of expressing your sympathy, then going on to say how you made cheerleading, it's nicer to write a focused card, and follow up later with chattier letters. Often the bereaved are deluged with letters when they are still feeling numb, but then nobody writes when the pain settles in.

If you chickened out of acknowledging someone's loss months ago, do it now. Some of my friends worried about writing a belated sympathy card because they were afraid they'd "remind" me of Dad's death.

Believe me, one mourns without reminders. And even when friends' cards made me cry, the tears were welcome and healing.

What do you write? "I was so sorry to hear about your mother's death. I know how much you loved her and how much she loved you. My thoughts are with you." Something like that, but in your own words. It doesn't have to be long. If you like, say something wonderful about the person or include a telling anecdote. "I'll always remember how your father took me to the Emergency Room when I cut my chin and my parents were at work. I was so scared, and your dad just kept making jokes and asking me about my teachers and boyfriends. He was a wonderful, funny, generous man."

Whether someone you love dies or someone you know suffers a loss, remember that brighter days are ahead. Time doesn't heal but it helps.

Dear Carol ...

Dear Carol,

I have a horrendous problem: my parents. I finally have a close group of friends and we go T.P.ing (toilet papering) on weekend nights and do the houses and never get caught. It's all in good fun. It lasts from about 9:30 to 11 (we need to do it while it's dark so we don't get caught) and I'm always home on time (before my curfew). Now my parents won't let me out anymore. They say they worry about me to the point of nausea. I'm a night person. I love black and I can't stand light. But now I'm forced to stay in all the time. What a crock! Thanks, you are the only one who could understand my free spirit.

That's a shame because even I am not gung-ho about free-spirited T.P.ing. It's all in good fun for *you* . . . but what about the people who have to un-T.P. their homes? Some parents are unfair, but some girls ask too much. The more mature your behavior, the more freedom your parents will give you.

Dear Carol,

I don't get along with my parents at all. They are from Italy and want to keep Italy's stupid customs. They don't understand that I like boys and some like me. If a boy calls, I get yelled at. If a guy stops by, they call me a slut. All my friends have boyfriends and their parents don't mind.

I get too much mail from the lovelorn to believe that *all* your friends have boyfriends, but your situation is difficult. Many kids have parents whose culture, religion, or background make them wary of American dating. If your parents are living in the Old World, you can't convert them. But you can reassure them that the guys in your life are just friends and that you don't intend to be serious about anyone for years. Try harder to understand them (Italy's customs are not "stupid"), and they may try harder to understand you. Who knows? Maybe you can arrange someday to visit relatives in Italy—and turn your troubles into advantages.

Dear Carol,

I read in your book about how you could write your mother a note that says "I love you" and put it on her pillow. I tried it. She read it, came up to me, and hugged me so hard I couldn't breathe. She said, "You're sweet when you want to be!" So I just wanted to thank you.

You're welcome! And here's a Polish proverb for you: The greatest love is a mother's; then comes a dog's; then a sweetheart's.

Dear Carol,

Hi. I have lettered in cross country and track. I went to the state twice as a freshman. But in the middle of the season, I injured my knee. My dad is a very competitive person. You could say he lives through me. When my times went down, he felt I was losing just to hurt him. I was running as fast as I could! I want a scholarship to go to college and run. But recently the morning of a race, my dad took me into the hotel room, locked the door, shut the blinds, and came after me with a clenched fist. I screamed. Luckily my mom's friend practically knocked the door down trying to get me out. Dad thinks that if I can't be a great athlete, I'm a loser. And now I feel I'm going to lose even before I get on the track. I told Dad I want to see a counselor and he said he would just lie to him. Who would you believe? A 15-year-old or a successful businessman?

A 15-year-old. Although family counseling would be ideal, going alone would be better than nothing. Your father is pushing too hard—literally—and that can psych out any daughter. I hope you win the college scholarship, but if racing ever stops being your ace in the hole, you're still not a loser. You have to separate your dreams from your father's, and you have to protect yourself from his anger. Easier said than done, but you *can* be a winner on and off the track.

Dear Carol,

I have a way of blowing a situation way out of proportion. Like I was yelling at my brother and my father told me to simmer down. But by then I was in a blind rage and I said my brother was a jerk and I hated my father (I said that!). After he left, a huge wave of guilt swept over me. He does his best to run our three-person (no mom) family. I told him I was sorry, but I want to work on my problem.

Recognizing a problem is step one to solving it. Since you know you have a tendency to fly off the handle, next time you're mad, take ten, take a walk, use "I" instead of "you" sentences ("I thought we made a deal," not "You jerk!"), and choose words carefully. Everyone gets mad, but the trick is to keep your temper in control. (It's easier if you're not starving or sleep-deprived.) Will Rogers quipped that people should live so that they "wouldn't be ashamed to sell the family parrot to the town gossip." That'd be a stretch for anyone. But since you told your dad you hated him, why not tell him now that you love him?

Dear Carol,

This year for Christmas I received a trip to Florida from my grandparents. They want me to escort my younger sister there for a visit in March. This might sound like a poor-little-rich-girl line, but I really don't want to go. I'm 14 and still not ready to fly from the nest. Is something wrong with me?

No. Many kids feel some separation anxiety, and it's as normal to want to stay in the cozy cocoon of your home as it is to want to flee from your family every chance you get. Nonetheless, since you have to leave home some time, visiting your grandparents might be an ideal first trip. Can you talk yourself into a weekend away?

Dear Carol,

I'm 15 and my parents just separated about a month ago. My mom moved out, and I'm now living with my dad. I've always had a pretty good life and I'm having a really tough time with this because I most certainly was not prepared for it. I always considered myself very lucky that my parents were happily married. I think my mom is going through a midlife crisis. I just wish everything could be back to the way it used to be. I'm not blaming myself the way some teens do. Sometimes I feel I'm walking through life in a daze. I'm sorry about your dad dying. That's really sad. Sometimes I even wish my mom would have died instead of moving out. At least that way no one would be mad at anyone.

They split up one month ago? Of course, you're having a tough time. It's better to cry buckets than to put your emotions in the deep freeze. After a separation (or divorce), life rarely does go back to the way it was, but it helps to remember that parents still love their children even when they're angry at each other. My hunch is that you probably don't really wish your mother had died, but it's OK to express your rage and hurt that honestly. After this confusing time, you and she can try to become close again—it'd be a shame to lose each other, too.

Dear Carol,

My mom recently died and my dad remarried. It didn't work, so he got a divorce. Now another girl moved in. They sleep together and I imagine have sex. They always bathe together, and it makes me feel ashamed. Or sometimes nervous or mad. Like she's taking my dad away from me.

Family matters . . . and death, divorce, and a father's sexuality are a lot for anybody to deal with. Not all stepmothers are stepmonsters, and you may end up forging a friendship with your dad's girlfriend. In the meantime, you can tell your dad (face to face or in a note) that you miss your mother and that you miss him and would love to go to lunch or a movie alone with him. Chances are he'll take you up on it. Do you have any friends whose parents are dating? It might be good to swap stories.

Dear Carol,

My mom divorced my biological father before I was even a year old. Then another man adopted me, but he and Mom got divorced when I was in third grade. She forces me to visit my adoptive father once a week, but I don't feel like he is my father. I like him, but I don't love him. Why did my real father give me up? Wasn't I good enough? I want to write him, but I don't know if I should.

If you really want to get in touch with your biological father, you can try to. But don't count on his spilling over with love and remorse. You can say that you'd like to see him, but keep anger out of the first letter. (The point is to get close to him, not alienate him.) Why did he give you up? It was your mother he wasn't getting along with, not you. And if being a parent was too much for him—that, too, is a reflection of him, not you. Curiosity about a biological father is natural, but since your adoptive father was there through the diapers, loose teeth, birthday parties, and school plays, don't rush to shut him out. He may be an ally or lifelong friend.

Dear Carol,

I am black and was adopted when I was four weeks old by a white family. Some of my black friends say I act too white and that if I didn't grow up in a rich neighborhood, I'd be better. But I have a family that loves me and I love them, so why should I worry about what they say, right? Wrong, because I do worry.

Lots of girls, black and white, wish they grew up in loving homes where money wasn't a constant problem. Your friends' criticism may be sparked, in part, by an envy that confuses even them. Finding one's identity is hard, and you may have to struggle more than the average teen. But crosscultural roots can be a plus, not a handicap. You can combine the privileges of affluence with the insights of being a minority in America. If you know other adopted kids or kids in multiethnic families, maybe you can start a group to talk about it after classes or Tuesday at lunch. If you go to a cool school and can sign up a teacher or guidance counselor, maybe you can even turn it into a course for credit.

Dear Carol,

I'm 12 and I've known my best friend since we were babies. Two years ago my sister and her brother got in a fight. My sister is now in a rehabilitation hospital. My friend's mother doesn't let me see my friend outside school. How can I convince her mother that it's not my fault that my sister is screwed up?

You could mail the mother a letter saying how much you've always liked and admired her daughter and how it's hard on you, too, that your sister doesn't have her act together, but that while you feel compassion for your sister, you and she are very different people. The mother may soften, and if not, your friendship can endure even without after-school dates.

Dear Carol,

I really like your book. My copy is dog-eared and worn, but you neglected to mention one thing that is supposedly common though rarely discussed openly: mental illness in the family. My brother acquired a drug problem in high school. He has never been the same. He ended up not graduating and now he can barely function. Either he sleeps for days at a time or he dominates the house with his hostility and crazy talk. Needless to say, my parents are heartbroken. I'm taking great pains to keep my friends from finding out for fear they will be too afraid to visit me. I have become considerably withdrawn. Before age 18, my brother had gone to rehab centers. After that, forget it, he legally refused. My mother says it's worse than if he had just died. When a loved one dies, eventually you move on. But it's like some monster is in his body tormenting the family and himself as well. I'm not really writing for advice, just to share this.

What a sad, sad situation for you and your family, and what a loss for everybody. I hope that with time, therapy, and medication, your brother can turn himself around. Meanwhile, try giving your friends more credit. They like you for you; your brother's illness doesn't have to shape their feelings. Besides, you need support. Get involved with activities outside your home so you'll feel less isolated. Extracurrics at school and community outreach programs may provide the outlets you deserve.

Dear Carol,

Have you ever tried to kill yourself? Probably not. Well a lot of kids want to die. A lot of kids have reasons, too. Like me. I had reasons. I was an alcoholic and on some drugs. (I went to a clinic and am better now although I still do pot, hash, uppers, and downers.) And I wanted to be free of this world. I'm not suicidal anymore but I still think adults just don't get it.

Being free of this world sounds romantic, but dead people aren't free to travel, sing, fall in love, eat chocolate chip cookies, talk on the phone, go to concerts, shop with friends, read books, rent videos, and pet purring cats. . . . They're just dead. At least that's what I think. You only go around once, and I can't see shortening the trip. No, I have never tried to kill myself. But that doesn't mean I've never felt morose or desperate. I'll be the first to admit that being a teen can be very hard. Kids today are growing up faster and faster, yet their support systems are often weaker and weaker. Where once the typical teen had Mom, Dad, relatives, neighbors, and maybe church or synagogue nearby, families are now scattered, and parents and neighbors are stressed and disconnected. There's no shame in being a sensitive person with deep and troubled feelings. But hang in there, get off drugs, get more counseling, and be glad you chose life. If Romeo and Juliet had been a little less rash, even they might have lived happily ever after.

Dear Carol,
   My brother gets more attention than I do. My parents hardly notice I'm around.

Parents can get so overwhelmed with their own lives that they don't always pick up on their kids' feelings. Can you try harder to communicate with them? Instead of being quietly hurt that they didn't ask about your art project, announce, "Let me show you my collage. The teacher loved it." Ask how their work day went or what they remember about being in the grade you are in now. Or try the direct approach. Place a note on their pillow that says, "I love you but it feels as though you pay more attention to Max than you do to me."

Dear Carol,
   I admit I have a pretty good singing voice. But whenever my family has a party, everyone pressures me to sing, and if I bail, I feel like I let everyone down.

You have two options. The first is to tell your parents (before the next party) to stop putting you on the spot. The second is to crank up your courage, despite stage fright, and take advantage of having a captive audience. A room full of clapping relatives may even rev you up to try out for the school musical. Your voice is your gift—why not share it?

Dear Carol,
   I have a boyfriend. We French-kissed. All my mother knows is that I like him. I really love him, but I'm only 12 years old. Should I tell my mother?

It depends . . . and it's totally up to you. What do you think she would say?

Dear Carol,

I'm always being blamed. My family went to the pool and my brother told me to splash my sister. So I did, and then I got in trouble. My mom asked me, "Why do you always start trouble?"

I see your point. Do you see your mom's? Next time your brother has a lousy idea, nix it instead of following orders.

Dear Carol,

My 4-year-old sister cries all the time, and my mother always falls for it. It's driving me crazy. I know I should love my sister but I can't.

Of course, you're mad at your sister—she's taking up a lot of your mom's time. (Even your mom probably gets a bit fed up with her.) Forgive yourself for having mixed feelings and start accepting that yes, you love your sister, and yes, she can drive you nuts. Once you stop expecting yourself to be a saint, it'll be easier for you to feel good about her—and yourself.

Dear Carol,

My grandmother moved in with us a few years ago. She always does weird things, often in front of my friends. She thinks it's funny, but I get embarrassed. What do I do?

Even if your friends think your grandmom is kooky, they won't think less of you. Is Nana humming Sinatra in her slippers? Give her a break. Or is she acting certifiable and dancing around with underwear on her head? Talk to your parent. Tread gently. Most people have many friends in a lifetime, but only one or two grandmoms.

Dear Carol,

I have a friend whose parents are getting a divorce. I want him to know that I know how he feels, but how do I tell him without upsetting him more?

He's already upset, and your caring support will help, not hurt. Pick a quiet moment and say, "I'm sorry about your parents. It must be hard for you." If your own parents are divorced, say something like, "When my parents broke up, it was awful at first." Then share any encouraging words or advice about how you got through it.

Dear Carol,

I have an uncle and when he comes to visit, he always touches me in the privates and I feel uncomfortable. Last time I ran to my room and shut the door.

That was smart. I hope you'll continue to trust your gut. Tickling is appropriate; intimate touching that makes you uncomfortable is not. Do not be alone with your uncle. If he tries to touch you again, say, "Don't touch me." And if possible, speak to your parent. Your uncle is troubled, and that should be his problem, not yours. When adults molest children, it's always their fault, never the child's.

Dear Carol,

My dad yells a lot. He's got a huge attitude problem. My friends' dads don't yell even half as much as he does. Sometimes he explodes and breaks stuff and sometimes he slaps me.

Some three million children are abused or neglected in the United States. When parents yell, they are usually mad at themselves or each other, not you, but kids suffer the brunt of their anger, frustration, or low self-esteem. Some girls who have lived with abuse at home end up thinking it's OK for boyfriends to hit them or curse them out. It's not OK, and the fact that you wrote me shows that you realize that your situation is not the norm and is not hopeless. For now, stay out of harm's way. Avoid pushing your dad's buttons, think about where you can spend occasional weekends (with a friend? aunt? grandmother?), and consider confiding in a guidance counselor or calling a hot line so your whole family can get some help.

Dear Carol,

I am so depressed. Not just depressed, but like wouldn't-wanna-get-out-of-bed-for-Disneyland depressed. It gets worse everyday. Your advice column in Girls' Life *is the only thing that has made me laugh in like a million years. I've talked to my parents, and they just say to get over it. I want a psychiatrist, but my parents say they're too expensive. Help!*

I'm glad I made you laugh, and I hope I can point you to someone who can get you smiling again. Therapy and medication can make a world of difference, and there are hospitals that charge on a sliding scale, as well as insurance policies that cover treatment for clinical depression. Talk with your parent, school counselor, or nurse, or call a hot line or hospital. Sadness sometimes lifts on its own, but this is your life and you're wise to want to consult a pro. Good luck.

Dear Carol,

I liked your book, but I've never met my father and my mother is in jail, so when I read the part about problems with parents, I felt like, at least they have parents. That's all I wanted to say.

That's saying a lot. And you're right. I talked about parents, single parents, and stepparents, but today over six million kids don't live with any parents and are being raised by relatives or in homes that keep changing. "Zero-parent" families are more common in inner cities where drugs, AIDS, and guns take a merciless toll. I hope you are being well cared for by relatives (or nonrelatives) and are finding support in your school, community, or church. Your path is not easy and I hope you'll feel free to write me again.

Dear Carol,

My parents got divorced three years ago. I just hate it. All of my friends at school have normal family lives. I just wish I was normal. Arrrggghh!

The pain of divorce can go on and on, and I do hope you have a good relationship with your mom and with your dad. As for your friends, please know that no one's family life is truly "normal." Everyone has problems and every family has troubles—even if things seem picture-perfect on the outside. Keep up your grades, and before you know it, you may be living on a college campus where nobody has parents around. And since we're talking school . . .

6 EDUCATION

Getting Through High School, Getting Into College

❖

Just the other year you were in kindergarten, and Mrs. Quintano had the whole class pledging allegiance and singing "Good morning to you, good morning to you; we're all in our places with bright happy faces. . . ." You looked up to the fifth graders and pretended you had lots of homework because it made you feel grown-up.

Now you have lots of homework. Does it make you feel grown-up? No. It makes you feel sick. You have a teacher you dislike and another who plays favorites. You're pressured by college and career decisions. You even have anxiety dreams. You're sitting naked in the stands during homecoming game composing essay answers to SAT math questions.

This chapter shows how to make the most of your school, even if it's a jail, zoo, or pressure-cooker. It includes what you need to know about study habits, teachers, harassment, learning disabilities, switching schools, studying abroad, and planning and paying for college.

Is School Unbeatable or Unbearable?

Adults tend to romanticize their long-lost school years. Many forget how they dreaded that first school day after summer vacation. How they struggled to intercept that first mailed-home report card. How they prayed for snow days. How they couldn't care less about what happens to the half-life of a radioisotope that combines to form a compound. How they felt trapped in a fishbowl during school hours and inundated by homework afterward.

School is no picnic. I remember that. And if I ever forget, I can always look back at my ninth-grade diary and reread entries, such as *"Classes warp creativity!"* or *"Someday I'll be a politician so I can express my views on education: It stinks!"*

Yet in all fairness, school has lots of pluses, many of which I did appreciate at the time. It was great having lunch every day with Judy or Jen or my boyfriend. I loved the English discussions about Salinger, Millay, Wharton, and Fitzgerald. I miss the two or three teachers who were truly inspiring. And I miss the variety of high school: the way I changed teachers every hour and courses every year. Sometimes I even miss the on-top-of-things feeling I'd get when I reached the QED of a geometry problem or figured out an obscure line of poetry.

Do you realize that one-third of the world's people are illiterate? Aren't you grateful to be among the other two-thirds?

Believe it or not, learning *is* often more fun than earning. In many ways, school *is* a picnic—a picnic complete with ants.

Why Should You Learn All That Irrelevant Stuff Anyway?

"They teach in academics far too many things and far too much that is useless." That's what Goethe said. But while you're in school, it's hard to judge what's relevant. When I took Psych 11a in college, I thought of it as just another class. It turned out to be one of the most useful courses I ever took, for my writing and my social life. When my husband took geometry, he had no idea that years later he'd be using it every day at work as he built props for TV commercials. A friend of mine joined stage crew in high school. Did she become an actress? No. She got interested in stage lighting design, then light in general, and now she's the most zealous (and well-paid) young physicist I know.

School exposes you to so much, from Einstein's calculations to Picasso's paintings to Rachel Carson's *Silent Spring*. Sooner or later, while you're writing a program in computer class, conducting a fruit-fly experiment in biology, racing around the track, singing in the chorus, or putting a pot in the kiln, you'll feel filled with energy and enthusiasm. You'll begin to figure out what you like to do, what you're best at, what fields of study to pursue, or what career to start aiming for. That's an exciting discovery. You'll also learn what you're not good at and not interested in, which helps in planning your future, too.

Whether you're in junior high or high school, dabble with electives, sports, and extracurrics. Balance your schedule without overloading it. The more you learn, the more things you'll enjoy and the more choices you'll have. If you can't type or aren't computer literate, you're limiting your marketable skills. If you don't like reading or theater or sculpture, you have fewer ways to enjoy yourself than someone who does. Do you know the basics of auto mechanics? You're one up on the person who panics whenever her car sputters.

You'll never regret having that education edge. School teaches you to think, to analyze, to solve problems, and to work with discipline. Not all your teachers are brilliant and amiable, but not all your future employers will be, either. Not every assignment is scintillating and important, but in the Real World, there are dirty dishes to wash and boring bills to pay, no matter how exhilarating your profession is. Besides, the best ticket out of a boring school is to do well there.

Your education, in and out of school, is for you—so you'll be able to lead your life instead of being led by it.

Cram Course in Study Habits

Students who always ask, "Whadja get, whadja get?" and teachers who give tests back in order with 98s on top and 38s on the bottom aren't on my Christmas list. I think working solely for a grade rather than working to learn is a shame. But grades matter. Especially if you are college-bound. If you're making As and Bs, you're probably learning a lot and feeling good about yourself, and since you're in school anyway, you might as well do your best.

A few natural-born brains make the honor roll without even cracking a book. Me? I got good grades by working my buns off. Some subjects came more easily to me than others, but I'm not a fast reader and I couldn't just coast along in anything. At times, I couldn't believe how much homework I'd have per class per day—some high school courses are more demanding than college ones—but I slogged through and it paid off. I'm glad I learned as much as I did in high school and I'm glad I got into the college I wanted.

There are many ways you can learn more and improve your grade point average.

1. *Aim high.* Shoot for 100 and you might get a 90. Shoot to pass and you might flunk. Spend a few minutes before each class looking over your homework and reviewing the assigned chapter. If you tune in, take notes, and move up a row, your classes will go by faster. Don't fall behind. And don't watch the clock and doodle, then, when called upon, have to ask, "What page are we on?" Try to excel in at least one subject. Acing one may inspire you to try harder in others. The cliché is true: The more you put into school the more you get out of it.

2. *Make lists.* Assignment pads are lifesavers. Write down which pages you have to read for history class and which problems you have to do for trig. Sometimes I'll even write down things like "work out" or "send Granddad a birthday card." It's not that I'd necessarily forget otherwise, but writing down plans frees my mind to think of other things. It also adds to my sense of accomplishment later when I cross off what I got done. (Am I making myself sound like a hopeless nerd in high school? I wasn't. I swear. Ask Judy.)

3. *Study actively for tests. Passive* studying means flipping through your notes and leafing through books. *Active* studying means taking notes on your notes, reading them aloud, reciting information to yourself, making an outline. If you own the book, highlight what's important with a yellow marker. Give yourself practice vocabulary quizzes or hard math problems to figure out. Have someone drill you on your foreign verb conjugations or write them out on a blank piece of paper.

Think up mnemonic (memory-boosting) devices. When I was studying for Mr. Wildman's essay test on the Renaissance, I concocted the word *pranchimy* to remind me to write about perspective, religion, anatomy, nature, classics, humanities, intellectualism, materialism, and youth.

Listen when your teacher explains what the test will cover, so you'll know what to study. I used to study for tests the night before, then look over the material again right before class. The risk of counting purely on last-minute cramming is that something may come between you and your books. The guy you like may choose that day to sit next to you in study hall. Or your teacher may have you hand out the tests when you were depending on those two minutes to commit a poem or formula to memory.

Before you begin an exam, look it over. Carefully. Find out how long it is. Read the essay questions. Pace yourself, leaving time to proofread or check your answers. If you have a lot of time for a short math quiz, you might even take it twice, then compare your results. Approach tests like sporting events—psych yourself for victory.

4. *Write and rewrite papers.* Second drafts are better than first drafts. Don't hand in a half-baked composition you scribbled off an hour before class. Don't think on paper, rambling on as you figure out what you want to say. Think first. Then write. Then do something else. Then return to your paper to proofread or revise it. Rewriting is extra easy if you have access to a computer, and since you'll have to type at college or on the job, you might as well get in practice now.

Be lively: Steer clear of stilted words, such as *thus* and *thereby* and bland, overused words like *nice* and *interesting*. Be succinct: Don't write *significant increase* when you mean *more* or *at this point in time* when you mean *now*. Be precise. Don't say *very, very worried* when you mean *frantic*. Be specific: Don't say, "Puerto Rico was a fun place to vacation" when you can paint a clearer picture by saying, "We waterskied and visited fortresses and even hiked in a rainforest." Eliminate unnecessary and repeated words. Read your paper aloud—does it sound OK? Check for spelling mistakes. (I dare you to find *drownded* or *alot* in your dictionary.) Watch your grammar—*between he and I* is wrong.

If you want to develop better writing skills, read *The Elements of Style* by William Strunk, Jr., and E. B. White.

Can't get your paper started? Pretend it's an essay question on a one-hour exam. Or pretend you're writing a letter to a friend. ("Dear Jen, Although Van Gogh died at the age of thirty-seven, his paintings . . . ")

5. *Cheat and plagiarize.* (Just kidding.) The problem with cheating is that you're only c_____ y_____ (fill in the blanks). As your grades go up, your self-respect goes down. Yes, you may get an A, but you know you didn't really get it.

I plead guilty. I occasionally planted myself near some know-it-all in the back so I could check my multiple-choice answers against hers. Then one day I stopped. It just didn't seem worth it anymore. I wanted to depend on myself. As Sophocles said, "I would prefer even to fail with honor than to win by cheating."

If you cheat in French in September, you'll regret it all year because you won't have learned the basics. How can you master the *passé com-*

posé if you don't even have the present tense of *avoir* down? Same principle in math. Besides, you'd feel like an idiot if you and Andy were the only ones to write 23,964 when the answer was 12.

Not that cheating is uncommon. A recent statistic revealed that over half the high school students questioned admitted to having cheated at some point. Many colleges try to solve the problem by using the honor system: No one proctors exams because administrators trust you; few end up cheating because few want to betray that trust.

Remember that cheating and plagiarism are illegal. If you're caught, some teachers will give you an automatic zero and some schools will suspend or expel you. The plagiarists who steal from Cliff Notes or turn in papers written by former students are often caught. I met a guy at college who was kicked out for a year for having plagiarized a paper. He'd copied it straight from an obscure tome—written by a friend of his professor's!

6. *Love your library.* Even if your desk at home is big and well lit, there are always distractions, from telephone to television. Some people can concentrate anywhere. Not me. I like studying where it's quiet, reference books are on hand, and desks are large enough to spread out on. A librarian can help you find back issues of magazines and ancient newspaper articles on the computer.

In high school, I often stayed after school and holed up in a classroom or the library to make a dent in my homework. That way I had fewer books to lug home and more free time at night.

Figure out where you are most comfortable studying.

7. *Leave the television and computer off.* A word about temptation. (Well, maybe a paragraph.) If I break down and buy a bag of Hershey's Assorted Miniatures, within a day or two, (quicker if I'm highly hormonal), I will have unwrapped and downed every single Mr. Goodbar, Krackel, and Special Dark, and soon even the Milk Chocolate bars (which I barely like) will start to disappear. Trust me: It is much easier to resist temptation one time in the store than 45 times at home.

The same goes for TV, computer games, and the Internet. Don't touch that button because it's harder to turn machines off than on and unless you're the Queen of Self-Discipline, you can lose two hours of homework time in what feels like mere minutes.

8. *Study when you're most alert.* I remember spending about an hour a page reading—or trying to read—*The Scarlet Letter* one night at about 2 A.M. Idiotic, because none of it sunk in. If you don't work efficiently late at night, go to bed and get up early. If it takes you forever to click on in the morning, don't expect to study well before school. Being well prepared is crucial, but so is being well rested. Give yourself study breaks, and switch subjects if you're getting drowsy. It may help to hit the books for an hour, take a fifteen-minute walk or phone break, then study for another limited amount of time. Or it may help to devise a study routine and stick to it.

You can also do some reviewing at the bus stop or in study halls or when you get to class before the teacher. Sometimes I used to study in the library the first ten minutes of lunch period—all I missed were long lines.

9. *Don't procrastinate.* Since you've got to do your homework anyway, you might as well get it over with. Figure out your priorities. Don't wait for enough free time to complete everything in one sitting. Instead, break your work into manageable pieces, and get started. You could even set your kitchen timer for thirty minutes and make a deal with yourself that you won't get up from your desk until the timer rings. Once you begin, it isn't so bad. I promise. The way to get into the work mood is to start working. Sometimes getting to your desk is tougher than the assignment. Often I'll write the lead paragraph before I go out. That way when I return, my essay is started, and it's easier to get back into the work mood.

Work has a bad name, but hard work usually makes you feel great, especially when it's behind you. Why not reward yourself by planning something fun to do afterward?

Do you do your term projects in a last-minute panic? Do you pull all-nighters? Try to start papers early and do them step by step before you become overwhelmed. It may help to schedule your work: By week one, you'll have completed the research; by week two, you'll have finished the rough draft; by week three, you'll have the project polished.

Have you ever brought homework along on a vacation? I bet you either didn't do it and felt guilty or did it and felt resentful. Next time try to finish it beforehand or be realistic when you pack.

10. *Get help if you need it.* Most teachers are happy to explain a lesson after school and answer questions during class. You can also get help

from friends, siblings, parents. Are you way behind in math? Don't suc-
cumb to math anxiety that could trip you up in years to come. Of course
you are *able* to learn math—you may just not be as quick at it as some
people. (Will Rogers wrote, "Everybody is ignorant, only on different
subjects.") Arrange for a tutor; then work on understanding the con-
cepts, not just getting correct answers. I used to tutor and I know the
one-on-one approach can work wonders. Tell your teacher you're getting
outside help. He or she will probably be eager to recognize improvement. Your school may be able to recommend someone, perhaps an
upperclassman who volunteers tutoring services. Some cities even have
homework hot lines staffed by people who will help you grapple with
tough questions. Don't wait until two weeks before finals—start catching up now before the ditch gets deeper.

11. *Adjust your attitude.* Don't believe for a minute that you're a terrible student. Maybe you *were* a terrible student, but as of now, you are a
good student. You weren't dumb; you were a professional under-
achiever. Get ahead instead of getting by because smart people (like
TV's *Daria*) often laugh last. (You have been trying your hardest but
have little to show for it? Read the next section with an open mind.)

And don't swallow any lines about girls not being good at math or
about guys preferring dumb girls. A few insecure dumb guys may, but
you'd rather date secure bright guys, right?

On the other hand, if you're a perfectionist, loosen up a little. Your
world won't cave in if you get a B. (It might even be good for you!) And
if you do nothing but study, you run the risk of burning out.

Straight-A students should also try not to flaunt their grades or
wail, "I flunked that test" when they missed only two questions. And
many still need to learn to accept criticism. Many overachievers have
mastered the art of studying, but haven't yet learned the art of relaxation.

Learning Difficulties: You Know You're Smart But . . .

It's one thing to have problems with schoolwork because you're skipping class or you're not taking homework seriously. It's another to have
problems when you really are trying to do well.

Maybe you need a tutor. Or a quieter place to study. Or better organi-
zational skills. But maybe, just possibly, something else is going on.
Many kids have learning disorders or disabilities. They aren't stupid

and they aren't lazy, but they keep hearing that they are and some begin to believe it.

I'm not a doctor, psychiatrist, or learning specialist, and I'm not big on labeling or rushing a diagnosis. But if you have a condition (mild or severe) that makes learning extra hard, it's important to recognize and address it. Your mother may say, "You just need to apply yourself!" Your father may think learning disorders are "bogus"—a justification for sloppy work.

Yet if you have, say, attention deficit hyperactivity disorder (ADHD), you may benefit from medication, rather than simply more structure, better study habits, or a swift kick in the pants. Or if you have, say, dyslexia, and pages look like mazes and your spelling is a joke, it's a relief to learn new approaches to reading and writing.

Around 15 percent of the U.S. population may have learning disabilities, which have been defined as an unexpected failure to learn, despite intelligence, instruction, and motivation. These disabilities are common; often run in families; and once discovered, can be compensated for. If you consistently have trouble with writing, math, memory, or "getting it," consider talking to your guidance counselor or a health professional. In public schools, you can get a free evaluation or assessment, and you have a right to special education. One girl I know said that when she got on track, it was as though a veil had been lifted. Another described her mind as full of doors; treatment meant finding the right combination of keys (therapy? medication? tutoring?) to open them.

Thousands of bouncing boys who are hyper and disruptive in grade school are diagnosed early with ADHD. But girls who are dreamy and distractible and who have the same disorder (or who have ADD—ADHD without the hyperactivity) often float through school, sometimes paying attention, sometimes not, and no one quite realizes that they are missing too much until years later.

Everyone's mind meanders, so don't immediately count yourself in, OK? But if you have always had problems focusing; you are chronically disorganized, tardy, and inefficient; and kids tease you about being ditzy or a space case, then why not talk to the school nurse or counselor? Everybody tunes out at times, but if you have trouble staying tuned in, find out why. ADHD is not an excuse for poor schoolwork, but it may be an explanation. And there are treatments.

Ritalin (methylphenidate) has been around since 1937. Is it overused in this country? Some say yes. Countless others, including many teens and parents, say that when it's properly administered (not abused!), Ritalin and other medications can make a positive difference.

What about dyslexia, the common disorder that affects reading, writing, and spelling? To dyslexics, *untie* may look like *unite*, *was* like *saw*, and *b* like *d*. You may have heard about Bill Cosby's tragically slain son, Ennis, who got his M.A. in education from Columbia. For years he was a terrible and terribly frustrated student. He knew that his failure was not his fault and that his grades didn't reflect his effort or his intelligence. But he didn't know why. "The happiest day of my life," Ennis Cosby wrote, "occurred when I found out I was dyslexic."

My hope is that things are bumping along smoothly enough for you and that you don't need any intervention. But if you happen to have ADHD or dyslexia or any auditory-processing or word-retrieval problem or neuropsychological disorder or even social phobia that hampers your performance in school, seek the advice of a pro. If something is causing you distress or dysfunction, get help. (Unfortunately, some kids with learning problems abuse drugs like speed or cocaine in a dangerous and illegal attempt to self-medicate.)

Go on-line or check library or bookstore shelves to read about learning difficulties or psychological syndromes. Enlist the support of a parent or adult friend. And keep listening for innovative programs, such as ReadNet, that can help kids read and help combat illiteracy at large.

If you think you have a learning disability, you may think you can't afford treatment. But the price of doing nothing is even greater, and treatment may be free at your school or covered by your parents' insurance.

Maybe you are a super student but you have a friend or family member with learning issues. Do you ever say, "Earth to Heather" or "Knock, knock, anybody there?" or "What'd you do, forget your pills?" I hope not. Brain chemistry is a given; insensitivity is a choice.

For more information, contact:

National Center for Learning Disabilities
(212) 545-7510
http://www.ncld.org

The Council for Exceptional Children
(800) 328-0720

Learning Disabilities Association of America
(412) 341-1515

The Orton Dyslexia Society
(800) 222-3123
http:\\ods.org

CHADD (Children and Adults with Attention Deficit Disorder)
(800) 233-4050

Teachers: They're Not In It for the Money

Give them some credit. Many teachers love their subjects and their students and can offer you a world of learning, guidance, and friendship. But teachers, like students, come in all types, and you may hit on a colossal bore or on a teacher who never tires of comparing you to your brilliant older sister.

I had a history teacher who was a windbag. He'd stare at the wall as he droned on and on. He'd show us a movie about the Incas on Monday; then on Friday he'd announce he had a movie about the Incas to show us. We'd watch it again. And again. He knew he was absentminded, but that just made matters worse. "I didn't give you this test yet, did I?" he'd ask as he passed out exams. "Yes you did! We took it yesterday!" we'd lie in unison. Most of us depended on his class to get our math homework done. (But now I wish I knew more about World War I!)

Are you having trouble with any of your teachers? Ask yourself whether you are being singled out. Maybe your teacher calls everyone "numbskull," and does so affectionately. (What a fella.) Or maybe he is hard on you because you've been loud or disrespectful or were caught cheating or passing notes. Or maybe you're called on often because you can be counted on to know the answer. Or maybe she wishes you wouldn't say *like* and *you know* every three seconds.

If you feel you specifically are being treated unfairly, try to make the best of it or speak to your teacher in private. Don't ask: "Why do you always pick on me?" Say, for instance, "I'm trying really hard, but I feel as though you still think of me as the class clown I was last year. I've grown since then."

Most teachers will respect you for coming to talk with them and will make an effort to judge your work or actions in a new light. So speak up if you think you don't deserve ten points off just because you spelled the last word in *A Separate Peace* as "Piece." I've even spilled tears in front of a few teachers, and although it's embarrassing, I survived.

What if your teacher is unreasonable or terrifying? What if Mr. Castel requires you to regurgitate his words verbatim on exams and docks points when you defend ideas of your own? Consider discussing the matter—gingerly—with your parents or principal or guidance counselor.

Is your school sexist? The American Association of University Women's report, "How Schools Shortchange Girls," says that girls receive less attention in class than boys. If boys call out, teachers listen, whereas if girls call out, teachers often tell them to raise their hands. (Isn't that pathetic?) The gender gap still rages on in math and science, too, and many teachers do not do enough to encourage girls to pursue technological and scientific careers. If you feel hampered by sexual bias from teachers, you can speak to your teacher or to a different teacher or to a counselor, principal, or headmaster.

Title IX of the Education Amendments prohibits sex discrimination in schools that receive federal funds. If you think your school is, for instance, giving more budget money to boys' soccer than to girls' field hockey or more space in the trophy case to boys' sports than to girls', you can speak up about that, too.

In the meantime, as Oprah Winfrey put it, "Excellence is the best deterrent to racism or sexism."

A few teachers are shamefully open with favoritism toward particular girls or boys. If a teacher takes to you, try to let that motivate you to learn more and to feel extra confident. But don't let it go to your head or cause undue pressure to make an A+ every time.

The situation can be a problem if the teacher dotes aloud and a lot about you and if other students, feeling left out, tease you or call you a brown-nose. Look, if you sincerely like Mr. Wollenberg because he is inspiring, that's wonderful. But if you are apple polishing because you hope he'll give you a higher grade or you're befriending teachers while estranging peers, who can blame classmates for resenting you?

I came across this item in one of my old diaries: "*You know who I despise the guts of? Myra! She's pathetic. She's a brain and every teacher's pet, but I don't feel any envy—just disgust.*" Now I can admit that I probably did feel envy, but if Myra had been as friendly to students as she was to teachers, she and I might have become buddies.

What about crushes? I had crushes on several male teachers from fifth grade on, and I looked up to a few female teachers, too. It's healthy to have role models besides your parents, and it's OK to have crushes—though I wouldn't make it obvious. A crush on a teacher, like one on a singer or an actor, is a fairly safe way to feel romantic. It can even put some zing into an otherwise dry class period.

In ninth grade, I had a certified crush on my bio teacher. I could handle it fine—until I confessed to my mother, who, on Parent's Night, asked him if he was married. Can you imagine? When he kidded me about it the next day, I nearly died. Fortunately, I soon got interested in going out with biology students instead.

A harmless crush can become harmful if a teacher tries to exploit it by becoming sexually involved with a student. Don't confess your crush to your teacher (it puts him in a bind). Most teachers welcome your admiration and have no intention of letting your friendship get out of hand. But in every truckload of melons, a few turn up rotten. And although sex with a minor is statutory rape, a few teachers do jeopardize job and dignity to take advantage of young women. (You, my dear, are jail bait.) If you are ever a victim of sexual harassment—for example, if a teacher says he'll up your grade or write you a shining recommendation in exchange for a sexual favor—report the incident to a family member, school counselor, principal, or headmaster.

(You're feeling heckled not by teachers but by students? If boys make repeated, degrading, and unwelcome comments or gestures that make it hard for you to do your work, that's sexual harassment. Say, "Don't talk to me like that," or "I'll report you if you grab me again." Then keep a record of the persistent and offensive behavior so you'll have evidence when you speak to a counselor or school official. Note: Some schools respond more quickly than others.)

A final word about teachers. A boring teacher can take the fun out of a course on modern movies. A great teacher can make any subject fascinating. In grad school, I took a course on the Spanish subjunctive at 8:30 A.M., and would you believe Jesús Fernández made it compelling? (On the other hand, don't start hating computers just because you hate the computer teacher.)

In high school, you may not have the opportunity to pick your teachers, but if you do, grab it. If your school's French teachers are considered terrible, but the Spanish teachers are terrific, and you're up in the air about which to take anyway, opt for Spanish. If you can choose one elective and everybody loves Mr. Stout, take his course—even if you don't know archaeology from a hole in the ground.

Good movies to rent about unforgettable teachers: *Dead Poets Society; Stand and Deliver; To Sir with Love; Goodbye, Mr. Chips; Lean on Me; The Blackboard Jungle; The Paper Chase; Mr. Holland's Opus;* and—why not?—*Matilda.*

When You Need a Change

Restless? Sick of school? Some students, like some batteries, have to be recharged once in a while. What can you do to liven up your education?

Plenty. Travel, switch schools, plan an out-of-the-ordinary summer, take a course at a local college, shake up your routine.

Not everyone sticks it out and gets that high school diploma. Thousands of kids quit school each year. The national high school dropout rate is estimated to be around 1 out of 5. It's higher among groups deemed "at risk": kids from low-income or single-parent homes or some minorities. Among Hispanics, the rate has risen to 32 percent. On the other hand, the dropout rate for African Americans today is half of what it was in 1970.

At first, dropping out may seem like a good move. You'd be making big bucks clerking or packing boxes. But what happens when you want to try more challenging work, meet new people, make more money? Since most jobs require a diploma, you could be left in the cold.

Studies show that high school graduates earn hundreds of dollars more on average each month than dropouts. College graduates often earn over $1,000 more each month. But we're not just talking money. Not having a diploma can eat at your self-esteem. And education opens doors and enables you to shoot high. (Sure it's great to sell blue jeans over the summer, but do you really want to do that forever?) Even if you are pregnant or have family problems, think twice before dropping out. A recent Louis Harris survey found that among women who were college graduates, 95 percent said that things were going fairly well, compared with only 3 percent of women who did not finish high school. Gives you pause, doesn't it?

If you leave school now, you could go back later, but it'd be a lot harder. You'd have to attend night classes with people of different ages, and you might have trouble summoning the discipline to study after years away from the books. Even if you end up passing the General Educational Development test (bravo!), the GED isn't worth quite as much as a high school diploma.

Some restless students drop out to become singers, actresses, models, athletes, or entrepreneurs. But if their dreams don't pan out? It makes sense to have a degree to fall back on. Don't cheat yourself. Nearly 77 percent of Americans over age twenty-five have at least a high school diploma. Dropping out is not the only way to shake up your life.

I was restless my junior year of high school. I'd been a student in the same public school since seventh grade, and I felt I'd already had all the best teachers and taken all the best courses. My brother Mark was in college, and my brother Eric and my boyfriend were both about to go to college. I was worried that all I had to look forward to was Senior Slump.

Then my mother found an enticing ad for School Year Abroad (Phillips Academy, Andover, Massachusetts 01810 [508]-725-6828), a small program that enables dozens of public school and private school students to study in France or Spain or China during their junior or senior year of high school. I applied, was accepted, and spent my senior year living with a French family!

It was expensive, but four of the credits I earned counted at college, so I made up the money. It was hard, but taking courses from native French teachers and Exeter and Andover professors made my transition to college easier. Mostly, it was wonderful. *Formidable!*

If you'd like to travel during the summer or school year, I highly (highly!) recommend you do so. Teens can travel more readily than adults because they have more time, can arrange to live with families, and can make dollars stretch further. Seeing a country from the inside is a great way to grow. You soak up another culture firsthand. Your history studies become suddenly vivid. Away from family and old friends, you become more independent. And because you're exposed to another nation's values, you rethink and gain a better understanding of your own views and background.

Ask your guidance counselor about travel possibilities. Your local Rotary Club probably offers study-abroad fellowships. Or call the American Field Service at (800) AFS-INFO. Or Youth For Understanding, an exchange program for fifteen to eighteen year olds at (800) TEEN-AGE. Or, my personal favorite, the Experiment in International Living at (800) 345-2929. I got a $500 grant from a local business and spent an EIL "home stay" summer with an enchanting farming family in the south of France, where I survived with no hot water, no indoor toilet, no English. Survived? I loved it! I helped vaccinate sheep, hunt for snails, bail hay, feed rabbits.... If *you* want to explore France or Kenya or Japan, give them a call. And phone the Council on International Educational Exchange at (212) 822-2600 to get an International Student ID card.

What if your grades have been mediocre and you don't think you'd be accepted by these programs (let alone receive a scholarship)? What if you want to create your own itinerary? Consider summer travel. Maybe an exciting summer is what you need, rather than a huge shift in your academic path. Do you know anyone who knows anyone who knows a foreign family? Perhaps you can arrange to live abroad and be a mother's helper for them. Afterward, if you'd like to return for a school year with credit, let the Eiffel Tower or Vatican City be your incentive to improve your grades. The world's the limit!

Now that I'm married and have two daughters, as well as professional commitments, it would be nearly impossible for *me* to finagle a summer abroad, much less a year. But *you* can do it.

Would a few weeks of summertime rock climbing or cycling appeal to you? Call Outward Bound at (800) 243-8520. It offers strenuous programs worldwide. Ask about financial aid. And find out about other field-study programs—check the Net or your school library.

What if you can't face another year in the same school but you're not up for anything as dramatic as dropping out or going overseas? Consider transferring to a different school, public or private.

Private schools are expensive. Choate Rosemary Hall, Emma Willard, and Deerfield, for instance, all cost over $20,000 per year. But need-based financial aid is available, and even middle-income families can sometimes receive a $10,000 break. Write the National Association of Independent Schools at 1620 L Street NW, Washington 20036-5605. Or check *Peterson's Guide to Independent Schools.* Applying to private schools can be as complicated as applying to colleges, so if you're in that boat, study the next section.

Do not enroll in a private school just to up your chances of getting into a good college. Your chances of getting a solid education and stretching intellectually will increase, but competition to get into "name" colleges is fierce among private school students. Instead of being the shining star at your public school and the only one to apply to Princeton, you could find you'd be just one more student, one applicant among dozens at your private school.

Still interested in applying to a new school? Visit it first to be sure it offers what you feel your school lacks, whether that means better facilities for sports or arts or a better atmosphere for learning. Would you be willing to take harder courses, meet higher expectations, and follow a dress code, as may be the case? If so, start selling the idea to your parents.

Would you be comfortable going from coed to all-girls or all-girls to coed? I went coed all the way, but some people like all-girls schools because they give girls a chance to assume all the leadership positions and to learn without the distraction of boys around. All-girls schools often do a better job than coed schools of addressing women's issues, from depression to discrimination to abuse. Nonetheless, if you do go to an all-girls school, and especially if you don't have brothers, try to join a sports or theater group or community service project or religious class or go to a coed camp in order to meet and mingle with boys. Boys represent half of the population, after all, and it's important to feel comfortable with them—not intimidated, not flirtatious, not shy, just comfortable. (Kids who are home-schooled also need to "hang around" with boys and girls and neighbors and teammates.)

Instead of switching to another school, coed or not, could you improve things at your own school? Join the student council and fight for changes. Ease out of a clique that has grown boring. Sign up for new electives, sports, extracurrics. (How about voice lessons, dancing, yearbook, chess, volunteering in a soup kitchen?) Or push administrators to set up a seminar about environmental or family issues. Do you want to improve your Spanish? Start a once-a-week lunch-time conversation table, and let everybody know *cuando* and *donde* it meets. Or get a discussion table started on surviving divorce or whatever interests you.

What if it's senior year, your parents are moving, and you don't want to start at a new school? See if you can arrange to stay behind with relatives or a best friend.

What if you're an amazing musician and you're ready to focus, even at the risk of narrowing your options? Consider applying to a music school. I know an actor who left public school after ninth grade to enroll in a performing arts school. He still earned a high school diploma, but he was able to devote a lot of time to his talent and he met people with similar aspirations.

Internships, apprenticeships, vocational schools, and junior colleges are also worth investigating, as are vocational-educational programs offered in some schools. Ask your guidance counselor or librarian or go cybersurfing.

If you want to skip senior year, your grades have been high, and you are self-reliant and adaptable, look into the possibility of starting college early.

You're wondering how hard college will be, or you're ready for one really rigorous course? Take a class or two in a local university after school. Or enroll in a summer program at a prep school, such as Dana Hall, or a college like Rhode Island School of Design, Syracuse, Georgetown, Northwestern, or the University of Pennsylvania.

For more ideas, go to the library or a bookstore and check out *Peterson's Guide to Summer Opportunities for Kids and Teenagers.* And while you're at it, take a peek, too, at *The Ultimate Guide to Student Contests, Grades 7–12.*

If you don't feel ready for college yet, apply for deferred or delayed college admission, get your high school degree, and take time off. Some students benefit from a year in the Real World. Many land a routine job, earn money, realize they don't want to wipe tables forever, and begin to appreciate and value education. Others work for free or for pay in a stimulating job that helps define their career interests. You can also spend an additional year at a private school to become better prepared academically for college. Or travel and become better prepared emotionally.

Your parents may scowl, but if you're buckling under the pressure and don't want to go from high school to college without a break, you don't have to. Explore your alternatives. Think about your short-term and long-term goals. Learn as much as you can. You're not running a race in which a diploma is the finish line.

College: Choosing and Getting Chosen

Mark Twain, who didn't graduate from grade school, said, "I never let my schooling interfere with my education." I agree that loads of learning occurs outside the classroom. And I take my hat off to all the accomplished people who never had the benefit of four years of college, from Henry Ford, Thomas Edison, and Eleanor Roosevelt to Abe Lincoln and my father.

Nevertheless, I think continuing your formal education is a privilege well worth taking advantage of. In your neighborhood, maybe almost everyone goes to college, or maybe almost no one does. Nationwide, over 60 percent of high school graduates enter college. Years ago, women didn't have the right to a college education. It was only in 1837 that the first woman was allowed to graduate from an American university. Today, because only about 1 in 5 Americans now twenty-five years old or over have earned a college diploma, that piece of paper still makes a difference when job hunting. It won't guarantee you a lucrative job right away, but it will provide flexibility and make it easier to find work. Besides, careers aside, college is a valuable time to grow. You have your whole life to be a wage earner and a homemaker, but only a short time to devote yourself entirely to improving your mind. And it can be unbelievably fun to meet young men and women who are interested in what interests you, be it film, marine biology, psychology, German, medicine, or graphic design.

If you are college-bound, remember that the admissions committees are sifting for gold, so your job is to shine.

1. *Think ahead.* That doesn't mean you should devote your four high school years to preparing for the next four years. But being suddenly impressive in twelfth grade may not impress the school of your choice. Be aware of what most college admissions committees look at: grades, board scores, extracurrics, recommendations, essays, interview. They scrutinize junior-year transcripts and study freshman-, sophomore-, and senior-year records. They look for a range of interests and a particular passion or commitment.

Enroll in serious, not watered-down, courses, and work hard. The most competitive colleges like to see three years of math, four years of English, and at least two or three years of history, science, and a foreign language. If you did well in any course that you will not take again (American history, physics), take the SAT II (Subject Tests, formerly called Achievement Tests) immediately afterward—not two years later. If you do well in Advanced Placement tests, you may be able to impress the deans of admission, place out of introductory college courses, and even earn college credit.

What about the other nationally administered standardized tests? Many sophomores and juniors take the PSAT (Preliminary Assessment Tests), which are scored on a scale from 20 to 80. The PSAT serves as a sort of practice SAT and helps you see where you stand (50 is average). PSATs are not required for college entrance, but do remain on your transcript. If you ace the PSAT, you become eligible for merit scholarships—and some colleges may even start contacting you.

Many high schools offer preparation classes, often free, for the Scholastic Assessment Test and American College Test. The ACT is popular in western and midwestern states and is scored on a scale from 1 to 36, with the average just over 20.

Every year 1,800,000 students take the three-hour SAT I: Reasoning Test. It consists of two parts, verbal and mathematics, each of which includes two thirty-minute sections and one longer section. (You may even have to sweat through an "experimental section.") Each part is scored on a scale of 200 to 800 and scoring was recentered in 1996, so that the average score is 500 (up from 430).

How to prep for your first exams? You can find tips and sample exams in workbooks and in software like *Road Trip for the SAT/ACT.* Coaching programs, such as Kaplan and Princeton Review, are expensive but effective. The best Web site on this is www.kaplan.com. Also good is www.collegeboard.org.

It is important to know what to expect before you sit down with your sharpened Number 2 pencil. In the verbal section of the SAT I, you'll find, for instance, analogies and sentence completions, and in the reading comprehensions, you'll do better if you study the questions before slogging through the text. For the math section, you may take along a calculator, and there will be fill-in-the-blank questions as well as multiple-choice ones. Overall, SAT I experts advise that you pace yourself, make educated but not wild guesses, and mark the answer grid carefully. In the future, instead of grids, tests may be customized and computerized so that each student has a keyboard and questions get progressively harder—until they're answered incorrectly.

You can't cancel your SAT I score once it's recorded, though you can cancel it within four days of taking the exam. About half the students take the SAT I again. Two-thirds improve their scores; one-third does worse. Colleges usually look at the highest scores. If you plan to take the exam a second time, call the Educational Testing Service at (609) 921-9000 to ask to buy a copy of your first SAT I answer sheet. Look it over to see where you went wrong—then bone up accordingly.

Did you know that when some colleges report their students' SAT I scores, they're reporting average scores, not median scores? In other words, many students' scores are lower, and if yours are, too, but everything else in your file is impressive, you may get accepted because the college is aiming to round out its orchestra, strengthen its basketball team, please its alumni, or achieve diversity. (If *you* happen to be an athlete, flautist, alumni—or legacy— child, foreigner, or Eskimo, see if you can make that work for you.)

OK, you're trying to do well in hard courses and on standardized tests. What else can you do?

Get involved. While I don't think you should sign up for an activity simply because it will look good on your application, this *is* the time to pursue interests and expand horizons. In the long run, if the only reason you join band, spearhead a recycling campaign, serve as class treasurer, or collect blankets for the homeless or money for the rainforests is to impress the deans of admissions, that still beats spending afternoons or summers sitting on your rump. Get a job, run an STD hot line, go to music camp, teach kids to read, work for Habitat for Humanity, or take a course at a nearby college. Do it for yourself: your here-and-now and your future.

And finally, start figuring out which teachers you like best. A teacher with whom you have a good rapport now will be willing to work overtime later to write you a sparkling recommendation. In borderline cases, that can make a difference.

2. *Explore your financial options.* Yes, college is expensive. Room, board, books, and tuition at private colleges can be around $20,000. Top-tier private colleges (like Bennington and Sarah Lawrence) can run over $30,000 per year. Even state schools (like the University of Vermont or University of California at San Diego) can cost $10,000 for in-state students. But the costs don't have to be so high. The average tuition for in-state residents at four-year colleges is a bargain at about $3,000. (Room and board cost another $5,000 each year.) And seven out of every ten college students go to a public college.

The latest on financial aid information is at these cybersites: http:// www.finaid.org, www.collegeboard.org, www.nasfaa.org, www.nelliemae.org, www.salliemae.com, www.rams.com/srn/search.htm/, www.ed.gov/offices/ OPE/express.htm/. Or ask your guidance counselor or librarian about long-term low-interest student loans and merit- and need-based aid and scholarships, grants, fellowships, college work-study programs, and part-time jobs. A lot of money has been earmarked for financial aid, and most students do not pay full freight. Your parents can fill out the Free Application for Federal Student Aid (FAFSA) and hand it in first thing in January of your senior year. (Money is given out first come, first served.) Call (800) 801-0576 for the form. Your parents may also need to fill out the College Scholarship Service Profile.

Call the Federal Student Financial Aid Information Center at (800) 433-3243 to learn about need-based Pell Grants (free money!) and Stafford and Perkins loans (these you'll have to pay back). Ask individual colleges for their specific financial aid applications and other monies. Some schools have huge endowments; M.I.T., for example, has over $1 billion. Others can sometimes give because they have received large gifts: Robert Woodruff, the chief of Coca-Cola, donated $105 million to Emory, and Bill Cosby gave many millions to Spelman.

Clubs, civic groups, foundations, and companies also have dollars to offer. Ask your parents to ask the human resources departments of their companies. Students who ace their PSATs can receive award money through National Merit Scholarships. If you are an outstanding student and want to become a teacher, ask about the Paul Douglas Teacher Scholarship Program—it could mean up to $5,000 a year.

Go to a college library and ask for resource books or computer programs on financial aid. Find out about "exotic" scholarships. Some unusual aid sources exist that offer scholarships to glassblowers, pig farmers, or descendants of a particular family. In Georgia, if your family makes less than $100,000 a year and you have a 3.0 grade-point average, you can attend a Georgia public institution free. Eugene Lang started the I Have A Dream Foundation in 1981 that has grown and paid the tuitions of many disadvantaged kids. To find out more about off-the-beaten-path scholarships, check the *Scholarship Book*. Looking for a sports scholarship? Hundreds of millions of dollars are awarded to teen athletes—a prestigious gift that they don't have to pay back! You may need a combined SAT I score of 820 to be eligible for athletic scholarships.

Most colleges don't let the fact that you're requesting aid affect their admissions decisions—they *want* students from diverse economic backgrounds. Do you think everyone in the Ivies is rich? Think again. Nearly 60 percent of all Ivy League undergrads receive some financial aid. Even way back in 1807, when Dartmouth cost only $20 a year, thirty-three of the thirty-nine seniors who graduated owed the college money.

It's easiest to receive aid if you apply early and demonstrate need. (If you have other siblings in college, say so!) Schools will want to know how much your family can contribute before they offer you a "package." Read the fine print. Are they offering a gift or a loan? Will it be ongoing or will it disappear next year? What are the terms for paying it back? If one school offers you money, but you like another school more, see if your favorite school will match the other offer. Some schools recruit with a passion.

I saved one full semester's tuition by converting my advanced placement (AP) scores into college credit and getting my diploma in three
and a half years. AP courses may exempt you from required college
courses and/or save you thousands, too. Many other students choose to
take more than four years, perhaps using time between terms to earn
money for tuition.

You can also save money by living at home or off campus. A recent
study by the U.S. Department of Education found that nearly 30 percent
of undergraduates live with their parents.

What? You won the lottery? Forget about asking for aid and hire a
fancy (and reputable, please) college consultant to help you get where
you're going.

3. *Find the colleges that most appeal to you.* You have about three thousand in the United States to choose from. Do you want to go near or far?
South or north? Urban or country? Do you want your school to be big or
small? Two-year or four-year? Private or public? Coed or single-sex?
Should it have a strong department of English or of physics?
Fraternities and sororities? Religious emphasis? If you attend a small
all-girls' prep school now, do you really want to go to a small all-
women's college?

What matters to you? Don't go by where your friends and boyfriends
are applying. College is your opportunity to strike out on your own.
Friendships and true love can endure separation, but if you follow their
lead and wind up in a school that doesn't suit you, you could end up
resenting your boyfriend (or ex-boyfriend!).

Visit your high school guidance office or library, attend college fairs,
look at college video guides, browse home pages, and take virtual tours
of the campus and community. (Click www.nyu.edu for a bite of the
apple or www.collegeview.com for general interactive information.) Buy
a guidebook, such as *America's Best Colleges* or the Fiske or Peterson
guide. Guidebooks describe the atmosphere, tell how many freshmen
returned for sophomore year (95 percent? 50 percent?), report student-
to-faculty and male-to-female ratios, and give the percentage of minority students and financial aid recipients. Guidebooks also list median
ACT and SAT scores, class size, cost, most popular majors, and statistics on how many people apply and how many are accepted each year,
as well as provide information about deadlines and where to write for an
application and catalog. (Schools love to send out booklets showing

attractive students playing Frisbee, lively professors leading intimate discussions, and ivy-wrapped buildings shining in the sun.)

It takes many hours and costs several twenties just to *apply* to each college, so make your decisions carefully. Did you know that Indiana University is a haven for musicians? That Tufts has language houses? That Colorado College offers a One-Course-at-a-Time program? That you can major in fashion design at Parsons School of Design? That Middlebury has its own ski area and a program that lets you spend junior year in Moscow? That Yale has an official Shopping Around Period in which you can sample classes for over a week before deciding which to take? That Rutgers offers Substance Free Housing? Did you know that some schools, like William Smith, have fewer than 1,000 students, while others, like the University of Minnesota, have over 50,000? Did you know that for anthropology, you can't beat the University of Michigan and for religious studies, the University of Chicago is tops?

Still looking for ways to cut costs? McGill is a good school in Canada that is cheaper than most American colleges. And you can save thousands (thousands!) by going to a terrific state school, even if you live out of state. Look into William and Mary, the University of Virginia, University of Wisconsin, University of California at Berkeley, SUNY at Binghamton, or the New College of the University of South Florida.

4. Go college shopping. You've narrowed your choices. And deep down, you know you'll probably have fun and get a great education anywhere. But how can you decide between Stanford and Cal Tech? Kenyon and Georgetown? Agnes Scott and Drake? Colby and Colgate? Whitman and Wooster? Bates and Bucknell? Keep reading and try to meet alumni. If possible, take a trip to the campus while it's in session, maybe on a weekday or spring break of your junior year. Go alone or with family or friends. Attend open houses. Take notes or photos, so you don't get your memories muddled. Revisit the campus on the Net.

Strolling among the dorms and buildings for the first time is both edifying and exhilarating. Are the students friendly? Is the campus pretty? Is the food palatable? Do you like the libraries? Do you feel as though you could fit in? Ask the students what they like and dislike about the school. (Sure they're content, but are they lukewarm or raving?) If you can, sleep over one night to get the best possible picture of UCLA or Swarthmore or Tulane. Even if you don't have a friend at the college you're visiting, its admissions program may be able to match you with a student host for a day or weekend. (Pack jeans, a sleeping bag, and a thank-you gift, like chocolate, and if you don't love the school, save the complaints for your parents, since your generous host is probably proud of her college.)

5. *Have an interview.* Interviews are usually optional, but if you present yourself well, they're a good opportunity for you to learn more about the school and for the school to learn more about you. If you are visiting a college, set up an interview beforehand. If you aren't, consider arranging one with an admissions officer at your school or a local alum who serves as a college representative. Tell your well-meaning parents to let you go to your interview alone. And try not to schedule your first interview with your first-choice college; get some practice first.

Don't let your impressions of the interview affect your impressions of the school too much. When I visited Harvard, it was a rainy day and my interviewer was snooty. So I didn't apply. When I visited Yale, it was a sunny day and my interviewer was charming. I ended up going to Yale and loving it, but the point is I shouldn't have let one day's weather or one man's personality color my judgment.

How do you prepare for the typical twenty- or thirty-minute interview? Dress neatly and fairly formally, read up on the university, arrive early, and be your most poised, mature self, a downright likeable leader. Yet relax, too. (You're not being grilled on *Nightline.*) Think up questions ahead of time. If you want to be a doctor, don't ask how many graduates got accepted by med schools because the answer is in the school catalog. Ask instead how long the laboratories are open and if it would be possible to see them. Ask about the role of fraternities. Or student life on and off campus. Or safety. Or foreign-study programs. Or work-study programs. Or whatever interests you.

Be prepared to answer the interviewer's questions, too. He or she may ask why you want to attend Brown or Bryn Mawr or Brigham Young. (Be enthusiastic!) Other probable questions: Where else are you applying? What out-of-school activity do you find most rewarding? What are your shortcomings? What can you, in particular, offer the school? (This is a biggie.) If the interviewers ask if you've done community service, and you haven't but you intend to, don't just say no. Say something like, "After studying, swim team, practicing violin, and working at the copy shop, I don't have much free time, but I plan to volunteer at the ASPCA this summer." (That'll spin their bow ties!) The interview is also your chance to explain why your grades recently plummeted (you moved, you were sick, your parents separated) and to ask (unless you're as chicken as I was), "Would you encourage me to apply?"

Toot your horn, but quietly. The woman who interviewed me at Wellesley complimented me afterward on my humility. Believe me, I got *everything* in that I wanted her to know, but subtly, and I'd told her what I learned from being defeated in Student Council. Don't be too modest, but don't be a nonstop boaster.

After your interview, write a thank-you note. It can't hurt—unless it's sloppy or misspelled.

6. *Consider applying early to your favorite school.* Say you're a good student at New Trier or Highland Park or Harvard-Westlake, and you have your heart set on Johns Hopkins or Wheaton, and you don't think you can wait until April to see if it has its heart set on you. Go for it! If you apply to one school in November, it may respond in December. It may accept you (hurray!), defer you (postpone the decision until April), or take a pass (fools—the school doesn't know what it's missing.)

Among the schools that admit students early, many (like Amherst, Cornell, Duke, Princeton, Yale) expect a commitment from you in return (Early Decision). Others (like Brown, Harvard, M.I.T., Michigan) are willing to have you string them along (Early Action or Rolling Admission).

You were accepted? Once you make up your mind, let the school and everyone else know—then jump for joy!

You were deferred, but the college is still your first choice? Ask the school and yourself if there's anything else you can do to show you're worthy.

You were turned down? Well, at least you know where you stand and can get busy applying to an appropriate new set of schools.

7. *Zero in on other schools and apply.* Most students don't have clear-cut favorites in November—let alone early acceptances in December. Most apply to four to six colleges or universities before January 1. These include one stretch or reach or long shot (you may not get in but it's worth a try) and one safety or fallback or backup school (the others may pass you up, but you're a shoo-in here). Don't forget that schools base their decisions not just on your strengths as a scholar, leader, athlete, humanitarian, and individual, but also on things like whether they're desperate for an oboist or a lacrosse goalie and who else is applying from your school. If all your friends are applying to Cal Tech (or Carleton or Wesleyan), your chances may go down. If all the kids from your school who have gone to a particular college ended up transferring or dropping out, the college will screen you carefully. If you're applying to a state school in another state, your chances are slimmer than the natives'.

Most students send for seven or eight applications the summer before and fall of their senior year and then decide which to fill out. Keep records and copies of what you send where. (An accordion file may help.) The applications may vary or they may all share one Common Application that you can fill out electronically. Forms may include questions about your parents' jobs and alma maters, but that information alone won't usually get you in or keep you out (unless your mom is a famous, well-liked millionaire alumna who has been sending fat checks to the school ever since her graduation). There will be space to write about any honors or prizes you have received, and you can even send in published articles, photographs, slides of your artwork, or a tape of your trombone playing. (Do so *only* if you're sure you're supertalented.) Other questions will ask if you need financial aid and what your career goals are.

It's OK to say your prospective major is "Undecided." It may be a plus to lean toward Middle Eastern studies instead of being one more English major. But don't lie! If you say you want to be a geology major and you have hardly taken any science courses, you'll look silly. And if you start out in prelaw or as a business major just because you think that's the way to get rich quick, you may regret limiting yourself. What if you're focusing on the University of Minnesota because of its excellence in chemical engineering? Point this out!

Recommendations? Find teachers (preferably of different subjects) who like you and know you well, and ask if they would write you positive and supportive letters. Ask at least one month before the deadline; then, two weeks later, politely ask if the teachers have sent them in. The forms they'll fill out will have questions about your academic performance, as well as personality, and ability to work with others. Refresh the teachers' memories by jotting down projects you did in their courses, as well as some of your other activities. Encourage them to keep a copy of the letter in case you need another one. Thank them afterward!

What if your aunt's ex-roommate's second husband's brother is the town mayor and might be persuaded to write a letter on your behalf? Don't bother. Letters should come from teachers, employers, ministers—people who really know and respect you. A so-so recommendation can sink you, so pick a person who will wax on about your intellect and character and who won't throw in any potshots.

8. *Take time writing and revising your essays.* Colleges may ask for a personal statement that is 250–500 words long. (One page typed double spaced is 250 words.) Think about the turning points and major influences in your life. About your favorite books and magazines (don't say *Tiger Beat*). About the extracurric you found most valuable. About political issues and, say, how working at a food pantry changed your views on homelessness. Many colleges ask just one or two predictable questions, while others ask several thought-provoking ones. Colleges often ask an open-ended, tell-us-more-about-you question. Your answer should be thoughtful, personal, honest, and clear. Not cocky, pompous, wooden, or fluffy. Beware of b.s. and polysyllables: Don't say, "I'm dedicated, diligent, and disciplined," or "I'm uniquely qualified." Don't just write what you think they want to hear. That won't make you come alive on paper and won't set your application apart from the fifty others on the dean of admission's desk.

When I finished writing my essays, I had my parents check them. You may want a family member or teacher to look over yours. It's a good idea to make a photocopy of the original application, type your essay on that copy, and make any last-minute changes in content or format (margins, spacing) before you fill out the original.

Here is part of one essay and a complete second essay that helped me get into Yale from Byram Hills, my suburban public school in Armonk, New York. I include them not because they are model answers but because they may help you come up with ideas. (Am I tempted to edit them now? Of course! But I figure you may be heartened to see that while you do have to fill a page, you don't have to be in line for the next Nobel Prize.)

Tell Us About Yourself.

It is hard to analyze one's own character, particularly when it is still developing. I'm told I'm competitive—I'd say hardworking. But I had to be. As the baby of the family, I had to catch up with two older brothers, and the competition was pretty rough. Mark had a poem published in *Jack & Jill* when he was four; Eric knew the E.R.A.s of all the Yankees. . . .

Then, I discovered French, and in eighth grade I received the "Excellence in French" award.

I'm told I'm thrifty—my brothers would say a miser. I do like to see money and time amount to something. But I'm not a miser because I parted with my entire life's savings two summers ago and bought a trip to France. . . .

Comment on an Experience That Helped You to Discover or Define a Value That You Hold.

Things are valued most after they are lost. While one is camping, one realizes the luxury of running water. During a blackout, one believes he will never again take electricity for granted. After one finds employment, one values leisure.

Life is different. It cannot be temporarily lost in order to be better appreciated. I learned to value life through someone else's death. When I was nine years old, I made friends with a nature counselor at a local day camp. I always rode on his shoulders and we told each other jokes and stories. I guess I was half in love with "Uncle Norm."

That autumn he joined the Marines. I wrote him and he wrote me from Virginia, Guatemala Bay, and finally Vietnam. Uncle Norm had been a teacher and had studied at the Sorbonne. His letters were always so imaginative. He prefaced one letter with "I haven't written you in such a long time, I know you must be mad at me. If you are, just throw this letter on the floor and stomp all over it before you read it." He wrote about spiders he met while hiding in holes, the stars, and once the "pweeng" of bullets and the "thhhump" of bombs.

I was surprised and worried when one carefree letter ended with "The war isn't going just real well; things could be worse, though."

Things did become worse, and that was the last letter I ever received from my friend. He was shot and killed by Vietcong mortar fire in South Vietnam.

I valued his kindness, intelligence, and curiosity about the world. His death made me value human life even more.

And now here's a slightly abridged essay that helped a woman named Jasmin get into Harvard from Trinity, a selective private school in New York City.

Evaluate a Significant Experience or Achievement That Has Special Meaning to You.

"Fa la la la, fa la la la, fa la la la." "Zing-bing-a ring aloha; ay yea, cuckoo, ay yea." This gibberish is more meaningful than it seems. I used these words daily for two years during the vocal warm-ups in an experience that I will always consider significant—being in chorus at Trinity School.

I joined Chorus in tenth grade for a change of pace. When I first joined Chorus, it was just a way for me to try something new. If I did not like it, I reasoned, I could always drop it.

My first day of Chorus was a shock. Hearing these absurd words, and having to sing them, seemed ridiculous. I could not imagine how people could like this class. But those people who had been in Chorus forever came to class and loved it.

As time passed on, even I found singing nonsensical words fun. I began to love singing and I became a "Chorus person," a person who would be happy singing just about anywhere. Chorus people at Trinity were forever humming, talking, singing, or just listening to the music around them. I made friends with other Chorus people as well. With new and old friends, I went around the halls of Trinity singing songs ranging from "The Hallelujah Chorus" to "Stormy Weather." During Christmas vacation that year, I taught myself to sight-read music so that I could understand the music better.

One day, a friend of mine told me that I seemed to be happier than before. Why? I cannot explain, but I was happier since being in Chorus. Chorus gave me something that I loved, and something I could always have with me—music.

Chorus gave me another important gift, the gift of performance. Before tenth grade, I hated going on stage. I did not like the attention. However, Chorus introduced in me a love for performing. The excitement and nervousness of the people backstage, added to the feeling of amazement and happiness while being on stage.

In Chorus, I learned how to listen closely to what is happening around me. I learned the importance of cooperation with others. Most important, I learned how to have fun with people with whom I had only one thing in common.

I look forward to singing in a choral setting in college. But whether or not I continue singing in the future, I will always have the memories of this experience that has literally changed my life.

9. *Keep things in perspective.* Unless you applied Early Decision, Early Action, or Rolling Admission, and heard good news, you probably have to wait until early April to find out which colleges have room at the inn for you. Naturally, you are anxious, *stressed, OVER-WHELMED.* But get a grip. Don't spend those months biting off your toenails with worry. Don't get too wound up in the trauma and drama. Don't have a Duke-or-die attitude. For sanity's sake, talk about something else. (Aren't you eager for me to start talking about something else?)

When the letters arrive, keep your chin up. If you get a rejection, it may not be because you're not qualified. It may be bad luck: Thirty other triple threats (valedictorian volunteers with varsity letters) were vying for the very same spot. And it's not the end of the world if Rice or Pomona or Stanford or Vanderbilt or Bowdoin turns you down. Other schools will snap you up. You're wait listed? Knock again on that door. Restate your devotion; ask if there's more you can do. Even though the college you attend does make a difference, you can surround yourself with friendly, thinking people and get a great education anywhere. (If necessary, you can also transfer. Ask about requirements and be sure to take serious courses that will translate into credits.)

Mid-April can put a strain on friendships. Be caring through thick or thin—whether you or your friends receive thick or thin envelopes. Notice whom you're talking to when you express your delight. You'd hate it if someone gushed about Mount Holyoke if Mount Holyoke just turned you down.

For now, feel pumped, not scared. I bet you'll wind up at a school you adore. So when the good news comes, celebrate!

Dear Carol...

Dear Carol,

I've been in the same school for seven years and now I have to leave. I've grown so attached to this place and I find saying good-bye one of the hardest things to do in the whole world. The teachers are practically family. I'm scared to go to junior high with different kids and teachers I don't know. I know I can't stop growing up—but I feel like I'm starting over and I don't want to lose my friends.

Dear Carol,

My family recently moved, and I am worried about school. I'll be a sopho-more and I don't know anybody. It's hard for me to meet people because I'm so shy. I'm also afraid I'll get lost. (This school has three floors and my last one had one.) Mostly I'm scared no one will like me. What can I do?

Whether you're starting a new grade or a new school, early September can make you jumpy. To meet people with your interests, get involved with a sport or band or coat drive or environmental club or whatever interests you. Stay open-minded and speak up. (But don't keep saying how great your old school was.) Tour the new school before it opens. And if you do get lost? That will give you an opportunity to ask for directions—and maybe make a friend.

Transitions are hard, but in some ways, everybody starts anew each year. Besides, you aren't just moving away from your comfortable old life—you're moving toward your exciting new one. The qualities that charmed your old friends and teachers will serve you well again.

Dear Carol,

I am 11. I am just going into middle school and I am pretty scared. My 13-year-old brother keeps telling me about "Kick Ass Corner," "Bully Boulevard," and "Dead Man's Hall" where kids beat you up. I am also afraid people will tease me about my chest. I'm flat-chested like you.

Flat-chested? *Moi?*

First, the grim news: Although the risk of possessing a weapon often outweighs the protection it can offer, over 125,000 students do carry guns to school each day, and many others may carry knives, box cutters, razors, or clubs. One-fourth of urban school districts use metal detec-tors called magnetometers or "mags." Many others have security guards. Teen violence is indeed a growing problem, especially in inner cities. After accidents, guns are the second leading cause of death among people aged 10 to 19.

Fortunately, in most schools, there are no Bully Boulevards, let alone armed thugs. Your brother's horror stories are probably worse than the reality, and you may be pleasantly surprised come September. In fact, school statistics show that there are many more injuries from sports than injuries from violence.

But what if your Sweet Valley High really is a haven for gangs and violence? Can you talk to your parents about moving? Girls who join gangs often want to quit but encounter pressure to continue stealing, drinking, or even having sex with other gang members. Your best bet at a tough school: Stay independent and keep a low profile. And keep talking up moving!

Dear Carol,

I want to attend a private school because my school isn't very good academically. But we don't have much money. Will private school cost a lot more? I haven't talked to my mother yet. She took a job as a waitress after my parents' divorce. My dad refused to help pay for my education and I'm not 16 so I can't get a job.

Dear Carol,

I want to transfer from my public school to a good private school. We can afford it, so that's not the problem. My mother is not against it; it's my father. He thinks all people who attend private schools are snobs. I want to transfer because our school system is terrible and I want to get a better education than I can get here.

Are you taking the hardest courses your high school offers and still not feeling challenged? You can supplement your education with extracurricular activities or a course at a local college.

But perhaps switching to a private school (or different private school) *is* the solution. Most day schools and boarding schools do offer some financial aid, and most strive for an ethnic and economic mix, so if you're qualified (are your grades good?), read up on and visit schools. Librarians, teachers, and guidance counselors may be able to help.

Are private school kids all snobbish? No! Some lead more sheltered and/or privileged lives than their public school counterparts, but who are we kidding? There are stuck-up kids everywhere. Friendly ones, too. I went to public school and my husband went to private school, and we're both pretty outgoing—if I do say so myself!

If you really think you would welcome a heavier workload and new social scene, investigate the possibilities. If you approach your parents armed with information and a desire to improve your education, they may treat your wish with the respect it deserves.

Dear Carol,

Even when my sisters weren't there, your book was. Thanks! When I changed schools in ninth grade, I thought, "I must be the only freshman staying home on a Friday night!" But by reading your book, I realized I wasn't a leper, I just wasn't getting involved in anything—so how could I meet anybody new?

I'm now a junior at a competitive public high school. My grades are good and I dream of studying in Spain my senior year. The addresses in your book made me realize it is possible. The first hurdle I must jump is convincing my parents (and me, totally) that it is the best thing for me. Is it as good an experience as I have heard? Did you feel you missed out on just bumming around with friends your senior year? Did you ever feel lost over there? Or really homesick? How did you take standardized tests and apply to colleges over in Europe? Did the good points outweigh the problems? I've lived in the same town, same house all my life and I feel the need to experience more before I enter college.

Dear Carol,

I have been thinking a lot about studying in England. You really only told of the advantages of studying abroad. What were some of the disadvantages? Would you do it again if you could go back in time?

Yes! Yes! Yes! And since I can't go back in time, I'm so glad that I did live with other families in other countries and that I did meet so many terrific French, Spanish, and American students. Living abroad is not for everybody, but if you are bold, flexible, friendly, open-minded, willing to try new foods, willing to expect the unexpected, and (the hardest for me) willing to be apart from your family, then go for it!

I missed hanging around with the seniors, but I hung out with Hannah, Norma, and Seth (who are still my friends), and I'm still friends with Jen and Judy (we didn't forget each other in one year). College applications? I finished as much of that as possible before leaving in September, then did the rest from afar. (A nuisance, but then the foreign stamps on my applications probably made them stand out.) The program I chose, School Year Abroad, made it easy to take APs and other tests. And since I was away senior year, coming home was not too anticlimactic—I didn't have to fit the new me into my old school, though I did return in time for the prom and graduation.

Sure, I was sometimes homesick for my family, friends, and boyfriend. But at home I might have sometimes been bored or moody too. And my life is richer for having traveled. French came alive when I walked down the streets. History came alive when I toured the beaches of D-Day. The world suddenly became both bigger and smaller. If you have the chance to travel and broaden your horizons, I say jump.

Dear Carol,

I'm worried I won't live up to my parents' expectations. My mother went to Barnard (she calls it Barnyard) and my dad went to Princeton and most of my cousins are Ivy League. My parents say to give it my all, but I feel like I'm getting obsessed with doing well.

Dear Carol,

I am a senior. My GPA is not the greatest, 2.5. I want to get into this one college and the Dean of Admissions and I have been writing back and forth. I'm pretty sure I'll get in, but now I'm not sure I'm ready for it. I would like to take it slow, you know, go to a junior college for a couple years, then transfer. But that's unheard of around here! My friends think that if you don't go to a prestigious university, you're a loser. I know I shouldn't base my life on others' opinions, but I do.

Pressure! You don't want to get in over your head . . . but you do want to aim high because you can always step back down. The reason for going to a good school isn't because it's prestigious but because well-known schools attract a high caliber of students and professors. Yet there are hundreds of excellent schools out there, so you don't need a "Barnard or bust" attitude. Can you do your best without getting obsessed? As you get older, you realize that pleasing yourself is more important than pleasing family or friends. And no matter where you go, you'll get out what you put in.

Dear Carol,

Some of my friends tease boys about their butts and stuff. Sometimes I do it, too. But when a boy snaps my bra or makes an obscene comment, I get mad. Is that a double standard?

It sure is. Sexual harassment goes both ways. If you and your friends want boys to treat you with respect, don't say, "Nice ass," when you mean "Hello." That just contributes to the confusion and blurs the boundaries between crude flirtation and sexual harassment, which, by definition, is unwelcome and pervasive. If you are the victim of lewd comments or grabbing, say an unamused, "Don't talk to me like that" or "Stop touching me." (And don't retaliate with sexually explicit remarks or gestures of your own.) If the abusive remarks come from a teacher or boss, keep a record and consult an adult you trust.

Dear Carol,

I have a very weird problem. I study way too much. I'm only in seventh grade, and everyone tells me, "Relax, it doesn't matter." I want to believe them, but when I study less, I start feeling sick to my stomach. It's so bad that I study an hour and a half just for little quizzes. At school I'm known for being "the study girl." Any suggestions?

Laid back you're not. It's good to value education, not good to be over-anxious. Why are you driving yourself so hard? If your school has a counselor, make an appointment to talk about pressure and ways to unwind and be nicer to yourself. It might also help if you schedule some down time—baking or biking or an extracurricular activity. Last but not least, picture the worst-case scenario: You bomb a quiz. What would happen? The sun would still shine, your dog would still wag its tail, and your parents would still love you.

Dear Carol,

I haven't been doing well in school lately, and my teachers are thinking about holding me back. I know they are trying to help me, but I don't want to be separated from my friends. I am also afraid I will get teased about being held back.

If you buckle down, can you bring your grades up? Can you find a tutor? Or enroll in summer school? Might you have a learning disability? Are personal troubles getting in the way of your progress at school? Figure out why you aren't doing well in school and what you can do about it (besides repeating the year). If you do end up repeating, please know that many kids do, and many reap the rewards of making new friends (while keeping old ones) and enjoying the confidence of being a successful student—instead of a struggling one.

Dear Carol,

I am trying to study harder, but I have this friend who keeps talking to me and writing me notes in class. How can I make her stop without hurting her feelings?

If you yell, "Quit bugging me!" you'll hurt her. Instead try: "I want to pay attention. Let's talk after class or sit together at lunch."

Dear Carol,

The boys in my class are all racists, and they make really rude comments. When I ask them why they make fun of people of different races, they say, "Why do you care?" I try to make them stop, but they just keep doing it.

It's hard to change people, but I commend you for trying. If racists would take off their blinders, they would see that there are good people and bad people of all colors. It may even make an impression on your small-minded classmates to see that slurs or stupid jokes can lose them the respect of someone as special as you.

Dear Carol,

I saw these two girls in my class throwing spitballs on the ceiling in the bathroom. What should I do?

Since their behavior is not dangerous, you don't have to do anything. But why not speak up? Instead of tattling, say, "You know, you're just making extra work for the janitor." Some kids court trouble to impress friends. So it's helpful when friends let them know that they couldn't be less impressed by vandalism, cheating, smoking, drugs, or spitballs.

Dear Carol,

I home-school and mostly I really like it but sometimes I worry that I'm missing out and that I'll freak when I get to college. What do you think?

A lot of kids your age worry they are missing out and are nervous about college—no matter what school they do or do not attend. Because you home-school, it's important to hang out with other kids and to meet the academic standards for your age group. Are you involved with kids your age? Are your parents on top of your curriculum? Are you taking standardized exams or preparing a portfolio? The certified teacher who evaluates your work each year can let you know how you're progressing. Hundreds of thousands of kids (many of them in Texas, California, and Ohio) experience the pros and cons of home-schooling and go on to do well in college. Still worried? Take one course at your local college now.

Dear Carol,

I am a 15-year-old junior at Antilles High School in Ft. Buchanan, Puerto Rico. I'm zeroing in on a college in upstate New York, but that's so far from Puerto Rico, and I would probably see my family only twice a year. What is it like to come home for vacation? Do you change? What about roommates, classes, food, etc?

Dear Carol,

I am preparing to enter my first year of college at the University of Richmond. I wish you had included a chapter on college life. I could use a whole book on the subject!

Everyone looks at the college years with some trepidation, but living and learning among peers can be really fun. I can't include a whole book here, just fifteen quick thoughts:

1. Sign up for freshman orientation—whether it's a two-day program on campus or a four-day backpacking adventure. Once a college accepts you, it *wants* to keep you. (Someone has to pay the professors' salaries, and 1 out of 3 freshmen nowadays does not return to the same school sophomore year.)

2. Don't decide that you hate your roommates. Make an effort to get along and learn from your differences. After an inauspicious start, my roomie Helen and I stayed together all four years.

3. Beware the Freshman Five. (That's pounds.) Just because food is abundant and available doesn't mean you have to eat everything in sight.

4. Stay on top of your workload. It's OK to cut corners; it's not OK to blow off assignments.

5. Be glad you're female. Upperclassmen will notice you, whereas boys go from sexy seniors to invisible freshmen. (But be selective, smart, and careful!)

6. Don't be in a hurry to hook up. If you're going to be sexually active, use condoms. One out of 500 college students is HIV positive, and 7 out of 100 college women has chlamydia. Sixty percent of college women with an STD were drunk when they got infected. (Why are you not surprised?)

7. Don't start smoking (around 15 percent of American freshmen smoke) and don't binge-drink (college presidents cite alcohol abuse as the No. 1 problem on campus).

8. Consult the Student Health Service for anything from chronic cough to severe depression. You don't need your mother to tell you when you're sick.

9. Dabble with theater, journalism, rowing, waterpolo, the radio station. Just because you already got into college is no reason to abandon extracurrics.

10. No matter how wired your campus is, know when to log off. Dartmouth has Blitzmail and Vassar has Broadcast, and virtually everyone everywhere E-mails their crushes and professors and friends near and far. But tête-à-têtes are what college is about, too, so don't get lost in cyberspace.

11. Take the best courses taught by the most dynamic professors. If you take Melodrama in Soap Operas instead of a course in the classics, you may wish later that you'd taken advantage of having a tour guide to lead you through Flaubert or Doestoyevsky. (You can watch *General Hospital* on your own.)

12. Don't go crazy with credit cards—you can get into debt and ruin your credit rating. Credit cards do not represent free cash, but high-interest loans that must be repaid.

13. Stay on campus. Many college students (not necessarily freshmen) live off-campus, but you are about to have a lifetime of cooking your own meals. And isn't there something to be said for having a true collegiate experience among all those other likeable leaders and intellects with character?

14. Consider going abroad for a college semester or two. Australia? China? Chile? Costa Rica? Join the 85,000 students a year who live and study overseas and still get credit at their American colleges.

15. Keep in touch with your family and high school friends and expect a few awkward moments when you first see them again. You'll all be excited and you'll all have stories to tell. You may even start getting along better with your siblings. Will you have changed? Yes. You will have grown. They will have, too.

7 MONEY

The Buck Starts Here

❀

Money isn't everything, but if music, movies, CDs, clothes, books, and travel appeal to you, then the more dollars, the merrier.

The problem? Some people become hung up on money, always counting pennies and envious of those with bigger bank accounts. Others forget that how you earn is more important than how much you earn and get trapped in high-paying jobs they can't stand.

That's why I'm torn about this chapter. Money is a ticket to fun and freedom, but "love of money is the root of all evil." On the one hand, I want you to know how to make and save money, become a better baby-sitter, find odd jobs, write a résumé, ace an interview, use connections, get employed, and ultimately find a career not by chance but by choice. On the other hand, I want you to chill out. In school, most of you can enjoy a fleeting luxury: You don't have to get hyper about bills and taxes. Look ahead, but relax, too. You probably can be whatever you want to be, and you have years to decide what that is.

Be a Better (and Better-Paid) Baby-Sitter

I baby-sat around the clock. I baby-sat for one family in the afternoon and another in the evening. I baby-sat my way to Europe, and in Madrid, I worked as a mother's helper. I baby-sat until I got baby-sitter burnout.

During my primo baby-sitting years, ages twelve to sixteen, I usually loved it. It was fun trying to answer children's questions. Four-year-old Adam, the first boy ever to take any interest in my stick-like figure, asked, "Do you have big boobies?" And John said, "We learned there is water in the air. Why isn't everything wet?" I liked letting Gary finish the sentences when I read *Goodnight Moon.* I even got a kick out of the Ice Cream Crisis. Leah wanted a taste of her cousin Tim's cone. "Give her a bite," I said. He did—he bit her arm.

Do you like children? Are you patient? Responsible? Diplomatic? Baby-sitting may be for you. Of course, baby-sitting is a misnomer. It's really baby-watching, baby-chasing, baby-feeding, baby-bathing, baby-changing, baby-reading, baby-bedding. Here are more pointers:

- When you say yes to a job, make sure the parent knows how late you can stay and how much you charge. Write down the time and date of the job; the parents' name, address, and phone number; and whether they'll provide transportation. (If you don't know them or know of them, be cautious. Ask your parents for advice.)
- Don't ever cancel at the last minute. In a pinch, call the parents as soon as possible and offer to find a sub—your best friend or one of the parents' regulars.
- Before you leave, let your parents know where you'll be and when you think you'll be back.
- Before the children's parents leave, get the number where they'll be, as well as numbers of the police, doctor, and neighbors. Ask for any special instructions about bedtime rules, pets, medicines, phone messages, what to do if the doorbell rings, or how to work the alarm system (if they have one). If you're in an area where the power sometimes goes out, ask where they keep a flashlight.
- Don't invite friends over unless the parents said you could.
- Lock all doors.
- Play it safe. Pick up toys on the stairs. Take the phone off the hook, or don't answer it while you bathe the children. Don't give pills to a sick child without permission. And if you're cooking, use the stove's back burners.
- Be fun but firm, too. If bedtime is at 8:30, don't let them have pillow fights and let's-pretend-the-bed-is-a-trampoline parties until all hours. Say, "This is the last story" in a tone that shows you mean it.

- Kids asleep? Neaten up the puzzles and dishes, but no need to go overboard: It's not your job to mop the floor.
- Don't snoop. (You can peruse bookshelves, though. While my charges slept, I dipped into fine literature—and racy trash!)
- Don't abuse phone or fridge privileges. (I especially wouldn't recommend sipping straight from the juice carton when wearing lipstick, or eating all the cherries out of the Cherry Garcia Frozen Yogurt.)
- In case of emergency, call the police at 911. In case of fire, grab the kids and run, then call the fire department and children's parents from a neighbor's.
- If you're really dedicated, take CPR or a first aid course. (You may even be able to raise your rate.)
- Try to stay awake until the parents return. A quiet house can be your opportunity to get paid while doing homework.
- When the parents come back, tell them what went on, but spare them the saga of the spilled fruit salad that you already cleaned up. Say, "I love your kids and I hope you'll call me again."

Want more jobs? Spread the word. Tell your parents, friends, the families you sit for. Post a notice at your local grocer's, club, church, synagogue, nursery or elementary school, or pediatrician's office.

If you become a family's favorite, ask them if they'd like to hire you for, say, every Saturday or Wednesday night.

Are you being paid fairly? Find out the going rate from your friends. When you take care of three rowdy children, you deserve more than when you stay with a sleeping toddler. Let the parents know ahead whether you charge extra for additional children or postmidnight sitting. Most parents will ask you back if their kids like you and you have common sense—even if you live farther away or do charge slightly more than the norm.

Don't get gypped! I once helped out at a five-year-old's birthday party. I brought Scott a small gift and did my best to entertain his twelve wild buddies. Afterward, the mother wrote me a check (I hated checks) for the exact amount of time at my minimum hourly rate—no tip! I barely broke even! I should have asked beforehand if she'd pay me more than usual. Or I should have expressed my disappointment then and there. Instead, here I am, years later, still peeved.

Speaking of being frank, if the parents ever return drunk, don't let them drive you home. Say your parents were planning to pick you up and call home.

Baby-sitting can lead to mother's helper or day-care jobs. One summer when my friend Jen and I were sixteen, we took care of eight four-year-olds every weekday morning at different parents' houses. The children brought their own lunch, and Jen and I came up with arts, crafts, games, even a few field trips. We had fun and earned more than we would have if we'd been baby-sitting on our own.

If you *don't* want to sit on a particular night, don't. Say, "Thanks, Mrs. Brennan, I have plans. I'd love to another time." And if *you* have baby-sitter burnout? Say, "Sorry, I'm not sitting anymore, but thanks for calling." Me, I used to say, "Aahhm, I'm not sure," then bellow, "Mom, can I baby-sit tonight?" while violently shaking my head no and waiting for her to get me off the hook. What a wimp! You can do better.

Beyond Baby-Sitting (But Before the Big Time)

It's hard for adults to find work; it's even harder to land a job if you're not yet sixteen.

If you are fourteen or fifteen, you can probably get a free work permit (through school) and social security number (through your local social security office). You are eligible for some jobs at small businesses or restaurants. In most cases, you may not work legally during school hours or after 7 P.M. (or 9 P.M. in summer) or in "hazardous" places, such as in a boiler room or meat freezer, or where there are explosives, alcohol, gambling, or dangerous machinery.

However, you may bag groceries, shelve merchandise, pump gas, be a cashier (if the bill came to $1.78 and someone handed you $2.03, you wouldn't panic, would you?), deliver newspapers, bus tables, help in a nursing home, be a companion to an elderly person, set up store displays, work on a farm, be a junior camp counselor, help clean pet stores or hotel rooms, or—these are a stretch—be a model or actress or Olympic figure skater. And the list goes on. Listen for leads and keep your eyes open for help-wanted notices in stores and newspapers.

At any age, you can make money doing odd jobs in your neighborhood. When my brother Eric and I were little kids, we used to go door-to-door shining shoes and selling homemade potholders. We always came home with candy money.

Are you good in the garden? Are you handy with repairs? A pro with paint? How do you fare at washing cars? Washing dogs? Walking dogs?

Raking? Baking? Hemming and sewing? Dyeing Easter eggs or wrapping holiday gifts? Can you give guitar lessons? Tutor children in English or math? Run a weekend art, sports, or exercise class for kids? Would your penmanship look pretty on invitations? Can you take care of a house while the owners are on vacation—feed the cat, water plants, bring in mail, turn lights on and off—without getting spooked? Are you a snappy photographer?

Yes? Then if you want work, don't just stand there. Hustle your bustle and get your rear in gear! Let your neighbors know how lucky they are. Get your parents' OK and then write your name, address, phone number, and special talents on a piece of paper. Make photocopies and leave them at neighbors' doors. Better yet, dress neatly, knock, hand out your flyer, and explain that for a fee, you're a Jill-of-all-trades.

A "try-me" attitude is helpful, but don't insist and don't wander into houses where you don't know anybody who knows the residents.

Every week one winter, a boy rang my doorbell and asked if he could clear our icy walk for three dollars. Partly to encourage him and partly to have an unslippery path, I always said, "You're on." If he didn't show up, shovel in hand, I wouldn't have advertised for a shoveler. But because he took that initiative, he made money in minutes at many houses on our street.

Come up with creative tactics. You could even offer to work for free for a limited time (an hour for an odd job, up to a week for a worthwhile summer job) so a reluctant employer can see how useful you are.

Once you're on the job, work hard without constant supervision. Don't be like the well-meaning teen housecleaner my working mother once hired who, every ten minutes, interrupted Mom to ask, "Now what?" Instead, you and your employer should thoroughly go over the chores (laundry, dusting, cleaning the refrigerator) when you arrive.

It's most ideal if you can snag a few regular, once-a-week jobs. It's most fun if you and a friend can work together, although you'll have to share profits.

When I was fourteen, I told my diary, "*I wish I could get a real job and make lots of $ working for a few weeks. That'd be great.*" Getting a "real job" when you're young is not easy. But if you narrow down what you'd like to do and go after it with gusto, you *can* make "lots of $." The trick is to find a balance: working for money without letting your grades sink or your friendships flounder or your family forget what you look like.

All in the Family

Families differ and allowances differ. If you think you're not getting enough allowance, you can ask for more. (Satisfaction not guaranteed.) Keep a list of where your money goes and be reasonable. Your parents probably aren't charging you for room and board, and they may be trying to set aside money for your college and future.

Perhaps your parents think seventh graders should get seven dollars a week, tenth graders should get ten. Perhaps you just found out that your younger second cousin—the one with the perfect little body and the long blond hair and the babe of a boyfriend—gets twenty-five dollars every single Monday. Before you blow a gasket, consider this. She may be expected to pay for her own school lunch, friends' birthday presents, haircuts, movie tickets, clothes, and even school supplies, whereas your parents may pick up some or most of those tabs. Or maybe her parents simply have more money.

Finances differ from family to family, so comparing won't get you very far. However you might consider asking your parents for more money upfront and saying you'll use it to cover more expenses. If you want to learn to manage money, now's a better time than when you're in college three states away. Learning to budget means paying for what you need and saving for what you want. Your parents can also take you to a bank where you can set up an account. And someday they may consider co-signing a store credit card with you—especially if you've shown fiscal responsibility (not gone into debt and expected them to bail you out).

Allowances aside, your parents may be willing to pay you to do work for them. I don't mean sprinkling you with megabucks for doing your usual chores. It's fair for parents to ask you to tidy your room, clean the guinea pig's cage, set the table, and put away dishes. But maybe you can make a little extra if you do a little extra.

If your parents work and you're a good cook, maybe you can have dinner ready on certain days. If they give a party, maybe you can clean up. If you drive (or live downtown), maybe you can run their errands. Would they consider paying you to sit for a sibling? To paint dingy closets? To do the family laundry? Polish silver? Would they let you arrange a garage sale? You do most of the work and get most of the profit.

Many teens work for their parents outside the home. Does your mother the caterer need a hand on weekends? Offer both of yours. Does your father the shoe store owner need help on busy days? You may be a shoo-in for the job.

Working for your parents has its payoffs. You don't have to go through the job hunt runaround. You may be able to call in sick once in a while to study for a final or go to a game. The transportation problem to and from work is simplified. You may be entrusted with extra on-the-job responsibility. And understanding what your mother or father does all day may bring you closer. There can even be tax benefits for all if your parents keep careful records.

Drawbacks? Plenty. Parent-daughter scolding often hurts more than employer-employee criticism. And other employees might resent you or defer to you rather than simply accept you. My friend Laura said she felt caught in the middle when she worked for her father. "The people I worked with felt so comfortable with me, they'd bad-mouth the boss—but the boss was my dad!"

Many disillusioned adult sons and daughters complain that because their parents needed them, they got stuck in the family business and never developed their own skills or tested their own dreams. If you work for your parents, let them know if you feel put-upon. But also if you're happy and grateful for the job.

Figuring Out Your Future

Once you're sixteen, you can get more jobs and more money. A recent survey showed that nearly half of teens between the ages of sixteen and nineteen had jobs. Yet some states still have restrictions to protect you, from working, say, more than twenty-eight hours per week or after 10 P.M. on school nights. Sometimes an entry-level job with training and room for growth at a store or fast-food chain is the ideal launching pad. But before you run off to apply to be a store cashier or fast-food counter person, take a minute—no, many minutes—to grapple with the old "What do you want to be when you grow up?"

You don't have to have an instant answer, but now is the time to ask yourself questions, whether you are college-bound or not. Do you have short-term and long-term goals? What are your interests and strengths? Some of you may think, "I'm good at lots of things." Some of you may mistakenly believe, "I'm not good at anything." And others may be good in one subject but tilt toward another. (Case in point: My math SAT score was 140 points higher than my verbal, but since I loathed numbers and loved words, I stuck with words.)

You have years to decide to be a teacher, advertising executive, surgeon, literary agent, real estate agent, computer programmer, flight attendant, geologist, pilot, social worker, health care coordinator, interior decorator, lawyer, or politician. (America could use some more women in Congress!) It's too early to worry about your future career, but it's not too early to think about it. Consider the Big Picture. Deciding what sort of job you want is a job in itself. But it's settling to find a direction. Though goals change, having a goal can add a sense of purpose to your studies and life. If you know what you're aiming for (I didn't), you may be able to get a part-time or summer job in your chosen field (I didn't). Don't let your parents or anyone else choose a profession for you. And don't worry that your decision is being set in stone.

Do you want a career? It's OK if you don't, but I hope you do. A career can offer money and fulfillment and friends. And it gives a woman options: She can be single and self-sufficient; she can be part of a two-career couple; she can support herself and her children if her-husband-the-good-provider dies or gets fired or files for divorce; or she can leave him if he becomes abusive or unfaithful or if she feels she'd be happier without him. Let's hope this is never your story, but approximately forty-three percent of married couples wind up divorced, and all too many divorced or separated women wind up on welfare. Furthermore, women live an average of eight years longer than men in the United States, and 50 percent of all women older than sixty-five are widows. In the world, 1 of every 3 households has a woman as its sole breadwinner. It's risky not to know how to take care of yourself.

And I quote . . .

Susan B. Anthony: "Woman must not depend upon the protection of men but must be taught to protect herself."

Margaret Bourke-White: "Work is something you can count on, a trusted, lifelong friend who never deserts you."

Gloria Steinem: "Some of us are becoming the men we wanted to marry."

A *New York Times* poll reported that even if they could afford to stay home, over half of American working women would rather work (though one-third of working women would choose part-time work). Me, I'd keep writing even if I won a million-dollar sweepstakes. Well-chosen work can be enjoyable. That's why rich filmmakers, business executives, and Pulitzer Prize winners don't quit and go golfing. If you're lucky, you can decide later to try life as a full-time mother or homemaker or volunteer, but keep your options open.

Today you may want just a job. Later you may seek a career. "Just a job" forever could be boring. It's sad to think that many people spend over forty hours a week selling their time for money and impatiently watching the minute hand creep (or the digit cards flip) until quitting time. The Thank-God-It's-Friday crowd isn't enjoying Monday, Tuesday, Wednesday, and Thursday enough. Years from now when someone asks you, "What do you do?" you'll want to feel good about your answer.

What kind of career matches your talents and interests? What are you naturally good at? Do you like working with people, or numbers, or words? Would you like the security of a nine-to-five job with colleagues and bene- fits, or do you have the discipline and desire to be self-employed? I love being freelance and being able to juggle when to work and when to be with my kids. Do you want the kind of work that blends well with family? Do you want to make lots of money or have lots of vacation time? When you're older, how would you like to look back on your life?

I'm not asking all this to worry you, but to inspire you. When I was in high school, I wasn't sure what I wanted to be. I thought I might become a writer or psychologist or teacher or chef or. . . . And I confess, one line in my diary reveals: *"I probably will get married, etc., rather than have a neat career."* As though it were either/or!

Take out a piece of paper (this is not a pop quiz) and write down your best and/or favorite school subjects. Next add the extracurrics that mean the most to you. If you're not the star of the track team or the lead of the musical, but you love running and acting, write that down. What do you do in your free time? Read? Make jewelry? Play tennis? How would you describe yourself? Open? Creative? Methodical? What are you secretly proud of? The way your room looks? Your eye for fashion? How you can smooth out arguments? What achievements do you feel good about, and which skills did they involve? What are some of your values? Friendship? Knowledge? Power? Helping others? Jot this all down.

You're on your way to writing a résumé (more on that coming up). For now, use this personal profile, and look for patterns and clues about what sort of job to head for. Persuasive sorts might enjoy sales jobs. At a sport- ing-goods store? Electronics outlet? Clothes shop? Quiet organizers might prefer clerical work. At a travel agency? Radio station? Government office? If you're good with numbers, you may become an architect, Wall Street analyst, engineer. Science is your strong suit? Maybe you'll become an oceanographer or a pharmacist. Language experts might look toward teaching, diplomacy, or international business.

Does your list say art, going to museums, sketching portraits, making clay figures? Do yourself a favor: Forget fast food and look for artsy employment. Aim to be the arts-and-crafts instructor at a camp, or ask if help is needed at galleries, graphic design businesses, nearby paint shops, or museums. Maybe a local artist or craftsman would welcome an apprentice.

Does your list say English, school newspaper, reading, writing letters, keeping a journal? If you're motivated, don't settle for a cashier job as I did; get a head start on a literary career. Work in a library or a bookstore. Call the local newspaper and ask if they need a messenger—or better still, a "stringer" to report school happenings. (Jody, a spunky fourteen-year-old I know, called a paper and offered to write sports features. The editors didn't just OK the idea, they paid for the columns.) Could you be an intern or go-fer at a local magazine, running errands while meeting editors and seeing the business from within? Or try to sell your own writing to a teen magazine. Study the magazine carefully before you send out your typed double-spaced masterpiece, or it may boomerang back. And if it does? Remember that it is better to have written and been rejected than never to have written at all.

Maybe, modesty aside, you are a head-turner or have an exotic or an all-American look. Many teens wish they could be models, but only a few can. So don't kid yourself. If you're petite and adorable, you are petite and adorable and probably not model material. But if you're healthy, slender, tall (we're talking five feet seven inches minimum), photogenic, out-and-out beautiful and have straight teeth and a perfect complexion (most of us would be quite content with two of the above, thank you), consider checking out a local modeling agency. Bring along recent pictures and a good attitude. (If they say no, don't fall apart. If they say yes, don't get too vain on us.)

Your school guidance counselor can provide more job opportunities as well as internship information. He or she can also tell if any alums from your high school are in your field. (I once had an Armonk student intern with me simply because she asked, and I've also had lots of Yale undergrads spend part of their spring break with me.) Many communities have federally funded youth employment placement centers and services. The library is a gold mine, too. A librarian can lead you to helpful reference books, such as the government's *Occupational Outlook Handbook* or *Writer's Digest's Internships* or *Summer Employment Directory of the U.S.*, which is updated annually and includes available jobs at camps, campuses, ranches, holiday resorts, amusement parks, and restaurants.

Adults don't get to try out different careers each summer, but you can. So experiment!

If you can afford to forgo a salary, don't overlook nonpaying work. Volunteer at a soup kitchen, hospital, YWCA, nursing home, veterans' center, children's museum, ASPCA, or Red Cross agency. Get involved with a Girls Inc. friendly PEERsuasion group. Your pay is the good feeling that you are helping others unselfishly. Plus you may become deeper, more confident, more mature. When you've spent the afternoon in a hospital with a life-loving boy who was seriously burned when his house caught fire, you stop feeling so annoyed that your cousin's allowance makes yours look like pocket change.

Still want to waitress? Stretch yourself by doing it in a new environment. Ask your aunt or grandparents if you could live with them one summer.

And don't forget that the odd jobs that were available to you when you were younger are still around—at higher wages. Do you have your license and access to a car? Add "grocery shopping" and "chauffeur service to the airport" to your flyer.

Don't wait until summer to apply for a summer job. The early bird gets the work.

Writing a Résumé

If you want a job, you've got to market your skills. That means you have to let the bosses out there know why they'd be lucky to have you. And that means you may have to write a résumé.

A résumé is like your scribbled list of strengths and interests but is organized, on one page, typed, and includes, in reverse chronological order (recent stuff first), your experience, education (including the year you expect to graduate), and any pertinent courses you've taken (like accounting) or skills you have (like you *do* do Windows—on your P.C.). From your résumé, an employer should be able, at a glance, to get an idea about who you are and what you've done.

When you write your résumé, sell yourself. If your grades are lousy, don't mention them. If you got a varsity letter in gymnastics, say so. If you speak Japanese, write that down. You may have talents that you take for granted but that could knock an employer's socks off. Remember: Everybody started with no experience. Save your résumé on a computer and update and customize it often to include new activities, jobs, or awards.

You may want to come up with more than one résumé if you are applying for different kinds of jobs. For instance, if you want to work in a summer repertory theater, write the theaters in the spring and make a big deal of your singing and dancing parts in school plays, your two years of voice lessons, and your ushering at a local theater. If you're simultaneously applying for an internship at a corporation and a job to assist a veterinarian, highlight other skills and interests. But limit yourself to a page. No one needs to know about every gold star you ever earned.

Maybe you think all you've done in the last few years is pass your courses and pig out on Twinkies. Think harder. There's bound to be something you can include in a résumé. No? You're sure? Then do yourself the favor of signing up for some extracurrics. Not just to add zest to your résumé but to add zest to your life!

Have a parent, teacher, or counselor check your résumé because it should be perfect before you make copies.

Send it with a neatly typed personalized cover letter to various individuals. If the employer is local, write, "Would you like to set up an interview?" Then cross your fingers. If two weeks pass and you don't hear from your prospective employer, you could call him or her. (Sound self-possessed, not apologetic.)

Here is a sample cover letter and résumé that a girl seeking a summer position as a camp swim instructor might send in the spring.

(P.S. If you're getting a funny feeling in the pit of your stomach and thinking, "But I'm still a kid," maybe *you* don't need to know all this yet. This book is your personal encyclopedia, remember? It's so you know where to find out about résumé writing—or breakups, or sex, or college applications, or alcohol—when you *do* want to know.)

10 Maple Way
Armonk, NY 10504

Month/Date/Year

Mrs. Lisel Jeffrey
Camp Clearwater
19 Asbury Avenue
Wilderness, VT 01010

Dear Mrs. Jeffrey,

I would love to be a swim instructor at your camp this summer. I have my lifesaving certificate, have worked as a lifeguard, and am an active member of my school and club swim team. I adore children and baby-sit often.

Enclosed you'll find my résumé. Thank you for considering me for the position. I look forward to hearing from you soon.

All the best,

Sue Denim

Sue Denim

Sue Denim
10 Maple Way
Armonk, NY 10504
(914) 121-2121

Education
  Byram Hills High School, Class of___

Experience
  Lifeguard at Windmill Club, summers
  Baby-sitter, mornings, for children of Mrs. Little, Upland Lane,
    Armonk, New York

Awards
  Most Valuable Team Member, Windmill Swim Team (include year)
  Third place, Westchester County 50-meter breaststroke

Skills
  Lifesaving certification, white-water canoeing, diving, two years of
    Spanish, driving

Activities
  Byram Hills Student Council, treasurer
  Candystriper at Mount Kisco Hospital
  Outdoors Club, secretary

Age
  16 (include birthdate)

References available upon request.

Acing the Interview

Whether you're interviewing for a job, an internship, or college, you want to come off as mature, intelligent, enthusiastic, polite, and hard-working. The tips given in the *Education* chapter apply at the workplace as well.

Don't say, "Yo, I want a job." Instead:

- Read up on the company and prepare questions.
- Anticipate the interviewer's questions and prepare answers.
- Dress neatly and conservatively. (Remove your nose ring and ear cuff.)
- Plan to arrive alone and early—count on a traffic snarl en route.
- Introduce yourself and shake hands firmly, maintain eye contact, smile, sit up straight, and use complete sentences.
- Don't gesticulate wildly, scratch, chew gum, smoke, or ramble on and on.
- As succinctly and positively as possible, state what you hope to offer the company, not what you hope to learn or gain from it.
- Sell yourself without sounding arrogant. Instead of "I can do anything," say, "I am very persuasive. I sold more Girl Scout cookies last year than anyone else in my school."
- Don't be bashful about discussing hours and wages. (Can you handle working more than fifteen hours in a school week? Are you available weeknights? Is minimum wage OK with you, or are you looking for more?)
- Don't knock your last boss.
- Shake hands again and follow up with a thank-you note.

Last week a friend had an interview at a bank. Together we staged a practice interview. She had terrific answers for "Why should I hire you?" "What do you expect to be doing in ten years?" and "Tell me about yourself." But when I asked "What are your weaknesses?" she blew it. She said, "I'm not good with numbers." A bank doesn't want to hear that! (Later she realized she shouldn't have been applying for a bank job anyway. That was her *father's* aspiration, not hers.)

If an interviewer asks about *your* weaknesses, don't volunteer that you're a procrastinator or are hopelessly disorganized. A better answer would be, "I'm a perfectionist," or "Sometimes I get so involved with a project I don't know when to quit." Don't lie, but put your best foot forward. Role play the interview with your mom or dad and then talk your way into the job!

Last but not least: that thank-you note. It can make or break you. Write to everyone who has been of service. Try to notice the assistant's name, too, then mention how much you appreciated Terri's help. The thank-you note can also be your chance to say anything important that you forgot to mention in person.

Hey, and try not to be discouraged if you don't get the first, second, or even tenth job. You need only one boss to say "You're hired!"

No one's nibbling? Then chow down some sour grapes and decide that for now you are better off being the star of a Minnesota ice hockey team rather than one more cashier at the Mall of America.

Connections

When my sister-in-law planned to apply to my alma mater, I planned to write her a glowing recommendation. Sally helped me edit this book, and I couldn't wait to tell Yale what an all-around smart person she is.

But then she asked me not to gush on her behalf. She nobly worried about the applicants who didn't have Yalie sisters-in-law, and besides, she wanted to Get In On Her Own. Sally ended up at a tiptop school, but the point is, it's not so terrible to let people help you get ahead. *Connections* is not a dirty word.

Many students resist connections. But no one is going to go out on a limb to praise a nincompoop. I wanted to write the letter not only for Sally's sake but for Yale's. A connection can be a two-way favor.

Not that my letter alone would have done the trick. Connections merely help you get a foot in the door. You still have to squeeze the rest of your body in by yourself.

Are they worth making? Absolutely. Networking by weaving and pulling strings isn't cheating; it's a skill—it's being professional.

It won't kill you to be nice to the head honcho your parents know (who could someday offer you a job), just as you should be nice to all your parents' friends. If you don't have any family connections, make your own. Meet people who know people. Work hard and develop confidence in your abilities. Find someone you admire and let him or her know it. Get over the idea that biggies are unapproachable.

It pays to have gumption. I had never interviewed anybody, and then I interviewed Joanne Woodward. She was performing at the nearby

Kenyon Festival Theater in Ohio, and I told myself, "You have nothing to lose, you have nothing to lose" as I circled my phone like a pilot above an airport. Finally, I dialed and, after preliminaries, asked, "May I interview you?" "Yes," she said. Just like that. (I even got to meet her husband, Paul Newman!)

My husband, Rob, got a job with Broadway director Hal Prince when he was fresh out of theater grad school. How? On day one, Rob saw and loved Prince's *Madame Butterfly* in Chicago. On day two, he spotted Prince at Northwestern University and congratulated him. On day three, Rob sent Prince a letter and résumé. Upshot: even Big Time Successes may remember that sometime someone somewhere gave them a break. During the New York interview that followed, when Prince asked, "What can I do for you?" Rob answered, "Hire me." Prince did. Just like that.

There is such a thing as the Old Boy and Old Girl Network, and you can use it if you want to. Everyone knows somebody who knows somebody who can be of help. And the contact you forge may lead to something big or to a mentor or role model.

In the future, you, too, can lend a hand to people who could use your help. For now, if you want a job, don't sit back and wait to be discovered. Be bold and friendly. Write a letter to someone you admire. Let your peers and adult friends know you'd like to meet someone in certain career fields or from certain colleges or that you want to intern or "temp." Don't give up your dreams before giving yourself a chance. As the poet Emily Dickinson wrote, "Luck is not chance/It's toil—/Fortune's expensive smile/Is earned." And as Oprah Winfrey put it, "Luck is a matter of preparation meeting opportunity."

Success with no strings attached is great. But it's OK to cultivate connections and tug strings without guilt or apology. It beats feeling beaten.

Once You're Hired, Don't Get Fired—Or Should You Quit?

It's more fun to be given a raise than to be given the ax, so on the job, try to be (take a deep breath) punctual, dependable, cheerful, honest, busy, polite, open-minded, neatly dressed, professional, able to take criticism, willing to do more than the expected, and (phew) not the first to leave at the end of the day.

But what if you decide enough is enough? You can't wash another plate, serve another salad, or tell another customer how becoming the yukky skirt looks. What if you've worked over a year and still get minimum wage even though you requested a raise (pointing out not that you need it but deserve it)? What if you've learned quite enough about dry cleaning, thank you, and want to explore other fields? What if you've tried but just can't get along with catty Connie or nerdy Newt? What if you're weary of being wary of lecherous Larry? What if you're not earning all that much anyway after taxes? (Don't assume you're exempt.) What if your grades are slipping, your friendships are threadbare, and you're always tired and stressed? In short, what if your job is no longer paying off?

Consider quitting. You're allowed. (Even Snoopy thought about leaving when he got tired of working for Peanuts!) Try to give two weeks' notice and leave without hard feelings. Tell your boss you enjoyed and learned from and appreciated the experience. Your last employer can be a valuable reference on your next résumé.

When to Be Cheap, When Not to Be Cheap

Many moons ago, my grandfather bounced me up and down on his knee and said, "Always save your money and be cunning as a fox, and you'll always have some money in the old tobacco box."

Money is for spending and enjoying, so you shouldn't save it all. And instead of a tobacco box, you should probably save yours in some kind of interest-earning account. But Granddad's message is a good one: It pays to be thrifty. For instance:

- If every dollar counts, and you're going to want a box of Raisinets at the movies, buy it at a store, not at the theater. You'll bypass lines, too.
- Compare prices, look for sales, and buy items out of season.
- Look for affordable clothes and sundries in thrift shops, Salvation Army outlets, and antique stores.
- For cheap chic, buy trendy costume jewelry instead of an expensive in-today-out-tomorrow item.
- Read magazines and check out books at the library. (Except, of course, this book, copies of which belong in your and your best friend's permanent collections. Only kidding.)
- Trade clothes, magazines, videos, CDs, and accessories with your friends and out-of-town cousins.
- If your message is short, send postcards instead of letters.
- Make or bake presents instead of buying them.

- When dimes count, order water in restaurants, not soda, or an appetizer instead of an entrée.
- When shopping, always check expiration dates. No point spending today's money on yesterday's yogurt.
- Don't buy a majorly-cool-but-about-to-be-history dress right after you cash your paycheck. Ask a clerk to hold it. Go home and see if your closet runneth over. If you still want the dress, then buy it. (It's dry clean only? Add those costs into your budget.)
- Check boys' departments for bargains on T-shirts and other androgynous clothes. Girls' clothes are cheaper than women's.
- Don't go for name brands if generic will do.
- When you go shopping, bring a short list and a restrained friend and leave your checkbook or credit card (if you have one) at home.
- No matter how cute, patient, or insistent the salesperson is, never buy too-tight shoes or anything else you don't want.
- Remember that the same restaurant is usually cheaper at lunch than at dinner, and the same movie is sometimes cheaper at noon than at night.
- Don't spend lots of money on your boyfriend. Spend lots of time with him.
- Try not to live by the adage, "When the going gets tough, the tough go shopping!" Heed instead the Jamaican proverb, "Save money and money will save you."

The other side of the coin is that you don't want to be a penny-pincher. Sometimes it's not worth it to scrimp. For instance:

- If you and two friends go out for dinner and their meals are a little more expensive than yours, split the bill in three anyway. It can be crass and mood-dampening to whip out your calculator after a fun evening. If *your* meal cost a lot more than theirs, put that extra amount in the pot.
- If you're only parking for ten minutes, put a coin in the meter anyway. Spending the quarter avoids risking the fine.
- If you're sending photos or a fat letter, stick on enough postage. It's worth another stamp for the letter to get there without delay.
- Get your silk blouse dry-cleaned and your leather shoes reheeled. You'll save in the long run.

- If you're making a major purchase that should last many years, like a car, CD player, computer, modem, or even beeper, it may be worth the extra bills to get the best product. Check *Consumer Reports.*

- If you're short on money and the gang is going for burgers, don't sit home. Go and order a drink or side dish.

- Tip. As a teen girl, you can probably get away with not tipping much, and, yes, you could even leave a lonely penny in the sundae sauce, but it's decidedly not nice. And if you ever work as a waitress, you'll know that no tips is no fun. (Waitresses are underpaid because bosses expect them to make up the difference in tips.)

  How much should you tip? Waiters and waitresses: at least 15 percent of the total bill. Taxi drivers: 15 percent of the fare. Hair-stylists: 15 percent to 20 percent, and give a dollar to the person who shampooed your hair. At the airport give a dollar per bag to the porter who helps you with your luggage. How about the person who checks your coat? The valet who parks your car? (My, you are fancy!) If no one else is covering for you, give a dollar, minimum. The lady in the ladies room? You could scoot by, but would you want that job? Put a quarter in her dish. When you are tipping, have a heart—round up. If you are at a club, you may not have to leave any tips. And in some restaurants, if eight or more of you gather for dinner, the tip will already be included in the bill.

Don't be a tightwad or a spendthrift. Money isn't fun if it's all stashed away. But if you binge-spend or never check prices, you may have to put yourself on a budget.

Money Miscellany

- One in 5 American children live below the poverty line.
- Almost one-third of minimum wage earners are teenagers.
- Women make up over half the American workforce.
- Nearly one-third of working married women earn more than their spouses.
- One in 20 working women is a teacher. One in 5 is a secretary or has a clerical job. There are more female than male nurses, librarians, psychologists, food service workers, and bank tellers.

- Seventy-five percent of working women still earn less than $25,000 per year.
- When a man and a woman do the same job, the man often earns more. (Fair? No.)
- Never sign a contract without reading it carefully and asking a trusted adult to do the same. (Everything is negotiable until you sign.)
- Balance your checkbook.
- Check out classified ads to see what jobs are available and at what salaries.
- Ask your mom about Take Our Daughters to Work Day in April if you'd like to see what she does when you're in school.
- Every contest has a winner. (But you or your essay or photograph won't win if you don't enter.)
- The T-shirt that reads, "Anyone who says, 'Money Can't Buy Happiness' . . . Doesn't Know Where to Shop" is funny, but wrong. The same goes for "Whoever has the most things when he dies wins."
- The song that goes, "All I need is the air that I breathe and to love you" is romantic, but ridiculous.
- Unless your boyfriend has an orchard full of money trees, share expenses when you go out. It's only fair.
- If you have a rich boyfriend, examine your motives. Be sure you'd love him if the stock market crashed. I went out briefly with a guy who always treated for lobster—lobster!—on a roll. I thought, "Boy, if we got married, I could travel to Rio, Cairo, Fiji." Then I thought, "I'd have to go there with him." We broke up. (They say if you marry for money, you earn every penny.)
- If you have rich parents, try not to become spoiled, feel guilty, or take material comforts for granted. Treat your friends once in a while, but don't try to buy friends. Do volunteer work. And hope that someday you can be generous with your children.
- If your parents don't have wealth to spare, try not to resent friends who are handed money when you have to work for it. You're learning the value of a buck and how to make a living. That gives you an edge. And since you know how much life costs, you won't be in for such a shock in the Real World.
- Stop comparing. There will always be people better off and worse off than you.

- When you first live on your own, half your salary may go toward rent and food. (Unless you live in Manhattan, in which case half may cover just rent. Could *that* be why New Yorkers stay slim?)
- Cars eat money. Don't buy one unless you need one.
- People who make fast money dealing drugs often wind up in jail (or cemeteries) before their time.
- Don't get robbed. Your purse should not be grabbable in a restaurant or bathroom, or as you walk. Don't carry more money than you need. On trips, take traveler's checks. Avoid cash machines at night.
- Theft is common; try not to get too attached to material objects. Remember the heirloom diamond engagement ring for which I stopped biting my nails? Well, I recently took it to a posh jewelers for a slight repair. When I went to pick it up, I was told it had been a small part of a huge jewelry heist! Yes, I was distraught. But the ring was insured, and at least I still have my nails—and my husband!
- Don't stuff loose money into your purse; put it in your wallet. If you do lose a $5 bill, think how happy the person who finds it will be. Then be more careful.
- From my teen diary: *"I wrote down 'Dad owes me $10,' but I can't remember why, so he won't give it to me."* Keep *your* IOUs and UOMes straight and complete with explanations.
- If you save $1 a day, you'll have $365 at the end of the year.
- There's usually just enough money. There's rarely more than enough.
- Don't sign up for a credit card until and unless you're sure you'll be able to pay off the bills. More than half of college students use credit cards: many get themselves deep into debt long before graduation. Yet having a shaky credit-card history makes it harder later to rent an apartment or buy a car. A credit card isn't free money. It's a high-interest loan that you have to pay back fast.
- If you do get a credit card, use it responsibly so you can establish a good credit rating.
- Having lots of credit cards is asking for trouble. Just because a company offers you one in the mail doesn't mean you have to use it. Cut it up instead.

- Try a debit card instead. Charges come directly out of your checking account and you won't get a monthly bill.
- Don't say, "Mr. Hollings is worth $3 million." If he's a decent human being, he, like you, is worth more than money.
- "What is a cynic? A man who knows the price of everything and the value of nothing." So wrote Oscar Wilde.
- What is success? Not a mountain of money. According to Ralph Waldo Emerson, "To laugh often and much; to win the respect of intelligent people and the affection of children; to earn the appreciation of honest critics and endure the betrayal of false friends; to appreciate beauty; to find the best in others; to leave the world a bit better whether by a healthy child, a garden patch, or a redeemed social condition; to know even one life has breathed easier because you have lived. This is to have succeeded."

Dear Carol...

Dear Carol,

At school I am in the popular group. All my friends know me as pretty, wearing nice clothes, and having lots of money. I don't think I'm that pretty, my clothes are just normal to me, and the last thing we have is lots of money! Here's why: About three months ago, my dad lost his job. I never told anyone, not even my best friends, because I was embarrassed. We can't keep our big house anymore; we have to rent a small one. And the house we're going to rent is right next to a car repair shop—about a car length away! Now what are my friends going to think when they see where I live? It'll be so hard for them to believe.

Does money affect friendships? I don't pick my buddies by the size of their homes, do you? Sure it's a fringe benefit if your friend happens to have a pool or country house (or cute brother or Dove bar-filled freezer or parents who own a skating rink or manage a hot musician's career). But that's not why you're friends. What could cause a rift here isn't your father losing his job, it's you holding out on your friends. They may whisper for a day or two. But as long as you don't become secretive, ashamed, or reclusive, friends worth their salt will stay as close as ever. And the others? Who needs 'em?

Dear Carol,

I'm rich. I live in a mansion. Most of my clothes are fancy dresses. My friends like to be in my house more than they like me. I'm embarrassed about my richness, but I don't know how to tell my parents.

Try not to define yourself by your wealth. You wrote, "I'm rich." But are you also funny, smart, artistic, athletic? Think of your wealth as an extra instead of an obstacle. As for your wardrobe, tell your mom that you want to dress like your buddies and go shopping for jeans and T-shirts. Some of your friends may prefer your home to theirs, but unless they avoid you at school or never, ever talk to you on the phone, why assume that they are using you?

Dear Carol,

I'm only 15, but I've thought A LOT about my future. I'm already "verbally" engaged, I know exactly what my career is going to be (fashion merchandising), I know where I'm going to study, where I'm going to live, EVERYTHING! Is that weird?

It's mature to think ahead, but it's wise to stay open to new possibilities. You may fall in love with someone new. You may choose to study medicine (or film or market research or landscape architecture or teaching English as a second language). You may visit California (or New Mexico or Nova Scotia) and decide you'd enjoy living there.

Look ahead but don't limit yourself. One of the great things about being young is that your future is wide open. (This is true even if your parents are the ones who have figured out your future.)

Dear Carol,

I read your Money chapter, and I'm wondering whether on my résumé I should list jobs like cleaning a neighbor's house. I've baby-sat for two different families and I want to advertise for more but my parents won't let me. By the time you get this, I will be 12½. What other jobs can I do?

Include housecleaning on your résumé if you're looking to clean houses. Don't if you're applying to intern at a television station. Your résumé will change along with your experience and goals.

If your parents don't want you to publicize your availability in the paper, maybe they'll let you put up a notice in a nearby private nursery school. And tell the families you baby-sit for to spread the word. Your phone will ring!

Other jobs—besides those I wrote about? How about giving a sidewalk sale? With a friend, collect "valuable junk" from your own homes. Then inform neighbors that you're having a sale on noon Sunday and ask for their donations—you'll do a pick-up Friday afternoon. (If they have large things, offer to give them half of what you make.) Put notices everywhere, price your wares, have coins and change ready, and sell brownies to browsers.

Dear Carol,

My parents own a grocery/deli and I'm expected to work from 11:00 to 1:00 on Saturdays. It gets busy and I often end up staying longer, mostly because my mother asks me to. Recently I handed in a research paper that could have used more time on it. If my mother keeps interrupting me, I know my grades will fall. And if I don't keep up my grades, I'll never get a college scholarship. Other people quit their jobs. Why can't I? I've even written up a resignation but I'm afraid to give it to them.

Most parents would be pleased to know their daughter cares so much about school. Yet two hours a week is not an unreasonable request (parents do a lot for kids, after all). Can you tell your mother why you feel you can't work beyond the agreed-upon time? I doubt the Saturday lunch crunch alone will affect your GPA—and it may give you valuable Real World insights. But discuss your feelings before you implode and see if together you can come up with a fair compromise.

Dear Carol,

I live in Nixa, Missouri, a small city far from New York. But I dream of going there and starting a modeling career. Should I send photos and a letter to agencies like Elite, Ford, Zoli, Generation, and Wilhelmina?

Modeling jobs are hard to get—especially if you live a long way from New York. Even in New York, girls have more "go-sees" (meetings) than "shoots" (paid jobs), and few girls make big money. Occasionally a teen magazine will advertise that they're searching for a cover model . . . but most teen fashion shoots make do with the beauties on hand. Discouraging? Yes. But look into *local* modeling agencies. (Check your Yellow Pages.) You can try your luck in the Big Apple when you're older—or if your parents are willing to relocate to New York one summer and an agency is willing to take you on.

Dear Carol,

I'm only in eighth grade but I'd really like to work in a zoo. When I get into high school and college, what classes should I take? How would I get a job there? And what other jobs involve animals?

Take biology and zoology courses and ask a local zoo about internships. Consider working at the entrance, gift shop, or cafeteria, then checking in frequently with the zoo personnel manager. And look in the Yellow Pages under Animals. Other careers with animals include being a veterinarian (four years of graduate school required), animal training (there are several show-biz agencies in New York and California), dog training (dog schools need helpers), owning a pet shop (can you start as a clerk or assistant at a store near you?), and conservationism (wildlife biologists sometimes spend years tracking wolves, turtles, beavers, eagles, you name it).

Dear Carol,

LIGHTS, CAMERA, ACTION! Yes, if you haven't already guessed, I want to be an actress. Not just an ordinary actress, though, a famous teen actress. Crazy, huh? My parents think so, too. I have no real experience but I was in a few school plays a long time ago and I'm going to take acting lessons this fall. What will happen when the lessons are over? How will I get an agent? I know acting isn't all sunglasses and autographs, but how can I convince my parents that there's nothing else in the whole wide world that I'd rather do than act? I need their support, but they think I'm just a dreamer. Maybe I am until my dreams come true.

Dear Carol,

I'm from a single-parent family. Mom works in a lab and money is scarce. Fortunately, my career goal doesn't require a college diploma. I want to be an actress. Where can I get an education and still have a flexible-enough schedule to take drama lessons, audition for parts, and have time to breathe?

It's good to have a goal, but smart to be realistic. Lots of girls want to be famous actresses, but most working actresses run anonymously from audition to audition and waitress to make ends meet. Stardom? Many would sell their souls for a role in a deodorant commercial.

On the other hand, people pooh-pooh would-be writers, too, and I'm glad I stuck it out.

So don't pressure yourself to become a teen idol, but do audition for parts in school, community, church, or synagogue plays. Take lessons and learn all you can from the students and teachers (ask *them* about agents). Act, act, act, and break a leg. But don't rule out college. Not only will it pay off in the long run, but many colleges have drama departments and offer drama majors. You can earn your diploma while learning about theater and performing in plays and musicals.

Dear Carol,

My dream is to become an author. Before I die, I want to write a book. How do I get started? I love to write stories, poems, anything that has to do with pen meeting paper.

Dear Carol,

My ambition is to be a newspaper reporter, so I'm very much into research. How did you get into the business?

Dear Carol,

My writing has been entered in several contests and been praised by my English teachers. I think I have what it takes. But I'm only 14. Am I old enough to start trying to get my writing published? Do you have any helpful hints?

Dear Carol,

I'm an aspired writer . . .

Aspiring. That's *aspiring.* . . . I got my start when I was a teenager, but I was 19, not 14, and even 19 was pretty young. I sent an article to *Seventeen* magazine—and they sent me $100. Later I wrote for other teen magazines (like *YM* and *Teen*) and I've done the HELP! Column of *Girls' Life* ever since the magazine began. I just finished a book called *For Girls Only,* I've written for magazines like *Glamour, Bride's,* and *Parents, and* I even got to talk on *Oprah* about writing quizzes for *Cosmopolitan.* I've also written adult fiction. I love my career: If you love to write, I encourage you to write. But don't be in too much of a hurry to get published, because your writing will improve from junior high to high school to college. You'll have more to write about, too. And if you think you'd get discouraged by rejection (I still get discouraged by rejection!), why rush into the line of fire?

If, however, you are feeling both brave and talented, consider submitting your work to a teen magazine's articles editor or fiction editor. A long shot, maybe, but they will read your polished first-person essays or short stories or letters to the editor or embarrassing anecdotes or maybe even poems. Send manuscripts typed and double spaced, keep a copy, and include a stamped self-addressed envelope. If you read the magazine and know what kind of stuff they publish, you'll quintuple your chances of getting a byline. You can also ask magazines for their Writer's Guidelines for teens. Find the editor's name on the masthead inside the magazine. Here are some addresses:

Seventeen, 850 Third Avenue, New York, NY 10022

YM, 375 Lexington Avenue, New York, NY 10017

Teen, 6420 Wilshire Boulevard, Los Angeles, CA 90048

Girls' Life, 4517 Harford Road, Baltimore, MD 21214

Other ideas? Submit your work or letter to the editor to your school or town newspaper. Or simply keep a journal, keep reading, and keep writing.

Perseverance can pay off. Singer Ella Fitzgerald said: "Just don't give up trying to do what you really want to do. Where there's love and inspiration, I don't think you can go wrong." Writer Anne Lamott put it this way: "This is what separates us from ordinary people: the belief, deep in our hearts, that if we build our castles well enough, somehow the ocean won't wash them away. I think this is a wonderful kind of person to be."

Me too. How about you?

8 SMOKING, DRINKING, AND DRUGS

And I Promise Not to Lecture

❋

I'm all for animal rights and gun control, but I think Joe Camel should be shot. With the help of Marlboro men and Virginia Slims women, Joe lured millions of kids and teens into nicotine addiction, each cigarette setting up a craving for the next. "Start 'em young," the tobacco executives reason. "Hook 'em for life."

What about alcohol? Your basic couch-potato teenager sees some 2,500 alcohol ads on TV each year. She may be a minor, but if she hasn't learned to say no, she may find herself with a cigarette in one hand, a drink in the other. And again, smug ad execs will have succeeded in creating a consumer.

Tobacco and alcohol, though legal, are responsible for more deaths than any other drugs. Adults wring their hands over teens using illegal drugs—and we can see why. But the number of teen girls who inject heroin is tiny compared to the number of girls who smoke and drink.

A girl may smoke to feel older now, but when she is older, she may want to quit smoking and find that it's difficult. Maybe her new boyfriend hates it or her roommate has asthma or she wants to start a family or she has a worrisome cough. Quitting is doable, but it's a challenge and a struggle.

As for drinking, a young woman can be a danger to herself if, for instance, she drinks and gets sloppy with contraception, or a danger to others if she drives under the influence. If she keeps drinking, she can become dependent on alcohol, making booze the focus of what might have been a much more interesting life.

Have you heard this all before? Did you know that if you smoke and take birth control pills, you're upping your chances of having strokes, heart attacks, and blood clots? That if you down a few tranquilizers with a few drinks, you could die? That today's marijuana is much more potent than the stuff your parents were offered? That if you share a needle with the wrong drug user, you could contract HIV? That if you smoke, drink, or do drugs while pregnant, your baby pays?

This chapter on substance abuse is not alarmist propaganda—though the facts are alarming. It's your choice whether to abuse or abstain. But the patterns you set now may be yours for keeps and will have an impact on your health and longevity. You owe it to yourself to know what you're getting into. You owe it yourself to take care of your body.

Tobacco: When It's Good to Be a Quitter

In 1604, when the real (not Disney) Pocahontas was a girl, King James I of England didn't like the idea of American tobacco arriving at his shores. "Smoking is a custom loathsome to the eye, hateful to the nose, harmful to the brain, dangerous to the lungs," he said most regally.

Today, nearly 400 years later, smoking is still loathsome and dangerous.

In the 1800s cigarettes were dubbed "coffin nails."

Today men, women, and teens still smoke "cancer sticks," and even cigars have become more popular.

In 1946, George Bernard Shaw wrote, "I have never smoked in my life and I look forward to a time when the world will look back in amazement and disgust to a practice so unnatural and offensive."

Today, people still light up despite the irrefutable link between smoking and cancer and addiction.

Cigarettes may seem cool, but disease is uncool. And smoking without realizing that you can get hooked is as naive as hooking up without realizing that you can get pregnant.

Take this quiz and test your smoking savvy.

1. *How much money does a pack-a-day smoker spend on cigarettes per year?*
  a. Under $365.
  b. About $500.
  c. Over $700.

2. *How much tar does the average pack-a-day smoker inhale each year?*
  a. A negligible amount.
  b. About two tablespoons.
  c. A full cup.

3. *How long does it take for cigarettes to do a smoker any harm?*
  a. About three seconds.
  b. About three weeks.
  c. About three months.

4. *What percentage of adult smokers in the United States would like to kick the habit?*
  a. About 30 percent.
  b. About 50 percent.
  c. About 90 percent.

5. *What percentage of lung cancer victims die within five years of diagnosis?*
  a. About 30 percent.
  b. About 60 percent.
  c. About 90 percent.

6. *What percentage of American high school students smoke cigarettes?*
  a. Almost 33 percent.
  b. Almost 50 percent.
  c. Almost 66 percent.

7. *True or False: Smoking affects the smoker's sense of taste or smell.*

8. *True or False: If a pregnant woman smokes, her baby has an increased chance of being born small, weak, or dead.*

9. *True or False: Smokers live longer than nonsmokers.*

10. *True or False: Of the 3,000 American kids and teens who start smoking every day, 1,000 will die a tobacco-related death.*

11. *True or False: Most adult smokers started as teen smokers.*

12. *True or False: Rates of teenage smoking shot way up when Joe Camel, dubbed a "smooth character," came on the scene in 1988.*

13. *True or False: Smoking burns off calories.*

14. *True or False: It's easy to quit smoking.*

And the answers are . . .

1. c. Think about the clothes, CDs, books, tickets, computer programs, and gifts you could buy! It's a lot of money going up in smoke!

2. c. Ugh. And tar, made up of thousands of solid chemicals, is carcinogenic (cancer causing).

3. a. One puff speeds your heartbeat, raises your blood pressure, decreases the temperature of your hands and feet, and replaces some oxygen in your blood with carbon monoxide—right when your accelerated heartbeat requires more oxygen. It takes a little longer for cigarettes to turn your teeth yellow, but they do that, too.

4. c. Most adult smokers want to quit. Only 1 out of 4 adult Americans still smoke, down from 42 percent in 1964. Many got hooked as kids before they knew how harmful tobacco was. And half of all living adults who ever smoked have now quit.

5. c. Frightening. Yet lung cancer, which kills more Americans than any other cancer, is usually preventable. About 90 percent of lung cancer victims are smokers. Even smokers who don't inhale risk mouth, lip, and tongue cancers. Skeptical? Call (800) 4-CANCER. Maybe you think: How bad can smoking be if your own grandpa has been puffing away for decades? Answer: Bad. Your grandpa is a very lucky man.

6. a. Around one-third of high school students smoke. Many more have tried cigarettes. Whites smoke more than blacks; dropouts more than college students.

7. True. Not only does smoking stink, smokers have smoky-smelling clothes and hair and sour breath (who was it who first said kissing a smoker is like licking an ashtray?). But the smoker herself may not notice because her sense of smell and taste are off. Food tastes yummier and flowers smell prettier to nonsmokers and ex-smokers.

8. True. If you're pregnant, you're smoking for two. Your fetus is not getting as much oxygen as it normally would and is growing more slowly and with more difficulty. Crib death is more common among babies whose mothers smoked during pregnancy.

9. False. An average smoker's life is shortened by about the number of minutes spent puffing away, usually about six to eight years. At every age, there's a greater percentage of deaths among smokers than non-smokers. (No, I'm not making this up. It's based on research of the American Cancer Society.) The good news: Once a smoker stops smoking, unless irreversible damage has been done, his or her body works immediately to clean up the mess and replace ravaged cells with healthy ones. Two days later her ability to taste and to smell improves. Two years later, her likelihood of having a heart attack drops to near normal. Ten years after a heavy smoker quits smoking, she has the same chances of living a long life as a nonsmoker does.

10. True. Every day about 3,000 teens and preteens light up for the first time, and 1 of every 3 of them will die early because of it.

11. True. Eighty-two percent of smokers began when they were under eighteen. What may have started as a lark became a need, an addiction.

12. True. Way to go, Joe. The ad campaign was a big success for cigarette manufacturers. Most kindergartners even recognize Joe Camel. Here's the equation: Since one and a half million people quit smoking each year and almost half a million people die from smoking each year, that's two million steady customers that have to be replaced for the tobacco companies to keep making "healthy" profits. What to do? Hook the kids! Fortunately, new regulations about advertising and selling single cigarettes ("loosies") may make it slightly more difficult for cigarette manufacturers to go after the youth market. Rest assured, they'll keep trying even though it's illegal to buy cigarettes if you are under eighteen. (Lots of kids' first introduction to nicotine is through candy-flavored smokeless tobacco like Skoal spearmint, a "starter product." Be savvy!)

13. False. How could that be? If you smoke instead of eat, you end up hungry later.

14. False. Mark Twain claimed that quitting was easy and said he'd "done it one hundred times." Quitting isn't easy. But nearly forty million Americans have done it. Some quit cold turkey; others taper off. If you smoke, cut down on how much you smoke, don't smoke each cigarette to the very end, and inhale less deeply or less often. Filter, low-tar, or low-nicotine brands may be less harmful than regular brands, but each puff still contains such treats as formaldehyde, hydrogen cyanide, ammonia, and lead. The younger you are when you start smoking and the longer you smoke, the tougher it is to quit. But if you make it through your teens without starting, you probably will never take up the habit.

To you, emphysema and ulcers may not seem ominous. So what if smoking accounts for nearly one-third of all cancers, impairs fertility, and triples your chance of heart attacks? No biggie. You may not even know where your pharynx and larynx are, let alone worry about their health and well-being. But even young smokers catch colds, get winded, cough, and notice their athletic abilities heading south more often than nonsmokers. The ads that show smoking skiers, dancers, and mountain climbers are misleading. I prefer the antismoking ads that begin, "There's a killer out there and what this killer does is to choke people very, very slowly. . . ."

If you don't smoke, don't start. It's easier not to take up smoking than it is to quit once you're dependent on the habit and on the nicotine.

How do you say no to smoking? What do you do when a popular girl or good-looking guy offers you a cigarette? You don't have to say, "Disgusting! Never!" or point out the inanity of courting cancer. Just say, "No thanks," or "No, it makes me cough," or "I don't like the taste," or "I'm allergic," or "It gives me a headache." Don't make a big deal of it, and no one will bother you.

While some people smoke for status or peer approval, smoking generates peer disapproval, too. Sure, some kids may think you look more cool or grown up if you smoke. But other girls and guys will think you seem less attractive, less mature.

Tips on Quitting

Millions and millions of Americans are ex-smokers. If they can quit, you can, too.

- Throw away your cigarettes, lighters, matches, ashtrays. (Or lock or wrap them up, if you're only at the cutting-back stage. Or buy a brand you don't like much.)
- Read the rotating warnings on cigarette packs and ads.
- Write your own "Why I Want to Quit" list.
- Try to feel virtuous—not envious—when someone lights up. Try to crave quitting—not smoking. Hurray! You've put an ugly smelly teeth-yellowing health-hampering vice behind you.
- If you smoke to relax, quit over vacation or after exams.
- Trying quitting on the third Thursday of November on the annual Great American Smokeout. Or set some other definite date.
- Have a friend or family member quit (or break any bad habit) with you, or bet someone $10 that you won't smoke for two weeks. Cheer each other on (and call each other up in weak moments).
- Think one day at a time. The first two days are the hardest.
- Spend those days in no-smoking places: libraries, movies, malls. (That should be easy in America where vehement nonsmokers can make smokers feel like pariahs. In many other countries, smoking is still the norm.)
- Tell friends you've quit.
- Tell yourself you are stronger than your habits. Prove it.
- Stock up on sugarless gum, mints, celery sticks, carrots, grapes, popcorn, and other low-cal munchies. Some quitters gain a little weight, but 1 in 4 loses weight, possibly because he or she feels more energetic, active, and in control after quitting.
- Have a coin or bead to fool with when your fingers are restless.

- Change your routine. If you love an after-lunch cigarette, get right up after lunch instead of lingering.
- Brush your teeth when you feel like a cigarette.
- If smoking gives you a lift, take walks and get more sleep so you won't feel tired.
- Reward yourself by stashing away your cigarette money. Then treat yourself to a little luxury. Think of what you want in terms of cost in cigarette packs.
- Ninety-five percent of ex-smokers quit on their own. But some heavy smokers succeed with programs for quitters or nicotine gum or slow-release skin patches so they can cut back without suffering severe withdrawal. Call (800) LUNG-USA.
- If you slip up, don't give up. Consider it a practice round. Lots of quitters conquer the habit on the third or fourth try.
- Dont' quit only to take up smokeless tobacco or cigars.

What If You Don't Smoke?

Congratulations. Unfortunately, your relatives, boss, friends, and car poolers who may blow smoke in your face are doing more than making your hair and clothes reek. They're increasing your chances of an unnecessary illness. Secondhand smoke is hazardous to your health. Pneumonia, bronchitis, lung troubles and future smoking are more common among children whose parents smoke than other kids. Regular exposure to secondhand smoke doubles your risk of heart disease.

Sidestream smoke is worst in closed or poorly ventilated rooms. When nonsmokers sit in a smoke-filled room, the amount of carbon monoxide in their blood doubles. The Environmental Protection Agency called passive tobacco smoke "the country's most dangerous airborne carcinogen."

My parents smoked, so when someone next to me lights up, I've never been one to protest or flap my arms. One winter years ago, I even bummed a few cigarettes from my friend John and asked him to teach me how to blow smoke rings. But ever since I read the American Lung Association and American Cancer Association brochures and saw their gross photos of diseased lungs, I haven't been at all tempted to smoke.

Still, while I've chosen not to smoke and I hope you have, too, that doesn't give us permission to be rude or to police each puff of everyone else. Smokers and nonsmokers both have rights. What to do? Leave a smoky room if you can. Be polite when asking others not to smoke.

And tell your family and friends that your room (or car) is strictly No Smoking.

Thinking About Drinking

There's a T-shirt that says, "I don't have a drinking problem. I drink, I get drunk, I fall down. No problem."

Is that funny? Sad? Or just confusing?

Drinking before age twenty-one is prohibited—yet commonplace. You've seen friends and cousins drink beer, wine coolers, and sweet drinks containing alcohol. At parties, you've seen classmates down four or five drinks in a sitting—binge-drink—and still not know when enough is enough.

What don't *you* know about alcohol?

1. How long does it take the liver to metabolize and get rid of twelve ounces of beer?

  a. Under twenty minutes.

  b. About forty minutes.

  c. Over sixty minutes.

2. What fraction of U.S. teenagers had a drink last month?

  a. Almost 30 percent.

  b. Almost 50 percent.

  c. Almost 70 percent.

3. What percentage of U.S. homicides involve alcohol?

  a. About 15 percent.

  b. About 30 percent.

  c. About 50 percent.

4. About how many calories are in a can of beer?

  a. 200.

  b. 150.

  c. 100.

5. If you've drunk too much, what's the best way to sober up?

  a. Sleep it off.

  b. Drink black coffee.

  c. Take a cold shower.

6. *If you've drunk too much and wake up with a hangover, what must you do?*
   a. Drink a small dose of alcohol—hair of the dog!
   b. Drink coffee.
   c. Wait it out.

7. *True or False: How drunk you get depends solely on how much you drink.*

8. *True or False: Alcohol abuse is the number one drug problem in the United States.*

9. *True or False: Longfellow wrote, "Touch the goblet no more, it will make thy heart sore, to its very core."*

10. *True or False: Moderate drinking (defined as one drink a day for an adult woman) poses as many health risks as heavy drinking.*

11. *True or False: It's safe for pregnant women or mothers who are breast-feeding to drink.*

12. *True or False: No matter how much beer you drink, you can't get as drunk as you would if you were drinking the hard stuff.*

13. *True or False: It is illegal for anyone other than a child's own parent or guardian to provide alcohol to a person under 21.*

14. *True or False: Alcohol is involved in 9 out of 10 rapes on college campuses.*

15. *How many synonyms for drunk can you come up with?*

And the answers are . . .

1. c. It takes the liver over sixty minutes to metabolize one can of beer, one glass of wine, or one shot of vodka. If you drink more than one glass per hour, you're on your way to getting drunk. Age, weight, and sex also affect tolerance. For most girls, a little goes a long way. Some adults who drink are careful to follow a glass of wine with a glass of water, alternating alcohol with H_2O throughout the evening.

2. b. Nearly one-half of teenagers drink each month. A few high schools even do low-tech breathalyzer tests on students to make sure they arrive sober to dances or proms. On college campuses, students are smoking slightly more and drinking slightly less than they did decades ago. But there is a core of men and women, about 1 in 3, who frequently drink to get drunk. A recent study found that while almost half of college students never drink beer, 86 percent of fraternity-house residents were binge-drinkers. Such drunkenness can lead to noise, harassment, vandalism, and even sexual assaults. Over ten million Americans are alcohol-dependent; for many, that dependence began when they were party-hardy students. And some fraternities are now banning alcohol.

3. c. Over half the murders in America are alcohol related. About one-third of traffic injuries involve alcohol, as do well over two-thirds of all fatal falls, drownings, and fire fatalities.

4. b. Most alcoholic drinks are caloric but not nutritious. Sweet rum drinks (e.g., Planter's Punch) or creamy liqueur drinks (e.g., Sombreros) have more calories than do wine spritzers or light beer. Plus, if you get buzzed, your willpower to resist the Doritos and dip goes down.

5. a. What do you get when you throw a drunk into an icy shower and administer coffee? A wet, wide-awake drunk. Fresh air isn't sufficiently sobering, either. Time is. Because alcohol poisoning can be dangerous, if someone really overdoes it, she should walk around before falling into a toxic sleep. If someone passes out and can't be awakened, call an adult or 911. Put the person on her side, not back (in case she throws up). Don't worry about getting the person in trouble. Worry about saving her life.

6. c. There's no surefire hangover helper. If you ever wake up with the morning-after blehhcks, pour lots of water and fruit juice into your dehydrated body. (It would have been better to do that, between hiccups, before you went to bed.) Munch something healthful, like a banana. To speed up your metabolism and help your liver get rid of the poisons you've subjected it to, take a cold shower or a power walk or run (unless your head throbs in protest). If you like, take aspirin or a nap. Alcohol disrupts the dreaming REM (rapid eye movement) sleep stage, so if you go to sleep drunk, you wake up less rested.

At the next party, instead of spending an evening getting drunk and the following day recovering, don't drink, sip just a little, or go for club soda. If someone is pushing you to drink, say, "No thanks," and ask yourself why they care if you imbibe.

By the way, although overindulging in beer can result in a hangover, it's more typical to feel awful after overdoing it on rum, brandy, bourbon or red wine or after mixing different drinks. The darker the drink, the higher its hangover potential. Some people get hung over after drinking next to nothing, whereas others drink with seeming impunity. But nobody's body is a sponge.

7. False. How drunk you become depends on how much you drink, as well as how much you weigh, how much and how often you tend to drink, how fast you drink, whether you've eaten, your body chemistry, your mood, where you are, and whether you want to feel drunk or sober. If a petite girl who has her period hasn't eaten and is not used to drinking chugs a beer at a party in a high-altitude city, it will go to her head much faster than the same drink would affect a large man sipping his daily beer over dinner in Manhattan. *What* you drink makes a difference, too: Straight liquor is absorbed into the bloodstream and makes drinkers drunker faster than liquor diluted with mixers.

8. True. Alcohol is a drug. Parents of alcoholics who sigh and say, "At least she's not into drugs" are deluding themselves. It's one thing to have a collection of old Absolut ads. It's another to guzzle the stuff.

9. True. Good message. Lame poem.

10. False. "What is moderate drinking?" is a tricky question. Adults who drink one or two drinks a night and do not become intoxicated are probably not risking heart, liver, or digestive tract problems. Some studies suggest that for *adults,* modest drinking can actually be healthful: A glass of wine with dinner can relieve stress and may decrease the risk of heart attack because it may inhibit cholesterol buildup. But mixing drinks with other drugs (legal or illegal) can be out-and-out hazardous, and drinking a lot can be, too. To put it plainly: Too much booze pickles the brain.

"One reason I don't drink," said Lady Astor, "is I want to know when I'm having a good time." Gertrude Stein said, "It is so much more exciting to be sober, to be exact and concentrated and sober."

11. False. Alcohol is the number-one cause of drug-related birth defects in the United States. Talk about sad: When a pregnant woman or nursing mother drinks, her fetus or baby also takes a swig. Women who drink heavily during pregnancy, especially during the first three months, up their odds of having babies who are abnormal, small, or have mental or emotional problems because the fetus can't metabolize alcohol efficiently. The notices in many bars and liquor stores say it straight: Drinking Alcoholic Beverages During Pregnancy Can Cause Birth Defects. Some experts believe that once a mother is nursing, it's OK to drink an occasional beer. But nursing mothers should certainly use restraint.

12. False. Alcohol is alcohol. Yes, ounce for ounce, whiskey is much more potent than beer, but beer, wine, wine coolers, and whiskey all contain alcohol. Drink a little and you get tipsy. Drink a lot and you pass out. Most girls don't know that one twelve-ounce can of beer has as much alcohol as a shot of vodka or whiskey. And many forget that if they drink, they won't be able to think as clearly or communicate as well. (Having sex while drunk can be a recipe for disaster.)

13. True. If your parents serve alcoholic drinks to your friends, your parents are breaking the law and are responsible for any injury or damage your intoxicated friend may cause.

14. True. In 90 percent of campus rapes, the man, woman, or both were drinking alcohol. Sixty percent of college women who have a sexually transmitted disease were drunk when they got infected.

15. I'm not sure if I'm giving or subtracting points for this one, but if you're smashed, trashed, plastered, plowed, sloshed, looped, wasted, hammered, out-of-it, crocked, soused, bombed, blotto, blitzed, tight, toasted, tanked, or tractored . . . you drank too much.

Many people don't drink. They don't like the taste, the calories, the blurry feeling. They're taking medication or are pregnant or are in training. They have bad associations with alcohol: a car accident, an abusive father, a negligent mother, a friend who got drunk and was taken advantage of. Or they just don't want to.

That's fine. That's smart.

It can be hard to resist peer pressure, but if you don't want to drink, don't. (Though some may scoff at you for teetotaling, others will admire your strength of character.) There's no point in breaking the law and messing up your body and mind. If you're offered beer at a party, say no thanks. You don't owe anybody any explanations.

If you do choose to drink, don't be stupid about it. Sip and nibble, rather than chug-a-lugging on an empty stomach. Know your limit and stick to it. Never mix driving and drinking and never mix alcohol with other drugs. If you take a cold pill or antihistamine with wine, for instance, you're combining two depressants, which is dangerous. If you're taking an antibiotic and drinking, the antibiotic may be inactivated. If you're combining an illegal barbiturate with booze, you may get so mellow that you never wake up again.

Alcohol is a depressant, not a stimulant. One drink may make you feel peppy and talkative, but that's because alcohol dulls judgment and inhibitions. It also dulls the body. Shakespeare elaborated on the paradox in *Macbeth* (II,iii): "Lechery, sir, it provokes and it unprovokes: it provokes the desire, but it takes away the performance."

When alcohol plays a part, some girls say yes to sex when they didn't mean to, and some guys hear yes when it wasn't said.

A lot of alcohol slows your brain, making you slur words and lose coordination. Too much alcohol too fast can even result in coma or death. That's why the party-till-you-puke, don't-leave-till-you-heave attitude is moronic. About a thousand Americans die each year from overdosing on alcohol alone.

Sound scary? It can be. But whereas you get hooked on opiates or tranquilizers in mere weeks, it usually takes longer to become physically addicted to alcohol. Of course, many teens are problem drinkers without being alcoholics. If you *regularly* drink to get drunk, throw up after drinking, kiss a guy when you didn't intend to, or make a spectacle of yourself when you are out of it, beware! Strive to control your habit before it starts controlling you.

Alcoholism

For many people, alcohol becomes a poison, a necessity, a nightmare.

You probably know a few alcoholics. One out of 10 people who drink becomes alcoholic. Less than 5 percent of alcoholics are bowery-bum winos or derelicts; most are ordinary working people. About 50 percent have an alcoholic parent. About one-third of alcoholics are women. No one is too young to be an alcoholic. Some alcoholics drink regularly; some go on sprees. Most suffer withdrawal symptoms if deprived of the drug.

Alcoholism is a disease. Alcoholics have lost control of their drinking and drink even though the habit wreaks havoc on their health and professional, academic, financial, and/or personal lives. Alcoholism, after heart disease and cancer, is the third great killer in the United States. Are alcoholics only hurting themselves? No. They are often hurting their families and co-workers, and if they drive drunk, someday they may inadvertently commit murder on the road.

Although alcoholism is a progressive illness, it is treatable. Recovery usually means forgoing liquor for good and forever. The thousands of alcoholics who have been helped through Alcoholics Anonymous (AA) swear off booze one day at a time. Families and friends of alcoholics have also found strength and some solutions through Al-Anon and Alateen.

AA got its start in Ohio. Now groups meet all around the world. At AA meetings, members are committed to staying sober and helping each other stay sober. They share personal stories about their battles with alcohol. The only requirement for AA membership is the desire to stop drinking. Meetings are free; donations are accepted. Members don't think about never being able to drink again for the rest of their lives. They think, "I won't drink today. I'll take it one day at a time."

AA is not associated with any particular religion, although there is an AA prayer:

God grant me the serenity to accept
the things I cannot change,
courage to change the things I can,
and wisdom to know the difference.

One more quick quiz. Answer the following questions *yes, no,* or *sometimes.*

1. Are your grades sinking because of your drinking?
2. Do you skip class to drink?
3. Do you lie about how much you drink?
4. Do you forget things or have blackouts because of drinking?
5. Do you drink to escape?

6. Do you drink in the morning?
7. Do you need a drink to feel self-confident?
8. Do you get drunk when you hadn't intended to?
9. Do you think about drinking a lot?
10. Do you drink on the sly or hide liquor or empty bottles?
11. Do you drink alone?
12. Do you drink instead of eating?
13. Do you drink a lot in a hurry?
14. Do you drink until you pass out?
15. Do you drink when you're angry or stressed?
16. Do you get into trouble when you drink?
17. Do you look up to friends who drink a lot?
18. Has your drinking affected your reputation, friendships, schoolwork?
19. Has your drinking lowered your ambition?
20. Have you tried to quit or cut down your drinking and failed?
21. Do you brag about drinking?
22. Do you become defensive if someone mentions your drinking?
23. Do you use alcohol as medicine—drinking when you're pressured or premenstrual?
24. If your parents knew how much you drink, would they worry?
25. If you had a daughter who drank as much as you do, would you worry?

Add up the *yeses* and *sometimeses*. If you have more than three, take it as a warning. Try a week on the wagon. Can't do it? Look up Alcoholics Anonymous, or call AA at (212) 870-3400. No one will know you went to a meeting unless you tell.

Or call the Alcohol/Drug Abuse Referral Hotline (800) ALCOHOL or National Council on Alcoholism and Drug Dependence, (212) 206-6770.

If you think if would be hard to stop drinking now, think how much harder it would be to stop later. As F. Scott Fitzgerald wrote, "First you take a drink, then the drink takes a drink, then the drink takes you." Many say you can control an addiction, but never cure it. So don't get dependent in the first place.

What if it's not you who is drinking? What if your problem is that a family member or friend has a problem? Call Al-Anon at (800) 344-2666 or Alateen at (800) 356-9996 for information and support. Then consider talking to the drinker directly—with love, not accusations. Say, "I've noticed that you've been drinking a lot and I really care about you so that concerns me." Some families team up to confront one member—sort of a surprise party with an agenda. The message is: "We love you too much to watch you drink your life away. Get help." The drinker's initial response may be anger or denial, but eventually, many drinkers become ex-drinkers, and many feel very grateful.

Drunk Driving

If you've ever been in a car in which the driver was drunk, consider yourself lucky to be here. About 17,000 Americans died last year because of drunk driving. Some were drunk when they fell asleep at the wheel or said hello to a tree. Many were perfectly sober, minding their own business, singing along with Whitney Houston on the car radio, when some inebriated jerk plowed into them. Police officers and coroners don't enjoy telling parents that their kid is dead, but they do it all the time. The number of highway crashes has gone down recently, but crashes are still the leading cause of death in the sixteen- to-twenty-five-year-old age group, and millions are injured yearly, too. Nearly half of all crash deaths involve alcohol. Half occur at night. Many occur on New Year's Eve, New Year's Day, spring break, and other holidays.

I knew people who died young because they mixed drinking and driving: the brother of a girl I used to baby-sit for, a guy I once worked with, the daughter of a writer friend. What a waste. It's too sad to run into the mother of a classmate at the grocery store and watch her eyes fill with tears as you mumble how sorry you were to hear about the death of her son. It's too sad to hear a middle-aged friend tell you, her voice shaking, that as much as she tries, she can't remember the sound of her daughter's laugh.

Frightening but true: On any given weekend night, many drivers who are sharing the road with you and me are not all there. Alcohol has dulled their reflexes, and if they are distracted for a second, they may crash smack into us.

Teens are just learning to drink and just learning to drive. When they combine the two, many are dangerous to themselves and to others.

The legal drinking age is twenty-one. But younger teens drink, get smashed, and weave their way back home. Most arrive. Some don't.

If a cop catches you driving drunk, you may be asked to touch your nose with your eyes closed, recite the alphabet, walk a straight line heel to toe, stand on one leg, pick up a coin, or perform other tasks that seem like no-brainers—if you're sober. You may also take a breathalyzer test. If you are arrested for driving under the influence (DUI) or driving while intoxicated (DWI), it could cost you hundreds of dollars in legal fees and higher insurance rates. If you have an accident, you could lose your license—or your life.

The legal limit for intoxication in most states is a blood alcohol content of .10 percent (measured in grams of alcohol per 100 milliliters of blood). Before you even feel drunk, your ability to drive safely goes down. If you've had four or five drinks, you are probably legally intoxicated. If you drive, your chances of getting into an accident quadruple. I hope you don't try to outwit the statistics. (And if you do, I hope I don't happen to be cruising along in the next lane.)

If you are drunk at a party, don't drive home. Have a friend drive or call your brother or sister or parents or a cab (always carry enough money to get home on your own). If your date has the car and is drunk, don't risk both your lives. Refuse to let him drive. In a nonchalant way, just say, "I'll drive." Don't say, "You're too drunk to drive," because he might disagree and get defensive. Do not worry about offending him when he is about to put your life on the line. Take his keys and have someone else do the driving. I know that's hard, but that's what friends are for. Do *not* let a drunk drive.

Some friends have a system: When they go together to a party, one member of the group is the designated driver and stays absolutely sober. At the next party, they alternate. Some schools have systems, too. Many have a number you can call if you need transportation home. And some friends hire vans or taxis or limos to ferry them safely to bars or to the prom.

It may seem cool to have "road pops," and backseat drinkers may seem more socially acceptable than backseat drivers. But it's not cool to die or maim or kill.

I often drive. I sometimes drink. But I firmly believe: none for the road.

For more information, write or call these not-for-profit citizen activist groups:

SADD (Students Against Driving Drunk)
255 Main Street
Marlboro, MA 01752
(508) 481-3568

MADD (Mothers Against Drunk Driving)
511 East John Carpenter Freeway, Suite 700
Irving, TX 75062
(214) 744-6233
(800) GET-MADD

By the way, even sober drivers aren't always safe drivers. A ton of moving metal can be a lethal weapon. When you're driving, drive. Don't kiss your boyfriend. Don't yak on a cell phone (that quadruples your chance of crashing). Don't speed or show off.

I still remember my boast to David, a blond junior I had an unrequited crush on. The car I was in won a race to the Bum Steer restaurant. "We got up to ninety miles per hour," I said, oh-so-self-impressed. "That was stupid," he snapped. My bubble burst, but I realized he was right (and wouldn't you know it?—his "caring" and maturity made my crush even stronger).

Reckless driving *is* stupid. Drive carefully. If possible, drive a car with air bags. Don't race through the red light on this block just to be first at the red light on the next one. Watch out for the other guy. Stay alert on long and short trips. Two out of 3 traffic deaths occur within twenty-five miles of the driver's home. And put your seat belt on—traffic cops hardly ever have to unbuckle dead people.

Enough. I know I'm getting heavy-handed and I don't want you to think I'm a pill. But uh-oh, speaking of pills . . .

Illegal Drugs

Jim Morrison, Elvis Presley, Jimi Hendrix, Janis Joplin, John Belushi, Len Bias, River Phoenix. . . .

Drugs kill. They kill musicians, actors, athletes, students.

Used according to directions, drugs can save lives. Misused, drugs can wreck lives, or end them.

About 1 in 10 teens recently reported having used an illegal drug (mostly marijuana) in the previous month. Forty percent of high school seniors said they had used illegal drugs in the past year. Drug use declined for a while but rose again in the mid-1990s.

After alcohol (the legal drug), women get into trouble most with marijuana. For many, cocaine, heroin, LSD, sleeping pills, and diet pills also become a problem. Some women become addicted to more than one drug. Some try things like ephedra ("herbal ecstasy") and mistakenly imagine that just because something is "herbal" and sold at a health-food store, it must be safe. (Wrong.)

Most students don't get into drugs, and I'm hoping you don't use illegal drugs or abuse legal over-the-counter drugs. Would you be able to get hold of illegal drugs? Probably. Would that be a good idea? No.

When you're a teenager, you're developing independence. Why become physically or psychologically dependent on a drug? Why take long-range risks for short-lived pleasure? When you're a teenager, you're forging your future. Why let chemicals slow you down? Why let drugs reorganize your priorities, leaving you listless? Why crash and burn?

Some people are in the money because of drug dealing. Others are in the slammer. Others are dead. Drug dealing carries all the risks of organized crime.

It's also against the law.

I knew someone in college who got caught selling LSD to a plain-clothes policeman. (Ooops.) He ended up spending most of his summer vacation in a drug rehabilitation center and most of his money on legal fees. And he was lucky: Instead of throwing him in prison for up to twenty years, the judge put him on probation and assigned him two years of community service work.

Most students who smoke weed or take steroids or sniff glue or inhale stimulants in the basement of suburban homes don't end up as thieves, prostitutes, addicts, or inmates. But drugs are always risky. If you are high, you're useless in an emergency. You could get pregnant or an STD when you hardly even remember saying yes to a guy. You could drive or accept a ride when you (or the other person) has no business being behind the wheel. You could lose your energy and motivation and watch your grades plummet, your days become a daze. You could overdose and die.

Many drugs stay in your body for weeks. And since drugs aren't government regulated, you can never be sure of what it is you're allowing to settle into your brain, tissues, and reproductive organs. Many drugs affect women's and men's health, fertility, and ability to ward off infection. Many can result in lifelong addiction—or sudden death.

How would getting high affect you? Some drugs magnify moods. If you're sad, you may get paranoid, withdrawn, depressed. If you're merry, you may get gales of giggles. Listening to music may seem more fun, and studying trees may make you feel you understand the universe.

But the distortion of your perceptions can be a problem if you make decisions while high. If you've smoked pot and are having a romantic time with a guy, for instance, it may have more to do with THC than TLC. (Tetrahydrocannabinol is the main mind-altering chemical in marijuana.) If you're having a bad trip on LSD, you may forget that the nightmarish hallucinations are drug induced and you may really freak out—and try to hurt yourself. If crack cocaine is coursing through your veins and you're angry, you may become violent and unreasonable. If you're busted by the police, you could do time.

Are you taking drugs to self-medicate? Some pills to perk you up during school, others to buoy you along when you're depressed, others to help you sleep? Talk to a doctor, counselor, or psychiatrist. Some kids' systems can use a little tweaking, but let a pro prescribe the right amount of the right drug and monitor the positive results and side effects. Don't play doctor, hit or miss. Your health is way too important.

If you've ever been the straight one in a room full of wasted acquaintances, you know that people who are high sometimes think they're being so insightful or hilarious that it's a shame nobody brought along a tape recorder. Yet you can see they're just acting hyper or stupid-silly or zombie-like. They think they're seeing God because the curtains are breathing; you realize it's a summer breeze. They find a cracker the most delicious thing they've ever eaten; you say a Wheat Thin is a Wheat Thin. They're diligently discarding the W's from a bag of M&M's; you're cheerfully eating them up.

Types of Drugs

There are lots of drugs out there. I don't recommend them; I recommend you know about them.

Are your parents very antidrugs? Or did they do drugs? Please remember that in the good old days of peace and love, unsafe sex wasn't quite as dangerous as it is now and teens who got into fights were rarely armed.

Marijuana has been America's most popular illegal drug for decades, but it's a lot stronger (and more expensive) than it was back in the late 1970s. Then one hit got users buzzed (not stoned), and many perceived pot as harmless. In 1978, half the high school seniors reported smoking pot and 11 percent did so *daily*. (That was when people were more into "mellowing out" than being productive.) Sinsemilla is an especially potent type of marijuana. Remember all those cigarette findings? Well, there's more tar in marijuana than in tobacco. Plus joints or blunts are smoked to the end and pot smoke is inhaled deeply and held inside for a long time—not good news if you're a lung. Marijuana makes some people happy but makes others lonely or paranoid. Some weight-conscious girls smoke instead of drinking, but then get the munchies, devour everything in sight, and hope that calories don't count if you're too high to add. More serious is getting high and then driving (poorly) or having sex (unprotected) or getting messed up repeatedly and not attending school. Some adults worry that marijuana is a "gateway" drug because it's usually the first that someone tries. But many teens who do smoke marijuana are not tempted to move on from there.

Hash comes from the same *Cannabis sativa* plant that is harvested for marijuana, but has more THC and is a stronger drug.

Cocaine is a powder made from dried leaves of the cocoa plant. Robin Williams said, "Cocaine is God's way to tell you that you're making too much money." Ever seen the bumper sticker "My other car is up my nose"? More expensive than gold, cocaine is a natural stimulant of the central nervous system and causes blood vessels to tighten, heart rate to quicken, and blood pressure to shoot up. It is associated with seizures and heart attacks, and hospital emergency rooms are clogged with cocaine casualties. Some people sniff or snort cocaine, which can damage the cells in the nasal passages. Others inject it, which produces a more intense euphoria (and subsequent depression) and, as with any intravenous drug, also includes the risk of disease, since many users share needles. Because cocaine is a seductive drug, many become quickly obsessed with reexperiencing its rush and will do anything for more. (I knew one guy in college whose values got so distorted that he robbed his roommate for cocaine. And I knew a girl who continued going out with a guy long after her feelings had faded because "he was always good for some lines of coke.") Cocaine was once used as an anesthetic and was one of the ingredients in Coca-Cola until the early 1900s. Hundreds of millions of tax dollars have been spent to wipe out cocaine and discourage its use. Yet cocaine is still around, still snorted, smoked, injected—although not as much as in the 1980s. Bill Clinton's half brother is a recovered cocaine addict. Questions? Call (800) COCAINE.

Crack cocaine is a smokable, purified form of cocaine that is sold cheaply in vials and produces an immediate, short-lived euphoria. It is horribly addictive: Many once-responsible people have become slaves to the drug. That first hit starts them chasing after more. Crack use was epidemic in the late 1980s, especially among violent urban gangs. Many babies of crack-addicted mothers were born damaged, addicted, and months premature. Hundreds of thousands of dollars later, many survived, some with severe disabilities or AIDS, some as orphans because their parents were already dead (because of overdose, murder, or AIDS). Not a pretty picture.

Stimulants or amphetamines speed up your nervous system, making you less fatigued and hungry but more restless or agitated. If you take "speed" repeatedly, upping your blood pressure and heartbeat, you reduce your resistance and literally wear yourself out. When you come down off speed, or "crash," you go from wired to tired, from manic and hyperactive to irritable and lethargic, and your appetite returns in full force. That's why some users do more—and overload their systems. Speed damages the liver and kidneys, can cause psychotic and violent reactions, and can kill. A friend confided, "When I was a college sophomore, I studied by pulling all-nighters with the help of speed. Trouble is, the next few days were torture. So I got more and more behind in my work." Ice, a crystallized smokable form of methamphetamine, produces a more intense reaction than injected speed. Methamphetamine has been responsible for hundreds of deaths in the past few years, particularly in western states. Women particularly have been using "crank" or "meth," getting addicted, and then having a horrible time trying to get off it.

Ritalin, or methylphenidate, has been dubbed the "smart pill" or "poor man's cocaine." It's a stimulant that is often prescribed to grade school kids with attention deficit disorders because it helps them focus. Some teens have used Ritalin in order to stay up and study (or party). But one person's prescribed drug can be another person's poison. And how do you know how much is too much? What may give you a harmless high or energy boost may give your best friend a heart attack.

Caffeine, by the way, is the most widely used and abused stimulant in America. Sure it's legal, but if you're downing coffee or cola or tea or chocolate all day long, you may be hooked, which means that without it, you can barely get yourself going. A little is fine, but if you start constantly needing it instead of just wanting it, cut back. Anything that speeds you up will eventually let you down—or leave you edgy.

Depressants depress the nervous system, reduce the heart rate, and s-l-o-w y-o-u d-o-w-n. If you grow used to them, you become less able to unwind and sleep without them. Depressants include sedatives, such as sleeping pills and barbiturates (like Seconal and Methaqualone) and tranquilizers (including Librium and Valium). They're addictive, overdose can be lethal, and mixing alcohol with downers is courting death.

Narcotics are painkillers that induce sleep and relaxation. Doctors recommend them to patients recovering from accidents or surgery, not to teens looking to jolly up Saturday night. Narcotics come in two types: opiates and synthetics. Opiates are made from the opium poppy; examples are opium, morphine, codeine, methadone, and heroin. Synthetics are made in labs; examples are Demerol, Percodan, Dilaudid, and Darvon. Extremely addictive, narcotics create tolerance, meaning addicts need more and more to get high and keep from getting sick. Heroin is gaining in popularity, with one in 100 high school seniors having smoked or injected it last year. But most of the 600,000 heroin users in America are adults. Steven Tyler, lead singer of Aerosmith, survived addiction and now cautions others that it's harder to stop than to start.

Hallucinogens, such as LSD ("acid"), Ecstasy ("X"), PCP ("angel dust"), psilocybin mushrooms, and peyote, are psychedelic drugs that affect the mind more than the body. A little LSD goes a long way and can trigger a whole kaleidoscopic sound-and-light show in your mind. (You've heard the Beatles' song "Lucy in the Sky with Diamonds"?) A trip may last three hours—or twelve—and may be profoundly pleasurable—or total hell. Some say Ecstasy, or MDMA, a combination of synthetic mescaline and an amphetamine, makes you feel social and loving and euphoric; others say it's psychologically addicting (because reality pales in comparison?) and that users run the risk of overdose and of winding up sleepless or depressed or of screwing up the serotonin systems in their brains. PCP is an animal tranquilizer with unpredictable effects. Psilocybin mushrooms and peyote offer a shorter hallucinogenic trip than LSD and also produce nausea.

Inhalants are chemicals that are sniffed, "huffed," or inhaled. They are cheap, accessible, and dangerous. The high is not mystical and lasts just a few minutes. The person who sniffs glue, gasoline, paint, paint thinner, spray air freshener, or nail polish remover may feel briefly drunk—or may OD or go unconscious and suffocate and die. Nitrous oxide, or "laughing gas," makes users giddy and dreamy. When inhaled, the gas replaces oxygen in the lungs. But if users are not careful to breathe in fresh air while taking nitrous oxide, they can die. Amyl nitrite ("poppers") and butyl nitrite (sold as room deodorizer or liquid incense) produce short, intense "rushes," with side effects, from nausea to lowered blood pressure to organ damage. Three out of ten people who die from "huffing" were doing it for the first time. The National Inhalant Prevention Partnership can tell you more; call (800) 269-4237.

In short, drugs are dangerous, expensive, and illegal.

Don't give up your long-term goals for short-term highs. "All dope can do for you," said Billie Holiday, "is kill you the long hard way. And it can kill the people you love right along with you."

If someone urges you to try drugs, don't launch into an unwelcome holier-than-thou, I-get-high-on-life sermon. More teens don't use drugs than do, and if you want to say no, say it. You're smart and you're not alone. Tell yourself: If it's risky or wrong, I won't go along.

If you are tempted by drugs, don't be an idiot about it. Remember how in the *Sex* chapter I said don't do it, but if you're going to, for God's sake, use protection? Well here again, I say don't do it, but if you're going to, at least follow these ten guidelines.

1. Never mix drugs and driving. You could kill someone, including yourself.
2. Never get in a car in which the driver is high.
3. Never mix drugs and alcohol. You could die.
4. Never mix different drugs. One plus one can equal five.
5. Never take drugs if you're pregnant, unless a doctor prescribes them. Your baby could be born addicted or with defects. (Playing with your life is one thing. Taking chances with someone else's is mean, even criminal.)
6. Never share needles. You could get AIDS.
7. Don't use illegal drugs blatantly. You could go to jail without passing go.
8. Don't abuse over-the-counter drugs. They can be legal but lethal.
9. Don't make big decisions (about sex or work or love or . . .) while under the influence. You could use bad judgment and regret it afterward.
10. Don't buy drugs on the street. The person pushing pills could be passing out poison. Or willing to murder for money.

If you have been using drugs and have questions or want to get your life back together, talk to a friend (not the one you get high with) or family member about your goal. You can also talk to counselors or go to treatment centers without getting into legal trouble. Many counselors are ex-drug users. They don't judge; they help. For a referral, call (800) COCAINE or (800) ALCOHOL (you can call anonymously about any addiction). Or call a local chapter of Alcoholics Anonymous or Narcotics Anonymous. Or (800) 729-6686 for the National Clearing House for Alcohol and Drug Information.

Step one to recovery is to eat well, exercise, get enough sleep, and take vitamins to replenish what drugs have depleted. Then comes the hard part: to relearn to respect your body and to stop being self-destructive.

What if you are with someone who overdoses on illegal drugs? Don't sit around worrying about the legal ramifications of getting help. Call a parent or an ambulance. Your friend could die while you're weighing your options.

Dear Carol...

Dear Carol,

About a month ago, I saw my mother smoking for the first time. A week ago, she did it again. I asked her why. She jumped down my throat and said, "It's not gonna hurt anything if every once in a while I smoke. I smoke when I get nervous." Three days ago, she came home from work and smoked. I asked if she was nervous and she said, "No." She even told me not to tell any relatives. Also, she inhales. I told her not to and why. She said, "I don't care. I'm older." Your book taught me a lot and I really want her to stop. I'm even trying to cut down on the few I smoke and I'm only 13. Maybe I'm just jealous, I don't know.

Kids used to sneak out for a puff. Now parents sometimes light up when children's backs are turned. Your concern is well meaning, but it's a drag to be a nag. You can tell your mom how you feel and even that she's setting a bad example and that you love her and want her to stick around. But you can't change her habits. Your mother may stop when she is ready. You, however, know enough to quit before you have a habit of your own.

Dear Carol,

Hi! I really need your help in a life-and-death situation. Not about me, but my dad. He smokes and he always has. He's addicted and can't stop no matter what my family and I do. Doesn't he realize he can do permanent damage to his body? Whenever my dad takes my brother and me to the beach, we bury his cigarettes in the sand. I went on a field trip this year and borrowed my dad's windbreaker, and it had burnt holes in it and smelled horrible. We had a long talk about him dying someday because of cigarettes (which made him quit for two weeks but he jumped back to it). Now what? I've got to make him stop!

You can't make him stop. Only your dad can break the habit. But your love and concern can help. Why not reverse your parent-kid roles? Make a chart and award him a gold star for every day without cigarettes. Five stars? Bake cookies for his office. Ten stars? Take him to the movies or have your mother buy him the latest hardcover by his favorite author. Whatever. In the meantime, keep showing you care but don't assume his days are numbered.

Dear Carol,

My friend smokes in front of me. How should I tell her I don't like it?

Say, "I like you but I hate cigarettes. Please don't smoke in front of me—the smell really bothers me." Something like that? Good friends speak up. At least once.

Dear Carol,

I spent the night with a very popular girl who is 11. When I was there, she closed her door, took out a cigarette, and said, "Do you mind if I smoke?" I said no but that I didn't want to because it makes me cough. She said she's been smoking since second grade. I couldn't understand why she would pollute her body like that. In school she makes good grades and is so popular. I didn't want to preach to her, but holding back my feelings was hard. Maybe she's rebelling, but the rebellion could become a hazardous habit. Write soon because I don't want her to get hooked and I don't want her to die of cancer.

In an ideal world, teens, preteens, and parents wouldn't smoke. In the real world, people do experiment with—and sometimes enjoy—things that aren't good for them. While it's great (wonderful! stupendous! terrific!) that you are staying away from tobacco, you can't dictate your friend's actions. You can have her take my tobacco quiz. You can request that she not light up in front of you because smoke bothers you. But you can't make decisions for her.

Dear Carol,

I guess you could say that I'm in the "in crowd" at my school. The problem is that more and more of my friends are turning to cigarettes, alcohol, and even some drugs (mostly pot). One of my closest friends got drunk last night. I'm highly against all that stuff, and my friends have promised not to pressure me into it, but I'm scared. I just got back from the mall where I was the only one there who was straight. I felt like such a prude. How can I stay out of that junk without losing my friends? It seems like I'm about the only (well, not the one and only) person from our gang that cares about grades and my health. Am I normal? I'm only 14. I can't believe I'm having this problem.

I get lots of letters like yours, yet none from "druggies" complaining about straight friends. Unless you turn preachy, your friends won't drop you. (*You* may decide to distance yourself from them.) You could show them this chapter (or book) if you think it might help. But reach out to other friends, too—the girls and guys who do care about school and health. Are you normal? Yes. The majority of teens don't smoke or do drugs, and millions like you don't equate drinking with fun.

Dear Carol,

This guy and I were best friends and then he had to move. I made him promise he would write me. He did and it was really cute because at the end he signed "Love." I wrote him back and then I got another letter from him telling me he was on drugs and in a gang. What should I do?

Poor guy—he made a move for the worse. Write and tell him how you feel. Say that you hope he takes care of himself because you liked him just the way he was—off drugs. Gangs and drugs are a dangerous mix. Your letter may have an impact on him, and it will make you feel better, too. (You'd feel uncomfortable writing that? How will it feel to remain silent?)

Dear Carol,

I'm happy to say I don't smoke and haven't come into contact with drugs (I don't plan to do them), but if you're thinking, 'If she doesn't smoke or do drugs, she must drink,' then you guessed it, I do. But it's definitely NOT a problem. I don't drink every weekend, maybe one or two weekends a month at the most. If my parents knew I drank, it would break their hearts (not to mention my neck, my arm, my leg . . .) I would be grounded until I was 40. My parents don't drink or smoke and I'm proud of them for it, but they think our neighbors that do drink are crazy, nuts, ruining their lives. I'll be getting my license next month and I know I'll never drive while under the influence.

It's admirable that you don't plan to do drugs and don't plan to drive drunk . . . yet, truth told, people rarely plan substance abuse ahead of time. One reason why drinking is illegal and dangerous for anyone under 21 is that many kids don't just have a beer or two, they get drunk. And when you're drunk, all those sensible plans and decisions get foggy. What if your crush offers to drive you home when you've both had one too many? Suddenly it's harder to say, "No thanks, I'm going to call my mother." If you do drink, be smart. It's more fun to be tipsy than sloppy. Know your limits and always make sure that someone is going to be the trustworthy designated driver—even if it's you.

Dear Carol,

Hi. I'm 14. My sister of 21 was in a two-car collision that involved a drunk driver. My sister was pregnant at the time. The baby survived because they took him out. My other nephew was thrown out of the car and had severe brain damage. My sister was in intensive care for several weeks. The doctors said she would be a human vegetable for the rest of her life, and they put a trache in her throat so she could breath. She tried to take it out though, so they had to tie down her hands. Well, one day a nurse didn't tie her hands down and she pulled it out. She was without air and died two weeks later. I can't get over the stupidity of that nurse! It's hard for me to think that my sister is gone. We kinda got along, but do you know any brothers or sisters who always get along? I'm tired of crying myself to sleep.

How unutterably tragic for your sister, your injured nephew, and all the survivors. I'm really sad for you. You feel angry at the nurse, but I think I'd be even angrier at the fool who mixed drinking and driving and caused the accident that brought your sister's life—and your child-hood—to a crashing halt. If you're still crying every night, get some counseling and start coming to terms with what happened. You could also contact SADD or MADD; some of their members have also lost loved ones to drunk driving. Maybe you can even start a group in your area.

Dear Carol,

Both of my parents do marijuana and have ever since they were in high school. I have grown up around it and it doesn't bother me as much as it used to. The other day I found one of my mom's empty compacts and it contained a razor blade, a thin straw, and a small bag filled with white powder. I'm sure it was cocaine. I also overheard my mom and dad talking about "speed" and "'ludes." I know I can't do anything about it, but it still scares me. They get really upset if I say anything about it. I'm joining Just Say No but what else can I do? The smell of pot gives me severe headaches.

Parents are supposed to act like role models, but many act like children, and some shirk responsibilities and break the law. There's not much a daughter can do except vow not to emulate their behavior. You can tell your parents that you love them but are worried about them (or even ashamed of them) and you can tell them about your headaches. You can also try to sleep over more often at friends' houses—and keep working toward college. Call a drug hot line anonymously for advice and support or Al-Anon or Alateen. Confide in a trusted adult. Not the local chief of police, but an aunt, uncle, family friend, or guidance counselor. If you have younger siblings at home or if your parents are ever violent, it's imperative that you get help quickly.

Dear Carol,

I'm on vacation with my family and in my brother's suitcase I saw little green and clear capsules with hot pink and white dots in them. He's gotten in trouble with drugs in the past and he said he stopped. My brother is a really great guy, and he just got his license. If he died in an accident, I would feel so guilty because I knew about it and never told anyone. Our parents are the best—really supportive. My dad is a vet so my brother has needles but I don't think he uses them. But I'm still so scared I don't sleep at night. Our family is really close and loving. So why this?

Some people experiment with drugs without dire consequences. Some use dirty needles or mix pills and driving and end up another statistic. Your brother is scaring you sleepless? Call, for instance (800) COCAINE or (800) 999-9999, for anonymous advice. Or talk to your parents or brother directly. A quick chat isn't going to change him, but knowing his sister cares and worries may make him think twice about running the most dangerous risks.

Dear Carol,

I'm really mad. My dad said I could sleep over at my friend's house after a party, but then he changed his mind. I think it's because there will be alcohol there. I'm just glad he doesn't know that someone is bringing pot. (I'd never touch it or any other drug.) I know he's looking out for me, but still! My next problem: I've been really depressed lately so I take two or three Vivrin every time I get down but then I get so hyper and then I get a major downer and I get shaky, head rush, and nauseated. I know I should stop, but nothing seems to go right and Vivrin really helps. I just hate the effects.

Run this by me again. You'd never touch drugs, but you routinely take Vivrin even though you hate the effects. What do you think Vivrin is? It's a drug. Like No-Doz, it's caffeine to keep you wide-eyed. Sure it's over-the-counter, but don't kid yourself. Taking legal drugs without medical supervision is dangerous and can lead to dependence. When you're down, take a stroll, take a nap, call a friend, rent a movie, read a story, get a haircut, walk a dog . . . but don't hop on the drug seesaw.

Dear Carol,

Thanks for answering my last letter. I've been going to an eating disorder clinic and it's helping. I'm still taking laxatives and a Valium occasionally, but I don't think that really matters. Oh and guess what? I got some really neat diet pills. They say: "Fast results." I hope so! I don't want to tell my counselor because she may not like the idea. But they're working—I'm not hungry. And it's better than pigging out and throwing up, isn't it? I just hope I don't start feeling weak again. Wish me luck!

You're going to need luck. Yes it matters that you're taking laxatives and Valium and diet pills. Your body needs fuel (food), not pills (drugs). Diet pills create tolerance, meaning you need more and more to achieve the same effect. But too many pills are poison—even over-the-counter drugs can overtake you. Since you go to a clinic and a counselor, learn from them instead of popping pills on the sly. "Fast results?" People who get fast results from gimmick diets usually gain the weight right back.

Dear Carol,

A few days ago, I left home because of a senseless argument with my mom. I stayed in a hotel from Thursday until Monday then went home and now everything is pretty cool. I do whatever I feel like, but I don't like the way I'm leading my life now. For example, today I got up at 6:30 P.M. and I usually don't get home until between 4 and 6:00 A.M. I have to figure out what to do with my life. My friends are worried about me. They think I'm taking after my dad (an alcoholic-cocaine addict). I will admit I drink a lot. I don't smoke marijuana or do cocaine too often, but I do it. I know it's bad, but it's not often.

I hope you don't think I'm totally worthless because I'm not. I'm intelligent and sorta good-looking. I do OK.

I don't think you're worthless, but you can do better than "OK," and you yourself know it. You don't like the hours you're keeping? Then sleep at night! If you're staying out to spite your mom, it's still you who pays. Sounds like you need more structure to your days, be it school, a job, working out, or volunteering. If figuring out what to do with your life seems too daunting, just figure out what worthwhile things you can do with yourself today and tomorrow. And consider getting counseling.

Dear Carol,

I found out that a guy I like takes drugs (all kinds) and lies a lot. When I call him, he is either waiting for someone to call or sleeping. I lent him $100 because he said he needed it badly. I know he'll never pay me back and he keeps asking for more. Whenever I say no, he says, "You don't love me," so I do what he asks. I don't like doing it, but I don't want to lose him. One more thing—he barely talks to me in school.

Lose him? He's a loser! Cut your losses and run. Start looking elsewhere for romance, and I bet you won't look back.

9 A QUARTET OF QUIZZES

Getting to Know You

❀

Are You <u>Too</u> Nice?

We all know people who would give us the shirt off their backs, and others who wouldn't give us the time of day. Which are you? After each question, circle the answer that best describes you. Then check the scoring.

1. *You just baby-sat from 9:30 A.M. to 2:30 P.M. The children's mother returns, takes out her wallet, and says, "Let's see, I owe you for four hours."* *You*

   a. point out politely that you believe she means five hours.
   b. accept payment for four hours because you hate to contradict her and you want her to ask you back.
   c. tell her you will not be cheated out of money you earned.
   d. say, "Hmm, 9:30 to 10:30, 11:30, 12:30, 1:30, 2:30" in a hesitant voice.

2. You don't like your date that much, but he did take you to a fancy restaurant for dinner. On the way home, he drives down a dark country road, pulls over, and turns to kiss you. You

    a. talk a mile a minute each time he leans toward you.

    b. push him away and demand he drive you home immediately.

    c. kiss him back—you figure you sort of owe it to him.

    d. tell him you enjoyed the evening, but you're not ready to start a romance with him.

3. Your class had an impossible pop quiz in history this morning. The teacher warned you not to tell the afternoon students because they'd take the quiz later and it would be graded on a curve. At noon, a girl with a locker near yours asks, "How was history?" You

    a. pretend you didn't hear her and compliment her blouse.

    b. say, "You'll find out," and walk away.

    c. tell her about the quiz, and when she pleads, whisper the questions, too.

    d. say, "Not much fun" and change the subject.

4. A guy invites you to the movies and suggests a gory film you're sure you'd hate. You

    a. say, "Sounds great to me. I've been dying to see it."

    b. ask, "What else is playing?"

    c. say, "I will if you really want to."

    d. say, "No. I can't stand violent movies."

5. You're cramming for tomorrow's French test when a long-winded friend calls. You

    a. say, "I just can't talk to you now."

    b. talk to her for nearly an hour.

    c. say, "Let's talk for five minutes, then I've got to go back to my studying."

    d. gasp, "My father is calling me—I've got to go!"

6. A classmate who has borrowed lunch money from you before but has never paid you back asks if you'll lend her a few bucks. You

    a. say no and remind her she still owes you several dollars.

    b. say, "I don't have any extra money today."

c. hand her $5.

d. say, "Forget it!" and grimace so she knows you can't believe she had the gall to ask.

7. *A friend is returning a yellow sweater she borrowed—with a brand-new chocolate stain in the front. You*

a. say, "How dare you try to give my sweater back in this condition!"

b. ask her if she tried hand-washing or dry-cleaning the sweater.

c. say, "Thank you" and pretend not to notice the stain.

d. hold the sweater up in such a way that she knows you see the stain and hope she volunteers an explanation.

8. *You and a dozen others are on a committee to plan a class picnic. A meeting was scheduled for tomorrow at 4, but the chairperson suddenly wants to switch it to 3:15. She asks you to phone everyone about the change. You*

a. say, "I won't be home tonight, so I can't help you."

b. start looking up numbers and plan an evening on the phone.

c. say, "I'll make a few calls, but let's divide the names."

d. declare, "You're the one who's changing things—you make the calls!"

9. *Every time you and your buddy Jim get together after school, you end up helping him wash his car or mow the lawn. Today he phones and invites you to keep him company while he builds a bookshelf. You*

a. say, "No. But if you're ever ready to do something fun outside your house, let me know."

b. say, "I'll be right over." After all, he does enjoy being with you.

c. say, "Sorry, I'm busy right now."

d. say something like, "I'll help you under one condition: Afterward we go for ice cream and a walk."

10. *Your elderly aunt has shown you two family scrapbooks, and you're feeling antsy as she opens the third. You*

a. politely ask, "Who is this couple and how do you know them?"

b. say, "I'm really tired of scrapbooks."

c. suggest you go for a stroll and save the others for later.

d. ask, "Aren't your eyes getting tired?"

11. *Five girls cut in line in front of you at a concert. You*

   a. step in front of them, shoving each slightly so they know you're annoyed.

   b. clear your throat several times loudly and stare at them.

   c. stand quietly behind them—no point in causing a fuss.

   d. say, "Excuse me, but the line starts back there."

12. *Your crush has finally asked you out, and you've ordered burgers at a crowded restaurant. Suddenly your next-door neighbor and her grade school son appear at your table. The mother gives you a cheery hello and asks, "May we join you?" You*

   a. bury your head in the menu until your neighbor, bewildered, walks off.

   b. say that you'll drop by for a visit later, but that you and your friend have a few things you need to discuss.

   c. say, "We're having a private conversation."

   d. hear yourself stammer, "Sure, pull up some chairs."

13. *A popular girl always asks for your help with math homework during study halls but barely speaks to you outside school. Here she comes, trotting over sweetly, geometry book in hand. You*

   a. say, "Get lost, you hypocrite!"

   b. help her, but make a point of sighing, drumming your fingers, and checking your watch.

   c. help her as usual—it's easier than making a scene.

   d. explain that you'd feel better about helping her in school if she were more friendly out of school.

14. *You've already put in plenty of overtime at the store where you clerk. Your quitting time is 5 P.M., but your employer begs you to stay until closing at 9. You're exhausted, you promised your parents you'd be home for dinner, and you have to finish reading a novel for English. You*

   a. say, "I have evening plans, but if you really need me, maybe I can stay."

   b. apologize and refuse to work because you have other commitments.

   c. agree to work without complaint.

   d. complain that she forgets you have a personal life.

15. *A guy you don't like at all keeps calling to ask you out. You've made umpteen excuses: baby-sitting, family plans, out-of-town guests, even washing your hair. But he never catches on, and he calls you again. You*

    a. hang up as soon as you recognize his voice.

    b. explain as tactfully as you can that you like him, but "only as a friend."

    c. say, "I have a lot of homework to do, but thanks for asking, and call again sometime."

    d. consent to go out with him, then kick yourself for being so stupid.

Scoring

Are you too nice? Not nice enough? Find out your kindness quotient by circling the number following each letter you selected, then adding up your score.

1.	a. 1	b. 3	c. 4	d. 2
2.	a. 2	b. 4	c. 3	d. 1
3.	a. 2	b. 4	c. 3	d. 1
4.	a. 3	b. 1	c. 2	d. 4
5.	a. 4	b. 3	c. 1	d. 2
6.	a. 1	b. 2	c. 3	d. 4
7.	a. 4	b. 1	c. 3	d. 2
8.	a. 2	b. 3	c. 1	d. 4
9.	a. 4	b. 3	c. 2	d. 1
10.	a. 3	b. 4	c. 1	d. 2
11.	a. 4	b. 2	c. 3	d. 1
12.	a. 2	b. 1	c. 4	d. 3
13.	a. 4	b. 2	c. 3	d. 1
14.	a. 2	b. 1	c. 3	d. 4
15.	a. 4	b. 1	c. 2	d. 3

15 to 25 Congratulations! You know what you want and you're strong enough to go after it, yet you always remember to take other people's feelings into consideration. When problems arise, you deal with them directly. Because you are courteous and confident, your peers respect you.

26 to 37 There are lions and there are lambs, and you fall somewhere in between. You usually manage to get yourself out of unpleasant predicaments, but instead of confronting an issue head-on, you often escape through the back door, hemming and hawing and saying, "Uh, I don't think so" or "I can't, really." The trouble with being wishy-washy? You find yourself in the same bind again and again. Your excuse may work once, but you have to keep thinking up new ones. Be sensitive, but start speaking your mind to eliminate the guesswork.

38 to 49 Giving, thoughtful, helpful: That's you. But being a pushover isn't much better than being pushy, so don't let your sweet generosity run wild. If you lend out your only umbrella when you're caught in a rainstorm, that's being nice to another but not nice to yourself. Many love you for your soft heart, yet others try to take advantage of you. Some sucker you into doing them favors, then, instead of showing appreciation, treat you like a doormat. When you're too concerned with pleasing others, you forget to please yourself. So give, give, give—but don't give yourself away. After all, *you* count most of all. Ask yourself what you want and learn to express it diplomatically.

50 to 64 Watch out! You're fearless and firm and you usually get your way, but your brusqueness may be scaring off friends. It's possible to be forceful without being rude and to make your wishes clear without hurting or alienating others. Brush up on your manners and imagine how the other person will feel before you say or do something you may regret later. Being assertive is one thing. Being aggressive is another.

How Well Do You Know Your Best Friend?

You know your best friend's favorite music and favorite ice cream . . . but do you know her future plans or hidden thoughts?

Take this quiz with your best friend at your side. Read each question together; then, on separate pieces of paper, write the number of the question and the letter of the answer that best describes your friend. She should choose the answer that best describes herself. When you've completed all fifteen questions, find out your score and see how much you really know (or don't know!) about her. Then take the quiz again and find out how much she really knows about you!

1. *If she could specify only one quality in a computer-matched blind date, she would ask that her date be*
  a. intellectual.
  b. handsome.
  c. sensitive.
  d. athletic.

2. *If a guy wanted to win her over, he'd do best by giving her*
  a. a framed photograph of the two of them.
  b. fresh bread that he baked himself.
  c. a roll of quarters for video games.
  d. a bouquet of wildflowers.

3. *She'll admit she's sometimes envious of you because*
  a. you get along with your parents.
  b. you're so popular with guys.
  c. you're so good at sports.
  d. you get such good grades.

4. *Provided she meets the right guy, she thinks a good age to get married is*
  a. twenty-one or younger.
  b. twenty-two to twenty-six.
  c. twenty-seven or older.
  d. never.

5. *If she won a lottery, she'd probably*
  a. buy a completely new wardrobe.
  b. travel around the world.
  c. contribute most of the money to a worthy cause.
  d. save most of the money for her education and future.

6. *The best way to snap her out of a bad mood would be to*
  a. take a walk and talk.
  b. accompany her to a movie.
  c. blast her favorite CD and dance crazily together.
  d. go out and splurge on everything from milkshakes to makeup.

7. *As for abortion, she*
 a. is strongly pro-choice.
 b. is strongly anti-abortion.
 c. is torn—she sees both points of view.
 d. knows little about it.

8. *Her second favorite subject at school is*
 a. math.
 b. foreign language.
 c. social studies.
 d. English.

9. *Which of the following situations would upset her most?*
 a. if she received a D + on a report.
 b. if a girl flirted with her boyfriend.
 c. if she saw a friend shoplifting.
 d. a political crisis in the news.

10. *If someone offered her a joint, she'd probably*
 a. ask, "What's that?"
 b. say, "Great!"
 c. say, "No thanks."
 d. steer clear of that person from then on.

11. *Her high hopes after high school include*
 a. getting a job.
 b. taking time off to work or travel, then going to college.
 c. immediately beginning two or more years of college.
 d. four years of college and then on to graduate school.

12. *If she could magically change one part of her body, it would be her*
 a. legs.
 b. bosom.
 c. hair.
 d. nose.

13. *She would most enjoy spending an afternoon*
 a. sunning at the beach.

b. hiking in the mountains.

c. shopping in the city.

d. playing or watching a ball game.

14. *At a school dance, she's most likely to wear*

a. khaki pants, a polo shirt, and running shoes.

b. a dress, high heels, and lots of makeup.

c. jeans and a T-shirt and some zany accessory.

d. all black.

15. *Her favorite kind of party is*

a. a slumber party, complete with séances, gossip, and raiding the refrigerator.

b. a big open house with old friends and new faces.

c. a small pizza party with her very best buddies, male and female.

d. a masquerade party.

Scoring

How well did you guess each other's responses? Compare your answers and add up the number of answers that match.

11 to 15 You know each other very well and you share the gift of true friendship. Your conversations are open and trusting, whether you're discussing parties, pastimes, or politics. You're both lucky. But remember, friendship is like an old house—the shelter is warm and the memories happy, but the roof may spring an occasional leak. Take care of your treasured bond and try not to let a new boyfriend, summer apart, or other circumstance weaken it.

6 to 10 You know a lot about each other, and you know you enjoy being together. Maybe the reason you can't predict every twist and turn of your best friend's personality is that her opinions change often or she's more comfortable keeping certain thoughts private. Perhaps, with time, you'll explore new topics of conversation and learn even more about each other. Meanwhile, your friendship is important to you both, and only you two know if it feels wonderful as is or if it needs a bit more talking, listening, caring.

0 to 5 Why so few answers in common? Is your friend that mysterious? That private? That shy? Or could it be that you've been doing all the talking? Maybe there's a reason she isn't opening up to you. Did she ever tell you a secret only to find out that you'd spread it? Or perhaps you never think aloud with her, so she hesitates to be the first to expose her innermost thoughts. Begin to share your thoughts and insights and learn to ask about and listen to hers. You'll both win in the long run.

Are You and He a Good Match?

Are you and your boyfriend right for each other? Are you like peas in a pod or apples and oranges—and which makes for a more compatible couple?

Like the friendship quiz, you two take this in tandem. Unlike the quiz, you each answer for yourselves. You and your boyfriend should each number a separate piece of paper from 1 to 25. Read the questions together, then write down the letter of your answer. When you finish, add up the answers you have in common and check the scoring.

1. Your bedroom is
    a. stylish, immaculate—right out of a decorating magazine.
    b. neat but "lived in."
    c. somewhat eccentric—there may be a huge mobile hanging from the ceiling or a hand-painted mural on the wall.
    d. buried under layers of books, clothes, letters, and catalogs.

2. If you've planned to meet a friend at 3 P.M., you arrive
    a. ten minutes early.
    b. at 3 P.M. exactly.
    c. ten minutes late.
    d. who knows? There is no pattern to your punctuality.

3. Which best describes your attitude toward animals?
    a. You're a cat person: Happiness is a kitten purring in your arms.
    b. You're a dog person: Nothing beats walking with a tail-wagging canine.
    c. You adore horses, parakeets, turtles—any creature with fur, feathers, or fins.

d. Animals? Yech! They bite and shed, they're noisy and messy, and some make you sneeze.

4. *On Friday, you're paid $50 for your part-time job. This weekend, you'll probably*
    a. spend $60.
    b. buy one big item that costs around $40.
    c. save $25 and spend the rest on little things.
    d. put it all in the bank.

5. *As for astrology . . .*
    a. when you learn someone's birthday, you feel you know a lot about that person's character. You read your horoscope every day, and if it says "Avoid travel," you stay home.
    b. you think sun signs have some effect on personalities, and you often read your daily horoscope.
    c. you'll admit some Virgos are perfectionists, but when you read your horoscope, it's just for kicks.
    d. you think zodiac signs and horoscopes are nonsense.

6. *When it comes to clothes,*
    a. you like being in style and update your wardrobe regularly.
    b. you favor the classic and conservative.
    c. you take it to the limit with wild colors and surprising combinations.
    d. you've never gone to school naked, but you hardly notice what you wear.

7. *Your feeling about school sports is that you*
    a. would love to be the most valuable player on the team.
    b. would like to at least make the team.
    c. enjoy going to games and meets.
    d. couldn't care less—they are beyond boring.

8. *In school, you especially enjoy*
    a. math and science.
    b. English, foreign language, or history.
    c. art and music.
    d. lunch period and the final bell.

9. *When a substitute teacher is at the desk, you*
   a. help the sub figure out who's who and what's what.
   b. neither help nor hinder.
   c. slam your books on the floor and fire spitballs at the blackboard. Your motto: Sink the Sub.
   d. skip class.

10. *It's 11 P.M., but you still have lots of homework. You*
   a. go to bed; sleep is important, too.
   b. stay up another forty-five minutes finishing assignments, however haphazardly.
   c. continue working conscientiously until you're satisfied with your efforts.
   d. set the alarm for 6 A.M.

11. *When you see two students comparing answers during a quiz, you*
   a. are appalled and tell your teacher to watch for cheating.
   b. wish you were sitting next to them—some tests are impossible!
   c. figure they're only cheating themselves and forget about it.
   d. feel angry that cheating is so commonplace and frustrated that their scores may upset the grading curve.

12. *Your ideal vacation is*
   a. skiing down snowy mountain trails.
   b. going to a city you've never seen and exploring restaurants, museums, shops, parks, sites.
   c. getting together with relatives at a family reunion.
   d. staying home and catching up on reading, seeing friends, and everything you don't usually have time for.

13. *If you spent a week on a warm beach, you'd*
   a. enjoy lolling around with no decisions to make except which flavor ice cream to order.
   b. use a lot of effort and oil to achieve the perfect tan.
   c. spend the whole time swimming and body surfing.
   d. complain about sand, heat, sunburn, and boredom.

14. *You've won a free round-trip vacation to anywhere, so you're packing your bags for* *a.* Tibet.

b. Costa Rica.

c. France.

d. Hawaii.

15. *Of the following meals, your favorite is*

a. a cheeseburger, fries, and a pickle.

b. garlic shrimp with peapods.

c. tacos and chili.

d. pizza.

16. *You find swearing in public*

a. the norm for guys and girls.

b. OK for guys but not for girls.

c. somewhat offensive.

d. totally vulgar and off-putting.

17. *Cigarette smoking is*

a. OK every once in a while, but you'd hate to be hooked.

b. enjoyable—you don't apologize for smoking.

c. not for you, but it doesn't bother you when others smoke.

d. unattractive, unhealthy, and even impolite.

18. *Regular exercise? Yes, you*

a. work out daily, rain or shine.

b. do sit-ups, pushups, or body-toning exercises every so often.

c. practice a sport regularly, on a team or solo.

d. make many round trips to the candy store.

19. *Which do you go to most often?*

a. Concerts.

b. Museums.

c. Movies.

d. Ball games.

20. *When you are eighteen, you*

a. plan to vote in every election and campaign for candidates.

b. plan to vote in national and local elections.

c. plan to vote only in the presidential elections.

d. doubt you'll vote.

21. *If you found $20 on the floor of a store, you would*

a. pocket it and feel giddy.

b. pocket it and feel guilty.

c. quietly ask, "Did anybody lose some money?"

d. turn it in to a salesperson.

22. *How long will you be a student? You'll probably*

a. get your high school diploma.

b. attend a two-year college.

c. graduate from a four-year college.

d. go to graduate school.

23. *Your ideal home is a*

a. modern condominium in the heart of a bustling city.

b. restored nineteenth-century farmhouse in the country.

c. brick house in the suburbs.

d. wood-shingle house at the seashore.

24. *You think divorce is so common because*

a. marriage itself is too limiting. It's unrealistic to expect two people to stay married forever.

b. people get married for the wrong reasons.

c. married couples don't try hard enough to get along.

d. women's and men's roles are changing too fast—no one knows what he or she wants.

25. *Children? Ideally you'd like to have*

a. none.

b. one or two.

c. three or four.

d. five or more.

Scoring

How many times did your answers match? Add up and see what your score means.

17 to 25 A toast to two of a kind! You and your special guy are well suited. You have similar values, tastes, opinions, and habits, and you are as compatible in school as you are in your leisure time. Enjoy yourselves, perfect pair, but be careful not to lose your individuality. In the long run, you'd be bored going out with your double. Continue to grow separately and together, discussing insights, feelings, and projects. Being a good match is a good start; the future is up to you.

8 to 16 You two have your differences, but many of your priorities, character traits, and viewpoints are similar. You and your boyfriend probably complement each other well and have a dynamic, exciting relationship, with plenty to talk about all the time. If you can learn to debate politics, religion, and which movie to see without causing hard feelings, you're all set. Compromise and tolerance are the necessary glues to keep you smiling for a long time.

0 to 7 You've just proved the old adage: Opposites attract. Lots of liberals and conservatives, spenders and savers, cat people and dog people, sloppies and neatniks make happy couples. If you can each allow for some give or take, you may find you get along as well as the couples who seem like identical twins. But your bond *is* more challenging. Little quirks can drive you crazy, like his being late when you're always early. And big issues must be reckoned with: If you want a Ph.D. and he wants to drop out after eleventh grade, you probably aren't a heaven-made match. For now, have fun, learn from each other, and enjoy finding out why your characters, values, and tastes are often different.

Are You the Jealous Type?

Nobody is immune to jealousy. But while the green-eyed monster makes some feel blue and makes some see red, others rarely suffer the aches of envy. Test yourself honestly in the following situations. Then check the scoring to learn how you can understand and tame the monster.

1. The science teacher assigned lab partners, and your boyfriend got matched with a cute girl who has a crush on him. You
    a. don't worry—after all, examining a paramecium together isn't in the same league as going out.
    √ *b.* quiz your boyfriend lightheartedly on everything the two of them say and do on lab days.

c. are very uncomfortable with the arrangement but don't say anything.

2. *You're upset, so you call a close out-of-town friend. You catch her in top spirits: She's made honor roll, has a new boyfriend, and landed a summer job on a cruise ship. You*

> ***a.*** listen, mumble "That's great," swallow the lump in your throat, and tell her your saga.
> ***b.*** are delighted for her, say, "Congratulations" and ask for all the details, not mentioning your woes.
> ***c.*** say that your mom suddenly needs to use the phone and cut the conversation short.

3. *Your sister never wears jewelry or makeup and is oblivious to fashion and diet. Yet she always looks stunning! You*

> ***a.*** wish she'd wake up, just occasionally, with a few pimples on her nose and forehead.
> ***b.*** often remind yourself that while she's particularly pretty, you're especially bright, funny, or artistic.
> ***c.*** are proud to have such a beautiful sister.

4. *Your boyfriend still speaks wistfully of his former girlfriend, who moved away last year. You*

> ***a.*** hope that if she ever comes to town, he doesn't find out.
> ***b.*** insist that if he expects a future with you, he must get over his past with her.
> ***c.*** think she sounds nice and are curious to meet her.

5. *Your teacher gave both you and another student As for your joint report on Lebanon, but in front of the class, the teacher lavished your classmate with compliments and didn't even acknowledge your contribution. You*

> ***a.*** don't mind; grades speak louder than praise.
> ***b.*** write your classmate a note saying you resent her not reminding the teacher of your share of the work.
> ***c.*** plan to find the teacher later and say something subtle like, "I'm glad you liked our project. We both enjoyed writing it."

6. *Your boyfriend loves bicycling. So much, in fact, that when he's not in school, at sports practice, or doing homework, he's cycling into the wild blue yonder. You* *a.* tell him you won't play second fiddle to his bicycle anymore: If things don't change, you want out.

b. don't mind: He's happy, you admire his athletic prowess, and better your rival be a bicycle than another girl—even if you hardly see him.

c. accept his cycling gusto but say that you want to be with him outside school at least twice a week.

7. *You've just seen a movie together. You're raving about the special effects. Your date is raving about the teen actress. You*

a. agree that she's a talented beauty and bring up other movies in which you've admired her.

b. point out that the male lead was sensitive and charming, then change the subject.

c. say that while she's not unattractive, you don't care for her acting.

8. *According to your mother, your brother can do no wrong. She recites the list of his accomplishments. You*

a. tune her out, feeling hurt and annoyed.

b. are glad to see her so proud.

c. listen, nod, and hint that you're nothing to sneeze at yourself.

9. *The guy you've secretly had your eye on for months just asked your best friend to the prom. You*

a. cry and decide you hate them both.

b. feel hurt but since nobody really betrayed you, you try not to let it drag you down.

c. figure it's no big deal. There are other guys out there and nothing could ever come between you and your friend.

10. *You visit a friend's house for the first time. House? It's a mansion! Her room has a water bed, and out back, there's a swimming pool. You*

a. say with a sigh, "This is the life," and enjoy yourself thoroughly.

b. are so overwhelmed by the contrast between your two homes that your stomach is knotted and you can scarcely keep afloat.

c. drift merrily but think with a passing pang, "I wish our home were half this size."

11. *You and a guy you've just met have been flirting at a party. Suddenly the new girl in town asks him to dance. He accepts with a big smile. You*

    a. glare at her and ask a good-looking guy to dance.

    b. smile at them and go talk with another friend.

    c. study the CD collection and consider cutting in if they dance the next number together.

12. *The teacher hands back the papers. You can't help noticing that both classmates next to you got an A while you got a B. You*

    a. are happy with your grade and don't think twice about theirs.

    b. wonder if their papers really are better than yours and why.

    c. wish you hadn't seen their grades—now you feel bad that yours wasn't higher.

Scoring

1.	a. 1	b. 2	c. 3
2.	a. 2	b. 1	c. 3
3.	a. 3	b. 2	c. 1
4.	a. 2	b. 3	c. 1
5.	a. 1	b. 3	c. 2
6.	a. 3	b. 1	c. 2
7.	a. 1	b. 2	c. 3
8.	a. 3	b. 1	c. 2
9.	a. 3	b. 2	c. 1
10.	a. 1	b. 3	c. 2
11.	a. 3	b. 1	c. 2
12.	a. 1	b. 2	c. 3

12 to 19 You are unselfish and unpossessive, and these qualities save you from many needless heartaches. But before you stick a gold star on your forehead, be sure you are being truly honest with yourself about your feelings, not just repressing emotions. Could your nonchalance be a mere facade? Don't be afraid to open up and deal with any anger and fears inside you. Some jealousy is perfectly natural.

20 to 27 You are in touch with your full range of feelings, jealousy included. Sure you'd be happy if your neighbor won the lottery, but you'd be even happier if you won. You are mature enough to recognize your occasional envy as natural and legitimate and wise enough to control it, rather than let it control you. When you are jealous, ask yourself why and explore it. For example, maybe you think your boyfriend is tempted to roam because *you're* restless and you're projecting your feelings onto him. Or maybe you're feeling insecure because things at home and at school aren't going well. If you think your jealousy is well founded, let it serve as a warning that you two need to reexamine your relationship. If not, work on getting busier and boosting your own confidence.

28 to 36 Nobody will ever steal your friends without a fight: You're the jealous type. You are also a devoted girlfriend, and you like commitment in return. Fine. But if debilitating jealousy often gets the best of you, it's time to defuse it. Talk your jealousy out with someone you trust. And work on staying busy, building on your good points, and bolstering your self-esteem. The better you feel about yourself, the less vulnerable you'll be to jealousy.

Goodbye

I was going to ramble on about kitchen sinks (some are porcelain, some are stainless steel, some feature dripless faucets, others have garbage disposals . . .) but my husband, Robert, said, "Enough! This book is getting too long!" And he's right. 339 pages is enough.

The thing is, I was trying to provide one book with all the facts you could possibly need, plus information about where to go for more. Or maybe I *was* trying to be your big sister, just home from college and ready to answer your most personal questions. I wanted to be sure that you'd never say, "If only someone had told me about . . . "

I guess this is it. I really am signing off. Take care of yourself. Work hard and have fun. Be sensitive and sensible. You have a lot to look forward to and you have hurdles ahead. Luck helps, and life gets easier once you get the hang of it.

One favor. If you liked *Girltalk,* please tell your friends or give it as a gift. Thanks.

Well, so long. I wish you all the best. And I'm rooting for you all the way!

Love,

Carol Weston

Carol Weston

About the Author

Carol Weston has been writing for teens ever since her own teens. She graduated Phi Beta Kappa, summa cum laude from Yale and has a master's degree in Spanish from Middlebury. She writes the HELP! column for *Girls' Life* and has also written for *YM, Seventeen, Teen, Glamour, Cosmopolitan, Parents, Redbook, Woman's Day, Ladies' Home Journal,* and the *New York Times,* and other publications. Ever since the first edition of *Girltalk* came out in 1985, Carol has received—and personally answered—thousands of letters from girls. She gives talks at schools and has been interviewed on National Public Radio's "All Things Considered" and on television shows, including those of Oprah Winfrey, Montel Williams, Ricki Lake, Sally Jessy Raphael, Phil Donahue, and *CBS This Morning.* Among Carol's other books are *For Girls Only* (forthcoming) and *From Here to Maternity: Confessions of a First-Time Mother* (1991). Carol lives in Manhattan with her husband and two daughters.